M000102160

IOWA

Perspectives on Today and Tomorrow

IOWA

Perspectives on Today and Tomorrow

by ROBERT JAMES WALLER

Iowa State University Press / *Ames*

© 1991 Iowa State University Press, Ames, Iowa 50014
All rights reserved

The author gratefully acknowledges the assistance of the Iowa General Assembly, which provided a grant in support of the research and writing of this book.

"Caribou" from *New and Selected Poems, 1923–1985,* by Robert Penn Warren. Copyright 1985 by Robert Penn Warren. Reprinted by permission of Random House.

Authorization to photocopy items for internal or personal use, or the internal or personal use of specific clients, is granted by Iowa State University Press, provided that the base fee of $.10 per copy is paid directly to the Copyright Clearance Center, 27 Congress Street, Salem, MA 01970. For those organizations that have been granted a photocopy license by CCC, a separate system of payments has been arranged. The fee code for users of the Transactional Reporting Service is 0-8138-0264-4 (cloth) and 08138–0263-6 (paperback)/91 $.10.

♾ Printed on recycled paper in the United States of America

First edition, 1991
Second paperback printing, 1993
Third paperback printing, 1993

Library of Congress Cataloging-in-Publication Data

Waller, Robert James
    Iowa : perspectives on today and tomorrow / by Robert James Waller. — 1st ed.
      p. cm.
    ISBN 0-8138-0264-4. — ISBN 0-8138-0263-6 (pbk.)
    1. Economic forecasting — Iowa. 2. Iowa — Economic policy. 3. Environmental policy — Iowa. I. Title.
    HC107.I8W35   1991
    338.9777 — dc20   91-25891

To all of the Iowans
who care deeply about this place of ours
between the two big rivers,
and who have been kind to me along the way,
as I have struggled to understand
what the future might hold for us.

CONTENTS

We do not know on what errand they are bent, to
What mission committed. . . . But
They must have been going somewhere.

Robert Penn Warren, "Caribou"

PREFACE

W e are born; then we die. In between we eat, drink, seek shelter, and conceive babies. Those are the basics — everything else lies at the edges of our lives, regardless of how important a new automobile or the trip to Paris may seem at certain times. Yet it turns out that our nonessential activities cannot be separated from the basics. For in seeking pleasure and ever-higher levels of what we call living standards — some call it progress — we are at the same time influencing our abilities to provide the basics. A simple illustration is the Sunday drive that produces carbon dioxide that in turn influences climate that in turn influences our ability to grow food and find water.

This is a book about those kinds of connections. Though I primarily am looking ahead, as the title states, I do not consider myself a futurist. In some ways, many ways, I am writing more about what must occur if we are to survive in style and dignity, than about what will occur. As such, I make no pretense at having produced an objective piece of work. My personal values are evident throughout the book, and I make no apologies for that.

Of course, my values cannot be taken as a proxy for the values of Iowans as a whole. For example, I'm opposed to recreational killing in the name of sport hunting, and I find the attention given to competitive athletics appalling.

But I was not asked to write a book representative of what all Iowans believe. Rather I was asked to produce what basically is a minority report on the future development of Iowa. That's what I've done. I talk about what I believe is a way of living and working that will help create a sustainable Iowa, maybe a sustainable world. If I have done nothing else, I'm pretty sure I've presented some conceptual frameworks useful for organizing what philosopher William James called the great blooming, buzzing confusion that is reality.

It's critical to remember this book is the product of a fifty-one-year-old man who has a secure job, a decent retirement fund, and some money in the bank. I've tried not to be too preachy, not too aloof and haughty, for I certainly don't feel that way. And I hope an attitude of "I've got mine, Jack," is not apparent. If it is, I apologize in advance.

It's easy to rail about the abuses of our natural environment. It's easy to chastise our treatment of the creatures sharing this earth with us and the less fortunate of our own species. I've done some of that. Yet I've also tried to point out ways of curing those ills.

We pivot here on the rim of massive changes in the world and in our individual lives. Most of the impacts are yet to come, particularly those associated with the degradation of natural systems (and of many social systems). Underlying virtually all of these changes is the notion of *scarcity* — dwindling resources and decreasing sinks where the results of our production and consumption activities can be washed from view. Simultaneously, we must scale back our expectations in some areas while expanding them in other realms. I speak directly to these issues. Along with connections, scarcity is a central feature of this book.

Anyone who attempts writing, or even reading, a book such as this should understand four things. First, there's a fine line one must walk, on a sentence-by-sentence basis, between being too specific and too general. High levels of specificity ensure the book will be obsolete on the day it's published. Too much generality and the ideas seem useless, at least to those who fancy themselves as practical. I have wobbled on this razor's edge continually.

Second, one must keep in mind that life goes on regardless of what you say. Developers keep on developing, entrepreneurs keep on entrepreneuring, and so forth. The inventor bent over a workbench in some Iowa garage or the contractor bulldozing the last patch of forest for a new housing project could care less about my view of what a viable future ought to look like.

Third, what's left out of the book is at least as important as what's included here. The sifting process, as you might guess, was enormous. At one point I spent four ten-hour days simply reviewing my reading notes, and that was only halfway into the writing.

Everybody has his or her own favorite topic. Therefore, some readers will be distressed that I did not devote a separate chapter, for example, to agriculture. But I talk about agriculture and its impact on Iowa throughout the book. As I point out, we should begin thinking of ourselves as a "land state" rather than a farm state.

One sifts and sorts and writes and rewrites. Finally, one says "Enough!" What happens is this: One never finishes a book such as this; one merely abandons it after a while or lets it run to several thousand pages or watches it become outdated before it's published. If your pet subject is omitted or treated in cursory fashion, that's why.

Fourth, the problems we confront call for subtlety of thought and close reasoning. Many of the issues require advanced knowledge in certain fields. I've attempted to write at a level somewhere below the specialist. The issues before us are difficult and complex and do not lend themselves to simplistic thinking. In general, though, the book is self-contained, in the sense that little in the way of outside knowledge is needed to follow my argument. Some perseverance and intellectual effort, however, are required.

As part of my research I spent a good deal of time traveling in Iowa. Parts of the book were written in motels or dictated into a small tape recorder as I drove. In terms of size, Iowa lies about in the middle of the states. Still the miles of highway and gravel roads seem endless out here between the two big rivers. The number of people doing interesting things and ridiculous things also seems endless. I've encountered both types; fortunately, most of them have fallen into the category of "interesting."

My work was financed under a grant called "Emerging Business Opportunities," given to the University of Northern Iowa. There is more to this grant than the present book. But I was specifically requested by members of the Iowa Legislature to carry out this piece of research and writing. Now that I've attempted it, I don't want to do it again.

I do, however, sincerely appreciate having been given the opportunity to try it once. I was not required to produce a book, only a final report. The Iowa State University Press expressed an interest in seeing the manuscript, and a book resulted. A generous portion of whatever royalties are produced by the book will be returned to the state of Iowa to help defray financing of the project.

Special thanks go to Neil Wilson, former Director of UNI's Division of External Services, and Karen Bramblette, who coordinates things in External Services, for helping me manage the details of the project. And Theresa Hammond ran down about two hundred articles for me at various stages in my research.

The Iowa State University Press allowed me to quote liberally from my two essay collections. I thank them for that. The people at the Press are kind and considerate. They do not push me, but they're ready with help when I ask for it. As with my earlier projects, Bill Silag, Assistant Director and Chief Editor, provided encouragement, always, and counseling services when I needed them.

A number of people reviewed the manuscript and offered helpful comments and criticism. Two of the reviewers were anonymous, as is the custom with the Iowa State University Press. Others who supplied reviews are Stanley Walk, Allen Kruger, Carol Johnson, Gary Goldstein, Bill Witt, J. R. Ackley, and John Warfield. And, as with previous works of mine, Shirley Koslowski provided voluminous comment that much improved the final draft. I am indebted to all of the reviewers; each of them added something, and none is responsible for any weaknesses the book may contain.

In addition, I wish to thank Dennis Keeney, director of the Leopold Center for Sustainable Agriculture, for responding to a number of questions. And, as with my previous book, Marilyn Keller has edited the manuscript thoroughly and professionally. A good manuscript editor is essential; Marilyn surely must be one of the best.

My wife, Georgia Ann, suffered my mumblings from the loft and scowling trips to the coffeepot as I muttered about things in which she has little interest, such as the history of American farm policy and its impact on soil erosion. Through all of it, however, she remained supportive. Well, most of the time.

Finally, thanks should go to Pickles, the family cat, who dutifully rose with me between four-thirty and five in the morning and sat on my lap while I typed. She was bored by the talk of economic development but liked the places where I discussed recreation or equality among all creatures.

A comment on my approach to references is in order. I've used a very informal, nonacademic style in this book. Readings pertinent to the subject matter of a given chapter are listed at the end of that chapter. I freely drew upon these sources for ideas. If the idea was obviously the product of original thinking, I've provided attribution by mentioning the appropriate name(s) in the text. Where direct quotes are used, I've also included the authors' names in the text itself in conjunction with the quote.

Two time frames are apparent throughout the book. Forever is one of them, particularly when I'm discussing sustainability. Most of what I say, however, is in the context of the next thirty years, out to roughly 2020. Why thirty years? The choice was somewhat arbitrary. But thirty years seemed close enough to see, yet far enough away for events and decisions to have created a different world from the one in which we presently live.

Without belaboring the point too much, I want to emphasize the futuristic orientation of the book. Some of what I say may appear wildly naive, or at least unworkably idealistic, when viewed in terms of current events and customs. So, keep in mind that we, you and I, are reaching far out across the years in the pages that follow. Incidentally, I never mind the charge of "too idealistic," but I do smart from accusations of naivete. Except for a few minor updates in census figures, the book is based on research completed by November 20, 1990.

Structurally, the book is organized into two parts. The first six chapters contain a framework I find necessary for thinking about development in all of its forms. I explore these frameworks using problems mostly drawn from the natural environment, since it strikes me as obvious that getting our ecological house in order dominates everything else we might want to accomplish. The last six chapters focus more specifically on Iowa and its problems, along with solutions to these problems. So in one sense, the book acts as a funnel, with the ideas moving from the general to the specific as the chapters go by.

Let us, then, move along.

January 30, 1991   ROBERT WALLER

IOWA

Perspectives on Today and Tomorrow

CHAPTER ONE

Time and Perspective

THE IMPORTANCE OF VISION

The image comes first. Then comes the future. Mostly, though, we seem to operate without an image, muddling along, doing what feels right and avoiding what feels bad on a day-to-day basis. On the face of it, the muddling approach appears reasonable, for isn't it true that only a fool or an ascetic chooses self-denial over pleasure? If the fire is hot, withdraw your hand. If, in any situation, there are two alternatives, one causing pleasure while the other causes pain, shouldn't we select the one that produces pleasure? Sometimes, but not always.

And therein lies a fundamental dilemma of humankind: At crucial junctures in our personal lives and in our civic lives, sometimes we must play the ascetic's role. Turned on its side, though, what appears to be asceticism really is enlightenment, wisdom — the bearing of short-term sacrifice for the long-term good, the triumph of judgment over desire, depriving ourselves of current pleasures for the benefit of a distant and ambiguous future. Others out there are counting on us to be so enlightened. Who are these others? Our local and global neighbors, our descendants, and those creatures who have less control over the general state of affairs than humans.

Jacob Bronowski, in *The Ascent of Man,* argues that an important feature of humans and other higher primates has to do with the role that the frontal lobes of our brains play in the postponement of gratification. Apparently, this section of the brain allows us to think of actions in the context of the future and to delay gratification now for future rewards. That's the kind of information delivered in middle school textbooks, and it carries with it a rather lofty view of human behavior and, not so incidentally, an implicit denigration of most of our animal friends.

Though we have the physical capacity to think about the future, that doesn't necessarily mean we will use that capacity in the way that Bronowski implies. In spite of the brain's frontal lobes, some psychologists believe that people vary in their ability to think about the future, or at least in their preference for doing so. Whether this is true, I don't know for sure, though I must admit there is a ring of plausibility to it.

So we whine: "It's hard! We want pleasure now — material goods and physical satisfactions. Somehow things will work out, won't they?" No. Not unless we make them work out. And to ensure things turn out well, along with the will and the ways to delay gratification, we must have some idea of what constitutes the "good." That is the role of vision.

A vision of the future is critical. Certainly, we live in turbulent times. Certainly, changes beyond our imagination, such as recent transformations in the political organization of Eastern Europe, can occur swiftly. And these events seem to obviate the need for long-range thinking, for what is the point of thinking ahead if the dynamics of the world scotch our plans?

A vision that is rich enough allows for such dynamism. A good photographer carries a vision of what he or she wants to produce. Events, shifts in natural light for example, can frustrate the fulfillment of this vision. But if the vision is clear enough, the photographer adapts to changing conditions, varies filters or films, exposure or composition, and nonetheless is able to move forward toward the vision in a craftsmanlike fashion.

The role of *vision* is to produce *objectives*. And the role of objectives is to produce *criteria*. And the role of criteria is to guide decision making on both a short-run and long-run basis. The meaning of these terms, which I will use often, is illustrated by the following example

Not long ago, the chief executive of a business firm asked me to help him and his associates sketch out a vision for the firm over the next fifteen years. I began by asking them to respond, in writing, to the following question:

> Suppose, in the year 2005, your firm is visited by the representatives of a major television network. Employees in your firm, from the lowest to the highest levels, will be interviewed and asked about the firm and what it's like to work there. Assume the employees will be

brutally honest. Your customers and suppliers also will be interviewed. Moreover, videos of all aspects of your operation, from lavatories to production line to office operations to the grounds will be made. The result will be a two-hour, prime time special that will be viewed by millions of people. What would you like the viewers to hear and see?

The responses to that question formed the raw material for the construction of a *vision*. When the responses had been sifted and organized, a rich portrait of how this firm would appear in fifteen years had been sketched. The most general outlines of this portrait formed the vision these managers had for the firm. And that vision was as follows, with certain information omitted to protect the identity of the firm: "We want to be the premier firm in our industry, in all respects, including employee satisfaction and creativity, state-of-the-art equipment, a high-quality physical environment, with each division managed by the best management talent available."

The components of the vision are high-level *objectives,* and the high-level objectives, taken together, form the vision. As we worked on ways of achieving the higher-order objectives, subobjectives were developed in ever more detail, until we had produced a long-range strategy for the firm. In specific, day-to-day decision making, subobjectives become criteria, yardsticks by which the worth of alternatives can be measured. For example, in the arena of employee satisfaction and creativity, some subobjectives were to provide challenging jobs, to provide first-class compensation programs, to provide quality in-house training, and to provide a quality working environment for all employees.

Thus, when alternative job designs are being considered, the objectives become criteria by which the alternatives can be measured, that is, challenge, how compensation will be calculated, availability of in-house training programs for the job, and the ability to provide a quality working environment for a particular job.

In discussing how to fund improvements in employee training and compensation, it became clear to the executives that their own self-interest was at stake, since their yearly bonuses were computed in such a fashion that diversion of monies to employee training would have a direct and negative impact on the executives' welfare. A classic case of short-term versus long-term thinking had arisen. Eventually, after considerable discussion, the managers chose a path that reduced their own bonuses in the short term, but appeared to benefit the firm in the long term. That's called enlightenment; that's called wisdom. It's in short supply.

I have since used this approach to construct visions for a hospital merger and for communities. It has worked well in all cases.

In all important decisions, we always confront the enduring trade-off between investment for the future versus present consumption. Scarcity, of time and money included, forces us into such choices. And at the heart of such decision making lies the notion of *criteria*. I hammer away at this notion, because I find the notion of criteria, how criteria relate to one another and how criteria relate to alternatives, one of the least understood concepts in decision making at all levels. Therefore, here's another example of criteria, unencumbered by talk of vision, that clearly illustrates the concept.

Consider the purchase of a video cassette recorder. The alternatives are the various models of recorders for sale. The list of such alternatives is what I call the "choice set" in a decision situation. What are the criteria? A partial list would include cost of the unit, quality of the warranty, features of the unit, size of the unit, perceived quality of the unit, and so forth.

Think of criteria as yardsticks used to measure the relative desirability of the alternatives. Thus, VCR number 1 might be the best in terms of price, while number 2 has more features and a better warranty. Comparing them involves trade-offs, which I'll discuss in detail later on. For now, all that's important is to see that criteria play a critical role in decision making.

In talking about a society, or a life for that matter, the criteria used in decision making ultimately flow from objectives, which in turn flow from an overall vision. In the example above of the business firm, decisions about the management of human resources will be made using criteria that emanated from the statement of an overall vision for the firm.

The construction of a vision is an output-oriented approach to considering the future. The simple diagram in Figure 1.1 will explain an output orientation. It's one I use in my executive development seminars. Read this diagram starting at the right-hand side, not the left. First, I list my objectives for the seminar, which are to develop an ability in the participants to handle groups in problem-solving situations, to increase the participants' abilities to think about complex problems, and to increase their skills in handling decisions when competing objectives are present. Those are the *outputs* I want to produce. Taken together, they form my vision for what I want to produce in the course of the seminar.

Then, I look at the transformation or production process it will take to produce these outputs. Finally, I look at my inventory—the *inputs*—

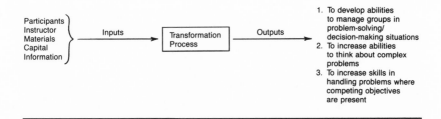

Participants
Instructor
Materials
Capital
Information

Inputs → Transformation Process → Outputs

1. To develop abilities to manage groups in problem-solving/decision-making situations
2. To increase abilities to think about complex problems
3. To increase skills in handling problems where competing objectives are present

1.1. Diagram of an input-transformation-output process.

to see what's required to operate the transformation process to produce the desired outputs. What if the necessary inputs are not available? If you truly believe that the output side — the *objectives* — are correct, then you set about trying to acquire the inputs to conduct the transformation.

Or if the inputs truly are constrained to what you have on hand, you can look at the transformation process and ask, "Can I produce the outputs I want with the inputs on hand by altering the transformation process?" That's called innovation or technological change.

It's possible that constraints on the input side, or in the transformation process, prevent the attainment of the objectives, thwart the realization of the vision. If that is truly so, then you may have to scale down or change the vision. Too often, however, that's exactly what people do prematurely, without really attempting to acquire the needed inputs or innovating in the transformation process. When someone uses the term "visionary," they usually are referring to a person who stops at nothing to acquire resources, or to modify the transformation process, or both, in order to attain the objectives making up the vision.

To digress for a moment here, our culture (as do most other cultures) distrusts visionaries and is recalcitrant when confronted with new ideas. People may enjoy novelty, but they are uncomfortable with real change. That has a certain advantage, for without some rigidity, our social systems would fluctuate wildly. But, as with all things, strengths become weaknesses at the extreme, and the old ostrich ploy can obstruct our view of what's coming toward us.

The perfect example of this occurs periodically in Iowa. Let someone, particularly someone employed by the state, suggest that red meat may not be the best diet for a healthy life, and the wrath of the cattle and hog industry rises up to smite the heretic, led by those red-meat proponents who also happen to be members of the General Assembly. A better approach is to ask, "Well, let's see what we have here," rather than rejecting ideas out of hand. To behave otherwise is to live in darkness and foolishness, to be overtaken by events. End of digression.

In problem-solving situations, people have a tendency to start at the wrong end of the problem. They make a list of what things they already have and try to create something out of that list. Don't get me wrong. A personal or community or state inventory is a crucial part of thinking about the future.

But this inventory is not the right place to begin the construction of a vision. The reason? If you start with an inventory of where you are now, your vision always will be limited by what you currently possess. It doesn't matter how much capacity you have in the manufacture of buggy whips if automobiles are going to be the dominant style of transportation in the years to come. It doesn't matter how much capacity you have in raising cattle if people decide to forego red meat.

The right place to start any problem-solving process is on the output side, not the input side. Ask: What is it we are trying to produce? What is the output we want? Put another way, What is the vision?

Then you can ask: What kind of processes will it take to produce this output? Then: Do we have the necessary inputs or resources to operate the processes to produce the output? This latter stage is where your inventory of strengths and weaknesses is brought to bear.

So once again, it is vision, the "what should be," that forms the basis for getting under way. Everything else flows from the answer to that question.

As you might guess, the process is not as clean as the diagram in Figure 1.1 implies. There is a constant moving back and forth among the input, transformation, and output stages. But the focus, continually, is on what you're trying to achieve, not what you currently possess. It's output-driven, not input-driven.

Suppose you accept this premise. Now what? If you gather a group of people in a room and say, "We need to create a vision for our community – any suggestions?" you're on the fast track to frustration. The typical meeting format is a disaster in problem-solving situations.

That's why meeting after meeting is called, why tempers flare, why certain people dominate the discussion, why nothing ever seems to get done. In the Appendix, you'll find a guide to organizing and managing problem-solving meetings. It's easy to use, and it's a nonskid, fail-safe approach to getting on with things.

I am so confident in the power of this approach that I believe if you use nothing else in this book other than the Appendix, you will be well rewarded for your efforts. I have used the techniques described there in roughly seventy-five situations, worldwide, since 1974. Some of these occasions were high-tension, big-dollar, politically charged predicaments. Others were more routine. The approach has never let me down. It will get you under way in thinking about your vision and, through repeated use, will help you move toward the vision, even in turbulent times.

What I'm talking about is designing the future, rather than just letting it happen to you. Good design is everything, in life and in your professional activities. Most of the problems around us now are the result of bad design and its attendant problem of emphasizing present consumption over investment for the future. And, as with the red-meat example, our problems also can arise from an incapacity to see the possibility of an emerging reality different from what we might prefer.

So objectives flow from vision, criteria flow from objectives, and vision is, simultaneously, both the parent and child of the objectives and criteria. Clearly vision is the parent of objectives and criteria, but how can it also be the child? It's simple. If we try to operate without a vision, if we focus only on means, muddling along and neglecting to think carefully and creatively about what we might like to be, the means we employ will fashion a world of their own, will create their own ends.

This state of affairs likely will be an unhealthy stew, which looks and tastes exactly like what it is — a concoction created by chance rather than design. The absence of an energy policy in the United States over the last two decades is an example of a complete lack of vision, and eventually (in the next ten to thirty years) we are going to find ourselves in chaos, unless a long-range strategy is formulated and implemented.

Here's a quote of which I am fond. Arizona, while exhibiting high economic growth rates compared with other areas of the country, has suffered terrible problems associated with its development. Among them are pollution, crowding, and degradation of water resources. Several years ago Shirley Agnos, who was president of the Arizona Academy, a kind of think tank on state issues, commented on the state's rampant growth and associated problems, "We've been so busy being we've never spent much time thinking about what we'd like to become." I rest my case on that.

TIME AND THE FUTURE

There is something about humans that works against perspective. We carry within us a peculiar kind of arrogance about our own self-importance in the grand sweep of things. This implicit arrogance, this excessive self-focus, causes us to overestimate the significance of our lives in a universe of incomprehensible dimensions, a universe ten to twenty billion years old by current reckoning. Astronomer Carl Sagan said it best: "We are like butterflies who flutter for a day and think it is forever."

Time is an elusive idea. St. Augustine asked, "What is time?" He responded to his own question as follows: "If no one asks me, I know. If I want to explain it to a questioner, I do not know." Alfred North Whitehead, one of the preeminent thinkers of the last two centuries, also struggled: "It is impossible to meditate on time . . . without an over-whelming emotion at the limitations of human intelligence." Einstein made things even more complicated by fleshing out the notion of relativity, which thrashed badly any notion of absolute time. So an anonymous sage tried to set things right, once and for all: "Time is just Nature's way of making sure everything does not happen at once."

Does time flow? We say that it does; it seems that way. Still, a decent philosopher can prove logically that it does not. But we have clocks, don't we? Those devices are just our way of giving successive happenings their place in our scheme of things — time as a sequence of passing events, as pendulum swings, as marks on a candle, as the run of sand through an hourglass, as the shadow cast by a stick in the ground. Human time.

Yet, in the depths of their genetic patterns, living organisms carry within them responses to light. These are called circadian rhythms. In humans, such rhythms control a daily ebb and flow of energy and emotion, the body and the mind changing in regular ways throughout a twenty-four-hour period.

There is some haunting legacy here of being attuned to sunlight and darkness. We are tired in the early afternoon, energetic just before evening, cold in the early morning as our body temperature declines, and sleepy at night. Some mystical sense of time as measured by the revolutions of the earth every twenty-four hours controls us, often in spite of our wishes not to suffer jet lag. These responses, of course, have nothing to do with our clocks, for clocks only reflect what we have learned about Earth's revolutions.

J. B. Priestley summed it up rather nicely: "Pursuing Time, we are like a knight on a quest, condemned to wander through innumerable forests, bewildered and baffled, because the magic beast he is looking for is the horse he is riding."

So what? If we're going to think about the future, about generating a vision and moving toward the realization of that vision, we're dealing with some idea of time. But, intuitively, we do not handle time very well. Even when we are defining time by our own devices, we err in our perspective. We see our own contributions to both the welfare and degradation of our cultures and our natural environment in one of two ways, neither of which is particularly accurate.

The first involves what I long ago began to call "the value of the small increment." By this, I mean that alterations that are imperceptible, or virtually so, over short intervals can result in changes of extremely large magnitude when eventually summed. Great violinists do not emerge full-blown, but rather are the result of some basic gifts *plus* seconds and minutes and hours and days and years of steady practice. The improvements in technique are not discernible on a second-by-second basis, but the sum of all those seconds results in soaring technical ability.

Compound interest is another good example. If you invest $100 today at an interest rate of 7 percent, it will be worth $107 a year from now. Pretty small stuff it seems. But in ten years your $100 will have doubled to $201. In thirty years, the original $100 will be worth $817. The increments are small, but the overall result is not, unless you're in a hurry, as measured by earth time.

The same is true of pollution. In the short run, whatever that is, one more piece of plastic tossed into the trash bag is of little consequence. But, obviously, the aggregate of all such behaviors can result in a formidable problem for the planet. Sheet erosion, where water or wind or both remove a thin layer of topsoil on farmland, is another good example. An average loss of one-quarter of an inch per acre per year is not noticeable, though such a loss amounts to about forty tons per acre. Over a sixteen-year period, the loss is four inches and *is* noticeable. A tree cut here, a wetland drained there, and the eventual result is a barren place, though it didn't seem that way when we were cutting and draining.

In the same way, the Upper Mississippi National Wildlife Refuge, stretching from Rock Island, Illinois, to Wabasha, Minnesota, has been degraded slowly, piece by piece. The refuge now is listed as one of the 10 most threatened out of the nation's 445 refuges. John Lyons, director of the refuge's McGregor, Iowa, district says (the italics are mine): "If we can't awaken in people an understanding of the finite nature of this resource, if we keep *nickel-and-diming* it, we'll go past the point where it is a significant resource."*

Lyons is referring to the steady thump of siltation, chemicals, vacation house trailers, river-front developments, and other intrusions, none of which by itself is disastrous in a given time period. And that's exactly the argument offered each time another intrusion is proposed — the damage from just one more development is not major, so we should be able to do it. Taken as a whole, however, we are destroying a magnificent resource. As Lyons notes, "Every compromise is a loss."

That's what I mean by the value of the small increment. We seem to understand best those events that are large and occur in a short time span (there's *time* again), relative to our lives. Earthquakes or tornados for example. When such catastrophes occur, U.S. presidents visit the afflicted areas and aid is sent in billions of dollars. Yet the natural environment has been suffering in all quarters for decades, and no president has visited, and little aid has been sent.

The United Nations Environmental Fund has received $30 million a year, often less, since it was established in 1972. This amount is roughly 40 percent of the annual budget for the University of Northern Iowa. Yet, we think nothing of sending $5 billion to an earthquake-ravaged area. The small increment is something we have trouble handling. Some of this has to do not only with our conceptions of time and magnitude, but also with the way we make decisions, which I'll discuss later on.

The reverse is also true. In a universe of incomprehensible dimensions, we attach undue importance to ourselves and the present cultures we inhabit. It's an arrogance of the worst kind, in some ways. Earth is part of a solar system within the Milky Way Galaxy. Our sun and its solar system came into existence about 4.5 billion years ago, which means that the history of the earth occupies a place only in the most recent fourth of cosmic history. A humanlike species has been present for about five million years.

The worn, but useful, clock example illustrates all of this rather well. If the history of the universe is placed in the perspective of a single calendar year, *Homo sapiens* (Man, the wise) arrives late in the day on December 31, somewhere around 11 P.M. (about 500,000 years ago). We are, however, still wanderers at this point, hunting and foraging for our sustenance. At 11:57, we develop forms of communication with some permanence, such as cave painting.

---

*Of course, the refuge is, itself, a product of economic development, a by-product of constructing a series of navigational locks and dams.

Agriculture arrives on the scene at 11:59, and we begin to settle down. The wheel is invented at 11:59:25; Christ is born at 11:59:45. The industrial revolution occurred only one and one-half seconds ago, by this clock, and we launched for the moon at 11:59:59.94. By contrast, the dinosaurs, whom we are so fond of ridiculing about their unadaptability to changing conditions, lasted for 150 million years. Not a bad run, and it's three hundred times as long as we have been around in the form of *Homo sapiens.*

It's worth noting that not all cultures view time the same way. The West thinks of it as a seamless thing. For the Bantu cultures of Africa, time has meaning only in terms of momentous events, such as The Time of the Great Invasion. As for the hours between such events, the Bantus see them as empty, involving no time at all.

Then there's what might be called "ecological time." We tango while the earth waltzes, and we are not in step with the earth. Nature's time scales do not conform to ours. In nanoseconds, our computers may flash information about lumber prices, but trees require decades to grow. Humans expend in a single year the amount of fossil fuel that nature required roughly a million years to produce.

The seas and rivers have the power to cleanse themselves, but not at the pace we ask of them. When sewage is dumped in a river at a rate beyond the capabilities of nature to deal with, the result is something called an "oxygen sag," and fish die. In terms of my earlier discussion, the inputs overload nature's transformation process, and the output is something other than we might prefer.

Natural processes require two hundred fifty to one thousand years to create an inch of new topsoil. The average depth of Iowa's topsoil was fourteen to sixteen inches, or more, one hundred years ago, when we first began to farm the land. Today, it's six to eight inches. A 1978 inventory by the Soil Conservation Service showed the average topsoil loss on cropland in Iowa to be 9.9 tons per acre, but the acceptable loss, in terms of natural replacement, is in the range of 3 to 5 tons per acre (some estimates are lower, in the range of 1 to 5 tons). The SCS notes, "Iowa has more acres of land with soil erosion above acceptable rates than any other state." In this fashion, by outrunning nature's clocks, we create scheduling problems and environmental deficits. The deficits accrue in small increments. We hardly notice them until things assume crisis proportions.

Even our measurement scales can delude us. What seem to be trivial changes, in fact, can be consequential. The earth's atmosphere is mostly oxygen and nitrogen. Carbon dioxide makes up only about .035 percent of it. A change from .035 percent to, say, .06 or .07 percent doesn't seem like much. But it represents a doubling of the CO_2 composition of the atmosphere, and that is enough to raise the earth's average temperature by 3 to 10 degrees Fahrenheit over the next fifty years. I am a little over fifty years old, and, looking backward, that doesn't seem like a long time. If the most sophisticated computer models are correct, we may be headed toward such a doubling, and the effects will be disastrous.

What I'm trying to do here is convey the sense of caution we must have in thinking about the future. When we fail to understand the great bend of time, we overestimate the importance of our present lives in the overall scope of things. Yet we also err in the opposite direction. We think our individual actions have little impact when, conversely, they have considerable influence on the direction of the planet.

We are butterflies laughing at the unadaptability of the dinosaurs. Our civilizations have existed for ten thousand years, $1/1250$ of the time the big and smaller reptiles managed to survive and dominate. Not all cultures have the same conception of time, and ecological time does not match our measurements. In thinking about the future, in counting down the years and making our plans, it's probably wise to keep such things in mind. I turn now to the idea of what constitutes a sustainable culture, one that can survive and prosper over time as we measure it, regardless of how time eludes our conceptual grasp of it.

FOR FURTHER READING

Bronowski, Jacob. *The Ascent of Man.* Boston: Little, Brown, 1973.

McKibben, Bill. *The End of Nature.* New York: Random House, 1989.

Pins, Kenneth. "Ducks' Brief Visit Signals Peril to Mississippi Habitat." *Des Moines Register,* November 20, 1988, pp. 1A, 10A.

Priestley, J. B. *Man and Time.* London: Aldus Books, 1964.

Soil Conservation Service, U.S. Department of Agriculture. "A Matter of Inches." Pamphlet. U.S. Department of Agriculture, Soil Conservation Service, Washington, D.C.

Waller, Robert James. "The Importance of Vision." In *Just Beyond the Firelight,* by Robert James Waller. Ames: Iowa State University Press, 1988.

CHAPTER TWO

Sustainability

The first task of any species is to sustain itself. In fact, sustainability might be called the "metavision" for a species. In the strict dictionary sense, *to sustain* means to keep in existence, to maintain. Currently, with all of the attention being given to world-class environmental problems, sustainability is usually interpreted as getting our ecological house in order so that a balance is struck between our use of nature and nature's ability to both provide resources and to cleanse itself of our leavings. As well as achieving peace with nature, there are other characteristics of a sustainable culture.

SUSTAINABILITY AND NATURE

The earth seems large. At the equator, it's 24,901.55 miles in circumference and has a diameter of 7,926.41 miles. Earth's area is 196,938,800 square miles. Viewed against the great sweep of the cosmos, however, Earth is small. Light, the measurement of preference for distances in the universe, can traverse the diameter of Earth in $\frac{1}{25}$ of a second, while the same light ray can go around (if light rays could "go around") the circumference seven and one-half times in a single second.

In a year, light moving at 186,000 miles per second travels nearly six trillion miles. The Milky Way Galaxy, in which our solar system resides,

is one hundred thousand light-years in diameter and contains hundreds
of billions of stars. And the universe beyond our galaxy contains other
galaxies. How many? At least as many as the Milky Way has stars.

Human existence takes place in a narrow band around the surface of
Earth and slightly above it. As Nathan Keyfitz points out, "If the earth
were represented as a globe two feet in diameter, most life would be
contained within the paint marking its surface, and the habitat of the
five billion humans would be a thin layer within that." Our daily business of working, loving, paying mortgages, exulting, and mourning occurs in a shallow cover on the surface of a small planet surrounded by a
universe that can only be conceived of in light-years.

We are destroying the paint. Humans, though, have a tendency toward psychological denial, a subject I'll address later, and there are still
Pollyannas among us who refuse to accept the reality of what we are
doing to our planet and, hence, to ourselves.

I think no one event better symbolizes the predicament we have
created for ourselves than the saga of the *Mobro 4000,* a trash barge
loaded with 3,168 tons of gunk. The story began several years ago in
Islip, New York, where a deal was cut to haul away the leavings of Islip
and nearby townships. Out to sea went the barge, pulled along by a
tugboat with the wildly appropriate — or inappropriate, depending on
how you view the situation — name *Break of Dawn.* Down the East Coast
churned the load of paper, syringes, and bedpans, the pilot looking for a
place to dump the festering cargo.

Rejected at North Carolina, the sad little tugboat and its even more
pathetic barge continued on to New Orleans. By now, the bales had
begun to ooze unspeakably hideous stuff, and even Louisiana, in spite of
an environmental record close to laughable, took one look at the mess
and sent it onward. On to Mexico. "Yankee, go home!" screamed the
Mexicans and put their navy on alert in case a full-scale repelling of the
barge was necessary.

Eventually the *Mobro 4000* returned to its starting place and the
load was disposed of somehow, somewhere, polluting another landfill,
or the atmosphere if it was burned. Keep this example in mind as you
continue through this chapter and, in fact, the remainder of the book.
One possible future is broadly hinted at by that epic journey.

I once mused about writing an article called "Cleaning Up My Files."
The idea was a simple one and occurred to me during a long day of
clipping articles and filing them for future use. I would simply list the
headlines or subjects of the articles I was filing and let people draw their

own conclusions. Though I never got around to writing the piece, the beginning of the list was as follows:

1. "About 3,000 miles of rivers — 15 percent of Iowa's 20,000-mile river system — have disappeared since the state was settled"
2. "Long-awaited rains may carry harmful acids"
3. "Coasts sink under development weight"
4. "Meanwhile, California drowns in autos"
5. "Restoring trees could slow Earth's warming"
6. "Harkin [U.S. Senator Tom Harkin] shown Red Rock sediment; study proposed"
7. "Superfund branded as 'ineffective' "
8. "Chemicals, silt tainting Iowa waters"
9. "U.S. study cites Iowa arms plant as polluter"
10. "Destructive cycle of Florida's highways"
11. "Dolphin deaths continue"
12. "Oil interests compromise Alaska wilderness [before the *Exxon Valdez* fiasco]"
13. "The toxic assault on the Rhine"
14. "Drift nets and the decline of the North Pacific"
15. "Farmers Home Administration yields to Congress, partly folds umbrella for wetlands"
16. "Poorer nations become dumps of rich nations"
17. "The complexities of acid rain"
18. "Ozone layer being destroyed more quickly, scientists fear"

Three aspects of this list should be emphasized. First, I do not look only for bad news. Second, the list was random; I merely typed in the title or subject as I worked down through the stack of clippings prior to filing. Third, in terms of being a full accounting of things going wrong, the list is far short of being complete.

Even if you're only half-sentient, a one-hour perusal of my files can be discouraging. Here's a brief tour.

Population

Since 1900, the earth's human population has more than tripled. At midcentury it was 2.5 billion. In 1987, it passed 5 billion. This doubling in roughly a forty-year period equaled the total increase of humans over the millions of years (say 5 million) from the emergence of a humanlike species up until 1950. Projection: Our numbers will reach 8.5 billion in the next thirty-five years. Less than 200 million of this increase will occur in developed countries, leaving about 95 percent, or over 3 billion, to the less-developed countries.

The good news is that recent data indicate the fertility rate (number of children per woman of childbearing age) is declining in all areas of the Third World. Unfortunately, the rate still remains far above the "replacement rate" required for a stable population. Even if the rate declines dramatically, our absolute numbers will continue to increase because the large base of children generated by past growth will eventually become mothers and fathers. The upshot is we'll probably have about 10 billion people on the planet by 2050 or sooner, double what we currently have.

The Atmosphere

In the last 200 years, the earth's atmosphere has changed significantly faster than at any time in human history. Whether by coincidence or cause, probably the latter, the change corresponds to the onset of the Industrial Revolution. The results include acid rain (50 percent of West Germany's forests had sustained visible damage by 1985), health effects, corrosion of materials in buildings and monuments, urban smog, a thinning of the ozone layer, and a projected rapid warming of the earth resulting from what is known as the "greenhouse effect."

In the United States, ninety-six cities were listed by the Environmental Protection Agency in 1989 as having serious health effects due to smog, an increase of twenty-eight over 1988. Pollution from human activities affects visibility over 90 percent of the time at the National Park Service monitoring stations in fifty national parks. Also, several thousand lakes in Europe and North America have registered increases in acidity to the point they no longer support fish life.

On May 25, 1990, scientists from the United Nations Intergovernmental Panel on Climate Change issued the following warning: Immediately reduce by more than 60 percent the amount of carbon dioxide and other harmful gases being emitted into the atmosphere or face potentially dire and unforeseeable consequences for humanity. If no action is taken, according to the group, global mean temperatures could rise by 5.4 percent in the next one hundred years, resulting in disaster. That was enough finally to convince former British Prime Minister Margaret Thatcher to join the activist group of national leaders committed to reduction of emissions. The Bush administration remained skeptical.

Water

Fresh water in all of the world's creeks, rivers, and lakes — water that is easily accessible — represents about .01 percent of the earth's total store of water. Rain or snow replenishes this supply, but now much of our precipitation is contaminated on the way down by gases and particles that human activity introduces into the atmosphere. Soil erosion carrying farm chemicals and other discharges is the major cause of stream pollution in Iowa. Warnings, sometimes in the form of handbooks, not to eat fish caught from certain lakes and rivers are issued regularly in such unlikely places as Wisconsin and Minnesota.

Fresh water is unevenly distributed over the planet, and population concentrations coupled with droughts in certain areas are causing shortages, such as the one in Los Angeles. Global water use has doubled at least twice since 1900 and probably will double again by 2010, and this must be matched against the predicaments faced by eighty developing countries, with 40 percent of the world's population, where water problems already are seriously hindering development.

In the 1980s, there were more than five thousand oil and chemical spills into the Great Lakes, the world's largest single source of fresh water. The overall picture of groundwater contamination, a quarter of the world's fresh water supply, is grim. A recent report states that much of the problem "is largely beyond the reach of remedial actions and contamination is essentially irreversible." Overall, plenty of fresh water exists on a per capita basis; however, its uneven distribution across the earth and our continued pollution of it is worrisome.

Biodiversity

The biological diversity of the planet is being reduced to the lowest level since the Mesozoic era, about sixty-five million years ago. The effects of this are unknown but are potentially dangerous to human survival and are irreversible. More than half of the estimated species live in rain forests, which cover only 6 percent of the earth's surface. A good estimate of loss from clearing the rain forests is four thousand to six thousand species per year. That's a rate ten thousand times greater than the natural rate of extinction that occurred prior to the arrival of humans on earth. An estimated one hundred thousand species of plants and animals became extinct in the 1980s alone.

The catastrophe is of such a size that even scientists have trouble grasping its dimensions and significance; the global extinction rate reaches perhaps twenty thousand plants and animals each year. If you like doomsday scenarios, the biodiversity area might be the best place to look. I'll return to this later.

Soil Erosion

Erosion and the consequent loss of productivity is significant around the world and is particularly bad in certain regions, including Nepal, some areas of India, the highlands of East Africa, and parts of the Andes. Since I will discuss soil erosion at some length later, I'll not say any more here, except to note that experts are in disagreement as to whether current rates pose a crisis in food production.

The Oceans

Debasement of the seas has been occurring for decades. Most people, however, have become aware of this only recently. Oil spills, particularly the disaster in Alaska's Prince William Sound involving the *Exxon Valdez,* have made the evening news. Bathers on eastern beaches have been horrified at the swill washing up on the sand—balls of sewage two inches thick, decomposed rats, drug paraphernalia, stained bandages, and vials of blood (some of which tested positive for hepatitis-B virus and AIDS virus antibodies).

Oyster beds in the Chesapeake Bay are decimated, and shellfish beds in Texas regularly are closed because of pollution. In Washington state, the posted signs are blunt: BOTTOM FISH, CRAB, AND SHELLFISH MAY BE UNSAFE TO EAT DUE TO POLLUTION. The Minnesota Department of Health has warned of chemicals in fish from 262 lakes and 45 river segments. Because of health threats related to pollution, the Soviets have periodically banned swimming in the Baltic, Black, and Aral seas.

Wetlands

Iowa has lost roughly 95 percent of its original four million acres of wetlands, mostly through tiling and other forms of drainage. The figure for the United States as a whole is over one hundred million acres. People wonder why ducks seem to be in short supply.

Forests

Destruction of the world's forests continues. In 1987 about twenty million acres of Amazonian rain forest were cleared, an area approximately the size of Austria; that estimate as an indication of today's situation should be viewed as far too low, since more recent data from Brazil indicate that the country is deforesting nearly twenty million acres *annually*. Desertification, the encroachment or development of deserts, is increasing by about fifteen million acres per year.

Ten trees are cut in the tropics for every one planted; the ratio in Africa is twenty-nine to one. One-fourth of all the drugs now prescribed in the United States contain plant compounds from tropical rain forests, and a number of other such drugs are being studied, for example, tree bark derivatives for treating arthritis and a wild mushroom that seems to stimulate the body's immune system. Clear-cutting of old growth timber continues on the slopes of the Pacific Northwest, largely for export to Japan. At the beginning of this century, 50 percent of India was forested; the figure now is 14 percent.

It goes on . . . and on . . . and on. We are ravaging the planet and ourselves and our fellow creatures with it.* All of this appears so unbelievably stupid that the entire justification for our species is called into question. For example, ask any Iowan about our natural gifts, and the rich soil upon which we built this state will be ranked topmost. Yet in the hundred or so years since we settled here, we have managed to decrease our topsoil base from its original fourteen to sixteen inches to six to eight inches presently. (I have mentioned soil loss before, and I return to it here, since for me no single environmental event symbolizes better our witless behavior.)

Much of the food for our world is grown on a thin, dark, fertile layer of dirt called topsoil. Because of its crumbly and porous structure, topsoil permits air, water, and nutrients to reach plants. Subsoil, which lies directly below the rich top layer of soil, is harder, heavier, and more cloddy. Consequently, air and water cannot permeate it easily, and rainwater tends to run off rather than soaking in to a depth where plant roots can reach it.

Two properties of topsoil make its preservation of critical importance, in terms of sustainability. First, there are no good substitutes for

---

*Even outer space is becoming less of a safe harbor. Some sections are becoming so clogged with debris — spent satellites, rockets, and other pieces of hardware — that astronauts may be in danger. Roughly seven thousand pieces of known debris are sailing around out there.

it. We eventually may find substitutes for fossil fuels, but not for topsoil, unless hydroponics, the growing of plants in water, accelerates at a dramatic pace. Second, the regeneration period for topsoil is a lengthy one. As I noted in Chapter One, up to one thousand years are required to replace one inch. In Iowa, five tons per acre per year is considered an acceptable loss, but we average seven to ten tons.

Through the use of fertilizers and more powerful hybrid seed stocks, soil loss can be temporarily masked. In this sense, there are substitutes; the fertilizers, however, along with pesticides and herbicides, seem to find their way into two-thirds of Iowans' drinking water. Moreover, the use of fertilizers to hide topsoil loss is, at best, an interim strategy. Eventually, all such variable inputs reach a point of diminishing returns, and that is occurring with fertilizers. Lester Brown of the Worldwatch Institute estimates that in 1970 each additional ton of fertilizer applied in the U.S. Corn Belt increased world grain production by fifteen to twenty tons, whereas today that increase is perhaps five to six tons. In part, this is due to nutrient buildup in the soil.

Along with the problems of decreasing food production and of stream pollution, soil erosion has other bad effects. Siltation of our rivers and lakes is an example. The annual sediment loads sent from Iowa into the Mississippi River may exceed two thousand tons per square mile. Sediment enters and ultimately fills the Iowa reservoirs used for flood control and recreation.

The Saylorville Reservoir, near Des Moines, for example, receives 4,500 tons per day, while Red Rock Reservoir averages 16,500 tons per day. From 1969 to 1977, Red Rock lost roughly 26,750 acre feet, or nearly 30 percent of its pool to sediment. The Coralville Reservoir lost over 52 percent of its pool during a seventeen-year period. The major threat to the Upper Mississippi Wildlife and Fish Refuge, an incredible resource for Iowa and the nation, is silt. Smaller lakes and marshes, not to mention rivers and streams, also are filling up from sediment.

In my files is a depressing picture taken by a resident of Greene, Iowa. The photograph shows dunelike piles of soil in her backyard, a legacy from the fall plowing by the farmer next door and the winter winds that swept the land. Iowa leads the nation in soil loss, with about 260 million tons annually, which is the equivalent of one-sixteenth of an inch across the state each year.

According to the study by the Soil Conservation Service mentioned in Chapter One, Iowa will look considerably different in the year 2020 if current rates of erosion continue. Currently 9 percent of our land is classified as severely eroded. In thirty years, 40 percent will be in that category. The present rate of erosion, statewide, amounts to 260 million tons lost from cropland each year. The Iowa State University Agriculture and Home Economics Experiment Station is blunt about this, stating that the lost soil "simply cannot be replaced within our lifetimes or those of our children. The eroded soil is gone, depleting the fertility of the land."

Similar depletion is occurring throughout the world. Estimates by the Worldwatch Institute of world soil loss are in the range of twenty-five billion tons annually, which is roughly the amount that covers Australia's vast wheatlands. The Soviet Union, in an attempt to increase its food supply, has ravaged much of its land over the last fifty years and has been abandoning roughly 2.5 million acres of cropland each year because of the land's degradation. China is in the process of doing that as well, washing over a billion tons of soil each year down the Huang He and into the ocean.

Australia is experiencing severe soil erosion, and a report from the U.S. embassy in Jakarta indicates that soil erosion is bringing on an "ecological emergency" in Java. Similar problems are occurring in Pakistan and in India's rich Punjab region (in spite of the fact that Nepal sends 240 million cubic meters of soil down its rivers to India each year), as well as in Mali, Mauritania, Tunisia, China, Thailand, and Brazil. In some developing countries, entire villages are being abandoned because of soil degradation.

Ethiopia is already a disaster. Lester Brown, in *Building a Sustainable Society,* cites a U.S. Aid Mission report: "There is an environmental nightmare unfolding before our eyes. . . . It is the result of the acts of millions of Ethiopians struggling for survival: scratching the surface of eroded land and eroding it further; cutting down the trees for warmth and fuel and leaving the country denuded. . . . Over one billion — one billion — tons of topsoil flow from Ethiopia's highlands each year."

Annually, according to Sandra Postel writing for the Worldwatch Institute,

Irreversible desertification claims an estimated 6 million hectares worldwide — a land area nearly twice the size of Belgium lost beyond practical hope of reclamation. An additional 20 million hectares annually become so impoverished that they are unprofitable to farm or graze. Most of the affected land, however, lies on the degradation continuum, somewhere between fully productive and hopelessly degraded. Unfortunately, much of it is sliding down the diminishing productivity side of the scale.

The results of a survey conducted by the United Nations Environmental Program in 1984, which remains the major source of available data on worldwide land degradation, showed that 4.5 billion hectares,* or about 35 percent of the planet's land surface, are threatened by desertification.

Recent evidence indicates that the great Mesopotamian civilizations along the Tigris and Euphrates river basin, what we learned to call the Fertile Crescent in our history studies, fell not because of invasion, but rather as a result of accumulating environmental problems. One such stress was salinization of the soil due to faulty irrigation practices.

Southwest across the Mediterranean from the Fertile Crescent, North Africa was once the granary of the Roman Empire. Today, Libya and Algeria import half their grain from North America. The Mayan civilization, considered one of the great cultures in history, apparently succumbed to soil erosion brought on by overdriving the land in response to population pressures.

Presently, about one-tenth of the land in the world is cultivated. This is most of the best farmland available. And we are destroying it.

Are we worried about it? Yes. A survey conducted in 1978 asked more than eight thousand Iowans in the state's one hundred soil districts to name the resource problems that most concerned them. Soil erosion was, overall, the major concern. Have we done much about it? No.

How can we do this to ourselves? Are we just dumb, or what? We consider ourselves rational. Would a rational organism destroy the foundation of its food supply even when it knows that such destruction is occurring? Well, it all depends on how you define rationality. (In Chapter Four I'll discuss how apparently rational behavior often can lead to irrational results.) It is self-evident that we are not behaving in a fashion consistent with sustainability. Soil erosion is only one problem in a mosaic of such problems.

The Gaia Hypothesis

Nonscientists tend to have a flawed view of what science is and how it functions. Because of advances in computers, medicine, and space exploration, to cite a few examples, people tend to think that scientists know a great deal more than they actually do about the natural world, including the human body. This breeds unwarranted confidence that scholarly looking people in white lab coats can always discover a new

---

*A hectare is approximately 2.4 acres.

technological fix to extricate us from our problems. It also causes an underappreciation for the difficulties of learning about truly complex systems, such as the ecology of rain forests.

Earth is complex, magnificently so. There is something quite strange, mystical perhaps, about this place where we live. And where mysticism meets measurement, science and religion (in the broadest sense) part company, or at least they have in the past. That might change.

In the early 1970s, inventor-scientist James Lovelock, working with microbiologist Lynn Margulis, proposed that Earth functions like a giant organism. All living things possess feedback mechanisms that maintain steady states, enabling the organism to survive. Humans perspire when they are hot and shiver when they are cold. Other creatures have similar devices. Those that do not, or those for whom environmental conditions exceed the ability of the system to adjust, perish.

From one perspective, life on earth should not exist. Consider our neighbors in the solar system. Both Venus and Mars are roughly the same size as Earth. All three planets were formed about the same time from similar elements in the universe. Suppose someone who was not aware that Earth existed, but who had the same data that we have about Mars and Venus, were to hypothesize a planet between Mars and Venus and then described the properties of this hypothetical planet based on interpolation of the Mars-Venus data. Our unknown scientist undoubtedly would describe a planet having properties quite different from those of Earth. Among other things, it would not have parameters making life possible.

As an illustration, Earth's atmosphere contains more oxygen and nitrogen, hundreds of times more, than it should, if purely interpolative data were used. Similarly, we live on a planet that ought to have more carbon dioxide and sulfuric acid than it does, again based on interpolation. Earth has fertile soil, but given an atmosphere with such a high oxygen content, acid should be raining down upon us.

And the sun itself is not a constant; it has been increasing its output during the last several billion years. Yet the temperature of Earth has remained quite stable. If the temperature had dropped only a little sometime in the past, due to changes in the atmosphere, some of the water on Earth would have frozen, as it did during the Ice Ages. The result of this should have been a substantial reflection of solar heat off the snow and ice packs, driving the temperature even further downward until an equilibrium was reached at something resembling a permanently frozen Martian landscape. That obviously did not happen.

Or if the temperature of Earth had risen (as it appears to be doing now), increased evaporation would have created a layer of water vapor that retained even more heat and caused even more evaporation. The conclusion of that scenario would be closer to a Venusian environment. In general, drawing inferences only from what is known about Mars and Venus, an observer would predict a terrestrial environment on Earth quite different from what we have.

Earth, in short, is an anomaly. Something seems to be in control here that preserves environmental conditions conducive to life. It almost seems that Earth *is* alive. That's Lovelock's point. His idea is called the Gaia hypothesis, the name taken from the Greek goddess of the earth.

Lovelock points out that oxygen levels on Earth have been steady at around 21 percent of the atmosphere for two hundred million years. Geophysical models of the atmosphere would have predicted dramatic oxygen fluctuations instead of stability. Above a 25 percent level of oxygen, spontaneous fires would occur. Below 15 percent, much of life would disappear. But as it turns out, there are biological governors at work.

Ocean algae produce oxygen through photosynthesis. Left unchecked, these creatures would produce a surfeit of oxygen. Fortunately, tiny ocean creatures called zooplankton consume both oxygen and algae. Balance, therefore, is created in this little subsystem. It's possible, though, for either the algae or the zooplankton to fluctuate in numbers. Too many algae, too much oxygen. Too many zooplankton, an oxygen deficit.

That would be a knife-edge kind of balancing act, if it were not for marine bacteria. These little folks act as managers for the subsystem. Along with oxygen, zooplankton also consume nutrient nitrogen. So do the bacteria. If there is plenty of oxygen around, the bacteria have less of an appetite for nitrogen, which lets the zooplankton prosper. That could cause a shortage of oxygen. But when the bacteria sense an oxygen deficiency, their appetite for nitrogen explodes, starving the zooplankton and allowing more oxygen to enter the atmosphere.

This is just one example, there are many more, of how we owe our existence to subtle and intricate relationships among the earth's parts, including evidence that Earth regulates its own temperature. We like to think of ourselves as a higher form of life, relegating creatures such as the three just discussed to the category of "lower." Our arrogance should be tempered by the realization that our global life-support systems are dependent upon the so-called lower forms. Looked at another way, we are mere parasites; the earth might get along very nicely without us. As cosmologist George Seielstad says, "Biologically we are superfluous."

And I find it more than passing strange that we can bring ourselves to a state of fury over the extinction of, say, elephants (marvelous creatures admittedly), when organisms visible only under the microscope may be more critical for our survival. That's why biologists fret over the loss of biological diversity on our planet as we cut and chop and plunder. Science does not yet understand, and may never completely understand, the linchpins that hold conditions for life on Earth together. Somewhere in the tropical rain forests being ravaged for grazing land or the oceans into which we disgorge our pollution or along the fencerows of Iowa may exist a creature whose presence is a key factor in the planet's life-support system.

Lovelock underwent severe criticism for his initial attempts at establishing the Gaia concept. Things are changing, though, and scientists are beginning to regard Gaia more seriously. In 1988, the first major scientific conference on Gaia was held, sponsored by the American Geophysical Union. When the meeting ended, the scientists in attendance, people not given over to exuberant charity, rose and gave Lovelock a standing ovation.

Earth, you see, might just be alive in its own way, and caution is in order, lest we maim it in some way beyond repair. Remember the famous photograph taken during a 1968 space mission? There was Earth, blue and hospitable, floating in lifeless space. When you see that photograph again, think of marine bacteria and algae and zooplankton. They're out there working hard, keeping us alive, while we dump oil and toxic waste and millions of tons of sewage on them.

Amenities

Does our destructive behavior toward our planet mean we won't survive as a species? Possibly. More likely, though, is this prospect: If we continue our profligate ways, we'll muddle through, in one way or the other, surviving some ecological disasters, adjusting as we go. Total apocalypse is probably not in the cards, at least for a while. But, that doesn't mean we'll sustain ourselves at a level resembling the world as we've come to think of it.

Economists speak of "amenities" to describe such things as wilderness, clean water for recreation, blue skies and peaceful vistas, crime-free neighborhoods, and uncrowded parks. In a way, it's an unfortunate term, for it carries the connotation of luxury. Since it's part of the jargon, however, I'll use it.

Systems can reach places of stability at various levels. Thus we might "sustain" ourselves as a species, but, in the extreme, we would endure meager diets, polluted air, dirty water, a scarcity of wildlife, and the like. That is *life without amenities,* life without those things that most of us cherish as critical aspects of being alive.

Not all of us view amenities in the same fashion. It's clear to me from reading certain columnists and listening to certain politicians, for example, that villas in Palm Springs, high-performance automobiles, good meals in luxury restaurants, and air-conditioned skyscrapers are what really count. They don't exactly say as much. But on a planet with finite capacities, that's what they're implying when they scoff at environmental problems and counsel ever more rapacious economic tactics, environmentally, with the sole intent of continuing what they consider the good life.

It goes further, though, than rubber tires tossed in your local river, traffic congestion in Des Moines, and smog in Denver. When Bill McKibben writes about "the end of nature," he's talking about a more profound kind of ruin. In his opinion, we are confronting an unprecedented situation in which nature is no longer a huge, mystical force "out there," but rather is part of human systems because of the way we influence the course of nature. McKibben states:

> When I say that we have ended nature, I mean not that natural processes have ceased but that we have ended the thing that has—at least in modern times—defined nature for us: its separation from human society. . . . Nature has provided a way for us to recognize God and to talk about who He is—even, as in Job, a way for God to talk about who He is. But now we have become Godlike, for we can transform nature and create it as well.

He continues:

> The idea of nature will not survive the new, global pollution—the carbon dioxide, the methane, and the like. . . . We have deprived nature of its independence, and that is fatal to its meaning. . . . There is nothing here except us. We have built a greenhouse—a human creation—where once there bloomed a sweet and wild garden. This alone changes its meaning completely, and changes our reaction to it.

One reads McKibben with kind of a creepy feeling along the spine.

This sensation only increases with the emerging popularity of phrases such as "managing planet Earth." Nature is not only no longer out there somewhere, but also now is subject to our management. What's even scarier is that we have only the most rudimentary sense of what it is we're trying to manage. Imagine you're in charge of a complex production technology in a large manufacturing firm that produces all the food, water, and air for five billion people. Imagine, further, that the technology sputters and begins to break down, but that you and your colleagues understand very little about how the technology works as a whole. That's where we are in managing our planet.

Who's responsible for destroying both natural amenities and nature in the more theological sense? Consider this. The United States has 5 percent of the world's population. On a yearly basis, we use 26 percent of the world's oil production, release 26 percent of the world's nitrogen oxides (a factor in acid rain), produce 24 percent of the world's carbon dioxide emissions from fossil-fuel combustion (CO_2 accounts for about one-half of the greenhouse effect, and nitrous oxide is an increasingly important contributor to this problem), and dispose of 290 million tons of toxic waste. Incidentally, the United States is the largest emitter of carbon dioxide, but the Soviet Union and China are gaining on us and may eventually surpass our output. It's a race we should care little about winning, for a change.

In that same year, the average American discards eighty-four pounds of plastic, uses thirty-seven thousand gallons of water, eats more than 110 pounds of meat, and burns three hundred gallons of gasoline. Our landfills are projected to decline from six thousand to two thousand in number over the next few years as we choke them with our leavings, which amount to 1,547 pounds for every man, woman, and child in the United States, based on 1988 figures.

How does this compare with the rest of the world? The Australians are the only people who are close to us in trash and garbage, with 1,498 pounds per person. The Japanese and Germans toss away about half as much as Americans. Apparently Californians are the most prodigious waste generators, with an estimated 2,555 pounds per person per year. Los Angeles produces enough trash and garbage to fill Dodger stadium every nine days. Michael Deland, chairman of the White House Council on Environmental Quality, made the rather obvious statement in 1989 that "this country is the most wasteful on the face of this earth."

About 20 percent of the world's population lives in the developed nations (primarily the United States, Western Europe, and Japan). Yet, on an annual basis, this portion of humanity consumes 63 percent of the calories consumed by humans, 59 percent of the protein, 76 percent of the fat, 92 percent of the steel produced, 93 percent of commercial energy, and 94 percent of paper (percentages based on figures taken from *Scientific American,* September 1989).

According to Jim MacNeill, secretary general of the World Commission on Environment and Development, from 1900 to 1989 the world economy expanded by twenty times, the use of fossil fuels grew by a factor of thirty, and industrial production increased by a factor of fifty. Incredibly, four-fifths of the production growth occurred since 1950.

Earth's population rose in 1989 by an estimated 87.5 million people, bringing the total to around 5.2 billion. This growth rate, if it continues, will just about double the number of humans by 2025. In Africa, 45 percent of the population is under the age of fifteen. Out there, beyond the boundaries of the richer nations, are four billion people with their faces pressed against the glass, looking in at us. That's a haunting image if you dwell on it. These people want the same things we have, and their national development plans are being designed to provide it for them.

It gets a little tight about here. Even ignoring population growth, if only 20 percent of us, the industrialized nations, have managed to put the entire planet in jeopardy with our mode of living, what's going to happen when the other four-fifths try to emulate us? Take China, for example. To power its vast development program, China plans to nearly double coal consumption in the next decade. By 2025 it may be the world's largest emitter of carbon dioxide, and China apparently cares little about what the rest of us think.

At a recent conference on the global environment, Mostafa Tolba, executive director of the United Nations Environment Program, was blunt about the prospects: "If the developing nations, home to 8 out of 10 people, repeat the pattern of development of the North, if they reach the North's levels of consumer goods and fuel consumption, and if they continue to clear the forests, then our mutual destruction is assured." Also, in spite of sunny rhetoric about self-sufficiency and the Green Revolution, Lester Brown of the Worldwatch Institute continues to maintain that global food production, even now, is trailing population growth. He argues that environmental degradation is reducing annual overall yields by 1 percent while world population is growing at a rate of 2 percent.

We live much closer to panic than Americans like to admit or even realize. In August of 1988, during the great drought conditions in the major food-producing states, the world stock of grains was down to forty-seven days' worth of consumption.

A useful concept here is that of "carrying capacity." Ecologically, it means the maximum number of individuals of a given species that can be supported by a particular environment. The idea usually is found in discussions of population growth and the tendency of natural populations to be regulated by the carrying capacity of their surroundings.

But, when it comes to human populations, there's more to it than simple head counting. Look at the following equations.

Total consumption = population × per capita consumption

Total pollution = total consumption × pollution per unit of consumption

Therefore,

Total pollution = population × per capita consumption × pollution
per unit of consumption

Thus, in a broader context,

Carrying capacity = amount of inputs available and ability of environment to absorb unwanted outputs of production and consumption activities

This can be viewed using a more elaborate version of the input-transformation-output diagram concept in Chapter One.

The outputs of our living can be partitioned into two classes, roughly. The first are what might be called "desirables." I put the word in

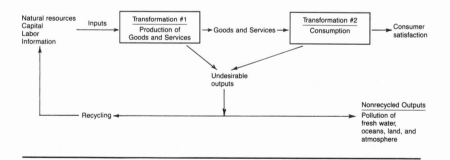

2.1.   Diagram of an input-transformation-output process illustrating production, consumption, and pollution.

quotation marks because whether or not the outputs of our production and consumption are desirable is a matter for discussion, a question of values. Economists sometimes call these "intended outputs." The ultimate output of these goods and services is consumer satisfaction.

A second class of outputs are the undesirables, or unintended outputs. This is what we commonly label "pollution." Pollution occurs both in the production and in the consumption stages, such as factory smoke and the disposal of household trash.

On the input side are the natural resources — along with labor, capital, and information — that we use to produce the outputs. To the extent that we drive our natural systems harder than they can supply resources or assimilate pollution, we have a problem. In other words, we exceed the carrying capacity of the natural environment to act as both a source and a sink for our activities.

What determines the level at which we ask our natural and human systems to perform in order to support us? Three factors, and you can see them in the equations above. First, there is population. Second is the amount of consumption each person effectively can demand. And third is the amount of pollution generated by each person's consumption.

Since consumption is the final result of all economic activity, economic growth (or economic development as it's popularly labeled now) implies ever-higher levels of consumption. Consumption of what? That's an interesting question I'll take up later.

For now, just notice that, other things being equal, more consumption means more use of resources and more pollution. Are other things always equal? Not in this case. There are at least three places where we can intervene in the system in Figure 2.1 to reduce resource use and pollution. First, both industry and consumers can recycle part of their undesirable outputs, given the appropriate technology and markets. Recycling reduces both the amount of pollution, defined broadly, and the amount of resources needed for another round of production and consumption.

A second place where intervention can occur is in the production and consumption processes themselves. We can find more efficient ways to use materials, thus using less of them as a percentage of output. Finally, there is always the possibility of finding substitutes for scarce resources, though this usually requires a retooling of production processes and perhaps convincing consumers that the new product is at least as good as the old.

Remember Gaia, though. We don't know to what extent we can intervene in Earth's processes without permanently damaging the complex relationships holding things together. We ask always for technological fixes to relieve us of our responsibilities for behaving better toward Earth. Science and technological innovation try to provide such repair, but if we do not understand what is breaking or broken, it's difficult to fix. The prudent course is *not* to jeopardize a system whose elements, and linkages among those elements, we do not understand.

Furthermore, there's the old problem of scheduling. The processes by which the environment handles our demands do not necessarily conform to the schedules humans devise. Likewise, there is no reason to suppose that the technology for solving problems develops at the same rate as the problems themselves, which is also a scheduling problem.

ECONOMIC GROWTH AND THE HIGH-CONSUMPTION SOCIETY

I am writing this chapter only two weeks before Earth Day 1990. Communities throughout the United States and the world are planning celebrations on behalf of our endangered planet. Universities and colleges are hosting the obligatory conferences. Newspapers and magazines are rife with stories surrounding the event. Environmental chic is in the air, along with various pollutants. In fact, a recent poll indicates that three of four Americans now consider themselves environmentalists, a result I have trouble accepting. In any case, the environment has become fashionable, temporarily at least.

Look closely at the popular proposals for getting us out of the mess we're in. You'll discover they mirror the three intervention strategies: recycling, more efficient use of resources, and finding substitutes for scarce resources. But there's still *another* solution, which few people want to mention — the very real possibility that we in the developed countries may not be able to continue living in the style to which we have become accustomed.

The words of Mostafa Tolba are worth repeating because they underscore a central issue before us: "If the developing nations, home to 8 out of 10 people, repeat the pattern of development of the North, if they reach the North's levels of consumer goods and fuel consumption, and if they continue to clear the forests, then our mutual destruction is assured."

In terms that are unmistakably stark, Tolba is saying we may have to reduce or redefine our standard of living. As before, bring the image to your mind of four billion people, many more in the years to come, looking at the developed countries and murmuring, "We want a piece of that." Then juxtapose that image against America's profligate ways, as illustrated by the data presented earlier concerning our production and pollution relative to our 5 percent of the world's population.

Though we should continue to applaud the democratic movements occurring all over the world, we also must recognize, simultaneously, that a major impetus for the dazzling shifts in political power is a desire for a higher material standard of living, as well as for political freedom. That's clear in every such movement, and nowhere is it more apparent than in the Soviet Union. It's not only clear, it's understandable.

Almost anywhere in the less-developed world, America is held up as the standard by which earthly paradise is measured, in economic terms. How, then, can we resolve the conundrum we face? How can the rest of the world live at the level we do without a complete ravaging of our planet? It seems they cannot.

Yet how can we ethically deny them that right? We cannot. That's why all the attention is being given to recycling, production and consumption efficiencies and to substitute resources. The only way the economic pie can grow in a world limited by resource availability and sinks for our offal is through a strategy involving some combination of recycling, innovations leading to more efficiency, and substitutes.

That may not be enough. Suppose it's not. The remaining option is a reduction of economic growth, not just a slowing down in the rate of growth, but a real, absolute decrease in our national product. There it is, written boldly.* We may have to reduce our level of consumption, or what is commonly called our standard of living. No politician, no business person, and few ordinary citizens want even to contemplate that possibility, let alone state it. In the construction of a viable future, however, it's necessary to look at all conceivable circumstances, and absolute growth reduction is conceivable, maybe even probable.

Economic growth—economic development—is so much a part of our cultural fabric that it has attained the status of a religion. Those who dare to question economic growth are branded as unpatriotic heretics, soft-brained, and sometimes elitists. Most people refuse even to discuss

---

*I'm simplifying things a little here. Obviously, recycling, technological innovation, resource substitution, and the question of economic growth are not mutually exclusive. They can be combined in various ways to produce a number of different alternatives. Moreover, recycling is one method of reducing the impacts of final consumption, a component of economic growth.

the possibility. A clear majority exists in favor of our unsustainable ways.

Forests are cut and agricultural land is taken and people are dislocated, all for highways. The justification is economic growth. We build highways to attract industry and people who will then require more highways that bring more people requiring more highways. The marshes of Louisiana are abused, and the justification is economic growth. States subsidize firms exhibiting questionable social and environmental practices, and the justification is jobs; read that "economic growth."

Growth is tracked via our national income accounts. The terms Gross National Expenditure (GNE) and Gross National Product (GNP) refer to two different ways of *measuring* national income; conceptually, except for errors stemming from measurement difficulties, the two approaches produce identical figures — the market value of the nation's output. Since both approaches produce the same total value, the terms tend to be used interchangeably. I'll use GNP, because it's the more familiar term for most people.

Consumption expenditures by individuals make up 65 percent of GNP. Such items as haircuts, medical care, legal advice, automobiles, groceries, and television sets are included in the computation of consumption expenditures. In order to arrive at the total output of our economy, three other sums are added to consumption expenditures: government expenditures, investment expenditures, and net exports.

One way or another, most of these latter three categories are consumption-driven, either by demand or anticipated demand, such as consumer demand for government services, for products produced by investments in machinery and residential housing (counted in the investments category), and for imports included in the net exports calculation, which is the algebraic sum of imports and exports. Of course, even our *exports* end up as consumption by somebody, somewhere.

Consumption, then, is the foundation of economic activity. From a purely economic perspective, that's not bothersome. People require commodities and services to survive. It's the job of the economy to supply these goods and services. What is something more than bothersome — frightening is a better word — is the status that consumption has attained in America.

Culture, a set of customs, laws, beliefs, values, and social conventions, is usually seen as encompassing more than economic activity. But steadily it appears that economic consumption and culture are converging to the point that economic consumption is the dominant cultural manifestation of Americans, as well as of residents of other countries. William Leiss speaks plainly on this point:

> The principle of legitimacy for modern society . . . now consists in a permanently rising level of consumption. . . . There is no apparent end to the escalation of demand and no assurance that a sense of contentment or well-being will be found in the higher reaches of material abundance. . . . In those societies where such a market economy already exists or is in the process of formation, a principal article of faith is that the economy should continue to expand and to offer an ever-widening array of commodities for consumers. And a principal concern for such societies is to ensure that sufficient quantity of energy and material resources will be available for this purpose.

It doesn't seem to be working. If our consumption were composed of necessities, nothing more, and we were running up against the limits of nature, that would be an entirely different problem from the one we presently confront. We still would be asking the earth to exceed its carrying capacity, but the dilemma would be purely that of a species over-reproducing itself relative to the tolerances of its environment, a dilemma common to nonhuman populations.

Although the rapid increase of population is a critical element in our current situation, that's only part of it. The equations presented a few pages earlier indicate that per capita consumption and pollution per unit of consumption also are important.

The realities press upon us. Nonetheless, few people are willing to even consider the possibility that we may not be able to continue our reckless and extravagant ways. Clearly, unless profound technological breakthroughs of a kind we have not yet dreamed of occur, we are not and will not be operating in a sustainable fashion, ecologically. And that's just in the raw sense of human survival.

Beyond that, we also confront the loss of natural amenities and, if Bill McKibben is correct, a revolution in the way we think about the relationships among nature, God, and ourselves. Finally, the technological fixes to extricate us from our dilemma have the allure of allowing us to continue our present behavior; that's why we scurry to discover them.

The Arguments for Economic Growth

The idea of economic growth is rooted deep within our thinking and is closely linked with another idea—progress. It's hard not to like economic growth. Ordinary folks like it, since, as usually interpreted, it means a rise in the standard of living (defined narrowly as the ability to purchase consumer goods). Business people like it. Growth for them means increased sales and all the joys that accompany that happy circumstance.

Politicians like economic growth. It relieves them, at least partially, from having to confront the nasty question of income redistribution as a means of helping the poor and attacking other social problems. "A rising tide lifts all boats," they are fond of saying. Nations like economic growth; their leaders see it as a way to world power, including the financing of military clout.

Even though the most vocal proponents of economic growth in America tend to be conservatives, the arguments in favor of growth have a decidedly liberal ring to them: Aside from augmenting a nation's economic and military clout, it's a way of reducing poverty; it's a way of increasing everybody's standard of living, of making everybody better off. There's even an anti-elitist undercurrent to the arguments, for if the common man can afford fast cars and nice houses, this reduces the visible differences between the middle class and the rich.

And oddly enough, an argument can be made that economic growth is the best way of dealing with the pollution of our planet. It runs like this. Population is the major cause of environmental damage. The highly industrialized nations have shown that economic development is the best means of population control. Such growth, accompanied by urbanization, rising income levels, improved education, and the increased status of women, has brought about slower rates of population growth or even negative rates in certain countries, such as West Germany and Sweden.

Thus if we want to control pollution and resource depletion, the best way to do it is through economic growth. As you can sense, there's a "kill-the-patient-to-save-him" quality to this reasoning. The caveats cited as part of the pro-growth argument have to do with finding more efficient means of using resources so that environmental damage is minimized while growth is taking place. When some level of development has been achieved (exactly where is not specified), apparently the patient can be resuscitated and stabilized.

Emotionally, I like this argument. In fact, I like all arguments in favor of economic growth, since I, along with many others, benefit. My university receives more money for salary increases, organizations can afford to pay me more for my speech making, magazines raise their payment rates for articles, and business firms feel better about hiring me as a consultant. My boat rises, too.

All of this, however, contains at least four important assumptions. First, it is assumed that the technological advances leading to more efficient use of resources will not only come along, but will also arrive at the proper time and be good enough to offset the problems accompanying growth. There is an element of blind faith here—like Dickens's Mr. Micawber, we believe something will turn up. Second, there is an implicit assumption that we are smart enough to handle the scheduling problems I have mentioned before. Nature does not conform to our time scales, and our desired growth rates may not match the earth's ability to supply resources and cleanse itself of pollution.

A third assumption is that any damage done during the drive to higher and higher levels of development will be reversible. The ozone problem may be reversible, over the course of a few decades. A warming of the earth is not reversible, at least not in any time frame humans find acceptable. Similarly, based on the information we currently have, tropical rain forests cannot be regenerated once they have been destroyed, though some small-scale attempts currently are being made. Nor can species be re-created once they are extinct.

The fourth assumption, perhaps the most critical of all, is that humans will be satisfied with some reasonable (whatever that is) amount of well-being. As I pointed out earlier, population is one part of the problem, but per capita consumption and pollution per unit of consumption are also important. Even rapid growth rates on a worldwide basis, say 4 to 5 percent, are unlikely to be rapid enough to satisfy the billions who want to share in what Americans and other residents of developed countries have defined as the good life.

And growth rates such as these cannot be generated or sustained without rapid and dramatic shifts in the way we deal with nature. That is, energy use must be immediately reduced through efficiency measures, the raw-material content of each unit of product must be drastically reduced, recycling far beyond anything we have conceived of needs to take place, and the nonrecyclable components of output must be disposed of safely. Only in the area of energy efficiency have the Western nations indicated that such progress can be made, and still we are using too much energy. The barriers to the improvements needed are as much, probably more, social and political as they are technological.

Earlier I provided data concerning the disproportionate consumption of resources by Americans. On a wider scale, the world's middle class uses between fifteen and thirty times as much oil per capita as does the poorer five-sixths of the population. If total resource consumption is taken into account, the middle class uses about five times as much of the earth's resources as does the poorer five-sixths. Bundling all of the assumptions together, along with the consumption habits of a middle-class world, I remain skeptical of the viewpoint that economic growth ultimately is the way to a more enlightened treatment of nature.

Therefore, the argument is no longer whether economic growth is a good thing. The reality of our predicament is that it simply may not be possible, may not be sustainable. And, remember, I like economic growth, other things being equal, which they never are.

Here's one more important idea. Growth has content in terms of what is being produced. Earlier I put the word "desirables" in quotation marks and indicated I did that because it has value connotations. Think about it for a moment. A nation growing via its production of garden tools, technology for recycling, devices for cleaning the oceans, and development of alternatives for nonrenewable resources is not the same as a nation fostering economic growth through the production and marketing of automobiles that can travel at speeds far exceeding posted speed limits, and of superfluous trinkets in general. (I'll return to this topic in Chapter Nine.)

Earlier, I provided a somewhat informal definition of sustainability. In light of what has been said about economic growth above and other problems discussed earlier, something a little weightier is required. William D. Ruckelshaus, who was administrator of the Environmental Protection Agency from 1970 to 1973 and again from 1983 to 1984, as well as a member of the World Commission on Environment and Development, says it well:

> Sustainability is the nascent doctrine that economic growth and development must take place, and be maintained over time, within the limits set by ecology in the broadest sense — by the interrelations of human beings and their works, the biosphere and the physical and chemical laws that govern it. The doctrine of sustainability holds too that the spread of a reasonable level of prosperity and security to the less developed nations is essential to protecting ecological balance and hence essential to the continued prosperity of the wealthy nations. It follows that environmental protection and economic development are complementary rather than antagonistic processes.

Ruckelshaus uses the word "nascent," which means "in the process of emerging." It's a wise choice of words. As I've said in several different ways, we have historically not understood, or have ignored, the bare and brutal fact that nature and economics are intimately linked.* Now we have begun to recognize that what Loren Eiseley called the old contract between man and nature is in the process of being rewritten. Slowly the notion that nature cannot be treated separately from economic matters is pressing its way into our consciousnesses. Slowly.

Ruckelshaus argues that a sustainable consciousness must include the following three beliefs:

1. The human species is part of nature. Its existence depends on its ability to draw sustenance from a finite natural world; its continuance depends on its ability to abstain from destroying the natural systems that regenerate this world.
2. Economic activity must account for the environmental costs of production.
3. The maintenance of a livable global environment depends on the sustainable development of the entire human family. If 80 percent of the members of our species are poor, we cannot hope to live in a world at peace; if the poor nations attempt to improve their lot by the methods we rich have pioneered, the result will eventually be world ecological damage.

The points made by Ruckelshaus are good ones. The first and third have already been dealt with. The second is focused upon in Chapter Three.

The sheer physical problem of sustaining ourselves via better treatment of our natural systems is, of course, fundamental. For creating an enduring society, that's necessary. But it's not sufficient. The sustainable society must also have other characteristics, if we take sustainability to mean something more than just base physical survival. I discuss some of these characteristics next.

SOCIOPSYCHOLOGICAL ATTRIBUTES OF A SUSTAINABLE SOCIETY

The truly sustainable society can be described, at least partially, as a caring, learning, thinking, creating, designing, preserving, saving, investing, enhancing, tolerating society.

The elderly and how we treat them is a good example. Data from

---

*For a lengthy discussion of the relationship between nature and economic development, see my article "Going Soft Upon the Land and Down Along the Rivers," listed in the readings.

1989 indicate that 31,000 Iowans age seventy-five or older live below the poverty line, meaning they have an income of less than $483 per month ($660 for the combined income of couples). One study reported that 42 percent of all Americans sixty-five years or older are living at or near the poverty level. The problem is more severe for women and minorities. For example, one-third of the women in Iowa who are sixty-five or older try to survive on incomes below the poverty line. And that's just the economics of it.

Social services people in Iowa list loneliness, isolation, depression, lack of independence (due partly to poor transportation), and other debilitating conditions as part of everyday life for many elderly Iowans. The idea, particularly for those who are unable to care for themselves and who are confined to care institutions, is to get them out of the way and keep them quiet, pacifying them with television or drugs. In 1990, one-fourth of Iowa's nursing homes were cited in a federal report for misusing drugs or physical restraints. This was twice the national percentage for such violations.

A U.S. House of Representatives subcommittee estimates 1.5 million elderly Americans suffer abuse each year, often administered by their children. What's the nature of this abuse? Systematic thefts of social security checks, rape, car theft by adult children, denial of food, verbal and psychological abuse, and other atrocities, including murder. According to the report, the incidence of such abuse is increasing. In 1980, 1 million cases were reported. Ten years later the number had risen to 1.5 million. Forty states indicated the problem is getting worse.

These people are our mothers and fathers. Now they have become an annoyance and an embarrassment, a drag on our fun. Why don't we do more for them? Money. That's the problem, part of it at least. All right, let's provide more money. But there's not enough to go around. Okay, raise taxes. No, the electorate won't put up with that. Why? It reduces the discretionary income available for private consumption, that's why. End of game, continuance of current conditions.

Twenty-five percent of American children live below the poverty level. Fifteen percent were in that situation in 1970, 20 percent in 1980. It's even worse when only black and Hispanic children are considered. Their poverty rates are 45 percent and 39 percent, respectively. Aside from the sheer inequity of it all, poverty engenders the risk of long-term problems for these young people, such as poor adult health, failure in school, teenage pregnancy, crime, and drugs.

But it's not just children who will suffer. All of us will. By our neglect, we are creating social costs that will be paid some time in the future in the form of welfare, police protection, a clogged criminal justice system, and violence that spills over into all segments of society. A modest example is this: The number of soup kitchens in New York increased from thirty in 1980 to six hundred in 1989. (I discuss these kinds of costs in Chapter Four.)

Mistreatment of the elderly, drugs, violent crime,* spousal and child abuse, infant mortality (the United States ranks twenty-second among industrial nations), bad design in products and lives, faltering educational systems, neighborhood deterioration, junk along the rivers and streets, undue attention to gossip and trivia—these kinds of attributes are not characteristic of a sustainable society or at least not how most of us would define that term.

The loss of natural amenities has social equivalents. Crime, fear of violence, urban blight, and crumbling infrastructures are examples. Yet it runs deeper than that. I suggest we are experiencing a loss of human amenities something like McKibben's end of nature.

That is, a clear conscience from the standpoint of how we treat the less fortunate among us is an amenity. A sense of using our creative powers to the fullest and pride flowing from good design and craftsmanship are amenities. Other examples are the quiet satisfaction that comes from attending to the preservation of our heritage and the equally quiet psychological benefits that come to us from being tolerant of others' beliefs. These amenities appear to be declining or at least are not moving toward the level one expects of an enlightened civilization.

Certainly, a society that allows five thousand to ten thousand children to work, illegally, in the sweatshops of New York's garment district every day cannot be seen as enlightened. Nor can a state whose child-labor laws permit children twelve and older to work from 7 A.M. to 9 P.M., for a maximum of forty hours. Iowa does just that, and the children most exploited are those of migrant farm workers. Furthermore, Iowa's services for those suffering from chronic mental illness rank thirty-eighth, nationally, according to a joint study by the National

---

*The Uniform Crime Reports for 1988 indicate that the number of violent crimes—including rape and robbery—increased from 1987's record high. In 1987, there were 1.48 million such crimes. The 1988 figure was 1.56 million. A record 20,675 Americans were murdered in 1988. The reasons for the continuing increases are speculative. Another source provides data showing that the number of state and federal prison inmates increased by 113 percent from 1980 to 1989. The inmate population of local jails grew at about the same rate from 1978 to 1988. In mid-1988, 703,677 of us were in prison (compared with 329,821 in 1980) and 343,569 were in jails. These numbers represent an increase of 54 percent since 1953 and 117 percent in a ten-year period.

Alliance for the Mentally Ill and Public Citizen.

If all this seems a little grim, it ought to, for grim it is. The United States exudes the characteristics of a culture that is staggering badly, that has lost its way and shows little evidence of finding its direction. Our sustainability depends on getting ourselves right with nature and developing, or perhaps redeveloping, other attributes of a sociopsychological kind.

I believe it's possible to devise an interim strategy, an approach to living that will enable us to treat the earth in a kindlier fashion while we're on our way to constructing a higher conception of what it means to live with nature and with one another. I will explore such a strategy in later parts of the book. As preparation for that, it's necessary to look at how we go about making decisions as individuals and as a society. I turn to that issue in the next four chapters.

FOR FURTHER READING

Brown, Lester R. *Building a Sustainable Society.* New York: W. W. Norton, 1981.

––––––. "Reexamining the World Food Prospect." *State of the World 1989,* New York: W. W. Norton, 1989.

"The Fight to Save the Planet." *Time,* December 18, 1989, p. 60 ff.

"Garbage, Garbage, Everywhere." *Time,* September 5, 1988, p. 81.

"Iowa Has Prominent Spot on 'Good, Bad, and Ugly' List." *Waterloo Courier,* March 20, 1990, pp. A1, A2.

Iowa State University Agriculture and Home Economics Experiment Station. "Our Thinning Soil." *Research for a Better Iowa,* February 1977.

Keyfitz, Nathan. "The Growing Human Population." *Scientific American,* September 1989, pp. 119–26.

Leiss, William. *The Limits to Satisfaction: An Essay on the Problem of Needs and Commodities.* Toronto: University of Toronto Press, 1976.

McKibben, Bill. *The End of Nature.* New York: Random House, 1989.

MacNeill, Jim. "Strategies for Sustainable Economic Development." *Scientific American,* September 1989, pp. 155–65.

"Panel: Elder Abuse Grows, and Government Ignores It." *Des Moines Register,* May 1, 1990, pp. 1A, 8A.

Postel, Sandra., "Halting Land Degradation." In *State of the World 1989,* ed. Lester Brown. New York: W. W. Norton, 1989.

"Report: Children in N.Y. Sweatshops." *Des Moines Register,* May 29, 1990, p. 4A.

"Report: Nation Failing Its Young." *Waterloo Courier,* April 26, 1990, p. A3.

Ruckelshaus, William D. "Toward a Sustainable World." *Scientific American,* September 1989, pp. 166–75.

"Scientists: Cut Harmful Gases or Face Disaster." *Des Moines Register,* May 26, 1990, p. 5A.

Seielstad, George A. *Cosmic Ecology.* Berkeley: University of California Press, 1983.

Waller, Robert James. "Going Soft Upon the Land and Down Along the Rivers." In *Just Beyond the Firelight,* by Robert James Waller. Ames: Iowa State University Press, 1988.

Washburn, Lowell. "What's the Point?" *Iowa Conservationist,* May 1990, pp. 16–19.

Wattenberg, Ben. "Lower Birth Rates Spell a Brighter Future for the Third World." *U.S. News & World Report,* December 18, 1989, p. 23.

Decision Making

O ne way or another, everything comes down to decision making. All of it — our lives, our world, and what we leave behind for others. In this chapter, I continue my discussion of sustainability, with more focus and precision.

THE BASIC MODEL

The study of decision making has attracted considerable attention from scholars over the last thirty years, though certainly not as much as it deserves, given the critical role that decision making plays in our individual and collective lives. Approaches to the subject range from anecdotal to psychological to mathematical. The following simple model, based on a car purchase, is useful, not only as an aid to making decisions, but also as a way of better comprehending the world we inhabit. I use this conceptual framework daily both in organizing my own thoughts and in attempting to understand why we humans behave as we do. For those disenchanted with mathematics, I'll keep things at a reasonably informal level.

Alternatives and Criteria

In a decision-making situation, *alternatives* are those elements under our control. For example, in considering the purchase of an automobile, we can choose among various models. Within the boundaries of our financial capabilities, the choice is ours. We control the selection. Thus if we're interested in purchasing an auto, our list of alternatives might include a particular model of Ford, a similar model manufactured by General Motors, and yet another produced by Toyota. I call a set of alternatives a "choice set."

When we start thinking about how to select the best alternative from among a group of them, however, things get more interesting. We need one or more yardsticks by which the relative attractiveness of the alternatives can be measured. In decision making, these yardsticks are called *criteria* (a term introduced in Chapter One in connection with the idea of vision).

In a decision concerning which automobile to purchase, some common criteria are luxury, appearance, prestige, purchase price, comfort, reputation of the dealer, and repair record of a particular model. Complex decisions involving the future always involve more than one criterion, hence the term *multiple-criteria decision making*.

In my management consulting work, I find no concept more misunderstood or elusive than criteria. People often confuse alternatives and criteria. For example, in the context of the automobile purchase example, you might hear a person say, "One of my alternatives is to purchase a reliable car." That's not an alternative; reliability is a criterion.

If you ask people what their criteria look like in a given decision problem, most will have trouble answering with any degree of completeness. They've never thought much about making such a list. With a little prodding, however, you can develop a set of criteria in any decision situation.

Criteria can be divided into two categories. *Absolutes* are those initial criteria that each alternative must satisfy if it is to be a candidate for further consideration. Any alternative not satisfying an absolute is dropped. For example, "I will not spend more than $14,000 on a car" is an absolute. If a particular model costs $14,500, presumably that model is no longer part of the choice set. Notice that in this stage the various members of the choice set are not being compared with one another, but rather are individually being compared with one or more absolute standards.

A second set of criteria are called *desirables*. Briefly, these are criteria by which the alternatives will be judged once they have passed muster on the absolutes. There's a small problem here. Some of the absolutes can also be desirables. An example will illustrate this rather easily.

Suppose, as above, a cost of $14,000 is an absolute criterion in purchasing an automobile. Now imagine you are comparing four cars, and three of them are less than $14,000. These three will be retained for further consideration, while the one costing more than $14,000 will be dropped.

If all of the remaining three alternatives cost exactly the same, then there's no problem. Chances are they won't. One might have a tag of $13,000, another of $11,500, and the third $12,000. These prices now become a way of evaluating the three automobiles relative to one another. Other things being equal, the least costly model will be preferred. Thus in some instances, an absolute can also serve as a desirable, after it has performed its function in the stage where alternatives are compared to absolutes.

But other things are seldom equal. This is where the concept of *trade-offs* originates. Car A may cost more than B, yet A provides more luxury. Likewise, B may cost more than C, but C is less attractive.

It can get nasty at this point, and trade-offs are critical in thinking about any kind of decision, particularly those involving the future of a society. In the social arena, one policy alternative (such as higher interest rates) may result in more savings in the economy, providing a pool of funds for future growth. But the trade-off is to have less consumption now, which may not be popular among the electorate or retailers.

Before I get to an examination of trade-offs, however, I need to say more about the relationship of the criteria to each other. It's difficult enough to get people to list their criteria in a decision situation, even though these criteria are present. It's even more difficult to obtain their rankings of the criteria relative to one another.

Suppose two people are considering the purchase of an auto and both of them have the same set of criteria: cost, quality of warranty, prestige, reliability, and gas mileage. There's no reason to believe that both people rank the criteria in the same order. Look at the example below, in which the criteria for each person are ranked in descending order of importance.

Person X	*Person Y*
prestige	cost
reliability	gas mileage
warranty	reliability
gas mileage	warranty
cost	prestige

It's apparent that these two people are going to evaluate various models differently. Person X is looking, most of all, for prestige, and cost is not very important, relative to prestige. Person Y feels quite differently. If these people are making their decisions completely independent of one another, there's no problem. Each can choose the car that suits him or her best.

Ah, but suppose these two people are members of the same family and only one car will be purchased. Obviously, given the difference in how the criteria are ranked, there's going to be some conflict. Incidentally, this example is not so hypothetical. Several years ago my teenage daughter and I debated, heatedly I might add, the relative merits of various criteria when it came time to purchase an auto for her to drive back and forth to school. She ranked appearance and performance very high; I ranked them low. She ranked cost and gas mileage low; I ranked them high.

Now think about the kinds of social decisions people in a democracy are asked to make via the process of government. This is analogous to the situation when two people with different criteria rankings set out to purchase one auto. Most business firms rank profit high and concern for the environment somewhat lower. Environmentalists see things differently. Developers wanting to build a strip mall in an area that is relatively undeveloped will rank profit high and traffic congestion or noise pollution low (they don't live there, for one thing). People who have residences or professional offices in the area are in favor of peace and quiet.

Consider the problem of disposable diapers and their impact on landfills. Proponents of the throwaways argue that the diapers only account for about 2 percent of what is put into landfills. This is another of those situations I talked about in Chapter One where our measurement schemes can lead us awry. Even if the figures are correct and the diapers do account for a mere 2 percent, the bulk and bacteria from the diapers are, nonetheless, a serious problem when we're talking about billions of tons of trash.

Eighty-five percent of the diapers used today are disposable. Seventeen billion of them each year wind up in landfills, and the average baby will consume twenty-six trees via disposable diapers by his or her third birthday. Though no one knows for sure, the decomposition period for disposable diapers is estimated at around five hundred years. Cloth diaper services have been available all during the time that people were switching over to the disposable alternative. Why have people chosen disposable diapers? Not on the basis of cost, since commercial diaper services are often cheaper than purchasing disposables.

Obviously, purchasers rank what they perceive as convenience much higher than either cost or the dilemma of overflowing landfills. Recently, there has been a shift toward cloth diapers. The reason for this seems clear. Some people have moved concern for the environment higher than convenience in their criteria set.

Kimberly-Clark is a major supplier of disposable diapers, under the gagging label of "Huggies." Procter and Gamble, which has about half the market, receives $3.6 billion, or about 17 percent, of its net annual sales from disposable diapers. Certainly these firms have known for some years about the bulk and bacteria problems of disposable diapers. They should have stopped manufacturing them, right?

People who argue for that kind of behavior simply don't understand much about pressures in a market economy. Based on the realities of the competitive world in which they do business, the criteria set of Kimberly-Clark quite obviously, and understandably, has profits ranked higher than concern for bulging landfills.

Automobile preferences are an even more dramatic example. Those of us concerned with the environment prefer that people compare small, efficient cars with the large, inefficient ones and choose the smaller autos. Yet present figures show that the top ten automobiles in the Environmental Protection Agency's fuel-efficiency ratings account for only 2 percent of the new cars sold in America each year.

It's reasonable to ask, then, why people continue to choose large, inefficient autos. Obviously those who purchase big cars rank criteria such as prestige and cargo capacity higher than environmental considerations, not to mention initial purchase cost and maintenance charges. I say this is a dramatic example of how criteria rankings influence choice, since we have known for years about our declining stock of fossil fuels and the impact the purchase of foreign oil has on our balance of payments and international political stability. Still, we have chosen to pamper ourselves, with the result that criteria favoring large automobiles have been dominant. Incidentally, safety is claimed to be an important criterion by some people choosing larger vehicles.

It goes beyond the simple ranking of criteria. The way the criteria are psychologically weighted relative to one another is just as important. Look at the following criteria set relevant to an automobile purchase, ranked in descending order: cargo capacity, impact on the natural environment, prestige, and warranty. The environment is ranked relatively high. But suppose cargo capacity is judged three times as important as impact on the natural environment. With this difference in criteria weighting, any models that score well on concern for the natural environment will have trouble in the choice process because of the criteria-weight difference between capacity and environmental concern.

This all assumes that certain criteria are *in the criteria set*. Clearly, if concern for the natural environment is not even a criterion, then any alternatives containing environmental benefits either will not be chosen or will be chosen only incidentally because the alternatives in which they are contained satisfy high-ranking nonenvironmental criteria.*

One other point. If people have strong absolute criteria, then certain alternatives that might fare well in terms of meeting socially desirable criteria may never be considered beyond the absolutes stage of decision making. Here's an illustration drawn from the auto example. Say the purchaser stipulates that any model chosen "must be equipped with four-wheel drive and be able to carry nine little league baseball players along with their equipment while pulling a three-thousand-pound trailer." Not many cars that are truly fuel-efficient will survive evaluation on those criteria.

I have been using the natural environment as an example. But the same logic prevails when analyzing other problems with a social component. Our infrastructure (roads, sewer systems, water mains) is crumbling around us. The estimates of the investments that must be made in correcting this state of affairs dwarf just about any other such problem you can conjure up, except for environmental repair. Why have we let this deterioration occur? Because we have assigned present consumption a higher rank in our criteria set than maintenance of the infrastructure.

Iowa has been concerned about the exodus of people from the state in general and particularly the exodus of young people, many of them with critical skills. Look at where they go and the jobs they accept. That will provide you with a pretty good idea of their criteria set. Getting these people to stay or return involves developing alternatives that appeal to the highly ranked criteria used in making relocation decisions. (In Chapter Ten I talk about location criteria and their impact on demographic shifts in more detail.)

Or how about care of the elderly? Like everything else, that's partly a matter of resource allocation. We could choose to devote more of our incomes to this problem and alleviate some of the current disturbing conditions. But we don't. Therefore, it can be inferred that we have other criteria ranked higher than improved care of the elderly.

---

*In Chapter Six, I'll demonstrate how certain criteria can act as a proxy for the natural environment; that is, the natural environment is taken into consideration indirectly.

Values, in terms of people's preferences, are another way of talking about criteria. In the case of the elderly, our values seem to be such that we judge present consumption or at least other social problems to be more important than treating our elderly in a more humane fashion.

The little model of decision making presented so far explains much in terms of the dilemmas we have created for ourselves. As a wise person once said, "Tell me what you're doing, and I'll tell you what your priorities are." Another version of this is the old observation that actions speak louder than words.

Both of these maxims are really nothing more than putting in a nutshell what I've said about criteria. Priorities are high-ranking criteria, values under yet another name, and much can be inferred about people's criteria and how important these criteria are to one another by watching what alternatives they choose.

Now let's look at what it takes to change people's behavior in terms of the basic model sketched thus far. I'll use the natural environment as an example, but you can substitute repair of the infrastructure, better care of the elderly, education, or any other area of concern in place of the natural environment, and the logic remains the same. If you find the ideas confusing, think of the automobile example as you move through the list. That should help.

1. The environment, in the form of a criterion (or criteria), must be part of a person's set of decision criteria.
2. The person must rank the environmental criterion (or criteria) relatively high in the criteria set.
3. The person must give the environmental criterion (or criteria) a large weight relative to other criteria.
4. The person must have in his or her choice set alternatives that will be favored by the environmental criterion.
5. The person must choose an environmentally beneficial alternative based on the rankings and weights assigned to the various criteria being used in the situation.

In other words, calls for a higher level of environmental consciousness are, in fact, pleas for manipulating a fairly complex set of arrangements in the structure of decisions facing people.

In the last several years, a group of environmentally conscious members of the Iowa General Assembly have shown great sensitivity to the problems of environmental decline. The groundwater legislation bill that passed in 1987, the Resource Enhancement and Protection Act (REAP) that passed in 1989, and the mandating of an energy-conservation program and an increase in REAP program funding in 1990 all are examples of intelligent environmental lawmaking that are receiving national attention and applause. The "bottle bill" legislated in the 1970s also is significant. (Certain members of the legislature, and presumably therefore Iowans who send these representatives to Des Moines, have escalated environmental criteria to a higher level in their decision making. I'll have more to say about this shift in environmental consciousness and the reasons for it when I discuss politics, democracy, and social decision making.)

When I'm using this decision model on a day-to-day basis for thinking about the problems we confront, I visualize it in a certain way. I call it a "decision matrix." Think of it as grid or table. Figure 3.1 shows what it looks like in terms of an automobile purchase. In this case, our hypothetical purchaser is considering a choice set made up of three different vehicles. These are alternatives. To keep it simple, I'm assuming the decision maker has a list of only four criteria. In the background are the absolutes, which are not shown here; for example, "must have at least 75 cubic feet of cargo capacity" might have been an absolute criterion. Another might have involved warranty coverage in months. The three models (alternatives) shown in Figure 3.1 are those that have made it past the absolutes.

No ranking of alternatives in terms of preference has been done yet. The criteria, however, have been ranked and are shown in descending order of importance (i.e., cargo capacity is the most important). Weights, in the form of percentages, also are shown. Notice that the percentage weights sum to 100 percent. Thus, cargo capacity accounts for 40 percent of the decision, appearance is worth 30 percent, and so on.

Alternatives	Criteria			
	Cargo Capacity 40%	Appearance 30%	Cost 20%	Gas Mileage 10%
Model A				
Model B				
Model C				

3.1.   Decision model for an automobile purchase.

Ordinarily it requires a good bit of fussing around to get the criteria generated, defined, ranked, and weighted. Moreover, a problem can arise even when the decision maker thinks the weights are correct. In the above example, cargo capacity is the most important criterion and will account for 40 percent of the decision maker's choice process. But notice that appearance and cost *together* account for 50 percent of the decision.

In other words, an alternative might not score well on the cost criterion but could make up its deficiency by scoring very high on the next two criteria and thus be selected over an alternative that scores high on the cost criterion. Maybe this should, in fact, occur. Maybe not. The only way you can tell is to examine the weights carefully and make sure they represent your true feelings.

Notice that gas mileage is ranked low. Inferring from the purchasing behavior of the American public, that's an accurate depiction. But from an environmental perspective, it's not a happy state of affairs. The problem then is to get the environmentally sensitive criterion (gas mileage) ranked and weighted higher. Moreover, since cargo capacity is so important in this decision, it's likely that small, fuel-efficient cars never made it into the final choice set, if the cargo criterion also was used as an absolute.

In terms of the intricacies of decision making, the model so far is a little simplistic. Still, it does illustrate the basic problems involved in getting people to behave in a way more consistent with what some of us might consider desirable social objectives. And though few people use such a rational process in making decisions, the model explains much about the problems we confront now and will confront even more in the future.

For example, in making an auto purchase decision, people tend to say, either implicitly or explicitly, "Well, I've *got to have* this, and this, and this for sure [absolutes]; and I'd also *like to have* such and such along with such and such [desirables]."

Let's add a little more information to the model. Notice the blank cells in Figure 3.1 where alternatives intersect with criteria. Each alternative can be assigned a score against each criterion. I have shown this in Figure 3.2.

Look at the intersection of "Model A" and "Cargo Capacity" (row one, column one). There are two numbers in this cell—.8 and .32. The .8 means that Model A satisfies 80 percent of the cargo capacity desired by this purchaser. And since cargo capacity makes up 40 percent of the criteria set, Model A scores a .32. That is, Model A satisfies 80 percent of a criterion worth 40 percent, and $.8 \times .4 = .32$. Now examine the

Alternatives	Criteria				
	Cargo Capacity 40%	Appearance 30%	Cost 20%	Gas Mileage 10%	Total Scores
Model A	.8 / .32	.7 / .21	.5 / .1	.1 / .01	.64
Model B	.1 / .04	.5 / .15	1.0 / .20	1.0 / .10	.49
Model C	.9 / .36	1.0 / .3	.6 / .12	.2 / .02	.80

3.2. Decision model for an automobile purchase, with scores inserted.

.64 number at the end of Model A's row. This means that, overall, Model A satisfies 64 percent of the purchaser's perfect world. Likewise, Model B's overall score is .49 and Model C's is .80.

Two clarifications are in order. First, none of the models scores 100 percent. That's always the case in a world of trade-offs. One can't have everything. Some automobile models are better than others in terms of one or more criteria and vice versa. Second, some of the models have been given a 1.0 on various criteria. This is mainly a convenience in the scoring procedure based on the properties of certain criteria.

As an illustration, consider Model B and the cost criterion. The 1.0 in this cell (row two, column three) simply means that Model B is the least costly, and this model is used as a benchmark against which the other models are scored on the cost criterion, that is, Model A is twice as costly as Model B, and Model C costs less than Model A but considerably more than Model B. All I'm doing with these details is developing a vocabulary that I can use to talk about certain ideas in a more precise way.

Notice how well Model B scores on cost and gas mileage but how low it scores on cargo capacity and appearance. Actually, this model would not even have made it past the absolutes if cargo capacity had been an absolute. But I included it for illustrative purposes. Model B appears to be an environmentally responsible alternative, based on its gas mileage score. But because of the high weights assigned to cargo capacity and appearance, Model B fares poorly in the overall decision, ranking a distant third.

Thus in decisions such as this one, if we want better treatment for the environment, including resource conservation and reduction of exhaust emissions, something has to change. First of all, the absolute criteria cannot be of the type that exclude environmentally sound alternatives without further consideration. Or, looked at another way, the absolutes must include environmental criteria so that those alternatives kind to nature are passed through, and those not so kind are rejected.

Once an alternative has made it past the absolutes, it must do well on the desirables to be chosen. What this amounts to, as I've said before, is getting environmental criteria ranked high and assigning them comparatively high weights. Moreover, we must ensure that environmentally sensitive alternatives are in the choice set at the very beginning. Up until now, consumers have been offered a paucity of environmentally sound purchase alternatives across the broad spectrum of goods and services. That's changing. And the main reason it's changing is that a higher proportion of people are demanding alternatives that meet environmental criteria.

Today is trash/garbage collection day on my street. In my living room I have several bundles of newspapers neatly stacked and bound with twine. I have not taken the papers to the street; I'm trying to find a place that will recycle them. That's not easy here in the spring of 1990. Rumor has it that a place north of town will take them, and I'm trying to locate that mysterious establishment.

Given the rudimentary state of markets for recycled newspapers, however, I'm guessing that the business firm, if it indeed exists, cannot handle a large volume of newspapers, no matter how neatly stacked and bound they happen to be. In addition, the cost to the environment in terms of fuel usage to get the papers to the firm likely is greater than just sending them to the landfill. My criteria are ranked appropriately, in terms of the environment, but I'm short on alternatives.

To emphasize this point, it's not enough to have your criteria, your values, in the right place. It's just as important to have alternatives available. One particularly interesting set of investment alternatives for people concerned about the environment and other social problems is now becoming available. Coming into existence are stock and bond funds investing only in firms that meet certain criteria, such as taking good care of the environment, treating employees well, and making high-quality products with concern demonstrated for customer well-being. I don't have much extra money for such things, but I'm putting some of what I do have in one of those funds, as a matter of conscience more than profit. (I'll mention these funds again in Chapter Six.)

When people call for more education as a solution to various social problems such as drug abuse and environmental damage, what they really want is for people to change their criteria sets in such a way that different alternatives are selected. I wish it were that easy. But I don't think it's quite so pat (I'll discuss that later, as well).

One final caution is necessary. A common error people make in attempting to list and define decision criteria is that of creating overlaps. In fact, the example I have just provided could use some sharpening in this area. Cost, for example, can mean original purchase price. But it also could mean original purchase price plus operating expenses, one of which is fuel consumption. If you're not careful, you can find yourself double counting certain costs.

Another way this could happen in a car purchase involves two criteria such as appearance and prestige. Conceivably, in fact probably, appearance is one aspect of prestige. Therefore, if appearance were treated as a separate criterion and also subtly crept in under prestige, it would be given undue weight in the process through double counting.

RISK AND PROBABILITY

Dog tracks, riverboat gambling, and betting on horses are forms of controlled risk taking, except for those who suffer from compulsive gambling. People like to sit at blackjack tables in Las Vegas or on Iowa riverboats because they can control their losses by simply walking away and because the games are played according to a well-defined set of rules with computable odds. Almost all of us, however, are averse to risk in our ordinary lives.

Think about homeowner's insurance. For any given individual, the probability that his or her house will burn down is extremely small. Yet people pay rather large sums of money each year to insure their properties against fire and other hazards. The homeowner basically has two alternatives: "insure" and "don't insure" (your mortgage holder may well insist you have only one alternative).

Statistically, homeowner's insurance is a bad buy, when the cost of insurance is compared to the chance that your home will be substantially damaged and nothing else is considered. But bring risk into the decision process and things change. We are willing to incur a certain (it has a probability of 1.0), relatively small loss now—the insurance premium—to avoid the tiny possibility of a large and possibly ruinous loss in the future.

In a decision situation, the range of possible outcomes that might occur if a given alternative is selected can be narrow, or broad, or anything in between. In the most fundamental sense, then, risk is a measurement of how widely the outcomes are dispersed for a given alternative. For example, consider an investment alternative that will return something in the range of 10 to 11 percent, compared with a second alternative with a range of 3 to 18 percent. The second option clearly has more risk attached to it.

But what if the second alternative had a range of outcomes from 10 to 25 percent? In terms of dispersal, the range is still 15 percent, and is no less risky in the dispersal sense than the 3 to 18 percent situation. But in this case, alternative two is not *seen* as risky. That's because we tend to focus on the degree to which outcomes are negative.

There's a classic kind of decision problem that occurs over and over again throughout our lives. It looks like this:

Alternative A: Do nothing or only a minor variation of what we're currently doing and remain at the same place.

Alternative B: Do something that can result in circumstances that are either substantially worse or substantially better than the first alternative.

How do people behave? Usually, they'll take Alternative A. It's a way of avoiding risk and the unpleasant feelings that may accompany it. Of course, the range of outcomes and likelihoods attached to the outcomes influence decision making here. If the worst outcome of Alternative B is the same as the certain outcome for Alternative A, most people will choose the second. To the extent that Alternative B has outcomes that are much worse than the present situation (Alternative A), people will choose the first alternative, even if the potential rewards from choosing the second are much higher and the probabilities of loss are low. It's the old house insurance example again. The same thing occurs in decisions involving job changes, deciding whether to get married or divorced, or even choosing a pair of field boots.

Thus, the range of possible outcomes and the probabilities attached to these outcomes influence our perception of risk. What else is involved? Some people tend to have more of a risk-taking attitude than others.

If you don't have much, just about any alternative looks good. People who get older, and whose level of well-being has increased over time, have more to lose. We call them "conservative." In other words, asset levels play a role. Still, assets can determine the willingness to take risks in just the reverse of a "nothing left to lose" situation. A rich person can afford to lose $1,000; I cannot. Therefore, the fat cat may toss a grand down on the blackjack table, while I timidly push out my red five-dollar chip.

And again, there's the matter of probabilities. In our daily lives, words such as "perhaps" and "maybe" and "possibly" are all ways of informally talking about probabilities, about the comparative likelihood of something happening. Humans are not very good at estimating probabilities. (If you don't accept that, read the book by Hogarth and the article by Tversky and Kahneman listed in the readings for this chapter.) Perceived probabilities play a major role in risk assessment, and we don't handle the task of assigning probabilities well.

Here's an example. College students, women voters, and business people were asked to rank the risk of dying from eating pesticide-contaminated food, using as a scale a ranked list of causes of accidental deaths. The college students ranked pesticides at about the same level as automobile accidents, which are, statistically, the number 1 cause of accidental death in the United States. The women voters ranked pesticides, on a 1–30 scale, at about 9, which is one rank below drowning. Business people ranked pesticides at 15, the same as home appliances on the 30-point scale. The data presented with the article indicates that pesticide danger should be ranked 27.

Let's assume the survey was valid and the other data correct. The conclusion is that people don't estimate risks very well. In this case, risk was treated as essentially being equivalent to probability. It's worth noting, however, that the baseline data (the ranking of pesticides as number 27) can be severely flawed. The fact is that we don't know very much yet about how such chemicals affect us over the longer term. Also, in this survey death from pesticides was compared with accidental deaths, and death from ingestion of contaminated food, while accidental in a sense, is not quite the same as death from power mowers (ranked 22). Nonetheless, in terms of what we do know currently, the probability estimates of the respondents were far removed from reality.

Another factor is that people can *choose* to drive a car or operate a power mower or go skiing. But until organic food is more widely available, most of us don't have the option of selecting such food and are dependent on what comes from the grocery store shelves, risky or not. Even then, poor people may not be able to afford the premium price at which organically grown food sells.

Then there's psychological makeup. In a case where two people confront exactly the same decision situation, have assigned the exact same outcome and probabilities, and have the same asset levels, one person may take greater chances than the other. The scientific reasons for that behavior lie beyond our understanding at the present time. Some reach for the latchkey; others reach for the road.

DISCOUNTING THE FUTURE

All decisions involve the future. And those of any consequence — including auto purchases, deciding to increase funding for care of the elderly, and choosing whether or not to restore lost wetlands — involve large streams of benefits and costs extending over long periods of time.

Monetary interest is a way of handling time in decision making, a method of connecting the present with the future. The prevailing assumption underlying discounting is that people prefer rewards now rather than later. Thus a premium must be paid for delaying gratification. Consider the following two alternatives:*

Alternative A: Receive $100 now.

Alternative B: Receive $100 exactly one year from now.

Alternative A is preferred for two reasons. First, if you have $100 now, you can put it to work for you. Second, if you wait, there's always the risk that something will happen to prevent you from receiving the $100 in a year. The second reason is easy to understand. The first may require some elaboration.

Receiving the $100 now allows you to invest it at some rate of interest making it worth more than $100 in a year. Suppose you can earn 10 percent interest on the money in a risk-free investment, such as government bonds. In one year, the $100 grows to $110. Therefore, it's obvious that $100 received one year from now is not worth the same to you as $100 received immediately. It's worth less, since if you had it now, you could invest it and have more than $100 in a year. That simple fact underlies the idea of discounting.

If receiving $100 in one year is less valuable than $100 now, just how much less is it worth? That is, how much should we discount it? First

---

*If you're put off by mathematics, don't worry about it. Just look for the overall impact of interest rates on decision making in the discussion.

calculate the monetary value of having $100 right now that you can invest for one year:

Future amount = principal + interest earned in one year

Let F = the future amount that will be earned in one year, P = the principal, and i = the rate of interest (assume 10 percent). Then

$$F = P + (P \times i) \qquad \text{or simply} \qquad P + Pi$$

$$F = \$100 + (\$100 \times 10\%) = \$100 + \$10 = \$110$$

This is no more than the ordinary calculation you carry out when, for example, you put money in a savings account. We can turn this around and ask, How much would you have to invest now to have $110 in one year, when the interest rate is 10 percent? Of course, we already know the answer — $100 — but doing the calculation will help establish a method that works when we don't know the answer at the outset. First, we'll simplify a little: $F = P + (P \times i)$ is the same as $F = P(1 + i)$. To check this, multiply the content of the parentheses by P, and you'll get $P + Pi$, which is what we had above. Factor out P from both terms, and $P(1 + i)$ is the result.

If, as we just observed, $F = P(1 + i)$, then dividing both sides of the equation by $(1 + i)$ produces

$$P = F/(1 + i)$$

Solving for P will tell us how much we need to invest to have F dollars in one year at interest rate i. Confirm this by substituting our original numbers in place of the symbols: F = $110 and i = .10. So,

$$P = \$110/(1 + .10) = \$100$$

If you want to confirm this, get out your calculator and divide $110 by (1 + .10): (1 + .10) is the same thing as 1.1, so $110/1.1 = $100.

Let's go back to our original set of alternatives: Receive $100 now or receive $100 exactly one year from now. You chose Alternative A because $100 a year from now is less valuable than $100 today that can be invested and be worth $110 in a year. But bringing in the interest rate of 10 percent gives us this second set of alternatives:

Alternative A: Receive $100 now.

Alternative B: Receive $110 for certain exactly one year from now.

Other things being equal, you'll be neutral between the two alternatives. If you're not, there's something wrong with the rate of interest being used. Suppose you still prefer the $100 now. Changing the interest rate to 15 percent:

Alternative A: Receive $100 now.

Alternative B: Receive $115 a year from now.

At some point, most people will be neutral between the two alternatives. Where is that point? It depends on the interest rate, which, as I pointed out earlier, is a device that rewards you for waiting. To the extent that the investment has risk attached to it, you'll demand an even higher interest rate to make you neutral between the present and future opportunities. That's why risk and return are positively related. The higher the degree of risk, the greater the potential return must be to overcome risk aversiveness.

In general, the value now of a sum received one year from now can be found by our earlier work:

$$P = F/(1 + .1)$$

Remember F is the future amount, so, $P = \$100/(1.1) = \$90.91$; $90.91 is called the *present value* of $100, when the rate of interest is 10 percent. This result answers the question posed earlier concerning the worth today of $100 received in one year.

Given this, you'll be neutral between the following two alternatives:

Alternative A: Receive $90.91 today when the interest rate is 10 percent.

Alternative B: Receive $100 exactly one year from now.

In other words, $100 a year from now is worth only $90.91 in today's terms. But $100 today will be worth $110 in one year. That's why you prefer $100 today. The future is *discounted* because it's not as valuable as the present, and the applicable rate of interest is the *discount rate.*

By simple mathematics (which I'll omit here), it can also be shown that the value of benefits received at the end of year two, rather than year one as we've been assuming, is given by

$$P = F/(1 + i)^2$$

For three years, it's

$$P = F/(1 + i)^3$$

For *n* years, it's

$$P = F/(1 + i)^n$$

Therefore, $100 received at the end of year two is worth only $82.64 today. The present value of $100 received at the end of three years is $75.13.

The key ideas here are, first, that benefits received in the future are worth less than the same benefits received earlier and, second, the magnitude by which they are less is determined both by *when* they are received and by the *discount rate* applied in the analysis.

To understand this second idea, focus on the denominator in the $P = F/(1 + i)$ equation. As i—the interest rate—gets larger, the present value of a sum received in a given year gets smaller, and vice versa. If $100 is received ten years from now and the interest rate is 10 percent, the present value is $38.55. If the interest rate is 20 percent, that same $100 is worth only $16.15 in present-value terms.

Again, there are two variables here: time and the discount rate. And they work in tandem with one another. Think about our original example one more time. If $100 a year from now is worth $90.91 today, what happens when we change either the time period or the discount rate?

Extending the time period to greater than one year results in *lower* present value.

Reducing the time period to less than one year results in *higher* present value.

Increasing the discount rate while keeping the time period constant results in *lower* present value.

Reducing the discount rate while keeping the time period constant results in *higher* present value.

Then, of course, there are all the combinations you can get from changing the time period and the discount rate in combination with one another.

One final point: Costs as well as benefits must be discounted back to the present. If benefits received in the future are less than they are worth today, then future costs will be less expensive to cover than they are today, *if* you invest money now to pay for these future costs. One simple way of handling this is to subtract costs from benefits in any given future year and discount the result, that is, compute the present value of net benefits.

RISK, PROBABILITY, DISCOUNTING, AND THE BASIC DECISION MODEL

Linking together several ideas here will serve us well in the chapters to come. This is a book about the future, and decisions are, to a large extent, what determine our futures. We confront alternatives, choose among these alternatives, and the outcomes follow.

What determines our choices? First, there's the matter of criteria — the content of our criteria set, how the criteria are ranked, and how the criteria are weighted relative to one another. The second determinant is the set of alternatives available to us.

Risk, probability, and discounting enter the basic model in the following ways.* Remember, we scored each alternative against each criterion. How do we arrive at the scores? Let's compare two hypothetical alternatives. If we're absolutely certain about how well Alternative A will perform on a given criterion, presumably our scoring will reflect that. Similarly, if we're uncertain, presumably the scoring will reflect that also.

---

*There are better methods of illustrating how risk, probability, and discounting influence decision making than the model I'm using. The advantage of this approach is its emphasis on multiple criteria, which is at the heart of much decision making. It is also much easier for the casual reader to understand than are the more advanced models used by economists.

Here's an example. Consider a farmer deciding whether to forego chemical use on his or her fields. Currently, even though a number of farmers appear to be making quasi-organic farming work, many others consider the potential for success too uncertain to take the chance on switching over. If a farmer currently using chemicals could be absolutely certain that yields would remain constant, and that the costs (including physical effort) would be the same or less, then more farmers undoubtedly would select the chemical-free alternative. As one agricultural official put it, the decision "turns on the bottom line." In other words, net revenue is the dominant decision criterion in this situation.

Imagine a farmer scoring the alternatives (1) reduce chemicals and (2) use the same amount of chemicals. One criterion will be *impact on yields*. From past experience, the farmer has good estimates of yields based on the use of chemicals. How do you think "reduce chemicals" will fare against the chemical alternative on the yields criterion? Probably not too well, due to the uncertainty involved.

Does that mean the farmer will necessarily choose the old chemical method? No. It depends on what other criteria are in the set. If *health risk due to polluted wells* is treated as a separate criterion and is ranked high, it's possible that "reduce chemicals" can still be selected. Note that risk can be handled in the scoring of alternatives relative to criteria or as a criterion itself.

Now to discounting. This usually enters via scoring against the criterion of *net revenue*. And note that *crop yields* might be considered as a subset of this criterion. If the farmer borrows operating capital at the local bank, he or she might use the bank's interest rate for the loan as the discount rate. Net revenue involves not only expected cash inflows, but also costs. And expected yields certainly influence revenues. But if chemical farming is more expensive on the cost side, some surprising results may occur.

There's one problem here, though. The benefits from a reduction in the dependence on chemicals may not start to show up in the farmer's income statement for several years. In this case, the higher the discount rate, with other things being equal, the worse the chemically free alternative will appear.

Complicated isn't it? Earlier, I asked how we can be so stupid as to destroy our earthly life-support systems. It's not all stupidity. Part of it has to do with the enormous complexity involved in making decisions. And the complexity escalates when it comes to making decisions in which more than one person is involved, that is, decisions of a societal nature. I turn to that next.

Just before moving on, let me reemphasize something. I make no claim for this model other than the one I made at the beginning of the chapter: It's helpful to me in understanding both individual and collective behavior and in formulating solutions to tough problems. I've used it many times. I'll use it again.

FOR FURTHER READING

Anthan, George. "Farmers Say They'll Keep Old Methods." *Des Moines Register,* April 1, 1990, p. 1A.

Ballard, Larry. "The Debate Rages On: Are Farm Chemicals Harmful?" *Waterloo Courier,* April 1, 1990, p. C1.

Hogarth, Robin. *Judgement and Choice.* 2d ed., New York: John Wiley, 1987.

Kepner, Charles H., and Benjamin B. Tregoe, *The New Rational Manager.* Princeton, N.J.: Kepner-Tregoe, 1981.

McKenna, Christopher K. *Quantitative Methods for Public Decision Making.* New York: McGraw-Hill, 1980.

Tietenberg, Tom. *Environmental and Natural Resource Economics.* 2d ed., Glenview, Ill.: Scott, Foresman, 1988.

Tversky, Amos and Daniel Kahneman, "Judgment under Uncertainty: Heuristics and Biases." *Science* 185:1124–31.

CHAPTER FOUR

Markets

I n the spring of 1990, the desire for freedom and its implementation are in ascendance throughout the Soviet Union, Eastern Europe, and other places in the world. There are two dimensions to this revolution, or perhaps evolution. First is the demand for political freedom, for governments elected by the people and responsive to the people's will. The second is a strong movement away from centrally planned economies and toward market economies based on private incentives. The propellants for the trend toward a market style of economic organization are, clearly, economic growth in general and a wider range of consumer goods in particular.

Onetime communists are running their own beauty parlors and opening their own auto repair shops in Moscow. The government of Vietnam, a country that has become economically prostrate, is experimenting with the encouragement of privately owned small business in the retail and service sectors. Bulgaria is doing the same.

Venture capital is supplied to local entrepreneurs in Hungary. Tanzania is cutting back on its public payrolls, Angola is trying to sell state companies to private entrepreneurs, and Nigeria has abandoned exchange controls. Meanwhile, India witnesses the rise of a large middle class demanding less governmental interference with its lives and businesses.

On the one hand, then, we should be jubilant. Freedom is afoot; unfettered commerce soars. At the same time, we are haunted by a growing sense that all is not well in the West, where political and economic freedom have a history of some length. Our social problems mount; our natural systems crumble.

Centrally planned economies have demonstrated that they are no better at dealing with social and environmental perplexities than are democracies; for example, Czechoslovakia suffers from almost unbelievable environmental degradation. But that's not the point here. The issue is this: Given the rising political and economic aspirations of much of the world, along with the unceasing demands for a higher standard of living by those in already developed economies, what can be said about the relationships among political and economic freedom, social dilemmas, and environmental degradation? In constructing a future for a state or a nation, how does the architecture of freedom influence sustainability?

There are, I think, three aspects to all of this. The first has to do with economic freedom, which I'll discuss in the context of market economies, their strengths and their weaknesses (especially the weaknesses, since rampant boosterism found everywhere takes care of the cheerleading).

Second, political freedom has its attractions. I love it, you love it. But freedom also has it liabilities, as we are discovering. The trick is to enjoy the benefits while circumventing, or at least mitigating, as many of the problems as possible.

Third, having laid the foundation in the discussion of economic and political freedom, I'll talk about how we can find ourselves in traps, in spite of our best rational efforts at constructing futures. (In this chapter I deal with the critical issues surrounding market economies and in Chapter Five the dilemmas of democracy and social traps.) The three ideas are not easily separable, since all involve freedom and the problems spawned by the practice of freedom. Each, in its way, has much to say about the difficulties of creating a sustainable state, nation, and world.

FREE MARKETS, PRICES, AND THE PROBLEM OF COST

Even though we live daily in the roll and toss of a reasonably free market system, most people have only a vague idea of how it really functions. There's supply and demand, of course. And capital markets. And the right to open your own restaurant or recycling business if you wish.

But it's a little more subtle than that, particularly in the area of cost and how we measure it, how we try to avoid it, and how governments — federal, state, and local — alternately demand we pay our way or allow us to escape the costs of our economic activities. To begin, here's a brief review of the principal characteristics of *capitalism,* the broad and frequently misunderstood term that describes the economic system of the United States and an increasing number of other countries.

The first characteristic is that *capital,* the means of production and the money to buy those means, is privately owned. As with all mixed economies, governments own some of the plant and equipment and land, but the basic idea is that, insofar as possible, private individuals should own the means of production. A second characteristic is *freedom of choice.* As consumers, we can choose to purchase or reject goods and services. Moreover, we can freely decide to enter whatever business we want, consistent of course with our financial resources and legal restraints.

A third aspect of capitalism is *competition.* Firms compete with one another for the consumer's dollar and for sales to other firms or to governments. Individuals compete with one another for jobs and for those goods or services in short supply. Finally, a fourth characteristic is the notion of *markets,* which is closely related to all of the first three. Markets are where buyers and sellers meet. If more is effectively demanded of a certain good or service, prices go up. The reverse is also true.

The meeting of buyers and sellers in markets determines prices. In a perfectly competitive market, the economist's utopia, all sellers bring an identical product to the market and no seller has enough market power to determine price in isolation from the market. Most of our markets, however, are less than perfect, except for certain areas of agriculture. Sellers have varying levels of market power whereby they can bring differentiated goods or services (for example, television sets) to the marketplace at a predetermined price. Though a farmer takes the price of corn posted at the local elevator as a given, General Motors sets the price at which it is willing to sell an automobile and then maybe bargains a little after that. Wal-Mart doesn't bargain at all but does raise and lower prices in response to consumer demand.

The key idea is whether the seller is a price setter or a price taker. Iowa corn farmers are price takers; they take the market price as a given. General Motors and Wal-Mart are price setters.

In any case, and few people seem to understand this, prices are really information devices. They signal what is wanted and what is not wanted, in terms of goods, services, labor, monetary capital, and so forth. Higher prices, other things being equal, send signals to producers that more of a product or service is wanted. Lower prices perform the opposite task.

The price system is the real magic (if that's the right word) of capitalism. In highly controlled economies, exemplified by the Soviets over the last seventy years, central planners confront an overwhelming array of decisions. They must decide on what to produce, how much of it to produce, where to produce it, who should produce it, when to produce it, and what price to charge for it.

These planners, as history has demonstrated, are simply overwhelmed by the complexity of their task. They cannot gather all the necessary information, process it, and make decisions in a way that assures products and services of the kind needed arrive at where they should be in a timely fashion. It's complexity that defeats them, whereas the price system in free markets makes these decisions in a more or less automatic, decentralized fashion. Along with the powerful thrust of self-interest, the prices and the information they provide are the propellants for capitalism.

If we judge an economic system by conventional standards of growth in per capita income, capitalism certainly seems to work. The performances of the United States, West Germany, and Japan over the last forty years are a testament to that. Yet, as I discussed in Chapter Two, things are not going as well as they might be. Not well at all, in fact, at least by my standards. Many of the problems are a result of what is called "market failure."

Costs and Market Failure

At the outset, let's agree that markets do not fail, cultures do. Any socially sanctioned market operates within a framework of laws and customs, which are products of the culture. Still, market failure is the customary term and is well established in the literature of economics, so I'll use it.

Markets are where buyers and sellers come together to conduct exchange. Usually, except for barter situations, goods or services are traded using money as an exchange medium. A driving force in market economies is profit—revenues minus costs minus taxes. I'll set aside the tax issue until later and concentrate here on revenues and costs.

Units sold multiplied by the selling price of the units determines revenue. Costs, as most people ordinarily think of them, are those charges that must be deducted from revenues to arrive at net profit before taxes. Common examples of costs are payments made to labor, suppliers of raw materials, suppliers of finished or intermediate goods, suppliers of information, and freight carriers, as well as costs for advertising, rent or mortgage or lease payments, utilities, and interest charges on borrowed money.

No problem so far. To the extent that the only costs incurred in the production of a good or service are those listed on the firm's income statement, all is well, economically and socially.* Things start to get shaky, though, when producers of a product or service do not have to pay for all the costs they incur, and that's the case for virtually all business operations. If you tell someone you're going to lecture on the subject of costs, you can be assured that a glaze of boredom will settle instantly over his or her eyes. To anyone interested in why things go wrong in our society and what to do about fixing them, however, costs are not boring. In fact, the subject of costs is a fascinating and fertile area for exploration into the failures of market systems to provide for care of the natural environment and various social ills.

Private costs are the kinds of costs most people think of, the ones that normally appear on the income statement of business firms. Suppose, however, that in the process of production, a firm dumps pollutants into the air or water or onto the soil. The owners of the firm are getting away with something. They're not paying all of the costs of production, since they've escaped paying cleanup charges.

Who *is* paying for these costs? Third parties—another individual, society at large, or future generations. These are called *social costs*. A classic example is that of a firm, call it Big Polluter, that has an outlet pipe from its manufacturing plant into a nearby river. Out of this pipe flows unspeakable crud—arsenic, lead, acid, and what-have-you. The river becomes polluted, the water undrinkable, fish die.

Those costs of production are being generated, but not being paid, by Big Polluter. The firm is sloughing off these costs onto someone else. Economists use the descriptive terms of "internal costs" and "external costs" to distinguish between private costs and those costs ladled off onto third parties.

When a firm externalizes part of its costs onto someone else, the

---

*I said all is well. Not quite. We can quarrel with *what* is being produced. Chrome on autos is not necessarily the same as food for hungry children. Economists do not like to talk about such matters and prefer to view markets as amoral. I am not an economist, however, and I'll get to those value judgments eventually.

signals from the price system go awry. If the firm is not paying for all of the costs it incurs, its prices can be lower. In the usual supply-and-demand situation, lower prices result in a larger quantity sold. Therefore, more of a given product or service is being sold than would be warranted if the true costs of production were taken into account. The market is failing to register accurately how resources ought to be allocated.

And right there, in the divergence between private and social costs, is the crux of our agonizing debate over the environment (and, to some extent, other social problems). Social critics, environmentalists included, demand that business firms pay the full and true costs of production. But if the full costs are paid, profits will be lower. If profits are lower, less money flows into the hands of business owners and managers; the firm's stock issues don't look as attractive, and neither do its bonds, and neither do its income statements being perused by lending institutions.

Recently, in Clinton, Iowa, a rendering firm operating under the name of National By-Products responded to complaints about odors emanating from the plant by telling Clinton officials that the firm is "in business to make money, not spend money." Exactly! And a good way, a real good way, to make money is to let someone else pay part of your costs.

Labor unions, and workers in general, are not all that fond of environmentalists when it comes to the crunch. Environmentalists demanding the full-cost treatment are implicitly arguing for higher prices, therefore less demand for the product, therefore lower demand for labor, therefore lower wages and fewer workers employed. Loss of jobs is one of the first objections raised when it comes to environmental issues, such as the banning of styrofoam containers.

Who else doesn't like environmentalists and other social critics? Lots of people. Anyone, in fact, who objects to paying the full costs of his or her own activities. Those politicians whose popularity hinges on promising ever-higher standards of living via economic growth may pay lip service to environmental concerns, but secretly they're nervous about the whole affair. Some are outright hostile. They know what the environmentalists are up to — paying the full costs of production is a real drag on economic growth, including job growth, for all of the reasons just listed.

How about consumers? As I said earlier, I don't believe that three out of four people are environmentalists, even though polls may show that. They may *say* they're environmentalists, but they haven't been asked to assume the true costs of their consumption activities yet.

Suppose your friendly banker asks for some financial information as a condition to providing you with a mortgage. Basically, he or she is going to look at your income and how much of that income goes for present expenditures — your cash flow, in other words — and how much will be left over for mortgage payments. Now in the last year you've dumped the following into your trash cans or down your drains: mouse poison, oil-based paints, turpentine, furniture stripper, silver polish, furniture polish, brake fluid, and used motor oil. In addition, you burned up 750 gallons of gasoline, which pumped ten thousand pounds of carbon dioxide into the atmosphere.

That's not all. Say you used twelve thousand kilowatt-hours of electricity, which is not unusual for people with all-electric houses. That required twelve thousand pounds of coal with a carbon dioxide output of twenty-four thousand pounds. If you used natural gas, you produced methane (one of the culprits in the warming-of-the-earth controversy). If you flew in an airplane, some more costs are added. In addition, you needed food and purchased other items that contributed to environmental degradation.

Your banker examines your income, subtracts what you think of as ordinary expenditures, and then further deducts for your impact on the environment. Suddenly your dream house is even further removed than you thought from your ability to pay. The full costs of your existence have just been assessed, and you're madder than hell at the environmentalists who pressured bankers into looking at things this way. As much as I want to believe the polls, I contend that three out of four Americans are *not* environmentalists, no matter what they say. They just haven't been assessed the true costs of their existence yet, either in higher prices for products or charges for disposal of the waste products from consumption.

How would you feel if your local state representative or senator proposed an additional $2 per gallon tax on gasoline? That wouldn't be exorbitant, in view of the problems caused by the burning of fossil fuels and by our limited supply of them. If three out of four of us were true environmentalists, we'd grit our teeth, vote for the politician, and bear it. My guess is that less than 20 percent of the population would agree to such a proposal. The remainder would throw the rascal out of office, along with his or her environmental cronies.

A recent poll commissioned by *Time* showed 94 percent of those Americans surveyed ranked environmental problems as very important. When these same people were asked if they would be willing to pay an extra $500 in taxes to clean up the environment, only 44 percent said they would. My guess is that the figure of 44 percent is overly optimistic;

if the respondents had been asked to produce a check for $500, the figure would have been much lower than 44 percent.

In a culture geared to maximizing consumption via wages and profits, strong incentives exist to hold down required expenditures in order to maximize discretionary income. Social costs are a deduction from wages and business revenues and, hence, reduce the discretionary income left over for consumption, executive perquisites, new university buildings, and so on.

If we really wanted cleaner air, we would long ago have demanded that automakers produce cars emitting less pollution, even though such vehicles would cost more. As Eugene Linden has remarked: "Just as middle-class voters routinely condemn 'welfare' while opposing cuts in the social programs that constitute such spending, a good portion of the voters who claim they would pay for environmental improvements balk when the bill is presented."

So we live with market failure because it's convenient to live with it; it's nice to have someone else, the future in particular, pick up part of our tab. We are beginning to confront the costs of having done so. Nature, you see, is a "free good," or so it appears. The sky, the earth, the water—we are used to thinking of them as free, when they are not. For generations we've been ignoring the full costs of our activities, shoveling them forward. In a world of scarcity on Spaceship Earth, this behavior doesn't work. Somebody, sometime, is going to pay those costs.

What we have done, and this is particularly insidious, is to incur costs associated with the natural environment without having paid for them. They are liabilities, and the payment is suddenly due. It's not much fun to foot the bill for the party long after it has passed, but that's what we're confronting. (Later I'll discuss nineteenth-century coal tar wastes in Iowa, the costs of which will be borne by current residents of Iowa.)

Since Iowa is a state with a considerable dependence on agriculture, let's look at farm operations and social costs. Suppose soil erosion exceeding the regenerative powers of nature averages ¼ inch every four years over the length and breadth of a 640-acre farm. That's 160 inches of soil lost. If the average depth of topsoil is 6 inches on this farm, nearly twenty-seven acres of soil is lost every four years. At a price of $1,200 per acre, that's $32,400 of soil lost. You don't have to be a master of arithmetic to understand that the soil-eroding farmer, when making up his or her income statement, is understating cost and overstating profit.

But isn't the soil loss a private cost? Yes and no. Part of it is private to the extent that land productivity declines and farmers must use more fertilizer to maintain yields. Yet society bears another part of the cost, since soil erosion is the prime culprit in surface water contamination from pesticides, herbicides, and fertilizers, along with its further impact on siltation of flood-control reservoirs, drainage channels, fish kills, and decline of recreational opportunities due to loss of boating and fishing areas. The Conservation Foundation estimates these costs to U.S. society at $6 billion per year. And, of course, to the extent yields decline, higher food prices constitute another such cost.

If we wish to measure the true costs of production accurately, farmers should be assessed a cost equal to what is needed to clean up the surface water pollution caused by soil erosion, to remove silt from behind dams, to replace fish, and to provide alternative recreational opportunities, along with a charge, however that might be measured, for the loss of a critical asset — a *depletion charge,* in other words. Topsoil, because of its critical importance to all of us, can be viewed as a kind of social asset, even though it's privately owned. From that point of view, society suffers not only the costs already mentioned, but also the loss of a social asset.

Direct Social Costs

The kind of social costs I have been discussing thus far are "direct social costs." Here are some more examples.

1. Noise pollution. Your neighbor plays a stereo so loudly that you are annoyed by it. You are paying a cost in annoyance for your neighbor's revenues in the form of enjoyment of loud music. It's generally accepted that sound levels exceeding 85 decibels — roughly equivalent to the sound level produced by a food blender or power leaf blower — are potentially hazardous. Of the nearly 30 million Americans with severe hearing loss, about one-third can attribute the loss at least partly to exposure to loud sounds.
2. Air pollution. The Davol Company of Cranston, Rhode Island, produces a useful chemical called ethylene oxide, which is the only chemical in the world that can sterilize many medical tools. The chemical is credited with saving thousands of people from death by infection. But in the production of ethylene oxide, Davol emits pollutants that, federal officials say, could significantly increase the risk of cancer for nearby residents. Most of the emissions can be trapped by pollution-control equipment costing $150,000. The company has

delayed purchasing the equipment for twenty years and only recently agreed to install it; that is, Davol has been escaping the true costs of its production activities.

As a result of laxity in federal laws, the dirtiest industries in the nation are spewing forth 2.7 billion tons per year of toxic substances: chloroform from Maine paper mills, trichloroethylene from Massachusetts computer companies, pollutants from midwestern utilities. Each such pollutant has its own configuration of risks, from cancer to birth defects to brain damage to spontaneous abortions to acid rain.

Emissions from copper smelters in northern Mexico have increased the acidity of rain in southern Iowa by a hundredfold. In Bombay, India, as well as Los Angeles, California, heavy smog is causing breathlessness, dizziness, and eye irritation.

3. Hazardous wastes. We Iowans generate about four thousand tons of hazardous wastes each year. In 1989, the Iowa Department of Natural Resources (DNR) listed thirty hazardous waste sites in Iowa. An additional thirty have been proposed for inclusion on the state's registry for such sites and another four hundred are candidates for that list. Charles City, Iowa, has three sites on the Environmental Protection Agency's Superfund list, which is an inventory of the worst hazardous wastes sites in the United States.

Mining operations are the leading generators of hazardous wastes, producing twice as much each year as all other industries and municipal landfills combined. In the nineteenth century, Iowans used coal gas as major source of fuel for lighting, heating, and cooking. Coal tar was a by-product of coal gas manufacturing. As a result, we have about 150 abandoned coal tar pits, many located in densely populated areas, which are considered serious environmental hazards by the Iowa DNR.

4. Farm pesticides. The U.S. Environmental Protection Agency has identified the presence of seventy-four pesticides in surface and groundwater in thirty-four states. Iowa farmers rank second (sometimes first) in the nation in pesticide use, applying it to 95 percent of the corn crop and 97 percent of the soybeans. The systemic effects of pesticide use are diverse. High levels cause fish and wildlife kills, or bring about behavioral and reproductive changes in aquatic organisms, or both.

Ultimately, some pesticides and herbicides enter the human food chain through concentration in plant and animal tissues. A study of the Iowa River in the 1970s and 1980s showed the following pesticides present in the water: Atrazine, Bladex, DDT, DDE, Dual, Dyfonate, Lasso, and Sencor. Dieldrin is being detected today in some Iowa waters, even though it has not been used in Iowa since 1977.

George Hallberg conducted a water quality survey for the Iowa DNR for the years 1988 and 1989. He states, "It is clear that 35 percent to 40 percent of all Iowans are using drinking water that contains some detectable concentration of pesticides during the course of a year."

5. Overcrowding of national parks. *My* enjoyment detracts from *yours* and vice versa. We are creating direct social costs for each other. The Boundary Waters Canoe Area (BWCA) on the Minnesota-Canada border is an example. Kevin Proescholdt, executive director of Friends of the Boundary Water Wilderness, says: "Canoeists run into crowds of other canoeists, which diminishes the BWCA's solitude. Visitors also are having an impact on its campsites and portages." This is what I earlier called a loss of amenities.

6. Stream channelization. In Iowa, the dredging, clearing, and straightening of stream channels and banks for purposes of flood control or to gain more farmland have taken about 15 percent of Iowa's twenty-thousand-mile river system since the state was first settled. That's three thousand miles. The costs are shifted to those who fish and boat, to people who like scenery, and to wildlife, among others. In addition, channelization contributes to the silting of dams, since streams flow faster and carry silt further. Martin Konrad, a fisheries specialist for the DNR, states, "The landowners say it's their land and they should be able to do as they please."

7. Oil spills. The polluting of Prince William Sound and surrounding environs in Alaska due to the running aground of the *Exxon Valdez* tanker is the most obvious example. Big Oil, though, is not the only sinner. In an average city of one hundred thousand people, residents dump 3.44 tons of motor oil into city drains each month. According to the American Petroleum Institute, the total amount of oil dumped by the *Exxon Valdez* is spilled every two weeks by do-it-yourself auto mechanics who change their oil, and then pour the used oil down the sewer. That's roughly 240 million gallons annually, or enough fuel to heat every home in Portland, Oregon, for a year.

8. Industrial injuries and faulty products. Russel Mokhiber, author and lawyer, has pointed out that, every year, roughly 28,000 deaths and 130,000 injuries are caused by dangerous products. At least one hundred thousand workers die from exposure to deadly chemicals

and other hazards. Workplace carcinogens are estimated to cause between 23 and 38 percent of all cancer deaths.

The *Des Moines Register* surveyed state occupational health and safety files for 1989. These records showed that Iowa workers were exposed to lead, asbestos, hepatitis, repetitive motion injuries, electrical shock, and other hazards. Fines were levied against firms in violation of the laws pertaining to these hazards, in a rough-hewn attempt to make the firms pay social costs.

9. Solid wastes. Americans generate more than three and a half pounds of solid waste per person per day. This is twice as much as many industrialized nations, and only about 10 percent of this waste is recycled. We create a social cost by our disposal of this waste (as was illustrated in the bank loan example earlier).

10. Radioactive wastes. Those who tout nuclear energy as the carefree answer to our energy and related environmental woes either do not read very much or are gamblers of the first order. Nuclear power plants have a nasty habit of creating by-products, inevitable ones, that are radioactive for up to three million years. This waste requires heavy shielding in order not to cause lethal damage to human or animal life straying into its vicinity.

The federal government has tried, and tried again, to find a satisfactory disposal site. The latest candidate is Yucca Mountain in Nevada; the government has spent $500 million over a two-year period on this project and has delayed the opening date of the site to 2010. Other alternatives explored and discarded include salt caves in the southern United States and granite storage dumps in Michigan and other states.

Nobody, it seems, wants to pay part of the costs of disposal in the form of risk by living near such lethal discards, and understandable reluctance known as the NIMBY (not in my backyard) principle. Nevada citizens, environmentalists, and scientists all are opposed to the Yucca Mountain project. Incidentally, the Department of Defense is one of the major producers of radioactive waste, from its weapons plants. Some engineers have suggested (fruitlessly, I note with relief) firing the wastes into outer space in an effort to have the universe beyond earth sustain part of our social costs.

11. Ozone pollution. Our use of chlorofluorocarbons in such products as air conditioners and insulation has damaged the ozone layer above the earth. Again, social costs are present. One of them is the current dramatic increase in skin cancer. A 1990 study by the Izaak

Walton League indicates air pollution is causing billions of dollars of crop damage for American farmers. The data from this study show ozone pollution to cause at least $3.1 billion per year in lost productivity for soybeans, corn, wheat, and peanuts. Ozone concentrations in most U.S. agricultural regions is estimated at two to three times higher than would be the case without human influence.

12. Trees. Iowa is one of the most treeless states in the nation, somewhere around fourth from the bottom. Still, we continue to experience a net loss of trees.* Iowa's foresters estimate that four or five trees are removed for every one planted in this state. Forester John Walkowiak, of Des Moines, says, "Some Iowa communities are at a critical point, where continued tree removal without replacement could make portions of their city or town treeless in ten to twenty years."

The major reason is economic growth and what is loosely referred to as development, which is accompanied by tree removal, little or no tree planting, and poor pruning efforts. Algona, Iowa, chopped down eighty-one mature oaks and maples in 1989 to make room for the widening of Highway 169 through the town. Most of the trees were from 75 to 150 years old.

The arguments in favor of the project centered around the benefits to economic growth that less than one mile of improved highway would bring to the town. A few citizens fought a court battle to save the trees but were overwhelmed by the Iowa Department of Transportation and those who believed economic development should dominate trees. Incidentally, the proposed benefits of the larger highway were questionable, resting as they did on traffic counts that were, at best, inconsistent.

Did the highway supporters in Algona generate a social cost? Yes. In addition to the considerable aesthetic benefits, which apparently not everyone experiences, trees give us shade. Air conditioning costs can be reduced by up to 50 percent with the right tree in the right location. Trees also provide habitat for birds and small animals, decrease air pollution, and reduce noise. We also seem to forget, somehow, that trees produce oxygen. Aesthetics aside, arborist Arnold Webster assigned a value to the Algona trees of $288,000.

---

*The data are a little shaky here. One recent study claims Iowa is showing a slight net increase in trees since 1974.

There are more examples of social costs. A lot more. Those cited in the above list, however, should be enough to convince any skeptic that we are not paying the costs of our production and consumption activities. Hence, we consistently overstate our joys of consumption, business profits, and the benefits of government expenditures.

National Accounting and Cost

Even Gross National Product, our revered measure of societal progress, is . . . well, grossly overstated. Basically, GNP is computed by toting up our expenditures on all goods and services. The sum is the market value, determined by market prices, of the nation's output. If markets are failing to provide us with the proper signals via the price system, however, something is wrong with our measurements. GNP omits certain benefits, such as the value of a scenic vista or the labor of homemakers (the old joke provided to generations of undergraduates goes like this: A man marries his housekeeper, and GNP drops). But it's costs we're interested in here.

If our national income accounts are limited to counting only market-determined values and prices are not reflecting true costs, then certain important costs are being omitted. It can get a little strange. Here's an example.

Beginning in the 1950s, the Shell Rock River in northern Iowa became badly polluted. Three sources were responsible for the pollution. Soil erosion was one. The second was sewage from towns and cities along the river. The third was the city of Albert Lea, Minnesota, and the Wilson packing plant in Albert Lea.

The river almost died. In fact, it was dead, devoid of life, for about fifteen miles below Albert Lea in the 1970s. Nowhere in GNP is the cost of a dead or dying river shown. Yet, when pressures were brought to bear and Albert Lea cleaned up its problems, the cost of constructing a new sewage disposal plant in that city was included in GNP. The same was true for the Iowa cities that reconstructed their sewage disposal operations.

So while the Shell Rock was being polluted, all of the economic activity along the river in two states was being counted as net additions to GNP. The social cost was not deducted from the total. When the problem was partially fixed by construction or modification of sewage plants and Wilson's disposal methods, those expenditures were also counted as additions to GNP.

We can't lose! Just keep counting the benefits and ignoring the costs, and everything looks great. Furthermore, though the river's condition has improved, agricultural runoff still is polluting it, and we are counting the value of crops and livestock taken to market but ignoring the pollution costs.

Is there a way out of this? Conceptually, yes. Even though the numbers are often hard to come by, it's worth a look at how we might go about getting a better measure of national (or state) economic performance. Take GNP and subtract from that figure the plant and equipment used up in the process of production (this is done in the national accounts). The result is Net National Product (NNP).

What we want is something that might be called Net Social Welfare (NSW), which includes all benefits and costs of our economic activity. Thus, add to NNP the benefits of economic performance that ordinarily are not counted. For example, futurists long have touted increased leisure time as one such benefit. I question whether our leisure time has increased. But for the sake of this example, let's say it has. Other benefits might be improved health and the accumulation of knowledge.

$$\text{NSW} = \text{GNP} - PE + B$$

where PE = the plant and equipment used up in production and B = the total benefits not counted in the computation of GNP.

We still have costs to consider. So let's subtract the kind of social costs I've been discussing. The result is

$$\text{NSW} = \text{GNP} - PE + B - SC$$

where SC represents social costs.

Because GNP less PE is called NNP, the last equation can be simplified to

$$\text{NSW} = \text{NNP} + B - SC$$

Though NSW is difficult, maybe impossible, to compute accurately, it nonetheless is a useful concept simply because it reminds us that certain critical elements are not present in our measures of national progress and well-being.

Without taking into account the real costs of our economic activities, claims made to substantiate something called progress are a joke. For example, Martin Anderson, a former advisor to President Reagan, has made the claim that $30 trillion of wealth was produced from 1982 to 1989.

First of all, Anderson's numbers are wrong, since they appear not to include price increases. Beyond that, however, is the fact that we created untold amounts of environmental and social damage in producing whatever wealth was produced. You can't talk with very much confidence about profits when major costs have not been deducted from revenues. Anderson's claims are a joke.

The next time you hear politicians crowing over the gains in GNP or Iowa Gross Product, remember the costs that are not being counted. They are real, and they can be heavy. President Richard Nixon recognized the problem of social costs. In his 1970 State of the Union address, he argued, "To the extent possible, the price of goods should be made to include the cost of producing and disposing of them without damaging the environment." No one was listening, or if they were, it all sounded rather unpleasant and somewhat inconvenient to pursuing the good life.

Accounting for Direct Costs

Assigning dollar values to direct social costs is not always easy. Often it must be done in purely qualitative terms, though in a society that loves numbers, no matter how error-ridden they might be, qualitative judgments don't carry much weight. Floyd Beams and Paul Fertig dealt with this problem in an excellent 1970 article, asserting: "Accounting is not passive. Accounting provides information on which decisions are made — decisions that result in economic and social actions. If the resulting activities disrupt the environment then accounting is, at least in part, accountable for that disruption."

What they are talking about is the sort of market failure discussed earlier. If a business person looking at his or her accounts sees product Z is selling extremely well, the incentive is present to produce more of Z. To the extent production of Z has attendant social costs, the decision maker is receiving erroneous information via the market and the accountants who keep track of things in conventional accounting practices. Beams and Fertig suggest that, in preparing the financial statements for a firm, both quantifiable and nonquantifiable social costs should be included, even if the nonquantifiable costs are presented in purely descriptive terms.

Notice that Beams and Fertig emphasize decision making. We are back to that. Things always return to decision making. If a manufacturer were looking at the true costs of producing something, his or her decisions about quality, quantity, and even type of product would be affected. In fact, a fair number of the products we produce would probably be operating at a loss, rather than a profit, if all costs were included.

Sometimes it is possible to assign numbers to social costs. Remember Big Polluter, the firm mentioned earlier? In principle, we can ask the towns downstream how much they are willing to pay to get the firm to stop its polluting activities. Whatever they are willing to pay can be taken as a rough estimation of the social cost, with one reservation: Future generations are not being included in the responses.

It's not always that theoretical, though. Des Moines has installed a $3.2 million system to remove nitrates from the city's drinking water, which will cost consumers about $1.50 per month extra on their water bills. The nitrates are a product of agricultural runoff and constitute a social cost not included in the market price of the grain fertilized by the nitrates. Note, this is only the cost to Des Moines. Other cities getting drinking water from the river, along with fish populations, animal populations, and anyone or anything else making use of the river, is sustaining a cost in addition to that paid by Des Moines.

The Clean Air Act of 1990 is estimated to cost U.S. citizens and companies $25 billion a year. The Environmental Protection Agency wanted a plan that would have cost $40 billion a year. President George Bush's plan was in the $14 to $19 billion range. The difference between the two plans was in how much of the pollution cost would be paid for. In any case, the expenditures will appear in GNP as an addition to national welfare, not as a subtraction for costs incurred in the process of fouling the air.

Iowa Southern Utilities, based in Centerville, has announced that its customers would face rate increases of 25 to 30 percent if the clean-air legislation in Congress passed (which it eventually did). The utility now estimates it will cost $203 million to install the necessary equipment at plants in Ottumwa, Burlington, and Sioux City. Of course, the increases will be most harshly felt by those on fixed incomes and the working poor.

That's called a distributional effect of social cost correction, and there are ways around such effects. The important point here is that direct social costs are being incurred but not paid for. Some estimates indicate that the cost of removing power plant and factory emissions contributing to our atmospheric problems could increase the production cost of electricity 50 to 100 percent.

Starkist and other, smaller producers of canned tuna have announced recently that henceforth their tuna will be "dolphin-safe," referring to the hundred thousand dolphins killed each year in the nets of tuna fishermen. The cost of this laudatory action is uncertain, but Starkist thinks it will add a few cents to each can of tuna.

Citing studies on the costs of air pollution damage in Europe, the World Commission on Environment and Development estimates damage to material (for example, buildings) and fish alone at $3 billion per year. Damage to crops, forests, and health is estimated to exceed $10 billion dollars per year. Studies done in Japanese laboratories indicate losses in wheat and rice production due to air pollution and acid rain can reduce crop yields by as much as 30 percent.

Here are two final examples of measurable social costs. For decades, gasoline has been leaking from underground tanks at service stations. Recent legislation in Iowa dealing with groundwater contamination has decreed this pollution must be rectified. The costs to individual service station owners are staggering—as high as $100,000 for removal of the old tanks, cleanup, and installation of new tanks. This is an environmental cost that has not been included in the price of gasoline. The stations, with some help from the state, are stuck with paying it. All of us should have been paying for the entire cost, however, a gallon at a time as we purchased gasoline.

Earlier, I mentioned coal tar pits as a serious potential environmental hazard. Estimated cleanup costs are $1 million or more for many of the sites. According to the DNR, taxpayers will carry the financial burden for much of the cleanup. Even when the firms originally responsible for dumping the coal tar can be identified and undertake cleanup operations, customers of the firms will eventually pay for the cleanup through higher general charges or special fees.

To repeat, some direct social costs are measurable, but some are more difficult to quantify. Nonetheless, the marring of scenic vistas, neighborhood crime and urban blight, the loss of opportunities to observe wildlife or being able to hear songbirds (yes, the songbirds are disappearing, too), and mental anxiety brought on by poor working or living conditions all are real social costs that are not measured by the price system.

Subsidies as Social Costs

Payments made directly by governments to individuals or firms are another kind of social cost. As a society, we tax ourselves and use this money for various expenditures. In the same way as with direct social costs, market failure is at the root of subsidies. We make collective judgments in some areas of life that free markets do not provide either the right kind of goods and services, or the right amount of these goods and services, or both. No matter how you view them, subsidies are social costs, a transfer of money from society at large to benefit individuals or management, workers, and customers of the subsidized sector.

State universities are a prime example. Students at the University of Northern Iowa pay only about one-quarter to one-third of what it costs to educate them. Society pays the rest, because society has deemed education important for its collective goals. Left to market forces, it's doubtful that the demand for philosophy professors would be high enough to attract people into this academic field. But we, as a society, believe that philosophy professors are important. Therefore we override the judgment of the market and use subsidies to ensure a supply of such people.

National defense is another illustration of subsidies, as are welfare payments. So are governmental allocations to farmers. In 1989, Iowa trailed only Texas in the amount of farm subsidies received, with a figure just under $1 billion. Overall, U.S. farmers received nearly $11 billion in direct payments from society in 1989.

One very interesting example of subsidies, though these subsidies are quite subtle, is the support of big-time collegiate athletics. State universities, and hence society, subsidize athletic enterprises in all sorts of ways, including the use of university parking lots, state troopers for traffic and crowd control, interest on dormitory construction (to the extent rooms are used to house athletes), and liability insurance. When athletic departments brag about their income from basketball and football, these costs are not counted.

Some of the costs are more direct. During the 1990–1991 academic year, the University of Northern Iowa will spend $1.6 million over and above gate receipts to finance its athletic teams. I recently proposed a free market solution to the problem of subsidizing athletic teams, but it has not yet caught on (see my article, "The Trials of Hunter Rawlings," in the list of readings).

Iowa has used subsidies, such as outright grants and low-interest or forgivable loans, as a method of attracting new business to the state. Certain communities have done the same. In addition, there are more subtle versions of subsidies used by some states, such as minimal occupational safety and health rules and lax public regulation. These latter subsidies are nothing more than indications to business firms that social costs will not be assessed, which is a kind of subsidy.

On occasion, subsidies become intertwined with the payment of direct social costs. In the case of leaking gasoline tanks mentioned earlier, the state of Iowa is providing assistance, a subsidy, to service station operators in the removal of old tanks and the installation of new ones.

Subsidies often are looked at as something of an embarrassment by those receiving them. Thirty years ago, President John Kennedy suggested that we do away with the complex structure of payments to farmers, which has horrendous administrative costs, and simply send checks directly to farmers. That idea resurfaces periodically, but the farm community rejects it, partly because it looks too much like an out-and-out welfare payment, which it is. But much of the current farm subsidies are nothing more than disguised welfare.

Not earning your living in the open market casts certain aspersions on either your ability or your ambition. That's nonsense. Markets sometimes fail to provide the kind and quantity of certain goods and services that society wants; therefore, society sets up its own resource transfer system in the form of subsidies. If markets were constantly wonderful, such transfers would not be needed.

Social Costs as Foregone Opportunities

Of all the social costs, *opportunity costs* are the most difficult to measure. They also have a heavy future orientation, and are critically important.

In the purest sense, the cost of anything is the value of what must be sacrificed to obtain it. If we choose to spend money on consumption goods and argue for lower taxes in order to have the necessary discretionary income for these purchases, the true cost of our behavior is the opportunities we forego. For example, we might spend some of this money on improving the deplorable condition of many county homes for the elderly. Therefore, one measure of the opportunity cost of additional private consumption is how this contributes to neglect of the elderly.

For those not used to thinking this way, the logical networks involved in opportunity costing can get complicated. The following case deals with private opportunity costs, but it's such a good general illustration of opportunity costs that I'll present it before turning to the societal version.

Iowa State University has a Swine Enterprise Records Program for hog farmers, offered through its University Extension Service. The program advises farmers to employ an opportunity cost approach to figuring profit and loss on their operations. For example, consider two hog farmers, one who borrows $400,000 for operations and equipment and a second who supplies the $400,000 out of his or her own funds.

Suppose the farmer borrowing money does so at a 10 percent rate of interest. Under what are called "generally accepted accounting principles" (GAAP), the approach used by accountants, this farmer's profit-and-loss statement will show interest charges of $40,000 at the end of a one-year accounting period. On the other hand, the farmer supplying his or her own monetary capital will show no interest charges using GAAP.

The Iowa State University approach recommends that the second farmer should deduct an interest charge equal to what owner-supplied capital could have earned if invested in a certificate of deposit. If the CD would have paid 8 percent, then this farmer would show an interest charge of $32,000 on his or her profit and loss statement. Why? Because this is the amount of money the farmer could have earned if the money had been invested in CDs rather than hog farming. It's the opportunity cost of using money in the hog business.

In truth, the interest rate should be higher than the CD rate recommended by Iowa State, since putting money in a CD generally is somewhat less risky than hog farming. Thus using the CD rate understates the true opportunity cost. Aside from that technicality, what's the problem?

Those who criticize the opportunity cost approach argue that Iowa hog farmers using opportunity costs look less profitable than hog farmers not employing this approach, since the opportunity cost charged is not really paid out to anyone. Bankers do not think about opportunity costs when looking at financial statements, relying instead on GAAP. The result is that loan officers, and farmers themselves, may be too cautious about expanding operations, since the so-called bottom line is much lower when using opportunity costs than when GAAP is employed.

The Iowa State University proponents of opportunity costing counter by saying that opportunity costs make comparisons easier between those operations supplying part or all of their own capital and those who are highly leveraged (operating on borrowed money). Who's right? Both sides. Those who argue in favor of the GAAP methods are merely recognizing that most people think of costing in terms of standard accounting principles rather than the opportunity-cost approach favored by economists.

The opportunity-cost approach is more appropriate for decision making. For example, a farmer who supplies his or her own capital has a decision to make each year about whether or not to stay in the hog business. Opportunity costs permit a comparison of hog operations with alternative uses of the money. Normal accounting procedures, which are geared toward keeping records for tax purposes and annual reports, do not. If you're thinking about leaving the hog business, opportunity costs will allow you to make comparisons with alternative uses of your money. GAAP allows a better comparison with those operators who do not use opportunity costs.

When my father died in 1979, he left my mother two farms of decent quality. The tillable land amounted to about 210 acres, total. Land prices at that time were escalating and reached their peak in July 1981. Using a simple model I built on my computer, my best estimate of the values of the properties, in terms of income produced, was about $1,300 per acre under the most generous set of assumptions, even though land of that quality was selling for around $2,000 per acre.

I suggested to my mother that she consider selling the farms at that point. Her opportunity costs in keeping the farms were very high. In fact, I estimated these costs at about $500 per week in lost income she could be receiving if the money were invested in other assets that were virtually risk-free.

She sold the farms, invested the money, and her income jumped by over $20,000 a year. That's using opportunity costs as a decision-making tool. There's a hitch in this kind of thinking, though. Psychological costs and revenues play a role, sometimes a large one, in decision making. My father received such returns from fiddling with the farm operations each year. He liked watching grain prices, liked watching the crops grow. My mother had no such attachments to farming, so these psychological revenues were not present for her. As I said, opportunity costs can get a little complicated; that doesn't mean they shouldn't be used.

In fact, opportunity costs are particularly relevant in thinking about many of Iowa's problems. One concern is the "brain drain" stemming from young people moving to other parts of the country once their educations are complete. The decision to leave Iowa for somewhere else is another multiple-criteria problem. One of the criteria, so people claim, is income potential. If young folks believe they can earn more money elsewhere, this figures heavily in their decisions to move. In short, what they are computing is the opportunity cost of staying in Iowa or leaving, in terms of income.

When we spend money on ways to shoot down enemy rockets in outer space with lasers or on new fighter planes or on aircraft carriers or to send troops to Arabia, the true cost of those expenditures is not what is paid to defense contractors, but rather the best alternative uses of this money. A 1990 report issued by the National Commission on Children indicates that half a million American children are malnourished and that a hundred thousand of them are homeless. It's even worse on a worldwide basis. Some forty thousand children die each day (each day!) from hunger and disease. You can feed, house, and provide medical care for a lot of children in the world for the price of one aircraft carrier. That's opportunity costing.

Opportunity costs get even more interesting when you start thinking about the future. Some of this is straightforward, some of it is not. Let's look at the obvious cases first.

The United States consumes somewhere around a third of the world's energy use each year. Iowans are among the most profligate. We use more energy per capita in our homes than people in forty other states. Furthermore, our industries are more energy-intensive and energy-wasting than industry in thirty-one other states. Incidentally, we are more wasteful than both Minnesota and Wisconsin, so climate is not a major variable here.

One way to look at the cost of this behavior, both in Iowa and in the United States as a whole, is what could have been done with this energy if we had not burned it to produce nonessential goods and Sunday drives. Our demand for energy, and the prices we are willing to pay for it, reduces the availability of energy to those countries trying to pull themselves out of economic deprivation. There is, clearly, a current opportunity cost to our behavior.

Viewed from another perspective, we are robbing the future of opportunities by our extravagances. Every ton of coal burned, every barrel of oil used, every cubic foot of natural gas consumed constitute opportunities lost for future generations. What this really amounts to is a loss of options. As I pointed out earlier, it's always best to have a rich set of choices before you in decision making. To the extent that we use nonrenewable resources now, we are stealing options from our children and their children.

This notion of options is worth exploring a little more, since it relates so directly to our collective future and how we move toward it. To the extent we use nonrenewable resources now, we create opportunity costs. A ton of coal, once burned, is not available for future use. By using that ton of coal now, we have removed an option that would have been available for ourselves or for someone else at a later time.

Earlier I said that the crux of the environmental debate hinged around direct social costs. I exaggerated a little. A second part of this problem has to do with present use of resources versus conservation. Commercial exploitation of wilderness tracts has a long-range opportunity cost, particularly if the exploitation involves irreversible decisions.

Here's an example. Canada's James Bay, on the border between Ontario and Quebec, is an inlet off Hudson Bay. The region is a large wilderness area providing a home for diverse wildlife, as well as fishing and hunting grounds for the Cree and Inuit inhabitants. Quebec's prime minister, Robert Bourassa, has something else in mind for this wilderness. Bourassa looks at the dozens of rivers in the James Bay region and sees hydroelectric power that can be used by Quebec and sold to the northeastern United States. Five dams have been built, six more are under construction. That's only one-third of the project, with the other two-thirds to be undertaken in the next fifteen years.

The James Bay case is a clearly defined illustration of opportunity costs and their relationship to future options. Alternative A is to keep the region as wilderness. Alternative B is to develop it. The opportunity cost of development is the loss of wilderness and, hence, the loss to future generations of experiencing this wilderness or perhaps developing it to their own tastes. When Prime Minister Bourassa looked at the wilderness in 1985, he was quoted as saying, "What a waste." For him, the opportunity cost of development approximated zero. For others, it has a much higher value.

Sometimes opportunity costs can be cast as direct costs. In the James Bay situation, one of the opportunity costs of development is the loss of land by the Cree and Inuits. This is also a direct social cost in this case. In an effort to assuage the native hunters and fishermen, Quebec paid them $500 million in compensation. Apparently, the opportunity cost was not zero, as Bourassa implied, but at least a half a billion dollars.

Beyond money, though, is the loss of options for the future. Once the dams have been built, the irreversibility of the process steals from the future the option of deciding how the James Bay wilderness will be used. In an excellent little book, *Economic Growth and Environmental Decay*, Paul Barkley and David Seckler point out that, as humans, we can commit two types of errors. Both of these errors relate directly to decision making, cost, and the future.

First, there are decisions that result in reversible consequences. If we don't like the outcome, we can, perhaps with a little effort, change things around. For instance, when tile drains on Iowa fields are shut, those fields that once were wetlands revert quite readily to their earlier state. Other situations, however, are irreversible. Cutting down old-growth forests and building hydroelectric dams in the James Bay region are illustrations. If, as many scientists believe, the earth is undergoing a warming due to human influence on the atmosphere, this could be an irreversible mistake of considerable magnitude.

The loss of options is one of the most critical opportunity costs we can generate. The Ogallala aquifer, which lies under ten high-plains states covering 180,000 square miles, is being pumped dry to produce crops that are already in oversupply. This aquifer and similar ones providing water in the desert areas of Arizona are rechargeable only over periods of time measured in hundreds of years. In using this water, we deprive the future, both ourselves and those who follow us, of choices.

One of the saddest situations is that of the Florida Everglades. It's hard to imagine an America without this unique wilderness. But the Everglades, at least what remains of it, is dying, a victim of urban demands, phosphate and nitrate runoff from farms, flood-control projects, and other causes.

More is at stake, though, than the loss of this remarkable area for future generations. It turns out that the river of grass is a key element in the water supply systems of coastal cities from West Palm Beach to Miami. If the Everglades, an area historically viewed as useless by some, succumbs, so might south Florida. The situation provides an interesting and tragic example of a mix of direct social costs today and opportunity costs for tomorrow.

Barkley and Seckler put it well: "As activities become less certain and as the possibility of irreversible consequences increases, society must take pains to keep open the option of future use. The great bulk of conservation controversies have revolved around this very issue." The World Commission on Environment and Development, organized by the United Nations, uses this theme as the basis for its definition of sustainability: "Meet the needs of the present without compromising the ability of future generations to meet their own needs."

Recall now my discussion of discounting in Chapter Three. The future is uncertain; it contains risks. The higher the risks, the higher the interest rate we demand to compensate us for taking the risks. So because the future is uncertain, we apply a high discount rate to it, which convinces us to expend nonrenewable resources now, and in doing so we take away choices that would otherwise be open to us in the future.

If we kill all the elephants, drive out the songbirds with deforestation and chemicals, and use the entire stock of fossil fuels on earth for weekend trips to regional shopping centers and cruising the strip on Saturday nights, we are removing future options. Our great-great-grandchildren may well see nature as it exists in our aquariums and zoos, not as it flourishes in the wild. They will understand the opportunity costs of irreversible decisions as they stare at caged elephants and piles of rusting automobiles in the junkyards we have bequeathed them.

FOR FURTHER READING

Barkley, Paul W., and David W. Seckler. *Economic Growth and Environmental Decay.* New York: Harcourt Brace Jovanovich, 1972.

Beams, Floyd A., and Paul E. Fertig. "Pollution Control Through Social Cost Conversion." *The Journal of Accountancy,* November 1971, pp. 37–42.

Borowitz, Susan. "How to Drown a Wilderness." *Sierra,* May/June 1990, pp. 82–83.

Carney, James. "Last Gasp for the Everglades." *Time,* September 25, 1989, pp. 26–27.

Hocker, Philip, and Stewart Udall. "What's Mined Is Theirs." *Sierra,* September/October 1989, pp. 20 ff.

Hubert, Cynthia. "Long-Buried Coal Tar Threatens Environment." *Des Moines Register,* May 25, 1990, pp. 1A, 3A.

Linden, Eugene. "Will the Ballyhoo Go Bust?" *Time,* April 23, 1990, p. 86.

Lipsey, Richard G., Peter O. Steiner, and Douglas D. Purvis. *Economics.* 8th ed. New York: Harper & Row, 1987.

MacNeill, Jim. "Strategies for Sustainable Economic Development." *Scientific American,* September 1989, pp. 155–65.

Mansfield, Edwin. *Economics.* 6th ed. New York: W.W. Norton, 1989.

"No Home for Hot Trash." *Time,* December 11, 1989, p. 81.

"Report: Nation Failing Its Young." *Waterloo Courier,* April 26, 1990, p. A3.

Rose, Carol. "Citing High Energy Use in Iowa, Study Urges Conservation Plan." *Des Moines Register,* January 12, 1990, p. 12T.

Soth, Lauren. "Reaganomics' Shadow Still Looms." *Des Moines Register,* February 26, 1990, p. 6A.

Ullmann, John E. *Social Costs in Modern Society.* Westport, Conn.: Quorum Books, 1983.

Walkowiak, John. "Trees in Our Towns: A Growing Need." *Iowa Conservationist,* May 1990, pp. 14–15.

Waller, Robert James. "Going Soft Upon the Land and Down Along the Rivers." In *Just Beyond the Firelight,* by Robert James Waller. Ames: Iowa State University Press, 1988.

————. "The Trials of Hunter Rawlings." In *One Good Road Is Enough,* by Robert James Waller. Ames: Iowa State University Press, 1990.

Democracy

W ord meanings are a danger in the use of terms such as "democracy" and "liberty." Comparative political systems, where such matters are discussed and evaluated at length, is an interesting topic, but it runs well beyond what this book covers. This is a book about the future of Iowa, and Iowa exists within the framework of American constitutional democracy, so when I talk about *democracy*, I mean the form of government practiced in America.

That's a little jingoistic, perhaps, but it keeps things at a manageable scale for my purposes. Most of what I have to say, though, applies to any nation where people freely elect their governments and where these governments are responsible in some degree to the will of the people. More than that, a reasonably large subset of the ideas here about the relation between short-term thinking and nasty long-run effects applies to any kind of political arrangement.

When I mention *liberty*, I'll rely on the conventional meaning of that term used in the liberal philosophy of the West. As such, liberty means that one should be able to do what he or she wishes to do, as long as others are not harmed and that irreparable harm is not likely to fall upon himself or herself.

This chapter is a revised version of "Democracy and the Natural Environment," which appeared originally in *One Good Road Is Enough,* by Robert James Waller, © 1990. Iowa State Univeristy Press.

THE RULE OF THE ELECTORATE

In the discussion of rights, our Declaration of Independence states, "That to secure these rights, Governments are instituted among Men, deriving their just powers from the consent of the governed." And, of course, from Lincoln we have: "Government of the people, by the people, for the people . . ." Furthermore, for good or bad, we live with the legacy of people such as economist/philosopher Jeremy Bentham, who said, "The happiness of the individuals, of whom a community is composed, that is, their pleasure and their security, is the end and the sole end which the legislator ought to have in view."

These principles, and others like them, illustrate part of the dilemma we and the emerging democracies now confront in dealing with the natural environment and all other problems requiring present sacrifice in exchange for long-term benefits. The natural environment is slow to anger, or so it appears. Like the quiet kid on the playground who suffers years of abuse before exploding in rage, nature has been quiet and resilient.

And until the last few years, when the effects of our abuse have become obvious, nature seems to have endured without complaint. Suddenly, or so it seems to many people, our water has gone bad, our soil has disappeared or become contaminated, and our air is fouled.

Were there warnings? It turns out that a nineteenth-century Swedish scientist, Svante Arrhenius, recognized that humans were in the process of "evaporating our coal mines into the air." A century before Arrhenius, Jean-Baptiste Fourier had speculated about this matter. The general scientific opinion, however, held that our oceans could absorb any excess carbon dioxide emissions. That rosy forecast was refuted in 1957 by researchers at the Scripps Institute of Oceanography. Another Swedish scientist, Svante Oden, published a 1968 report, "The Acidification of Air and Precipitation and Its Consequences on the Natural Environment," warning of what has become known as acid rain.

Thomas Jefferson was an eloquent and ardent spokesman for soil conservation, recommending contour plowing, clover planting, and crop rotation to retain soil and soil fertility. And Hugh Hammond Bennett, the grand old man of soil conservation, was convinced of the dangers of soil erosion by 1903. He spent his life studying, writing, and speaking about the problem and published a U.S. Forest Service Report, "Soil Erosion: A National Menace," in 1928.

There were others, many others, who warned us. Rachel Carson, in her book *Silent Spring,* spoke of the dangers of chemicals in our biosystems thirty years ago. In 1970 we celebrated Earth Day and promptly forgot about the earth. The first studies warning of problems in the ozone layer appeared in 1973. Worries about the clear-cutting of tropical rain forests have been around for years. But you don't need science, or even prophets. Anybody who has been looking at rivers and forests and birds knows what has been happening. We've been trashing the place.

Why? We consider ourselves God-fearing and prudent and forward-looking. We spend fifty-two cents of every tax dollar on military preparedness and threaten to wave lasers around outer space against those who might harm us. Given our fear of God and our potential enemies, how is it that we have been able to ignore the destruction of our life-sustaining systems? If another country had poisoned our water, we all would be in military uniforms by now. In a manner of speaking, however, we have invaded ourselves.

Some say it's biblical, that certain convenient interpretations of Christian scripture both allow and promote our dominance over the natural order. Certainly, a casual reading of Genesis conveys a sense of such dominion. Others think it has to do with old habits stemming from a time when we confronted an unspoiled continent and, hence, saw no restrictions on exploiting resources and ridding ourselves of trash.

I think it runs deeper than that. Besides, those explanations, which probably have some truth attached to them, don't promise much in the way of getting out of our current mess. Arguments about religion are unproductive, and the limits of nature have been breached. I think it has to do with the liabilities of freedom and, more generally, the way we go about our daily business.

There is, I suggest, a rather natural, though not necessarily admirable, tendency to apply a high discount rate to the future. (I talked about this in Chapter Three.) Given two alternatives, one which brings rewards in the short run but has great long-run costs, and another requiring present sacrifice but with possible and uncertain long-range benefits, it does not require much change in the discount rate as applied to flows of costs and benefits to make the short-term alternative dominant.

And, clearly, we manipulate, either overtly to suit our most pressing current needs or covertly, in a psychological sense, our discount rates to match our preferences for short-term gratification. As every student of basic finance knows, the short run always triumphs over the long run when that occurs.

This phenomenon is equally present when we are dealing with long-term tangible problems, such as decay of the physical infrastructure, that is, the repair of sewers, roads, water mains, and so forth. It is even

more true when the short-term rewards are increases in tangible commodities versus more distant and intangible matters of beauty or wilderness or kindness or the survival of a species, including our own.

Alexander Hamilton, in *The Federalist Papers,* said: "Momentary
passions and immediate interests have a more active and impervious
control over human conduct than general or remote considerations of
policy, utility, and justice." Keep Hamilton's observation in mind as you
read this chapter.

Why do we choose the short run and refuse sacrifice for benefits in
the longer term? Are we evil? Ignorant or stupid? Surely we are not evil.
Ignorant and stupid, maybe. Among other things, we lead busy lives.
Consider the natural environment. Is it on your list of things to do
today? For most people, probably not. It's not pressing, or so it seems.
It doesn't fax you and ask for an immediate reply.

Connected with this is our system of learning that gets us by on a
day-to-day basis. In simplistic terms, this system can be described as, "If
it feels good, do it." Put another way, in light of the complexity we
confront and the difficulty of detailed planning and decision making
under such conditions of complexity, we respond to rewards and avoid
punishments—overall, not a bad strategy for daily survival.

The problem arises when the long term must be taken into account.
Sacrifice doesn't feel good; therefore, we don't want to do it, and we
don't, most of the time. Who, then, should be taking care of the long
run? If the electorate tends to favor the moment, then our elected officials are supposed to be those with the long view.

In the ideal world, a workable democracy must always involve some
compromise between what a strong elected representative believes is
right and what his or her constituents say. But that's not the way it's
working. Politicians are constantly running for office, attempting to
keep everybody happy. If the pronouncements of our Declaration of
Independence and of Lincoln and Bentham are to be taken seriously, this
apparently is as it should be.

But we have been successful at transferring our short-run inclina-
tions into our political preferences and demand that politicians accede to
them. When it comes to matters requiring the government to ask us for
self-sacrifice, we behave in much the same way that we do in our daily
lives, choosing short-run rewards and avoiding punishments. And we
transmit our feelings via the mails or lobbyists or the campaign fund or
the ballot box.

The legendary columnist and political philosopher Walter Lippmann
put it well:

Faced with . . . choices between the hard and the soft, the normal propensity of democratic governments is to please the largest number of
voters. The pressure of the electorate is normally for the soft side of the
equations. That is why governments are unable to cope with reality
when elected assemblies and mass opinions become decisive in the
state, where there are not statesmen to resist the inclination of the
voters and there are only politicians to excite and exploit them. . . .
Democratic politicians have preferred to shun foresight about troublesome changes to come, knowing that the massive veto (from the electorate) was latent, and that it would be expensive to them and their
party if they provoked it.

Lippmann wrote that over forty-five years ago. Things have not
changed. No politician that I know of has come forward to say, "Citizens, the natural environment is in danger; you will be asked to sacrifice
for the future good of us all." Some have hinted at the problems; none
has asked for sacrifices of such magnitude that votes might be in
jeopardy. Even the power-holding conservatives are worried. Kevin Phil-
lips, a conservative analyst, described the current state of things as a
"frightening inability to define and debate America's emerging problems."

And President Bush's Director of the Budget, Richard Darman, in
the summer of 1989, blasted both the government and the voters for
mimicking spoiled children with demands of " 'now-nowism,' our collective short-sightedness, our obsession with the here and now, our reluctance adequately to address the future." A few months after Darman
spoke, Bush joined with leaders from Britain, the Soviet Union, and
Japan in blocking a sixty-eight-nation conference from adopting specific
annual goals intended to cut carbon dioxide emissions by the major
industrial countries.

In addition to short-term thinking, there is the problem of knowledge. In general, Americans have a distaste for the study of science, an
even greater dislike for mathematics, and a complete misunderstanding
of how knowledge is built. Add to this an intolerance for ambiguity, and
you have the makings of ignorance and impatience with an ecological
science that must talk in terms of estimates and probabilities, at best.
The problems confronting us are too new and too complex for quick and
easy answers of the kind that both the electorate and politicians favor.

The cause-and-effect chains are long and subtle, with feedback effects and surprises present at nearly every stage. For example, the greenhouse effect may feed on itself once it gets under way. One possibility is
that as carbon dioxide and other gases trap solar infrared radiation and

the atmosphere warms, additional water vapor will be created, leading to further warming and even more water vapor. Or, the warming may melt the northern permafrost, releasing methane contained within the permafrost, which in turn leads to more warming.

It's all very subtle, all very complex, and apparently beyond our reach. An anecdote provided by Curtis Moore illustrates this: A commuter in smog-choked Atlanta maneuvers his out-of-tune Chevrolet through backed-up rush hour traffic, and three years later trees die on a North Carolina mountaintop.

At the moment, we know only four things. First, there will be unpleasant changes in our natural environment. Second, some of these changes are going to be irreversible. Third, we are uncertain about the magnitude and timing of these changes. And, fourth, someone will have to pay to fix it.

Americans tend to be impatient with such uncertainties. In the absence of anything approaching conclusive proof, probabilities are necessary. Thinking about the future always involves probabilistic reasoning. But, as I said, humans are not very good at estimating and using probabilities and tend to have a low tolerance for ambiguity overall. For example, there is plenty of evidence showing that humans assign higher-than-warranted probabilities to desirable outcomes and the reverse to unwanted outcomes.

This amounts to a kind of psychological denial. Adlai Stevenson said: "Given the choice between disagreeable fact and agreeable fantasy, we will choose agreeable fantasy." And, I might add, when it comes to the natural environment, we deal with probabilities in a mighty curious fashion.

Here's an example. The Food and Drug Administration demands years of proof before a drug is released for human consumption. In other words, we ask for proof of safety. Yet, in terms of environmental impact, we forge ahead and are asked to prove harm before questionable manufacturing or other practices are ceased. From a decision-making point of view, we employ a criterion of unwarranted optimism when it comes to nature and the reverse when it comes to pharmaceutical drugs, even though both enter our biological systems.

In general, then, we favor the short term, while nature and other social problems require long-term thinking, and we emphatically forward this preference to our elected officials or those seeking office. The fault, ultimately, is in the electorate and not in our public officials. I used to think it was the reverse, but eventually I came to understand that blaming politicians simply is a way of excusing ourselves. Another form of denial. In other words, we get the kind of leadership we deserve (or demand!).

Eventually, in a democracy, events begin to outrun us. Though it's hard to imagine a United States without the Everglades, this sea of grass does appear to be dying, irreversibly so (and I am given to wonder at the "Ever" in Everglades). We see it happening, we don't want it to happen, but like the narcotics addict, every time we think about a cure, it seems worse than the disease, for it means short-run sacrifice for the long-run good.

Then there are the worldwide environmental problems, such as the greenhouse effect and the thinning of the ozone shield. Here we have something similar to what occurs within a democracy, in the sense that nations pursue their own self-interests. Each nation is independent, yet we seek to have all agree to ban, for example, chlorofluorocarbons or dirty coal-burning processes, when it is not in the short-term interests of any of them to do so.

Even the developed countries have been slow to act on these matters, and understandably so, for they are the major contributors to both of these problems. Now we ask the underdeveloped countries to come into line with us on restricting chlorofluorocarbon emissions and other such problems. Why should they? It's not in their interest to do so in the short term, and they have plenty of short-term problems to solve without cooperating in the solution of problems caused by those countries who have been so wanton in the use of the world's resources, countries that themselves are reluctant to change.

POVERTY: A DIGRESSION

One of the problems confronted by both developed and less developed countries is poverty. Just as high-intensity consumption is a contributor to environmental and other dilemmas, poverty also is a major obstacle to intelligent treatment of the natural environment.

The poor, with severely constrained sets of alternatives confronting them and criteria oriented to the short run even more than the rest of us, surely cannot afford to treat environmental protection and enhancement as important criteria in making decisions. As a Jesuit priest from South America once told me, "You don't preach religion to people with empty bellies."

Or as Thomas Fuller observed, "He that has nothing is frightened of nothing." Those who are hungry, poor, and thirsty are not frightened about the condition of the river or acid in the rain, let alone the probabilistic forecasts about melting ice caps in the year 2050.

When you are poor, you get what you can today and let tomorrow take care of itself. As Indira Gandhi remarked, "Poverty is the biggest environmental problem in India."

So, along with the basic injustices, suffering, and human indignities that accompany poverty, we have a second-order effect in that deterioration of the very ecosystems that sustain us all will be encouraged, particularly as the developing nations attempt their long climb toward prosperity.

It's important to remember, for example, that 45 percent of Africa's population is under the age of fifteen. These people, understandably, want food and air conditioning and automobiles and the rest of what they see highly industrialized economies enjoying.

And the cycle starts to close. For as we now must devote more and more of our resources to crash programs for cleaning up the environment, undoubtedly the poor, those with the least political clout, will suffer as resources are transferred to other priorities and costs of environmental cleanup increase.

SOCIAL TRAPS

There's a useful way of looking at these ideas. It's called social traps. I first encountered this notion in the early 1970s, in an article by John Platt. Platt and three others at the University of Michigan had been meeting informally for several years to discuss difficult problems, what caused them, and how we might go about extricating ourselves from them. In 1981, John Cross and Mel Guyer published a book summarizing the group's deliberations. The book was simply called *Social Traps*. It's a concept I've used over and over again in my thinking, in my consulting practice, and in my years as a university dean.

The first thing to understand is that the social traps concept, for the most part, is just a new way of packaging old ideas. That does not mean it's superfluous. The power of this way of thinking stems from being able to see diverse problems as having similar structures. For example, smoking, soil erosion, and inflation all exhibit similar characteristics when viewed from the traps perspective. As someone once said, science searches for similarities, the humanities search for differences. The traps approach is one of looking for similarities. And notice, as you read, that traps always flow from multiple-criteria decisions where certain criteria, particularly those promising short-term pleasures, dominate others.

Underlying the traps way of thinking is that humans prefer rewards over punishments. Muddling along, doing what feels right in a given instance is not a bad way to cope with the complexity facing us in our day-to-day decision making. Sometimes, though, this kind of behavior eventually leads us to punishment, even though we have been consistently seeking rewards and behaving in what seems to be a rational manner.

Here's an example. University department heads have a tendency to write evaluation letters for faculty that are either complimentary or bland, with common innocuous phrases such as, "One would hope to see additional progress in your research efforts over the coming year." If the faculty member is struggling in the research arena, surely a better phrase is this: "If you do not publish at least three articles in the next two years, you will be denied tenure."

But, in evaluating the performance of a faculty member at the end of an academic year, a department head likely will suffer acrimony from the faculty member if a really tough evaluation letter is written. Like all of us, department heads prefer to avoid punishment in the present — thus the bland evaluation letters. The result, however, is often a serious battle when a faculty member eventually is denied tenure. Like a mouse whose innate caution is overcome by the lure of cheese in a mousetrap, the department heads have ignored the ultimate punishment and concentrated on the short-term reward (which is really the avoidance of punishment, in this case).

The classic social trap is that described by Garrett Hardin in his article, "The Tragedy of the Commons." It works like this. In the early days of New England, each village was surrounded by common ground used as grazing land by all. One person looked at that expanse of meadow and said, "It won't hurt if today I take just one more cow to graze." That's true, from an individual perspective.

But others also had the same idea. As each person brought more and more cows, eventually the land was spoiled for everybody. A social trap was created.* The degradation of the Upper Mississippi National Wildlife Refuge, mentioned earlier, perfectly illustrates a commons type

---

*Notice the close relationship between social costs and social traps in the examples presented here. Social traps create direct social costs, or social opportunity costs, or both.

of trap. These traps usually are characterized by comparatively small events, each one the results of an apparently reasonable decision, that eventually results in tragedy.

Overcrowding in popular national parks, such as Yosemite, is a serious problem. No one plans to create this situation, while sitting around in kitchens or living rooms, saying, "Let's go to Yosemite for our vacation." That's a perfectly reasonable choice to make. Yet when a large number of people all make that choice independently, the commons syndrome emerges, and nobody has a good time because of the crowding. As one Yosemite tourist waiting in line for a back-country hiking permit said: "It's miles overcrowded. I know it sounds silly, because I'm a tourist myself, but you come here to get away from people." Our hiker is caught in a social trap.

Here are other examples. If only one factory poured its emissions into the air, nature could handle it. But each factory manager sees the atmosphere as a commons, and each therefore, rationally and independent of others, makes the decision to pollute. The result is, of course, disaster for all.

Likewise, if only one farmer eroded land or polluted waterways, the situation would be manageable. When many do it, a critical resource disappears and water becomes polluted. If only one Indian peasant gathered firewood from the nearby forest, things would be all right. When all do it, the forests disappear. If only one or a few fishing boats trawled a limited fishery, there would be enough fish for each boat. When a large number of boats do it, the fish disappear.

Some traps are a result of errors of *commission,* while others are errors of *omission.* Factory pollutants are errors of commission. The problem is caused by some action being taken. The department head example is an error of omission; the problem results from not taking action.

Only 40 percent of Americans regularly visit dentists. They'll pay for that neglect sometime. Others do not carry the proper kind or amount of auto insurance. Those are both errors of omission, but they differ in terms of who suffers the consequences. In the dental situation, the individual suffers the cost of neglect, unless society through a social program pays for dentures or the treatment of gum disease.

The auto insurance case is another illustration of people getting themselves trapped, but if you are involved in an accident with someone in that situation, you or your insurance company will probably pay the damages and your insurance premiums will increase if your insurance company does pay. In this instance, the uninsured motorist has created a trap but has offloaded the punishment onto you, via a social cost. You have been trapped by someone else's behavior.

It gets even more interesting. By our emphasis on maximizing present consumption in this society, we create traps not only for ourselves, but also for those coming along behind us. It's easy to neglect repair of sewers, water mains, and so forth. Those elements of the infrastructure are underground, out of sight, and their maintenance costs money, which means more taxes and less private consumption. We'll pay for a massive reconstruction eventually, instead of maintaining things as we go along. That's a trap, like the commons syndrome, and it results from errors of omission.

The same thing is true of environmental abuse; we are merely shoveling our social costs forward. To deal with these costs now means punishment. We prefer the short-term rewards that come our way from ignoring such costs.

There's a particularly insidious kind of trap where the rewards and punishment shift over time so that only punishments are forthcoming. Drug addiction is one such trap. The more complete the addiction, the more punishment there is in getting out of the trap; withdrawal and a life without the artificial support of drugs. Yet remaining addicted also has severe costs associated with it. Two alternatives, both having punishment as an outcome. It's not a nice place to be.

Polluting the atmosphere has many of the same characteristics as drug addiction. We are receiving severe punishment in the form of smog, ozone depletion, acid rain, and the like, and it promises to get worse. Yet when President George Bush looks at his alternatives, he sees only more punishment, in the form of decreased economic growth and increased taxes, if the hard steps needed to address our impact on the atmosphere are taken. Punishment is the outcome whichever way he turns. The tactic in cases like this is generally to call for more research or more education, which are just ways of ignoring the situation and avoiding hard decisions.

Farmers are faced with another similar trap. The costs of addiction to high chemical usage are apparent. Still, there is considerable motivation to continue using chemicals, since reduction in their use promises equal or greater costs to the individual farmer (that may not be true, but it's what many farmers believe).

Cross and Guyer present a classification of traps that, while not entirely satisfactory, provides a way of thinking about many diverse problems that have similarity in their underlying structures. Recognition of such likenesses is a way of reducing complexity, for what seem to be many problems turns out to be relatively few when the similarities among them are recognized. The pragmatist philosopher, William James, spoke of the "great blooming, buzzing confusion of reality." The traps notion is one way of decreasing confusion, and the classification follows.

1. Time-delay traps

How the trap arises: One alternative action followed by a delayed reward, and another alternative followed by an immediate reward. It is the second that is likely to be chosen repeatedly, even though the first alternative may produce a much more desirable outcome over time. Another way of looking at this is not taking some action now, even though it will prevent punishment in the future, because the current action will result in unpleasant consequences, that is, avoiding punishment now results in even greater punishment in the future.

Examples: smoking, AIDS, drug usage, dropping out of school, not passing tough environmental laws, farming practices leading to soil erosion, cutting of forested hillsides for profit or firewood.

2. Ignorance traps

How the trap arises: Lack of knowledge or highly attractive and immediate rewards that inhibit reflection or search for better information.

Examples: impulse purchases in general, use of chemicals such as DDT or products such as asbestos before bad side effects are recognized, AIDS, using chlorofluorocarbons for packaging and refrigeration without an understanding of their effects on the ozone layer—and, of course, certain matters that transpired in the Garden of Eden. A particularly macabre instance was the use of arsenic as an embalming fluid in the nineteenth century. Though banned in that application around 1900, arsenic is a stable element. As wooden caskets deteriorate, the arsenic is released and may percolate into groundwater. John Konefes, director of the Iowa Waste Reduction Center at the University of Northern Iowa, estimates that Iowa's 4,156 cemeteries could hold up to ninety tons of arsenic. This is an example of a time-delay trap due to ignorance.

3. Sliding-reinforcer traps

How the trap arises: Behavior in the present leading to punishment in the future because current behavior reaches forward to encourage continued destructive behavior even when punishments are being encountered. Sliding-reinforcer traps include a temptation to repeat the behavior simply to relieve the punishment brought on by the behavior itself.

Examples: two that have been discussed earlier are drug addiction and the use of pesticides, where the costs of stopping are matched against costs of continuing, and the individual or society confronts only costs no matter which way they turn.

4. Externality traps

How the trap arises: Situations in which one individual acting in his or her own best interest makes decisions that have an impact on the welfare of others. This kind of trap has been discussed extensively earlier in a number of contexts, particularly in Chapter Three in the discussion of costs.

Examples: noise pollution, pollution of a stream by a manufacturing plant, acid rain, a person in a neighborhood not maintaining his or her property.

5. Collective traps

How the trap arises: An expansion of the externality trap. Here there are several individuals (or groups or nations) behaving in such a way as to influence the welfare of each other. That is, a collective trap is a situation in which entities are all involved in creating punishments for each other as well as themselves.

Examples: the Commons Syndrome, deterioration of national parks, overcrowded beaches, traffic jams, decimation of ocean fisheries.

6. Hybrid traps

How the trap arises: Combinations of the types of traps already listed. Most truly complex problems incorporate more than one type of trap.

Example: the greenhouse effect involves time-delay (the bad consequences come later), ignorance (in spite of early warnings, solid evidence of the effect has been forthcoming only recently), and sliding-reinforcer (we suffer costs if we continue in our polluting ways and costs if we try to escape the trap).

IRREVERSIBLE VERSUS REVERSIBLE DECISIONS

Some decisions are reversible while others are not; this is a particularly critical issue. It's likely we are creating for ourselves, by our decision making, traps from which we have no escape, or at least an escape that will be a long time in coming. A decidedly unpleasant thought.

Acid rain is a good example. It's one thing to create the conditions for acid rain. It's quite another to reverse the effects. The simplistic, nonscientific view is that we can install scrubbers on smokestacks and burn low-sulfur coal to alleviate the problem. Certainly such measures will help reduce the most obvious effects. But complex systems don't remain motionless while we humans decide to tinker here and there. Once initial disturbances occur, cause-and-effect chains are created that continue even when the initial disturbances are ceased.

Thus alterations begun by human impacts on nature, perhaps along with natural perturbations themselves, can produce strange and threatening cause-and-effect sequences. In the case of acid rain, the decline of forests has resulted in gaps in the forest canopy. These gaps, in turn, lead to more light and increased soil temperatures, which then lead to changes in the kind of plant life on the forest floor. Where these changes are taking us and whether or not they can be reversed is entirely open to question.

In complex systems, things can get out of control very fast without our even noticing changes. As we try to correct one problem, other changes many steps removed from first causes are in progress and we are not even aware of them or, if we are, we do not understand them. In terms of traps, the acid rain situation is a hybrid of time-delay, ignorance, collective, and sliding-reinforcer traps.

Likewise, the heavy use of pesticides over the decades has created and is creating systemic effects that trap us in several ways, as biologist Michael Zimmerman has pointed out. First, there is the obvious problem of food and water contamination. Second, and this is still not well understood, pesticides form chemical bonds with other substances, which fosters durability for the pesticides and keeps them around much longer than we originally guessed.

Scientists at the Connecticut Agricultural Experimental Station have discovered that toxic ethylene dibromide (EDB), a carcinogenic pesticide used throughout the United States as a control for rootworms from 1948 until it was banned in 1983, is found in significant amounts under Connecticut housing developments constructed on former cropland, where the last applications of EBD were made twenty years ago. Sensitive tests conducted on stored grain, which is routinely sprayed with pesticides on its way to storage, have shown that much more of the chemicals remain attached to the grain than was previously believed.

The pesticide usage constitutes a time-delay trap born originally of ignorance. But it runs deeper than that. It turns out that the pesticides have, in fact, created new pests by destroying the natural enemies of certain insects. The Western corn rootworm and the cotton bollworm were trivial in their impact fifty years ago, but with their natural enemies obliterated, they have become serious problems.

Nature provides defenses for its creatures. Hence, some pests have evolved resistance to pesticides. Of our worst agricultural pests, twenty have developed immunity. Examples are the Colorado potato beetle and the green peach aphid. So we use even more pesticides to try to control the problems the pesticides have created. Structurally the pesticide issue is much the same as drug addiction. More leads to more and the costs, real or perceived, of getting out of the trap keep us in the trap. By the way, entomologist Robert Metcalf of the University of Illinois states that our current crop loss to insects (about 20 percent) is the same as it was in 1900.

Groundwater contamination also has irreversibility connected with it. The Congressional Office of Technology Assessment assembled an eighteen-member panel to assess this issue. The panel reported that groundwater contamination from farm chemicals is "essentially irreversible." The pollutants are long-lasting, stubbornly hanging on for a long time. The panel also reports that only 1 percent of pesticides reach the desired target, with the remaining 99 percent doing all sorts of potential damage, including finding their way into your glass of iced tea.

Similar irreversible effects appear to be at work in destruction of the rain forests and the decline in biodiversity. Still we tinker; still we deny; still we take risks that we would not think of taking with our personal bank accounts. When a species is extinct, it's gone. That is irreversiblility of the most profound kind. Read my article, "I Am Orange Band," for an account of the final days of the dusky seaside sparrow. And see Les Kaufman and Kenneth Mallory's book, *The Last Extinction,* for tough, literate essays by natural scientists that contain many examples of irreversibility.

After reading a review I wrote of the Cross and Guyer book on traps, a colleague of mine, John Warfield, suggested that a distinction between escapes from traps and releases from traps might be worthwhile. I suggest we tend to seek technological fixes to our problems, since this approach provides release by others, while escapes often require individual effort and grinding behavioral change. The idea of traps is both fascinating and practical. I've provided only a synopsis in this section of a fairly elaborate set of ideas; the Cross and Guyer book gives much more information.

Understand, sketched out here are the problems associated with democratic societies. There are plenty of countervailing advantages, of course, not the least of which is sheer economic performance. The economic output of the United States makes up about the same proportion of world output as it did in 1960, even with the large strides in economic production accomplished by such countries as Japan and West Germany. Solutions to our problems require that we make democracy and markets operate better, not do away with them.

PROPERTY RIGHTS

The Basis of Property Rights

As I said in the Preface, I am not a futurist. When it comes to property rights, however, I feel safe in making an unqualified prediction: Property rights will be one of the major areas of debate and litigation in the next few decades, and we will undergo a cultural revolution in our view of these rights.

On April 6, 1989, the Iowa Senate Environment and Energy Committee killed a measure that would have required Iowa farmers to leave an uncultivated strip sixteen and a half feet wide between their fields and nearby waterways. Such spaces, called filter strips, are designed to impede the runoff of water and soil, and therefore chemicals, into our rivers and streams. The 1990 General Assembly passed the measure in a weakened form. But during the 1989 debate over filter strips, Senator H. Kay Hedge, a Republican and farmer from Fremont, was quoted as saying, "It bothers me that we'd set a precedent of being able to go in and remove privately owned land from production."

What Senator Hedge apparently does not understand, or at least the comment implies such a lack of understanding, is the difference between property *ownership* and property *rights*. They are not the same, and the distinction is a critical one. Someone who owns a piece of land has the right, by virtue of ownership, to make certain uses of it, to prevent others from using it, and to gather the benefits from using it.

The same rights apply to automobile ownership. But you are not allowed to drive your car in the wrong direction on a one-way street or to operate the vehicle while intoxicated or to drive it on pedestrian walkways. You may purchase ownership of a gun, but your rights do not extend to shooting others with it or discharging it within city limits. The United States shares in the heritage of the English common law, which recognizes that the rights associated with property ownership have limits and qualifications attached to them.

Property rights are determined not by gods or by signatures on a bill of sale, but rather by law and custom. Such rights flow ultimately from culture (beliefs and values), the relative values of resources, technological shifts (for example, possible risks associated with biotechnology), and the degree of social interdependence involved. Property rights are an artifact of civil society, not something ordained by the highest power in the universe.

Once we cared little about factories pouring smoke into the atmosphere. Now we do care. As values shifted, as there were more of us crowded into limited space, and as clean air became scarcer, we began to complain about the *right of manufacturers* to infringe upon *the public's right* to breathable air. Recently we have demanded by force of law that certain factories and utilities clean up their emissions.

One clean-up method is the installation of smokestack scrubbers to remove some of the harmful discharges. A filter strip along agricultural land next to a waterway is nothing more than a different type of scrubber. Nor is it any different from the noise suppressors on jet airplanes or the catalytic converters that remove lead particles from automobile exhausts, both of which have developed as responses to changing definitions of property rights.

Part of our concern over agricultural practices has to do with cultural evolution in response to technological change. Farm chemicals are technology. So is monocropping (also called monoculture) and "up-and-down-the-hill" farming instead of terracing. Our emerging concerns are responses to alterations in the way we do things. One hundred years ago, though soil erosion was already serious in certain parts of the United States, we did not have to contend with chemicals whose effects are long-lasting and potentially lethal. Technology can change rapidly; social evolutions such as property rights take longer. And that returns us to the scheduling problem I spoke of earlier.

I emphasize that property rights are a product of people, not gods. As such, they are open to change over time. In discussing the problems of stream channelization (in Chapter Four), I quoted Martin Konrad, a fisheries specialist for the Iowa DNR, as saying, "The landowners say it's their land and they should be able to do as they please." No they shouldn't. Society confers both benefits and responsibilities on property ownership. Those who fall into the category to which Konrad refers either are totally ignorant of the history of civilization, or spoiled brats, or both.

Where Private Rights Meet Public Rights

An interface is the point (or points) where two components or systems meet. In spite of the corruption from overuse and misuse of the word in recent years, including its modification into verb form, it nonetheless remains a good concept.

Much of the conflict we experience today, particularly environmental conflict, occurs because of friction at the interface between the two systems of rights—private and public. You have a legal claim to the right of sale of your automobile; you do not have a right to drive the vehicle while intoxicated. You may own a factory with which you have polluted the atmosphere for decades, but, clearly, the public has some claim on pure air at the point where your private rights meet the public rights.

A farmer has the right to farm his or her land, or to sell it, or to rent it but does not have a right, in my view, to pollute surface water and groundwater. On a more lofty level, a case can be made, and undoubtedly will be pleaded in the courts at some time, that farmers have no right to erode topsoil through shoddy agricultural practices. The basis for that case will probably hinge around the public's right to protect its food supply. Beyond human rights, there are the rights of plants, animals, and, in fact, nature itself. If that sounds strange, watch the future as it unrolls.

It's pretty clear that nowhere, by the granting of property rights, have we also granted the right to despoil and plunder, to exercise what the distinguished English jurist, Sir William Blackstone, in his *Commentaries on the Laws of England,* long ago called "the sole and despotic dominion" over the land and the resources of nature.

Walter Lippmann, the famed political columnist, also commented on the problems of property rights in democratic society, quoting key phrases of Blackstone's as part of his argument, though he disagreed with and was puzzled by Blackstone's ultimate support of absolute property rights. Lippmann said:

> The ultimate title does not lie in the owner. The title is in 'mankind,' in *The People* as a corporate community. The rights of the individual in that patrimony are creations of the law, and have no other validity

except as they are ordained by law. The purpose of laws which establish private property is not to satisfy the acquisitive and possessive instincts of the primitive man, but to promote 'the grand ends of civil society' — which comprehend 'the peace and security of individuals.' Because the legal owner enjoys the use of a limited necessity belonging to all men, he cannot be sovereign lord of his possessions. He is not entitled to exercise his absolute and therefore arbitrary will. He owes duties that correspond with his rights. His ownership is a grant made by the laws to achieve not his private purposes, but the common social purpose. And, therefore, the laws of property may and should be judged, reviewed and, when necessary, amended, so as to define the specific system of rights and duties that will promote the ends of society.

This, then, is a doctrine of private property that denies the pretension to a "sole and despotic dominion." Historically, we saw a regression (in England) to a notion that property had only rights and no duties. Here's Lippmann again, talking about property rights in England, and in his words you'll find some jarring similarities to our own time: "Absolute private property inevitably produced intolerable evils. Absolute owners did grave damage to their neighbors and to their descendants: they ruined the fertility of the land, they exploited destructively the minerals under the surface, they burned and cut forests, they destroyed the wild life, they polluted streams . . ."

So the public philosophy, via Lippmann, Aldo Leopold, and others of similar mind can be stated as:

The earth is the general property of all humankind and the creatures who share it with us.

Private titles of ownership are assigned by lawmaking authorities to promote the grand ends of civil society.

Private property is, therefore, a system of legal rights *and* duties — a product of culture rather than of divine origin.

At the interface where private rights meet public rights, the key question is, Which rights should prevail? That, as J. H. Dales points out, "is always, and inescapably, the great question of social justice."

You can view these issues in one of two ways, or both if you like. First, we are entering a period where property rights accruing to those who own property — individuals, organizations, and governments — will be modified or reduced. Alternatively, you can see it as an expansion of public rights. I like the second approach, but either will take you to the same place, eventually. Technology runs ahead of us, commodities such as air and water are no longer free, soil must be preserved for all of us, and our values are shifting to account for these changes.

Property Rights and Social Costs

A close relationship exists between the idea of property rights and social costs. In fact, they are basically two different views of the same phenomenon, addressing the issue of who profits at whose expense. Yet these two views can lead us in different directions in terms of how we go about solving the problems before us.

If you see the problems in terms of property rights, you'll seek redress through the law. Economists, on the other hand, tend to view the problem as one of misplaced incentives and argue for correction via markets. Extremists see no alternative but complete social revolution (only to find, I might add, the problems are still there). In the next chapter, I'll talk about various methods of handling disputes and what I believe is the best way to get us pointed in the right direction for a sustainable future.

FOR FURTHER READING

Baden, John, and Richard Stroup. "Property Rights, Environmental Quality, and the Management of National Forests." In *Managing the Commons,* ed. Garrett Hardin and John Baden. San Francisco: W. H. Freeman, 1977.

Cross, John G., and Melvin J. Guyer. *Social Traps.* Ann Arbor: University of Michigan Press, 1980.

Dales, J. H. "The Property Interface." In *Economics of the Environment,* 2d ed., ed. Robert Dorfman and Nancy S. Dorfman. New York: W. W. Norton, 1977.

Kaufman, Les, and Kenneth Mallory, eds. *The Last Extinction.* Cambridge, Mass.: MIT Press, 1987.

Klein, Richard M. "The Complexities of Acid Rain." *Chemical and Engineering News,* October 24, 1988, pp. 49–50. (This is a review of Chris C. Park, *Acid Rain: Rhetoric and Reality,* New York: Methuen, 1988.)

Lippmann, Walter. *The Public Philosophy.* Boston: Little, Brown, 1955. (The quotes by Sir William Blackstone were taken from this source.)

Moore, Curtis A. "Does Your Cup of Coffee Cause Forest Fires?" *International Wildlife,* March/April 1989, pp. 39–41.

Waller, Robert James. "I Am Orange Band." In *One Good Road Is Enough,* by Robert James Waller. Ames: Iowa State University Press, 1990.

CHAPTER SIX

Incentives

W e want a bountiful present and a future with promise. We also want freedom, liberty, and a range of choices over which to exercise our freedoms and our liberties. Yet, it is clear that our present choices often damage our future prospects. In decision making, the future suffers in comparison with the present. If we are to choose wisely today and insure a rich, amenity-laden future, then we must search for ways *to bring the future back to the present in such a way that the future carries weight in our current decision processes.*

MORAL EXHORTATION

One approach to wise decision making for the future is moral exhortation — people up on podiums or in front of television cameras to tell other people what's good for them. "Don't pollute!" "Just say no!" "Conserve for the future!" Does this work? Yes and no. Mostly no. When the cause is focused, such as protesting the Vietnam War, and many people are involved in the shouting, politicians and business leaders can be moved. But they are, I believe, moved more out of fear than conscience. Politicians worry about votes, business people worry about markets and image (image is one part, an important one, of an overall marketing strategy).

Moral exhortation would be a cheap way of getting things done, if it worked. If merely bringing problems to the attention of people and instructing them as to appropriate behavior were enough, moral exhortation would be both an efficient and effective method of solving problems. But in dealing with such dilemmas as the natural environment, the polluters are scattered, are culpable at various levels, and react more strongly to concrete incentives than to vague precepts of moral coaching. Appeals to conscience are nice, but like patriotism, you don't like to count on them except in the most extreme cases.

Moral arguments do, however, produce two beneficial effects. (I have thought long and hard about this, since I write essays, many of which can be categorized as moral exhortation.) Here's the value of such arguments. First, they bring to the surface and place in people's minds the fact that problems exist and something must be done about them.

Second, certain kinds of moral exhortation renew the fervor of the already committed. I'm not cynical about this latter benefit. There are dedicated people who have fought for social justice or environmental preservation for years, and they continue to fight. But, met with constant rejection or indifference and little visible progress, even those with great missionary zeal can tire. Good arguments on the side of causes in which they already believe have a renewing effect and recharge their commitment.

On the other hand, if we are to carve out a viable future for ourselves, I'm skeptical about the use of moral exhortation all by itself. Environmentalists are fond of calling for something they label an "environmental ethic." I'm not sure what that means, literally, but I do know what they're trying to accomplish. It's the same thing that all moral exhortation tries to accomplish. Environmentalists want people to behave differently, to choose different alternatives from the ones they now choose, and moral exhortation attempts to change the content and weighting of the criteria set (see Chapter Three).

If moral exhortation were enough, we would be in good shape right now. From Thomas Jefferson to Henry David Thoreau to Hugh Hammond Bennett to Rachel Carson to Barry Commoner to Paul and Ann Erlich to Bill McKibben to the lofty speeches surrounding Earth Day 1990, the calls for a reranking and reweighting of our criteria sets have echoed over the generations. Yet we have gone forward with our pollution, our erosion, and the general destruction of our own earthly life-support systems. Something's not working in this approach to solving problems.

As we see that pure rhetoric is not accomplishing what we want, a rather natural lurch occurs in the direction of two other approaches. One is education; the other is the law.

EDUCATION

I have only a little more faith in the efficacy of education as a way of changing behavior in the short run than I do in moral exhortation. Basically, education, in the way that term is loosely used, as we think of it in terms of correcting wrongs, is expected to do the same thing that rhetorical argument is supposed to do, which is to change the content and weighting of the criteria set.

The prevailing assumption is that if people truly understand the impact they are having on the environment or on any other problem of a social nature, then they will behave differently. But we've seen that even when environmental knowledge is present, such as in the case of disposable diapers, other criteria easily can dominate environmental sensibilities. A brief stroll through university campuses will convince you that knowledge and intelligence, if you assume that both of those characteristics can be found on our campuses, are not enough. The parking lots are full of large automobiles, until recently styrofoam cups were everywhere, and the waste of paper is absolutely incredible.

We tend to see education as a panacea for all of our problems, and we assign the possession of pure knowledge a greater role in decision making than it warrants, whether the problems involve drugs or the natural environment. As soon as virtually any kind of problem arises, you can count on calls for "more education." Robert Hutchins, the renowned philosopher of education, once made the following observation: "To say that education will overcome such and such a problem amounts to saying: 'If we were wise, we would know what to do. Therefore, let us have education.' " In other words, education, in some respects, has become a very large closet into which we shunt our problems.

Personally, I think such calls are frequently a convenient excuse for delaying action that may require difficult decisions. So does Hutchins, for he also stated:

> One who proclaims salvation through education evades the necessity of doing something about the slums. One who sees education as the prime requirement of the poverty-stricken nations does not have to try to keep them from starving. Those who talk of education as the sole

means of solving the race problems, or of obtaining lasting peace, or of curing juvenile delinquency, often seem to mean that they have not much interest in these subjects, certainly not much interest in inconveniencing themselves about them.

Why some people will sacrifice in the cause of environmental preservation while others will not is something of a mystery. Looked at another way, a small minority of people have the natural environment as a highly ranked criterion in their decision making and live their lives consistent with good treatment of nature.

Tom Tanner, professor of environmental studies at Iowa State University, carried out a study several years ago designed to discover why some people "strive for the preservation of a habitable, resource-rich planet to pass on to posterity." His conclusions agree exactly with something I argued when I was part of a team looking at environmental education in the 1970s. Tanner says:

> I discovered an overwhelmingly clear common pattern: As children, my subjects had spent many hours alone or with a few friends in relatively pristine habitats that were usually accessible every day. The nature of these habitats varied with the settings of the respondents' childhood homes; they included vacant lots, undeveloped city parks, and farmlands.

Tanner also notes that studies in Illinois and Maine resulted in similar conclusions. The problem comes in providing that kind of environment for all children. Unfortunately, the increasing urbanization of America along with competition from television and other distractions seem to work against it. Like Tanner, I have doubts about the efficacy of standard classroom instruction, occasional field trips, or brief outdoor camping experiences as methods of creating environmental awareness at a level where the individual's decision processes are profoundly influenced.

Education certainly has a role to play in problem solving and preparing people for the future. But I don't believe pure academic instruction is sufficient to solve our problems, nor do I believe education, even if it were so powerful, can respond rapidly enough in most cases.

LAW AND REGULATION

When moral exhortation fails and the calls for education have been issued, the next phase of problem solving usually involves a spasmodic lurch toward legislation prohibiting certain kinds of behavior thought to cause the problem. As a society, we shout, "Stop that behavior or we'll fine, imprison, or kill you!" From a decision-making viewpoint, prohibitive legislation does not, by itself, change the set of alternatives or the criteria set.* Rather, punishment-centered laws attach an undesirable outcome to the set of outcomes from a given alternative (think about the cells in the decision matrix in Chapter Three). This creates a risk that if the perpetrator is apprehended and prosecuted the formerly desirable outcomes flowing from the given alternative will be replaced by a punishment.

Certainly, tough laws, stringently enforced, can have an impact on behavior in certain situations. But several problems are inherent in using a punishment-centered, legislative approach to correcting behavior. First, most laws can be evaded, at least for a time, and the monitoring and regulation activities flowing from prohibition are cumbersome and costly. Second, when people are ordered not to do something, they like the situation a good deal less than if they had freely chosen not to do it.

Third, by its very nature, law is an adversarial process. There are winners and losers. Hence, due to fighting between potential winners and losers, the passage of laws can take a long time in the political process. Meanwhile the problem, such as environmental degradation, continues to worsen. Fourth, even when a law is passed, enforcement and prosecution can also require long periods of time for a resolution of the issue. Large corporations or wealthy individuals or governments have the resources to carry on their litigation indefinitely.

Fifth, in the environmental field (and many other areas), each problem has its own unique characteristics, with the adjudication of one case not necessarily applying to other situations. Thus policy via law is carried out on a case-by-case basis—piecemeal decision making, in other words, sometimes resulting eventually in judicial precedent.

Sixth, in the complex world of social and environmental affairs, matters of probability always are present. Honest disagreement can occur based on differing estimates of what kind of impact a particular alternative can have and the probability of the impact occurring at all.

---

*If apprehension and punishment are certain, then the alternative set *is* modified, since only a masochist would continue choosing the banned alternative.

Seventh, above all of these drawbacks is the notion of liberty. The passage of laws is nearly always an attempt to reduce freedom of choice, though sometimes the intent is to expand and clarify the opportunities for ethical, socially responsible choice. Year after year, as legislatures and Congress meet, laws are being passed. Many of these are of a prohibiting, as opposed to an enabling, kind. Each prohibition is another limit on choice. Tied in with this is the fact that certain critical situations relevant to the future of Iowa are not amenable to solution by any lawmaking that prohibits one or more behaviors, given our heritage of liberal democracy. For example, forbidding rural people to shop at regional malls and mandating they spend their money at small-town stores.

Finally, note that the use of legislation to accomplish social goals has many of the same characteristics as centrally controlled, command economies. Decisions about how much pollution is required or whether a particular wetland should be drained have to be made on a case-by-case basis. The same complexity that has defeated central planners in the Soviet Union confronts those who must carry out the regulations stemming from laws. The same lethargy appears, the same cumbersome bureaucracies responsible for decision making and enforcement must be established. In terms of regulation by standards, the problem exists of applying a single set of regulatory standards to businesses and other organizations with widely differing production functions, which hinders the search for efficiency characteristic of firms in a market economy.

If moral exhortation or education or law, or some combination of the three, were truly effective, then the narcotics problem in this country would have disappeared by now. It has not. Aside from moral exhortation, education, and law, what else is left? In a large number of cases, particularly in the spheres of environmental and social problems, I believe the answers lie in one word: incentives.

INCENTIVES

*The Case for Incentives**

Consider the following decision situation. It's a general model for most of the problems discussed thus far in the book and is an especially good model for the tragedy-of-the-commons type of problems.

---

*In some of the examples discussed here, incentives are really disincentives. The arguments hold either way.

Alternative A: The outcome is one that is good for the individual in the short run, but bad for the larger group in the short run, or long run, or both. The "group" here might be a neighborhood, a community, a state, a nation, or nations. Likewise, the "individual" might be a firm or a town or a nation.

Alternative B: The outcome is less desirable than the outcome of Alternative A in the short run for the individual, but is beneficial for everybody from a larger and longer perspective.

As I have suggested all along, people respond to short-run incentives, and in many cases the alternatives chosen on the basis of these incentives have damaging effects in the longer run. Often, in fact, the individual eventually is snared in the same trap as the larger group. Examples here are agricultural practices promoting chemical pollution of groundwater, the Sunday automobile drive contributing to atmospheric pollution, the disposal of used motor oil down the household sewer drain, and the decision to shop at regional malls instead of patronizing local merchants.

In attempting to deal with these kinds of problems, we can try moral exhortation, or education, or legislation, or some combination of the three. Or, we can look at the structure of the decisions confronted by people and try to discover how we might manipulate incentives in such a way that people behave differently. Here's an interesting example from the social welfare arena, which is based on an actual case.

A young, unmarried woman has a child and is currently receiving government support (a social cost in the form of a subsidy) via Aid to Families with Dependent Children (AFDC) and food stamps.* The woman has no salable job skills beyond those of a minimum-wage worker. Society criticizes her for being on welfare and offers advice such as "pull yourself up by your own bootstraps." The advice is useless. Look at the woman's situation from the viewpoint of decision making.

Alternative A: Stay on AFDC and food stamps.
Outcomes: $5,600 per year in income, medical expenses covered, no baby sitting or transportation expenses.
Alternative B: Look for a job.

---

*The dollar figures used in this example are those from the original case and are slightly out of date, but that does not affect the ideas presented.

Outcomes: Failure to find job or finding poorly paying job with minimal or no medical benefits; transportation and baby-sitting charges incurred, along with income taxes (depending on income level) and social security payments.

Can anyone blame the woman for choosing Alternative A, even though she is well below the poverty line in this situation? No. This is a perfectly rational choice, and many of us in her position would make the same choice. The overall result is that the woman lives a life on welfare, has little opportunity for pride in her accomplishments, endures the scorn of larger society, and society bears the cost of supporting her and her child.

Moreover, apparently there is a self-perpetuating aspect to this kind of existence. A reasonable chance exists that the woman's child will follow her way of life and exist on government transfer payments. Poverty has its own vicious circles. In cases like this one, the road signs guiding our decision making are fouled up.

Suppose we offer the woman an enriched choice set through something called an "Employment Training" (ET) program, adding another alternative to her choice set that looks as follows:

Alternative C: Enter an employment-training program providing basic job skills for which a market exists.
Outcomes: The program provides short-term child care, medical coverage, and transportation subsidies while the woman is receiving employment training, and the promise of a job paying some reasonable wage that will enable her to care for herself and her child at the end of the program.

The woman's choice set now looks considerably different. In the case I'm describing, which happened in Massachusetts, the woman and many others like her chose Alternative C. The changes in the woman's life-style and attitudes were dramatic, and society eventually did not have to support her.

Yet, nobody forced her into the ET program. Quite simply, the incentives present in Alternative C were such that this alternative became more attractive than either of the other alternatives confronting her. Incidentally, the social workers involved in this situation were buoyant about the program, since their roles shifted from policing the woman's behavior to helping her into the ET program and placing her in a job at the program's completion. Incentives did the work, the woman made a free choice, and both society and the woman escaped a trap.

For the skeptics, I'll admit there are potential flaws in this approach. One has to do with the availability of a job at the end of the program. Whether a state or local or national economy can make this promise is questionable.

In addition, these schemes, overall, have not met the expectations for them. One study showed that such programs have raised the employment rate for welfare mothers by only 3 to 9 percent. Still, there is a basic logic to this approach, and the problems may well lie in the character of the incentives, the alternatives available, dissemination of information about the programs, and other aspects of multiple-criteria decision making that can be improved. The pessimistic view, however, would be that the habits and attitudes of those on welfare are such that nothing can be done.

Iowa has given some recognition to the problem of incentives in the welfare arena. For example, the state has participated in a national self-employment demonstration project sponsored by the non-profit Corporation for Enterprise Development. In this program, welfare recipients are provided special assistance in developing self-employment jobs for themselves and are given waivers for a period of time from welfare regulations that might disqualify them from receiving public assistance, such as a reduction in benefits if a recipient acquires too much in the way of capital assets.

Examples abound paralleling the welfare example just presented. For example, the history of farm programs in the United States is, with only a few exceptions, a textbook on how to promote soil erosion. The occasional nod toward soil conservation primarily has been in the form of education, a few weak economic incentives, and voluntary cooperation. Data from the Organization for Economic Cooperation and Development indicate that farm subsidies cost Western governments more than $300 billion a year.* As Jim MacNeill points out: "What conservation programs can compete with that? These subsidies send farmers far more powerful signals than do the small grants usually provided for soil and water conservation."

---

*Farm subsidies in developed countries have another detrimental effect. One of the key ingredients in getting a poor, developing country under way is the establishment of a solid agricultural system. Subsidies from the West, however, undermine this effort by encouraging the production of surplus crops that are then dumped in developing countries, which holds down the price that local farmers can receive for their crops.

Provisions in the Food Security Act of 1985 marked a turning point in the relationship of farm subsidies to soil conservation. Under the "swampbuster" and "sodbuster" provisions of the act, farmers producing commodities on highly erodible land, as defined by the Soil Conservation Service, are barred from receiving price supports, federal crop insurance, disaster payments, Farmers Home Administration loans or loan guarantees, and storage payments by the Commodity Credit Corporation. If a farmer converts wetlands into cropland, the same penalties apply. For erosion-prone land taken out of production, the Conservation Reserve Program section of the act pays farmers an average of $48 per acre over a ten-year period if they plant the land with grass or other noncrop cover. The key point is that the farmer *has a choice* of whether to participate in these various provisions.

In Britain, farm subsidies of the type used in the United States are a comparatively recent phenomenon. As farmers adapt to the subsidies, people have begun to notice the degradation of the famed English landscape. Bogs are being drained, overgrazing occurs on the moors, meadows are plowed under, hedges and stone walls are removed. The *Economist* magazine has this to say, in an article called "Green and Unpleasant":

> Supporting farmers with guaranteed minimum prices is lethal to the environment. It reduces risk. Fear of fluctuating yields once led farmers to hedge their bets, keeping pigs in their orchards and cows in their stubble fields. The less prices fluctuate, the greater incentive to abandon mixed farming for monoculture, which is generally uglier and more polluting. Payments linked directly to output encourage farmers to raise yields beyond the natural capacity of the land.

There it is. The same old song, the same disastrous consequences of ignoring the power of incentives operating under conditions of self-interest. In decision terms, the situation appears as follows:

Alternative A: Drain bogs, plow meadows, tear down stone walls, and remove hedges, all designed to bring more land into production.
Outcomes: Farmer gaining more land on which to raise crops and, therefore, receiving more money in subsidies. Social costs to society are the loss of beauty and diversity. Property rights prevent society from changing farmers' behavior or make it difficult to do so.

Alternative B: Leave land as is.

> *Outcomes:* Farmer receives less income, society benefits from preservation. Farmer is praised, maybe, as good steward of the land.

Based on the current behavior of English farmers, we can safely judge that revenue maximization is the dominant criterion, which is not surprising. Without changing criteria or even alternatives in this case, the farmer's behavior can be changed by altering the outcomes. That's what the *Economist* proposes, in the form of a "stewardship fee." The idea is to stop paying farmers to produce excess crops and, instead, pay the same money to farmers (and other landowners) for protecting the countryside. The *Economist* argues, and I agree, that everyone is better off under the stewardship-fee arrangement.

There are, of course, three other courses of action possible here. One is to exhort the farmers to leave the countryside as it is. The second is to "educate" the farmers on the importance of preserving a visually attractive landscape. The third is to launch legal action, on a case-by-case basis, against farmers who try to remove bogs, moors, walls, and so forth. But, it's simpler and more effective just to pay them a stewardship fee in the first place.

That is, let self-interest handle the dilemma by making the fees high enough so that farmers *prefer* to be stewards rather than maximizing the number of acres farmed. But democratic societies surely seem to have trouble grasping the elegance and power of the incentives approach. There must be something more at work here, and there is: fairness. I'll come to that in a moment.

Here's a third example. (As I describe it, understand that I do not believe in killing for sport. But I am also a realist.) Just about everyone has heard of the problems with Africa's great herds of wild game. Poaching is one problem, of course, and I'll come back to that shortly. Beyond poaching, however, is the situation confronted by the typical African living in game country. To this person, usually a small farmer, the animals represent a nuisance, destroying crops and competing with the farmer's attempt to support himself and his family. Now look at this from the decision-making perspective of the farmer.

Alternative A: Do no harm to the animals.

> *Outcomes:* Crops destroyed, family hungry, relatively wealthy tourists pleased that wild game is available to observe and photograph.

Alternative B: Destroy the game.
Outcomes: Crops protected, family fed at very modest level, tourists not happy.

So we sit in our living rooms in America or Germany or Japan and shake our heads at the disappearance of the Africa that has represented a kind of Eden for us, even if we never travel there. We resent the loss of options. For the African farmer, however, this is not Eden; this is reality, and hungry children must be fed. Like the welfare example, this state of affairs can be turned into a win-win rather than a win-lose situation. Zimbabwe has been doing it for some time, and other African nations are starting to follow.

What's needed is a modest restructuring of incentives. It works like this: View the animals as a natural resource to be managed and exploited, and make sure the farmer participates in the benefits of this exploitation. Many of the benefits accrue from wealthy foreigners who pay large sums for hunting safaris and others who come only to photograph or watch. If the animals produce revenues for the African peasant that exceed the benefits derived from killing them, then a strong financial incentive exists for preservation of wild game and the habitat it takes to support the game.

Zimbabwe is now sprinkled with hundreds of so-called game farms where hunters pay stiff fees for killing trophy animals. In addition, the government sells wild animals to zoos or culls the herds and sells the meat.* Game ranching has at least two benefits, according to Marilyn Achiron: "Not only does it conserve animals and habitat, it has the potential for getting money into the pockets of local people whose poverty is a prime cause of environmental degradation everywhere."

A specific case in Zimbabwe involved the southeastern Shangaan tribe. The nearby Gonarezhou National Park contained large numbers of elephants that crossed the park boundaries and destroyed the Shangaan's crops. The Shangaan, in turn, entered the park and killed the elephants to prevent the crop damage. That was before 1982, when a local rancher convinced the tribesmen that money could be earned by protecting the elephants.

---

*I don't cotton to words like "harvesting" as glamorized descriptions for the killing of animals. We talk about "slaughtering" cattle or hogs, but when it comes to animals viewed as being more romantic in stature, we insist on euphemisms. One of the worst, which is prominent in some hunting literature, is "collecting." We kill the animals. Period. Someday we'll all become adults and stop trying to prettify our behavior and salve our consciences by treating killing as anything other than it really is—killing.

Now the Shangaan act as hosts to hunters, as trackers and skinners, as meat processors. Achiron says: "Within a year, the rate of poaching in Gonarezhou had dropped 90 percent and the Shangaan had earned more than $9,000 in trophy fees and skins—and had collected hundreds of dollars worth of meat."

Wildlife lovers tried moral exhortation. They also tried banning the killing of game. Nothing changed, and the game continued to disappear. But harnessing self-interest in the form of incentives is doing what neither screaming about morality or prohibitions could do.

For some people, there's a moral dilemma in the Zimbabwe experience. It has to do with decision criteria and alternatives. You can argue that killing the animals to save them is wrong. In a perfectly enlightened world, all of us would contribute enough money to pay the farmers to let the game roam at will and have nature take its course. As in the case of the English countryside, we would pay stewardship fees.

That has not happened and appears to have little chance of occurring in anything resembling the present or near future. It's one thing to cluck in disapproval while watching the evening nature special on television; it's quite another to fork over $100 to save zebras.

So, what's more important, the criterion preserving game species in Africa from extinction or standing on the principle/criterion that it's wrong to kill for sport? I can't answer that for you. For me, I have something of a utopian dream that enlightenment will come, eventually, and that people will act on strong philosophical beliefs a good share of the time rather than self-interest. For now, I vote to preserve the animals, even if, perversely, it means killing some of them. It comes down, as always, to decision making.

Obviously I like the idea of incentives. The effects of using them are powerful, they tend to be easier to swallow politically than outright legal suppression of behavior, and they are self-policing (in many cases) in a way that laws are not. The latter idea deserves reinforcement here, for it is a key aspect of an incentive-based approach to solving problems.

In the Zimbabwe example, no regulation and policing of the kind normally associated with laws are required. The reason is a simple one. The incentives for protecting the animals are guiding behavior through self-interest. The animals produce benefits in excess of those received from doing away with them. Hence, tribesmen protect the animals. It's an elegant, promising solution to a complex problem.

In the late 1970s, President Jimmy Carter went on television and told Americans that they needed to conserve energy. As far as I could tell, most people went straight out and bought gas guzzlers. But as gasoline prices began to rise, the demand for small, fuel-efficient automobiles increased. Incentives via the marketplace accomplished what even a president's moral exhortation could not. If gas prices had remained high relative to incomes, as they should have, the incentive would have been present to continue the purchase of small cars.

In this context, economist Charles L. Schultze makes a classic statement on the use of incentives:

> If I want industry to cut down on pollution, indignant tirades about social responsibility can't hold a candle to schemes that reduce the profits of firms who pollute. If I want drivers to economize on gasoline usage, advertising appeals to patriotism, warnings about the energy crisis, and "don't be fuelish" slogans are no match for higher prices at the gas pumps. In most cases the prerequisite for social gains is the identification, not of villains and heroes, but of the defects in the incentive system that drive ordinary decent citizens into doing things contrary to the common good.

In 1973, we were shocked by dramatic energy price increases. No long-term plan existed to deal with such a situation, but those firms with the most to gain responded, based on self-interest, and created technological change that reduced their energy requirements 25 to 40 percent over five years. The increases in energy prices were a result of market power by energy producers, rather than any true scarcity of energy in the short run. Eventually prices dropped, and the incentive to seek efficiencies and substitutes evaporated.

Here are three personal observations that go far to explain why I like the incentives approach. The first one stems from a speech I gave in about 1970 to a group opposed to the Vietnam War. My topic was the military-industrial complex. Hot-blooded and wild of eye, I began my extensive research for the talk expecting to find villains of the worst kind. I was looking for evil. As I read and thought, however, I had trouble locating a group of all-powerful, thoroughly menacing conspirators composed of the Pentagon and big defense contractors.

Instead, I found managers worried about their careers, generals worried about promotion, and workers trying to pay mortgages. In other words, incentives were driving the whole system. Okay, I also found some stupidity and some ignorance and some greed, but I found no evil in the most profound sense of that word.

When I reported my findings to the group that invited me, I was not received warmly. They wanted evil—evil generals, evil captains of industry, evil engineers drooling as they designed more powerful weapons. "Sorry," I told them, "that's not what I found."

That speech, or rather the research and reflection that went into it, was a significant turning point in my thinking. I began to see *the power that incentives have in influencing behavior.* And I also began to understand that *removing "evil" as a source of our problems has some real benefits.* That's the second observation. There is not much to be done about true evil, except to kill it or lock it away. Yet there are behaviors appearing to be evil that are nothing more than rather decent citizens responding to the incentives before them. Much of our soil erosion problem in Iowa is just like that.

Third, and this idea came to me only after years of trying to fit much of the misbehavior I see into the framework of decision making, *it's not necessary to change people's criteria set in order to change behavior.* Instead, change the outcomes of alternatives via incentives (or disincentives). Because criteria are closely allied with basic human values, they are difficult, maybe impossible, to change.

But the natural environment can be represented in people's criteria set through *proxy devices.* Take the gasoline case. If gasoline prices rise and people turn to smaller autos, nothing has to have transpired in terms of their criteria to make this choice. What has happened is this: the natural environment is represented in the criteria set under the heading of cost. In fact, the term "natural environment" does not even have to be in the individual's criterion set. Yet it's there, in the form of cost.

Think back to the decision matrix in Chapter Three. Suppose the natural environment is not even included in the criteria set as a separate criterion. Even so, it can be present, because cost is there, and cost usually is ranked high for most financial decisions of any kind. *If incentives are manipulated correctly, cost becomes a proxy for the natural environment.* Revenue also can serve as a proxy for the natural environment when rewards rather than penalties are the incentives. Stewardship payments to land owners are an example of this, and no reliance on social conscience is necessary, since the environment is implicitly taken into account via revenues.

All of the efforts to create an environmental ethic have been attempts to change content, rankings, and weights within the criteria set. By changing the outcomes of alternatives, however, one can leave the criteria alone and still get the behavior desired. As biologist David Ehrenfeld says, "I believe that *the ultimate success of all conservation will depend on a revision of the way we use the world in our everyday living when we are not thinking about conservation.* If we have to conserve the Earth in spite of ourselves, we will not be able to do it."

Product Market Pressures as Incentives

I am no apologist for American business (including agriculture) or the market system in general. If that's not apparent already, it will become so before you finish this book. But I can get a little short with people who demand that business people behave in certain ways without fully appreciating the competitive pressures under which they live. I wish McDonald's would have done away with styrofoam containers ten years ago, instead of announcing a phaseout of them in the fall of 1990. And I wish General Motors would produce automobiles that have a lower negative impact on the environment.

Well, we should stop buying McDonald's products and demand smaller cars with higher fuel efficiency. Business people are not moral philosophers. In fact, their training, based on the structures and strictures of American business schools, is almost exactly the opposite. You'll often hear the term "level playing field" in discussions about the social responsibility of business. What business people are saying is this: "I'll consider a change if you assure me that all of my competitors must change at the same time."

If you want business people to modify their behavior, the easiest method is through the market. This is just another way of talking about incentives. If people demand small cars instead of large ones, Detroit, Japan, and Germany will produce small cars. Automakers may try to convince you that larger autos are superior, because the net profit is higher on larger cars, but if you persist, you'll get smaller cars.

If a firm is polluting the environment or is treating its employees in an inhumane fashion, refuse to purchase its products because of those reasons. Almost magically, the pollution will begin to decline or the treatment of employees will improve. Managers want to keep their jobs and pay their mortgages. They have an allegiance to what sells, and those who wish for change can take advantage of that allegiance. These kinds of incentives operate on the output side of the diagram in Figure 2.1.

Capital Market Pressures as Incentives

The Coalition for Environmentally Responsible Economies (CERES) is a consortium of fourteen environmental groups and 325 members of the Social Investment Forum. The latter is a national trade association of money managers, brokers, bankers, analysts, and other socially concerned investors. Through CERES, pressures in the form of incentives are being brought to bear on major U.S. corporations.

In addition, investment funds are now available that specialize in companies exhibiting socially responsible behavior. When people invest money, they expect or hope for a monetary return. The socially responsible concept adds another alternative to investment choices and allows the use of criteria other than financial return. Thus, as people examine investment alternatives, companies can be judged not only on their ability to produce investor returns but also on their corporate citizenship.

While the concept of socially responsible investing is a matter of an enlarged choice set for investors, it also involves incentives for companies who need capital. If this idea grows to the point that a substantial amount of capital is being moved around on the basis of corporate behavior as well as monetary returns, the pressures on business firms, including agribusiness, to respond will increase. Potentially, this is a powerful use of incentives on the input side of business firms (see Figure 2.1).

Law and Incentives

Lawmaking has an important role to play in the incentives-based approach. But it is *enabling law* instead of *prohibitive law,* and it creates additional alternatives rather than attaching punishment to existing ones. For example, stewardship fees will require laws permitting and structuring them, and farmers still can choose to accept or reject the stewardship alternative.

Also, it's a little simplistic to believe that incentives can solve every problem. Poaching is one such instance. Presumably, we could pay poachers not to carry out their dirty business. But then all, or almost all, would declare themselves poachers in order to receive the payments. It can be argued that stewardship payments fall into the same category. Like many things, behavior lies on a continuum, and judgment must be applied.

In a very real sense, though, prohibitive law, as I pointed out before, is a matter of adding unpleasant outcomes and risk to certain alternatives. In that sense, it involves incentives. Richard Leakey is director of Kenya's Wildlife and Conservation Management Department. He sees wildlife, elephants in particular, as a natural resource for economic development. But poachers long have been decimating the elephant herds. Leakey equipped his rangers with Land Rovers and weapons, instructing them to shoot first and query later. In the four months after Leakey's appointment, thirty poachers were shot. Elephant killings declined from three a day to one a month.

I doubt, however, if we are prepared to shoot farmers who practice poor land stewardship or executives who pollute rivers. Laws enabling the use of incentives seem to be a better approach.

Cost, Crisis, and the Future

Earlier I mentioned that a recent poll shows three out of four Americans consider themselves environmentalists. Another study, this one by Cambridge Energy Research Associates, suggests that we are prepared to sacrifice for the environment. More than 60 percent of respondents in the study indicated that they are willing to accept a lower standard of economic activity if they could be certain it would lead to a cleaner, safer environment. Similarly, a *Time* poll showed that 94 percent of those surveyed believe environmental protection is a very important issue.

Let's take the sunny position that these studies are an accurate reflection of current American values. Does this represent a sudden escalation in the environmental conscience of Americans, the flowering of an environmental ethic? Maybe. If so, it doesn't have much to do with morality.

Instead, fear is at work. The two C's—*cost and crisis*—are great motivators. Cost operates as an incentive/disincentive. Crisis, and the fear that accompanies it, *can* change criteria rankings and weights. Suddenly, so the polls claim, people have elevated the natural environment in their criteria set.

For example, Iowa farmers are concerned about the use of agricultural chemicals. A minority have worried about chemicals for years, and a subset of this minority based their worries on a genuine concern for the natural environment. But there's nothing quite like having your hogs die from drinking the well water or seeing bare subsoil appear in your fields to shift your criteria rankings. Fear, not morality, is at work.

Thus some Iowa farmers are switching over to alternative methods of crop production, including lower use of chemicals, crop rotation, and, in general, what is called sustainable agriculture. A group called

Practical Farmers of America has led this movement over the last decade (in fairness, I should note that some members of this group have acted out of moral concerns, as well as fear).

The same kinds of fears are driving American consumers, who worry about their air and food and drinking water. While eminently laudable, the precedent-setting groundwater law passed in the 1987 Iowa General Assembly was not a response to some abstract notion of environmental consciousness. It was a direct response to fear about water quality. A response to crisis, in other words, that escalated the natural environment as a criterion in voters' and legislators' criteria sets.

West Germany firmly opposed anything resembling stricter air pollution controls until 1983. Suddenly the West Germans supported a Scandinavian proposal calling for each member of the U.N. Economic Commission for Europe to cut sulfur dioxide emissions by 30 percent.* Why the sudden rise in consciousness? Because a 1982 survey showed that air pollution and acid rain were the probable causes of trees dying in the legendary Black Forest and elsewhere.

Patriotism soars in times of external menace, and people become environmentalists when they see a genuine threat to their well-being. But crisis is what we would like to avoid. And, as mentioned earlier, the problem is bringing the future back to the present. Incentives can help do just that.

In these terms, bringing the future back to the present, one of the most powerful social tools ever invented in this country was the Individual Retirement Account. First, the IRAs allowed a credit against taxes due. Thus a short-term incentive was present. Second, the proceeds from the IRA were out there compounding and could not be touched until age fifty-five. Thus individuals were providing for their own futures while also receiving an immediate benefit. Third, the pool of funds generated by the IRAs increased the amount of money available for investment in a nation with a notoriously low rate of savings.

Except for some equity problems, which could have been fixed with a little tinkering, the IRA had everything going for it: short-run rewards and long-run benefits for the individual, long-run benefits for larger society. In the tax reform frenzy of 1986, most IRAs were disallowed. One of the arguments given was that "taxes should not be used as an instrument of social policy." That's poppycock. Taxes are one of the few

---

*Opposition by the United States, the United Kingdom, and others prevented adoption of the proposal. Subsequently, though, the "30 percent club" was formed by a subgroup of nations committed to the idea.

surgical instruments available to governments for influencing citizen behavior.

If you want to avoid crisis, you must bring the future back to the present. The IRA is a good model to keep in mind when thinking about how to handle the problem of sacrifice in the present for the benefit of the future.

Short-term thinking pervades the American business community. Some of the most important reasons for this have to do with incentives — managers tend to be rewarded for short-run rather than long-run results. Hence, the reward systems for managers need to be changed. R. Stephen Berry mentions several possibilities. One is to make the monetary return from executive retirement programs contingent on the performance of the firm's future performance. Likewise, the deliverance of various perquisites, such as shares of stock, can be made in the future rather than the present. These, like IRAs, are methods of bringing the future back to the present.

Incentives and the Question of Fairness

Not everybody likes incentives as a tool for solving social problems. In fact, a good many environmentalists object to them. One of the major complaints lodged against an incentive-based approach has to do with fairness. Basically, the argument runs as follows: It's not fair to pay people to do what they already should be doing as a matter of conscience. That's one part of it. The second part is the mirror image of the first: If you pay polluters to stop polluting, you are being unfair to those firms who have been responsible in the past.

I understand and am sympathetic with both of these arguments. The second problem can be handled by providing extra payments or some other reward to those who have a history of responsible behavior. The first is more elusive and strikes at the heart of what it means to live in a responsible fashion. In fact, it has to do with how one views humans as sentient, rational beings of conscience.

Applause always accrues to those who do the right thing at the cost of personal sacrifice. Mother Theresa, known for her efforts on behalf of the poor in India, is virtually above reproach in the conventional wisdom. Some wish for a world of Mother Theresas. But we do not have one. There are those who throw themselves on daggers to save their comrades, and their heroism is recognized and acclaimed, as it should be.

We are, however, a long way from having a world of heroes. I hope for such a world in the future. Still, my rational self tells me we are some distance away from it. Until then, we must do what we can to save our social and natural systems from destruction, all the while applying efforts to engender a greater social conscience in the individual mind.

In the view of environmentalists and some others, the basic problem with an incentive-based approach is that it does not stigmatize behavior. That is, if somebody is behaving badly, they need to know they are wrong. Incentives don't operate this way. Incentives merely sit there and alter behavior without making judgments about right or wrong.

Of course, those who develop the incentives are making such judgments, but rational calculation is more evident than is stigmatization. With incentives, it appears that people are being allowed to violate moral rules without censure. In fact, they sometimes are rewarded for it, when positive incentives such as stewardship fees are used.

This argument was raised over and over again in the recent debates involving the use of filter strips along waterways in Iowa. Many of those who favored the strips objected to any proposal that included payments to farmers for installing the strips. In the 1989 Iowa General Assembly, a measure for mandatory filter strips without compensation was defeated. A revised, weaker law was passed in 1990 that gave farmers the option of putting in the strips. If they do, the state will reimburse farmers for the vegetation planted as part of the strips.

Clearly, the filter strip situation involves many of the decision-making factors discussed in the last two chapters. First of all, there is the social cost of soil runoff and the chemical pollution it carries with it. Second, there is the matter of property rights. And, third, there are incentives present. To the average farmer worried about maximizing net revenues, the situation looked like this as debate took place in the Iowa Legislature:

Alternative A: Put in filter strips.
  Outcomes: Less net revenue, some distant applause from society at large.

Alternative B: Don't put in filter strips.
  Outcomes: Maintain current net revenue, receive criticism from larger society.

The 1989 proposal would have eliminated Alternative B and forced the implementation of filter strips. But, and this is crucial, it didn't make it into law. So we had another year of soil erosion and pollution, while environmentalists criticized farmers, and the farmers planted right up to the river edges. I argued for Alternative A with the proviso that farmers be paid for putting in the strips and extra payments be made to those farmers who had already done so as a matter of good stewardship. My dominant criterion was "get the erosion and pollution stopped." I felt the same way in 1990 and would have been willing to pay more taxes to compensate farmers in the ways I just specified. What we have now is a fairly weak system of incentives that may or may not accomplish the desired objective.

We live in a political world, and politics must be taken into account when thinking about strategies. My judgment is that farmers would support filter strips if they are compensated appropriately, and that that alternative would become politically acceptable. Machiavellian? Maybe. But I often wonder how committed some people are to environmental improvement when they argue for social conscience while the rivers die. Moreover, in a country so concerned about liberty, I am always amazed at how ready we are to reduce freedom of choice. While I am not sympathetic to the old cry, "This is my property and I can use it in any way I want," financial payments for installing filter strips is a nonpunitive method of dealing with the private property issues discussed earlier.

There are other problems with incentives. One is the "distributional effects" of incentive systems, that is, in any approach to solving problems, some people are going to better or worse off than before. Gasoline taxes, for example, are regressive taxes, penalizing those at lower income levels. Some compensation scheme must be worked out in those cases. (The books by Charles Schultze and by Thomas Schelling in the readings list further explore some of these dilemmas, none of which are insurmountable.)

Steven Kelman presents a well-argued case against the use of incentives. His case rests largely on the issues I have just mentioned. After reading his book, however, I had a question: What have you got that's better? The silence thundered.

Obviously, incentives have their limits. Sometimes prohibitive laws and rigorous enforcement of these laws is the only answer. But, if we wish to preserve democracy and all that democracy means, while successfully handling the problems that press upon us, the shrewd use of incentives is a powerful approach to getting things under control, changing the outcomes of decision situations while we're trying to raise consciences through moral exhortation and education. Many of our problems won't wait until the long process of modifying values has succeeded, if it ever does succeed. And during this time of values reorientation, we can easily and unwittingly commit ourselves to courses of action with irreversible effects, such as species extinction and the warming of the earth.

If you look carefully at the problems recounted in your daily newspaper, you'll see, over and over again, incentives at work. In many — most — cases, the incentives are misplaced and are leading us in the wrong direction. Brazil provides subsidies that lead to tropical deforestation, and people collect welfare because it's the best option available to them.

Yelling at Big Polluter to change its ways is likely to have little effect. Suppose, however, you run a hose from BP's outlet pipe by the river right back into the executive offices. You'll get change, right away. Now, think about how you can run that hose to the executive offices in a little more subtle fashion using incentives.

Still, the lack of sensitivity to the power of incentives by policymakers and lawmakers is amazing. A mix of policies, regulations, laws, and government budgets generate the structure within which an economy functions. And contained within this structure are various incentives that signal people to behave in certain ways, both in production and consumption activities. Often these incentives contradict one another or, worse, promote economic activities at the expense of the natural environment. The first two questions to ask about any law or policy or budget are: (1) What signals does this send to producers and consumers and (2) how will these signals affect their decision making?

NEGOTIATION/MEDIATION

The basic decision model sketched in Chapter Three is a useful device for understanding the source(s) of disagreements among parties to a dispute. One can ask if the disputants disagree over what is in the criteria set, how the criteria are ranked, how the criteria are weighted relative to one another, the magnitude of the outcomes estimated for the individual cells in the matrix, the probabilities assigned to outcomes, attitudes toward risk, and the discount rate being used if the decision involves long time periods.

If you're at loggerheads with someone else, whether in marriage or environmental affairs, the source(s) of the disagreement will lie somewhere in one or more of these aspects of decision making. The problem is locating the source(s) and then negotiating a settlement in those areas where divergence of opinion is present.

Moral exhortation does not attack problems this way. Neither does the law with its adversarial methods, limited scope of judicial review, and win-lose outcomes. In addition, lawsuits often are fought on spurious grounds, using surrogates for the real problem. For example, the lengthy and costly litigation concerning protection of the spotted owl in Pacific Coast lumbering regions is fundamentally an argument over whether the old growth forests will be saved or clear-cut. As a result, the real issues underlying such disputes are usually not solved.

And public meetings, or just the typical meeting conducted as a free-for-all, are almost totally ineffective in resolving differences of opinion where money, ego, and similar matters are on the line. Thus mediation (using a third party to assist in negotiations) and arbitration offer some real possibilities in conflict resolution. Moreover, using a decision model of the type presented provides a mediator a way of finding the key points of dispute, which is critical if negotiation is going to proceed. In my experience, people tend to agree on an amazingly high percentage of all elements of a problem; the difficulty is finding the real sources of disagreement.

Even with negotiative approaches to problems, incentives play a key role. As I've pointed out, incentives really are entries in the cells of a multiple-criteria decision matrix where alternatives and criteria intersect — outcomes, in other words. Thus, if parties in a dispute are to reach consensus, it's likely that the outcomes of various alternatives will have to be manipulated in such a way that one alternative can be agreed upon by both parties. The trick is to find what is called a BATNA (the best alternative outside of a negotiated agreement). Then alternatives can be explored and outcomes changed so that at least one alternative in the negotiated settlement is preferred by all parties to the BATNA.

Obstacles exist to negotiation, however. First, negotiation is costly; it takes time, money, and skilled labor. Second, it may be in the interest of some parties to delay any resolution. Third, negotiation requires that all parties recognize the legitimacy of the other parties. The history of the American labor movement or the history of post-1948 Middle Eastern politics illustrates just how large an obstacle that third point can be. Fourth, as with the law, problem solutions are reached on a case-by-case basis.

Perhaps the classic problem requiring negotiation lies in the commons syndrome, situations where goods such as air and water are held in common. Disputes involving ocean fisheries, acid rain, pollution of the atmosphere by countries, and devastation of the tropical rain forests are prime candidates for negotiation. No one party has an incentive to change behavior; consensus must be achieved that fosters simultaneous change by all affected parties.

Conflict resolution techniques, based on decision making, will no doubt be employed more frequently in disputes of all kinds. Moral exhortation doesn't work. Prohibitive law, while necessary at times, fails to encompass the richness of many current problems. Yet, one way or the other, negotiation involves decision making, and decision making involves incentives. So the negotiative approach to problems can be viewed as a special case of incentive-based methods for resolving dilemmas. (Two good books on dispute resolution, one by Laurence Bacow and Michael Wheeler, the other by Scott Mernitz, are listed in the readings.)

PROTEST AND CIVIL DISOBEDIENCE

Contemporary governments, bound up as they are with politics and special interest groups, can be excessively sluggish in responding to social and environmental ills. Similarly, businesses attuned to the market system and its demands can be equally reluctant to change behavior. Moral exhortation is ineffective; the law is slow, limited, and costly; incentives often require government legislation of an enabling kind; and negotiation has its own substantial costs.

Hence, I expect to see the rise of civil disobedience as a strategy for creating change, particularly in the environmental sphere. Earth First!, an aggressive environmental group in the Pacific Northwest, is a primary example. Greenpeace also uses such tactics.

There is a thin and tenuous line between outrage and radicalism, and it's not difficult to understand why some people decide to cross that line. Anyone who believes that public protest, including civil disobedience, did not have a hand in our withdrawal from Vietnam or did not influence the granting of civil rights to African Americans is naive. When governments and other organizations do not respond sensitively in anything resembling real time, often the only course open, in the view of some people, is radical activity.

An article I started in 1987 but never finished was titled "Watch Out Iowa, Here Comes the Animal Rights Movement." Apparently, the animal rights people have had and are having considerable impact on the treatment of our fellow creatures, using tactics ranging from violence to peaceful protest. A precipitous decline in the purchase of natural fur garments is one indication of the movement's success. Even a recent world-class meeting of hog producers, held in Des Moines, had a seminar on animal rights included in the program. That would not have occurred in 1990 if animal rights activists, through protest, had not brought the issue to the forefront.

We can't escape decision making and incentives. And, one way or the other, protest and civil disobedience are aimed at getting behavior changed by jarring people into revising their criteria set or their outcomes and, hence, choosing different alternatives than they now are choosing. If a radical animal rights activist sprays green paint on mink coats, the wearer of such coats confronts a new and enlarged set of alternatives:

Alternative A: Continue to wear the coat.
        Outcomes: Risk having paint sprayed on expensive coat; suffer verbal attacks on the streets; enjoyment from wearing the coat.

Alternative B (a new alternative): Do not wear the coat.
        Outcomes: No risk of damage to coat or public harassment; less enjoyment (perhaps) from not wearing the coat.

Even if concern for animals is low in the coat owner's criteria set, the greatly increased outcomes of a negative kind associated with wearing the coat can override the pleasures of wearing such garments and cause the wearer to select Alternative B. Thus decision making and incentives are at the heart of these tactics as well. Protest, civil disobedience, and more radical tactics are all attempts to manipulate one or more elements in decision making.

A SUMMARY CASE

American farmers have faced a confusing array of incentives and disincentives for decades. Some signals come from the marketplace, others come from the federal government, and often these conflict. A study by the University of Minnesota's Center for International Food and Agriculture Policy concluded that farmers in the upper Midwest plant corn year after year and douse their crops with chemicals, including large amounts of nitrogen fertilizer, because it's the most profitable mode of operation for them. No surprises there.

Another study carried out by the National Academy of Sciences contains basically the same conclusions. Federal farm programs encourage high levels of chemical use and, at the same time, discourage crop rotation beneficial to the environment. The Minnesota report says this:

> If the government pays well above the market price for corn, farmers will be inclined to plant corn. . . . If retaining eligibility for government price support payments for corn requires continuous cropping, then farmers will be inclined to forego more traditional rotations of corn with other crops. . . . If government payments are based on a farm's or a county's average yields, farmers will be inclined to raise yields, beyond the point that market forces might dictate.

The Minnesota study was reported by George Anthan in the *Des Moines Register.* In the same issue, on the same page, was an article titled "Scores of Rural Iowans Drinking Tainted Water," which summarized the results of a research project conducted by the Iowa Department of Natural Resources and the University of Iowa's Center for Health Effects of Environmental Contamination. Wells were tested in all of Iowa's ninety-nine counties, and the results showed, "More than 94,000 rural Iowans drink water that contains one or more pesticides, most commonly atrazine, and 130,000 rural residents consume water from wells that contain high concentrations of nitrates."

Any farm chemical is, of course, potentially damaging to humans when consumed in large enough amounts. For example, according to that report, "Nitrate contamination has been linked to cancer, birth defects, and blue-baby syndrome, a blood disorder that reduces the ability of an infant's bloodstream to carry oxygen throughout the body."

These studies illustrate virtually everything I've said thus far in the book. First, of course, there is the assault on our life-support systems — soil and water, in this case. That's the sustainability issue. Second, the situation is a perfect example of decision making that appears rational in the short run, but results in traps in the longer term.

Third, the political problems of democracy are implied by the confusing menu of incentives flowing from a mix of farm programs and markets. Fourth, the power of incentives is clearly at work. Fifth, moral exhortation, education, and prohibitive laws have not succeeded in getting us out of the situation. Sixth, the issues of social costs and property rights clearly are involved here, including what I called shoveling the costs onto future generations, particularly babies in this case. Seventh, the questions of time, lack of vision, and the future are wending their way through the entire mess.

Markets are signaling one thing, while excluding consideration of social costs. Government programs are overriding the market incentives and creating social costs of their own; the future is heavily discounted. Multiple-criteria decision making is evident. Democracy is running in all directions. And, of course, incentives, ill-conceived and conflicting in this case, are propelling the whole business.

All of this is enough to drive one in search of monastic solace in the high mountain country of Asia. Farmers confront poisoned wells, city dwellers build systems to remove nitrates from their water, and surplus crops are being raised in a fashion destroying the environment. Nobody has constructed a vision of what ought to be, including what it is we want from farmers and what farmers want from us, and the logical swamp just described illustrates the results of piecemeal design where events produce a future nobody wants.

You can argue all you care to that an incentives-based approach to controlling social behavior contains an assumption that humans are something less than morally responsible, thoroughly gracious creatures. We are, in fact, something less than we would like to think we are, and our pride gets us into trouble. We respond to incentives, and we may as well be honest about that, harnessing the self-interest that drives us, while we're on our way to some higher plane of enlightenment, if that plane actually exists somewhere.

As William D. Ruckelshaus points out, three things are needed to bring the powerful forces of self-interest into congruence with social and environmental requirements. First, someone, leaders perhaps, must articulate a clear set of values. In my language, these are criteria, and Ruckelshaus is implying that not only must the values be articulated, but they also must be ranked high and weighted heavily relative to other values.

Second, Ruckelshaus argues that appropriate motivations must be established supporting the values. He's talking about incentives here, in terms of outcomes in the decision matrix. Third, institutions are needed to effectively apply the motivations. His last point involves passing enabling legislation establishing entities — regulatory bodies, or government departments, or both — that transmit the values into the correct incentives.

FOR FURTHER READING

Achiron, Marilyn. "Making Wildlife Pay Its Way." *International Wildlife,* September/October 1988, pp. 46–51.

Anthan, George. "Farm Programs Send Mixed Signals – Study." *Des Moines Register,* February 14, 1990, pp. 1A, 4A.

Bacow, Lawrence S., and Michael Wheeler. *Environmental Dispute Resolution.* New York: Plenum, 1984.

Berry, R. Stephen. "Our Energy Future: Time Horizons and Instability." *Environment,* July/August 1989, pp. 5, 43–44.

Brown, Lester R., Christopher Flavin, and Sandra Postel. "A World at Risk." In *State of the World 1989,* by Lester R. Brown et al. New York: W. W. Norton, 1989.

Ehrenfeld, David. "Life in the Next Millennium: Who Will Be Left in Earth's Community?" In *The Last Extinction,* ed. Les Kaufman and Kenneth Mallory. Cambridge, Mass.: The MIT Press, 1987.

"Green and Unpleasant." The *Economist,* April 14, 1990, pp. 17–18.

Hutchins, Robert M. *The Learning Society.* New York: Praeger, 1968.

Kelman, Steven. *What Price Incentives?* Boston: Auburn House, 1981.

MacNeill, Jim. "Strategies for Sustainable Economic Development." *Scientific American,* September 1989, pp. 155–65.

Mernitz, Scott. *Mediation of Environmental Disputes.* New York: Praeger, 1980.

Rose, Carol. "Scores of Rural Iowans Drinking Tainted Water." *Des Moines Register,* February 14, 1990, pp. 1A, 2A.

Ruckelshaus, William D. "Toward a Sustainable World." *Scientific American,* September 1989, pp. 166–75.

Schelling, Thomas C. *Choice and Consequence.* Cambridge, Mass.: Harvard University Press, 1984.

Schultze, Charles L. *The Public Use of Private Interest.* Washington, D.C.: The Brookings Institution, 1977. (This book is considered one of the classic arguments for the use of incentives in environmental affairs.)

Soth, Lauren. "A Soil-Saving Program with Teeth." *Des Moines Register,* June 15, 1987.

Two Plans, One Future

For several decades following World War II, Iowans felt secure with their niche in the world economy. We produced food—grains and meat—along with the equipment and other inputs needed for food production. In addition, we had a scattering of nonagricultural industries ranging from consumer durable goods to insurance. There were economic cycles, of course, and things went up and down, from good to not so good and back again. But the basic economic structure remained in place, and we knew who we were, economically. By the 1970s we were even a little smug, calling ourselves "recession-proof."

In the 1980s, the foundations began to quiver, and the old, comfortable structures shifted. No one event caused this; complex problems seldom have one propellant. The smaller nations on the Pacific Rim became powerful manufacturers; the 1979 grain embargo on the Soviets was imposed; the Green Revolution enabled countries to produce much or all of their own food; and other places, such as South America and Australia, became major competitors in the international food markets. All of this was coupled with soaring interest rates in the United States and a speculative binge that sent land prices to record levels before they began to collapse in the summer of 1981.

Iowa suddenly seemed rusty and poor and unwanted. We lost our confidence, people exited the state looking for work, communities withered, and hand-wringing was evident everywhere. Our initial response to these hard times was childlike. We whined, asked the federal government for more help, chased smokestack industries and pleaded with them to send some largess our way, and generally flailed about in all directions looking for guidance. But the market system, for all its strengths, lacks a heart, and it took no pity upon us. Along the farm-to-market roads and in the industrial centers of Iowa, there was despair coupled with bad thinking, a common associate of despair.

By the mid-1980s, it was clear that something fundamental had to be done. The world had evolved, and we began to look for new directions. The language changed: "more industrial diversification," "less dependence on agriculture," "entrepreneurship."

These new directions are, perhaps, best summarized by a review of the economic development plans generated by various agencies. Two of the most prominent, and the ones I'll focus on, are those by the Iowa Department of Economic Development (DED) and a study conducted by the SRI International (SRI) under the sponsorship of the Iowa Newspaper Association. The SRI study is commonly called the "Iowa Future Project."

The DED has prepared a five-year economic development strategy, which is updated periodically, and uses this framework to produce short-term "action plans" containing more specific recommendations. A twenty-year plan currently is being developed.

The DED document reviewed here is the five-year plan titled *Directions for Iowa's Economic Future.* SRI's study has two titles — one on the cover, the other on the title page (why that occurs is not clear). The cover title is *Iowa's Future: A Quality Economy for Tomorrow.* The title page reads *Commitment to Quality: A Six-Point Action Program for Iowa's Economy.*

In addition, the cover design of the SRI report is worth noting. It features a sketch of the state with tiny human figures in what appears to be executive clothing either facing, walking toward, or standing within the state. One such figure apparently has a basket on his or her head. But the most interesting aspect is the long shadows cast by the figures. The direction of the shadows indicate the time is late, just about sunset in fact. One supposes that rendering is accidental, a matter of design aesthetics, and not prophetic.

I'll present the major themes of the two plans, with an editorial remark here and there. Then I'll offer some critical observations about the plans and later in the book I'll provide more detail on topics covered in the two documents.

HUMAN CAPITAL

Both the DED and SRI studies begin with people and their importance as "human capital." The idea is that the primary component in economic development is a skilled and adaptable work force. Appropriate genuflections are made to the current Iowa educational system, and this praise is then muted by the recognition that we must become better than we currently are.

A dominant theme in both studies is that education must be revamped to meet the needs of economic development. Just how this might be done is contained in a fair number of recommendations: holding a summit conference on Iowa education, using telecommunications for educational enhancement, developing various incentive and encouragement schemes for lifetime learning, and others.

The SRI report also recommends that private and community colleges become involved as partners in local and regional economic development activities. The universities are seen by SRI as producers of ideas and state-of-the-art research. The DED tends to focus a bit more on the details of various educational schemes, such as developing intervention programs to assist disadvantaged youth and the retraining of middle-aged workers.

FINANCIAL CAPITAL

The need for financial capital—money that can be invested in productive resources—is not limited to capitalism.* Economies can grow only if there is an excess of savings over consumption, since savings provide a pool of funds for the acquisition of additional productive resources, which, in turn, provide more incomes and thereby more savings. Availability of financial capital is a central ingredient in bootstrapping an economy upward.

Both the SRI and DED reports recognize the important role of financial capital in economic growth. And both see attitudinal and structural difficulties in Iowa's capital situation. Bankers are treated gingerly in the reports, but the implicit criticism is clear: Iowa bankers (and other

---

*The qualifier "financial" is attached to capital in certain instances to differentiate money from the broader use of the term that includes plant and equipment. Financial capital, one way or the other, is money available for investment.

suppliers of capital, such as state government) are too conservative in their lending practices. A second problem is that Iowa's financial structures are ill-designed for a modern economy.

Iowa has a substantial pool of financial resources potentially available for investment, but according to the reports, these funds have not flowed to areas where they are most needed. Examples of such areas are venture capital to support new and somewhat risky businesses, agricultural innovation, the financing of industries designed to increase the value-added component of Iowa production (such as the production of soybean oil in Iowa rather than shipping raw grain elsewhere for processing), and enabling existing firms to shift into new markets. SRI summarizes the problems as follows:

1. Iowa's investors and bankers may not be experienced enough in today's new environment of investment financing.
2. Iowa's entrepreneurs and small-business owners may also lack experience regarding financing options.
3. Iowa does not itself enjoy a fully developed system of financial service providers such as investment bankers, financial advisors, and brokers.
4. Both investors and those seeking capital are too often hampered by poor access to information.

The recommendations provided by the reports cover a range of possibilities:

1. The Iowa legislature should act to encourage private investment by providing tax credits as an incentive. (SRI)
2. The state should assume more public debt to be used in innovative investments of a specialized kind in education, community infrastructure, and specialized laboratories or technology transfer capabilities at Iowa's universities. (SRI)
3. A statewide information network and finance service center should be established to enhance information and "deal flow" in the state. (SRI)
4. It must be ensured that capital is available to support the strategic needs of agriculture. (SRI)
5. New pools of capital should be formed for business start-ups, expansions, new product lines, and modernization. (DED)
6. Laws and regulations governing financial institutions and securities should be revised to meet current market conditions and demands. (DED)

In addition, the DED provides several more specific "action steps" that provide detail for its overall strategic recommendations.

Overall, Iowa is seen as capital-rich but investment-poor. The reasons for this are conservatism in both private and public finance coupled with structural parameters that are ill-suited to modern economies.

TECHNOLOGY

As with education and financial capital, both the DED and SRI are concerned about technology. Neither attempts to define exactly what is meant by the term. Here's a way of looking at it. In the most basic sense, technology is simply a tested, rationalized way of doing something. The opposite of technology is trial and error. Technology may grow out of trial-and-error efforts, but technology itself implies a generally accepted way of accomplishing a task. Technologies, viewed this way, lie along a continuum that measures the probability of achieving an output X given the application of technique Y. For example, the probability that John Deere can produce a tractor it has produced many times before is 1.0 or awfully close to it. On the other hand, the probability that a psychiatrist can produce a healthy patient is something less than 1.0, since the techniques of transforming mental illness into mental health are not as well understood and well structured as those for producing tractors, due mainly to the differences in the complexity of the tasks. Likewise, the probability that we can launch humans into the far reaches of space and have them return in healthy condition is 0.0, given our current technical knowledge.

Everybody talks about technology, but nobody really thinks very much about what it means. The DED and SRI both are talking about not just technology but rather technological change that results in one or more of the following:

1. Developing new, more efficient and effective ways of producing existing products
2. Modifying existing products in such a way that new markets for them are opened
3. Developing new products

The first two clearly involve technological change. The third is not technological change, but rather the output of such change.

Overall, the sense is one of becoming modern, of getting out at the frontiers of economic activity, of one-upping the competition through newness (in all things), efficiency, and effectiveness.*

SRI is relatively buoyant about Iowa's technological capabilities, citing strengths in basic research and technology application but finding weaknesses in the area of applied research, which is the linchpin between basic research and industrial application. The DED also finds much to like in this area, but sees several problems that must be overcome:

1. Low levels of research and development investment
2. A lack of venture and seed capital (which relates to the arguments given previously under financial capital)
3. The state's outmigration of the past decade (it's not clear to me how this relates to technology)
4. A low level of entrepreneurial activity
5. An absence of mechanisms to transfer technology from the laboratory to the marketplace

I judge the DED to have a more accurate representation of the state's technology situation than SRI's, particularly in its emphasis on the lack of technology transfer. SRI predicates its judgment of strength in this area on the recently established Henry Wallace Technology Transfer Foundation, which holds promise but which is still in its start-up phase.

In general, the recommendations in both reports involve more research of all kinds and the importance of transferring technology from the laboratory to industrial applications. One particularly interesting suggestion made by the DED is this: Develop Iowa's amenity base, including recreational and cultural development, to make the state more attractive to highly skilled persons. I'll have a great deal to say about that subject later.

COMMUNITY DEVELOPMENT

Community development is a fourth area given attention by both SRI and the DED. In reading the reports, one gets a little tired of the

---

*Efficiency is producing something with the least possible amount of inputs while preserving existing standards of quality. *Effectiveness* means being able to produce something, period. Thus you may have a process that is effective, but not efficient.

gaseous reverence paid to eternal verities, such as the quality of small-town life. The assumption is made that quality of life in small towns, and in Iowa in general, has been wonderful but is in danger of declining. The problem is how to preserve that perceived quality that apparently already exists. (In subsequent chapters, I'll take a hard look at these matters.) I do not necessarily agree with the assumption that things have been just fine in the past. If, for example, small-town life were as exquisite as myth proclaims, then small towns would have a whole lot less difficulty attracting new residents, a problem that most of them have.

Floating along just beneath the surface of economic development discussions in Iowa is the recognition that many small towns are in serious trouble. While most urban areas of the state have recovered from the economic downturns of the early and mid-1980s, much of rural Iowa has been bypassed in this recovery. Shifting demographics, the inability to generate or attract job-creating businesses, problems with infrastructure, and inadequate housing are among the liabilities these communities have in sustaining themselves. Both SRI and the DED, though they tread softly in this matter, conclude that some towns are going to die off. The DED sees the need for transitional aid to residents of those towns.

SRI and the DED both favor what has come to be known as "community commonwealths," where smaller towns form partnerships to share facilities, business recruiting efforts, health care, police protection, and so forth. Several such clusters already are operating in Iowa (these will be discussed later in the book in the chapter on rural development). Neither of the reports specifies in any detail just what a successful commonwealth might look like.

Furthermore, recognition is given to the importance of information sharing via library networks, leadership development, and the formation of linkages between major industrial centers and rural areas. Increased flexibility in governmental structures and taxing authorities also is necessary, with the redrawing of current governmental boundaries being a critical aspect of this flexibility.

QUALITY OF LIFE—ARTS, RECREATION, AND THE NATURAL ENVIRONMENT

In the panic that surrounded Iowa's economic decline, almost no attention was paid to quality of life. The focus was on jobs, and a kind of naivete existed about what it took to attract jobs. Quality-of-life issues were either ignored or assumed to be taken care of, and the focus was on creating incentives through taxes, state subsidies to businesses, good highways, and all the other emoluments business is supposed to demand in exchange for locating somewhere.*

SRI comes down firmly in support of the arts and recreation. The DED has little to say about these matters except for the suggestion to "build up local and regional recreation, amenities, arts, and cultural resources." (The use of the word "amenities" is slightly redundant in that passage.) I sometimes feel the DED is a little embarrassed to say much about the arts, as if such attention would imply an elitist view of what constitutes the good life.

In any case, SRI sees the arts as a critical component in attracting and retaining highly skilled workers to the state. The recommendation is for a public-private partnership to increase support for the arts, since Iowa currently ranks a dismal fifty-first out of the fifty-six states and territories in per capita support for the arts. SRI also suggests new initiatives for the encouragement of amateur sports in Iowa, as part of the recreational component in quality of life.

The natural environment is treated in two ways: first, as a factor in the quality of life and second (primarily by the DED), as an important component in other areas of economic development. Obviously, people prefer clean air, clean water, and safe disposal of wastes, if they are going to live in a place. This is the quality-of-life perspective.

Both reports wisely recognize that the natural environment cannot be separated from economics, though that separation has been dominant throughout the history of the United States and, for that matter, the history of humans on this planet. One suggestion by SRI is of particular importance: "An organization should be mobilized to serve as a focal point for dialogue between parties interested in economic development and parties interested in environmental protection."

Humans have, it seems, a natural tendency toward hierarchies, and we tend to structure our organizations in that fashion. Hence those activities that do not fit neatly into conventional organizational lines of responsibility or that overlap more than one department are not handled very well. More linchpin devices, such as the one recommended by SRI, are needed to ensure that the natural environment (and the arts for that matter) does not fall through the cracks between boxes of assigned responsibility. Eventually we will come to realize that the old hierarchical

*For a detailed discussion of the quality-of-life issue and its relationship to economic development, see my article, "Going Soft Upon the Land and Down Along the Rivers."

forms of organization do not fit many of the tasks before us very well. The SRI suggestion moves us closer to that emerging reality.

The DED also pays considerable attention to the critical problem of energy, arguing that we do the following: (1) "Integrate energy efficiency considerations into economic development efforts" and (2) "explore the feasibility and cost-effectiveness of Iowa-produced substitutes for imported energy sources."

In addition, the DED sees potential for economic development in dealing with problems of the natural environment. This amounts to identifying "business opportunities associated with environmental protection, cleanup and energy efficiency." And examining "the economic development potential of production waste streams, waste recycling, waste minimization, biodegradable products and re-manufacturing."

COMPETITIVE CLIMATE, SMALL BUSINESS, AND DEVELOPMENT

After some years of chasing large, established firms of the Fortune 500 variety, those interested in economic development in Iowa have finally recognized that most new job growth flows from small and medium-sized businesses. A new emphasis on entrepreneurship and the encouragement of local businesses with potential is therefore emerging. With this comes the consequent realization that state regulatory measures must be streamlined, taxes must be judged with an eye toward not thwarting business growth, and sources of venture capital must be located. Both the SRI and DED reports focus on such issues.

A common theme is the lack of entrepreneurial spirit in Iowa.* Iowans are seen as "maintaining and conserving" rather than "innovating and growing" by SRI. Though the DED does not actually say as much, it's clear that the same assumptions underlie their recommendations.

Entrepreneurship is not necessarily the same thing as simply starting a small business. For example, one might open a new hamburger franchise, but this hardly qualifies as entrepreneurship in the same sense as a person who invents a computer circuit board and attempts to produce and market it.

---

*The appendix to Chapter Nine contains a discussion of entrepreneurship and its role in the Iowa economy.

In general, both reports concentrate on the importance of business growth and how this growth might be better fostered by the state. The latter suggestions range over a broad area of possibilities: inventors' networks, providing technical assistance to small businesses, the expansion of the business incubator concept, educating Iowans about the importance of entrepreneurship, and making sure that Iowa's overall business climate is competitive in a global economy.

OTHER ISSUES

The topics covered thus far are those contained in both the SRI and DED planning documents. SRI's recommendations cover the following six areas: human capital, financial capital, technology, entrepreneurship and small business formation, quality of life and community development, and something called "other actions," which is a catchall category for miscellaneous recommendations.

The DED covers two additional subjects—infrastructure and the image of Iowa. Infrastructure maintenance and construction (roads, sewer systems, water mains, and the like) are national problems that haunt us. It's one of those areas that lacks glamour and is easy to ignore, particularly if higher taxes are required, but obviously it's also critical.

Furthermore, the contemporary world demands a broader definition than the traditional one, according to the DED, and it recommends the inclusion of air services, data systems, and telecommunications as part of infrastructure. The overall thrust here is quite general and suggests more education of the public about infrastructure needs along with better planning for facilities replacement.

There is, however, one slightly ominous, but appropriate, statement in the DED document: "Develop criteria and mechanisms to target limited resources toward locations with future development potential and toward communities that have demonstrated strong local commitment to their own development." In other words, if you want economic development support, stop whining and show that you deserve it.

The DED should be applauded for tackling one other issue, even though the analysis and recommendations concerning it are weak. That's the problem of Iowa's image. According to the report, Iowa lacks a strong image in the minds of people residing elsewhere. The belief is that "Iowa's [image] problems seem to lie more with attitudes and lack of promotion, rather than tangible deficiencies." My personal experience indicates that all of this is true.

THE DED ACTION PLAN, 1989–1990

The DED's action plan statements are designed to add more detail to its long-range strategic plans. The first was published in October 1989, and the second is supposed to be forthcoming in the next year or two. From the five-year plan a strategic issue (for example, human capital) and a strategy associated with it are selected, and then an "initiative" is developed that will help implement the plan. Following that, the DED identifies who will be involved in carrying out the initiative, when the initiative will be completed, the amount of resources it will require to study/implement the initiative, and what results can be expected.

A CRITIQUE OF THE STRATEGIC PLANS

Initially I was puzzled as to why the SRI plan was undertaken. In the opening section of its document, SRI states that while the DED project "offers a public-sector perspective, this project offers a private-sector perspective on how Iowa should proceed. In combination, the two independently developed plans provide a comprehensive and complementary set of initiatives for moving Iowa's economy forward."

Most of that statement is simply not true. The SRI document is no more private-sector oriented than is the DED's. Moreover, both cover roughly the same ground. Each report contains a few ideas not found in the other, and to that limited extent, they complement one another. The scope of both reports is broad, lending some justification to the assertion of comprehensiveness (though "comprehensive" is, indeed, a large claim, and neither of the documents strikes me as being truly comprehensive).

My guess is that some people felt the DED could not be trusted to produce an objective piece of work and that whatever was produced would be purely a product of a government bureaucracy not necessarily reflecting the sentiment of Iowa's citizens. That brings me to one of the fundamental weaknesses of all such plans undertaken by state agencies. In many ways, the DED report is a political document as much as an economic one. By itself, that does not make it a bad piece of work, but it's important to recognize the constraints that such planners confront.

Decisions to exclude or include something from a strategic plan, or how to treat it if it is included, are just that—decisions. And the selection among alternatives, as always, is guided by criteria, outcomes, and risk. It's necessary to be aware of that in reading such documents. The content is the result of people making decisions about exclusion and inclusion, along with depth and style of treatment of various subjects. And the criteria or other aspects that governed the preparation of the documents, in addition to decisions made about what was appropriate to study in the first place, are hidden from view.

The DED gets its funding through appropriations, which must be approved by both the legislature and the governor. Furthermore, the governor appoints the heads of agencies such as the Iowa Department of Economic Development. To believe that political pressures play no role in the formulation and construction of such plans is to exhibit considerable naivete.

By the same token, SRI is a commercial research organization that depends upon consulting contracts. Again the real world of money and clout enters, and one may presume that SRI is reasonably careful not to offend important suppliers of funds.

The word "vision" appears in both documents. SRI states: "The primary purpose of this document is to lay out a vision of Iowa's future to which both public and private leaders in the state can commit themselves, and a plan for achieving that vision." That, too, is a substantial claim, and I believe the SRI report falls far short of anything resembling a complete vision of a future Iowa. What they have produced is a set of ideas, in six categories, designed to promote economic development in a midwestern state, or just about any state for that matter. There is nothing very customized about SRI's work, in other words.

The DED is more restrained in its use of the word vision and merely suggests, in this context: "The overall goal for Iowa's economic development efforts should be continued growth and a higher standard of living for its citizens. The best single measure of our standard of living is Iowa's relative performance in terms of real per capita income—the amount of income per person, after controlling for the effects of inflation." Almost as an afterthought, the DED notes, "Nonmonetary aspects of standard of living, such as environmental quality, should not be forgotten, however."

In the executive summary of the plan, the DED does become somewhat more expansive:

The strategic plan update envisions a future for Iowa in which there is continued, positive growth in employment and economic well-being. If the plan is followed, more Iowans should be employed in better jobs. Unemployment should continue to fall. Iowans' standard of living should improve steadily. The economy should become more diverse and less susceptible to swings in performance. Businesses should be viable and profitable. Iowa's population should grow steadily. And all parts of Iowa, urban and rural, should share in the state's growth.

Here's the real difficulty I have with both reports. If vision produces objectives, which it does, and objectives produce criteria, which they do, then everything will be judged by the contribution it makes to economic development. A careful reading of both reports, in spite of the modest disclaimers such as the one just mentioned concerning the natural environment, produces the conclusion that art, nature, and education clearly are servants in the household of economic growth.

Even human development via education is seen as a means to no higher end than increases in the standard of living. "Human capital" is the phrase. Clearly, all roads lead to economic growth.

There are unrecognized cycles at work here. It's true that art and education, for example, can be seen as precursors to economic growth. That's not complicated. If you want talented people to remain in or emigrate to a state, such amenities are important. But it has always seemed to me that the *reason* for economic development is to provide the wherewithal for higher pursuits than simply earning a living.

There is a real and present danger in not recognizing the fairly complex cause-and-effect relationships between art, education, and nature, on the one hand, and economic development on the other. And this danger has to do with the notion of criteria. Furthermore, there is the potential for a particularly insidious trap here.

Consider education as an example. Throughout both the SRI and DED documents, reference continually is made to the importance of education in economic development. Here are some samples from the DED plan (the italics are mine):

Continue to improve primary, secondary and higher education to *better prepare youth for work*

Continue to revise school curricula and educational programs to *better reflect current economic and technological trends*

Encourage *greater involvement by business in public education and training programs*

No matter how you read them, these are statements of criteria, and I find them alarming. Suppose a decision must be made between retaining or instituting a course in oil painting versus a course in computer literacy; it's the sort of decision continually made in all educational systems. Now look at the three criteria statements taken from the DED plan. Which course do you think will be favored? When accountants are needed, send out the news to produce more accountants; if there are too many plumbers, cut the plumbing program.

It runs even deeper than that. Both the DED and SRI recognize the necessity of a clean, attractive natural environment. But the importance attached to nature flows directly from its ability to provide clean water, quality air, a place for waste disposal, recreational activities, attractions for tourists, and so forth. This is the same old attitude that got us into our present environmental predicament. The only difference is that the natural environment is at least recognized as a constraint on our economic activities.

When we're talking about the role of business in determining educational or environmental priorities, it's important to remember the source of business values: the market. Markets couldn't care less about the loftier, long-term goals of education for enlightenment or preserving the natural environment for future generations or for a wilderness experience. To the extent that the business community, and hence the marketplace, is allowed to impose its criteria—its values—as the arbiter of what should be taught or what should be conserved or what should be esteemed, a continual retreat from wisdom and respect for nature will be the marching orders issued.

This has nothing to do with whether business people are good or bad, smart or stupid. Rather, it's a simple recognition that what business requires in a market economy is what will sell, and grand ideas involving beauty and enlightenment and a humble view of ourselves in the great sweep of the cosmos never command much in market exchanges.

In short, education, art, recreation, and nature are seen, tacitly, by SRI and the DED as part of an overall infrastructure supporting economic development. Just as airports and sewer systems are critical parts of the infrastructure supporting development, so we apparently must have an arts and culture infrastructure, an educational infrastructure, a natural environment infrastructure, and a recreational infrastructure, all in the service of economic development.

People involved in the arts and education have a nose for funding opportunities and pick up on what such plans say about what is important and what is not. They respond to incentives like anyone else. The tendency then is to couch artistic and educational proposals in terms of the criteria and reward-punishment structures implied by the plans, to justify whatever it is they want to do in terms of its importance to economic development. That is a dangerous and limiting approach to the arts and education, for obsequiousness to the market replaces the truly visionary thinking that is a critical role for both art and education.

For example, cozy relationships between university professors and business or government have a clear and decidedly deleterious effect on scholarship.* I have done enough consulting and contract research to be certain of this. If you're supported by a chemical company, through a research grant or contract, to study the effects of pesticides on humans, you're not going to be allowed to write papers critical of the firm's products, even if that's what your research discloses, and still maintain your source of funding (thus, you should be aware that my funding for this book eventually was funneled through the DED, though members of the legislature originally proposed the project and allocated the funds).

Just that sort of thing has occurred for decades in the land grant universities, and those institutions bear substantial blame for the environmental problems associated with agriculture today. Many of the professors in those institutions have, in fact, been critical of the ideas of sustainable agriculture or low-input agriculture. Given the lucrative research funding that flows from various suppliers in the agricultural industry, these professors can hardly be expected to perform as unbiased participants in debates over high-input, chemical-based farming versus more organic methods.

Here's another example of how the economic development mentality influences people's view of things. Neal Smith, a U.S. Representative from Iowa, recently persuaded Congress to appropriate $6 million for a 3,800-acre wildlife refuge in south-central Iowa near Prairie City. A member of the Prairie City Economic Development Committee was quoted as saying, "If it included a lake, it could be fantastic." Clearly, from this person's point of view, a refuge for wildlife is all right, but a lake—now that would really bring tourists into the area. Representative Smith wisely replied, "A lake would be for people." He envisions the wildlife refuge, quite reasonably, as a refuge for wildlife.

Before going on, I should admit to being a little unfair to the DED vis-a-vis its attitude toward the natural environment. In the "Natural Environment and Energy" section of its report, concern is expressed for

---

*For a case study of just how economic development can influence academic research and the claims made for it, see my article "Lasers, Dreams, and Real Money."

the impact of economic development on nature. For example, the DED recommends:

> Recognize the impact of economic development policies, programs and projects on environmental quality; also, recognize the potential cost to economic development of existing or proposed environmental protection legislation and regulations.
>
> Invest in carefully targeted infrastructure projects that will maintain the quality of the environment while allowing development to occur.
>
> Invest in public open spaces, forests and other recreational facilities and amenities that improve the quality of life and maintain the quality of the natural environment.

Furthermore, in an appendix titled "Key Threats," the DED cites the following environmental threats: drought potential, environmental degradation/global warming, energy shortages, and price increases. But when it comes to which elements of the plan will be tackled first, as illustrated by both the action plan and the executive summary of the strategic plan, the natural environment is omitted except for one action plan dealing with energy efficiency, and energy is one of the most obvious components of the natural environment in economic development.

Nonetheless, the natural environment is at least mentioned prominently in the strategic plan, and that's a long step up in enlightenment from where things rested only a few years ago. None of this, however, nullifies the clear implication that nature's key role is that of one component in an overall economic development strategy.

In addition, it remains to be seen whether or not sentiments about environmental concern are given real weight in decision processes where the choice is between environmental degradation or economic growth. Neither the DED or SRI says much about the kind of trade-offs discussed in Chapter Three, trade-offs that are inevitable.

Furthermore, the DED's action plans — the nitty-gritty of implementation — flow directly from the larger strategic plan. Thus, to the extent that initiatives are omitted from the strategic plan now or in the future, the presumption is that action will not be taken on them.

Here's an example. Suppose the following hypothetical initiative were stated in the section on education: "Inculcate in people the idea that education is primarily for leading a happy, fulfilling life and only secondarily serves as a means of getting a job." That point of view is not expressed in the plan; hence, it's unlikely that any effort will be taken to implement it.

In other words, the list of initiatives in the DED plan is a short list. What's omitted is just as important as what's included. Those people who are concerned about elements that are not included in the strategic plan should be wary, for their concerns are not going to be addressed unless the plans are modified to include them.

On the positive side, the DED, and this is one of the overall strengths of its report, sees the need for information networks and/or clearinghouses of various kinds. Just what these networks might look like and how they could be expected to function is not clear. Nonetheless, in a world and society increasingly based on rapid information exchange, such devices are critical. This topic will emerge again in the chapter on rural development.

A major omission in both reports, an omission that has been consistently present in state discussions of technology for decades, is the implied emphasis on "hard" industrial technology and the absence of any attention given to "softer" technologies. For example, more money is wasted on unproductive meetings than in just about any other organizational activity conceivable. There are, indeed, technologies for making meetings more efficient, and they are just as important as industrial technologies, but they go wanting in discussions of technology.

Similarly, the notion of incentives is a technology for accomplishing certain ends. Yet we spend little time and money developing such rationalized approaches to problems. Consideration of such technologies is dwarfed by concerns about whether or not we are the first to produce a new gizmo.

The DED has received much criticism over the years. Some of it is justified. For example, the department has not displayed much skill or sensitivity in dealing with entrepreneurs; I know this from talking with a number of such people, some of whom have succeeded in spite of what they view as poor treatment by the DED. Though I should note that entrepreneurs are not always skilled at presenting their cases or necessarily patient themselves with people who do not immediately grasp the eternal glory of the entrepreneur's ideas, still, there's a fair amount of anecdotal evidence to suggest the DED has fallen short in an area they continue to tout as important.

Criticisms directed at the DED's planning efforts have included the following: too broad, no real attempt at dealing with real issues at the community level, too passive in business development, more politically oriented than economic development oriented, and no means of measuring success.

But it's important to study the entire set of three documents (a fourth will be the promised twenty-year plan)—the executive summary, the five-year plan, and the action plans. Several of the above criticisms are understandable if only the first two documents are looked at. The action plans, however, begin to supply much detail that is missing in the more general statements of intentions. For instance, issues connected with community development are dealt with quite explicitly in the first action plan (1989–1990).

As for the political orientation of the DED's work, it's unavoidable, given the funding and administrative structures within which the DED operates. We need to recognize this reality and make sure that such tendencies receive countervailing pressures from the larger community. The fact is, at the moment, the DED is the primary planning game in town in terms of a consistent, ongoing effort (though SRI promises a continuance of its work). It's incumbent on the rest of us to correct whatever weaknesses we see in the plans.

The conceptual framework being used by the DED makes it easy to see just what is being treated as important and what is not. That in itself has considerable value and is a major strength of the planning process being used. If you don't like the way a threat or initiative is stated, or if you don't like what is included or excluded, at least you can locate these areas in the planning framework. Such clarity is an advantage that flows from all formal model building; the model provides a framework for debate.

I think, taking into account all of the above warnings and complaints, the DED has produced a reasonable first draft of some fairly complex ideas. It's incomplete and philosophically repugnant to me in certain places, but I have a decent idea of what it is I want to complain about. That's not the case in the ordinary smoke-and-mirrors approach of most public bureaucracies.

I would be remiss also if I did not credit SRI with the overall thrust of its recommendations, which is that Iowa should become known as a "quality economy." Just what that means is not entirely clear, but the implication is that Iowa should seek and find niches for itself in those domestic and global marketplaces where quality of production takes precedence over quantity. That's a valuable idea, which fits well with some forthcoming discussions in this book. In fact, the emphasis given to the notion of quality in SRI's efforts may alone justify the study, and the DED should pay close attention to the quality-economy notion espoused by SRI.

SRI also claims to have built a base of 3,000 Iowans who have agreed to participate further in the planning process. That being so, and if the project continues with vigor, it may provide a useful, citizen-oriented approach to economic planning that will serve to counter the self-serving, bureaucratic tendencies that most state agencies exhibit.

Major irritants in both documents, particularly SRI's, are the continual lurches toward gratuitous praise (pandering in other words) for the people and the state of Iowa. A good example is the first paragraph of the SRI report:

> Iowa is a state whose residents have always been able to balance the immediate needs of the present with the long view of the future. Perhaps this ability comes from the state's history — the early settlers who recognized that accepting hardship in the short term would make life better in the long term. Perhaps it comes from the state's farming heritage; a century of tilling the land makes clear the need to plant first in order to harvest in the future. Whatever the reasons, Iowa is a state whose people have always been uncomfortable with inaction in the face of uncertainty.

That's so much gibberish. It's also insulting in its palpable lack of truth. In a state that has depleted 50 percent of its topsoil, destroyed 99.9 percent of its prairies and 95 percent of its wetlands, cut 80 percent of its forests, lost more than one hundred species of wildlife since the place was settled, poisoned its water supply, and did little long-term thinking until crisis was upon it, are we supposed to believe that we have taken the long view? Nonsense.

And "tilling the land makes clear the need to plant first in order to harvest in the future" sounds like dialogue from an old Peter Sellers movie, *Being There,* that spoofed philosophical-sounding blather via a character named Chauncey Gardener. It's the kind of language you get from people being paid to please, and it took a sizable effort toward objectivity before I could recover from the negative feelings I had after reading that opening paragraph of the SRI document.

The DED is to be commended for setting forth measures by which the success of its plans can be judged. SRI does not do this, at least explicitly. The DED yardsticks, which really are high-level objectives, are the following:

1. Consistently positive performance in other common economic indicators, including new job creation, unemployment and business starts and failures
2. Growth in nonfarm, real per capita income at least as great as the

U.S. rate and a convergence of Iowa's income toward the national
level
3. An improvement in the relative diversity of Iowa's economy, as
measured by a "diversity index"
4. Positive and sustained population growth, at approximately the
same rate as the rest of the Upper Midwest

Finally, neither of the reports mentions anything about *what* we
might want to produce in Iowa. One inference that can be drawn is that
we will watch for what's selling well and make sure we are among the
first to get there. SRI emphasizes the notion of quality, but you can do a
quality job on the most useless kinds of trinkets that the market indicates
are in demand.

And, of course, neither SRI nor the DED addresses the question of
whether continued economic growth is possible or desirable. In the reports, the bald assumptions underlying both of these issues are that yes,
it's possible, and yes, it's desirable. Those who want to keep their jobs in
state government or who want more consulting contracts know something about what assumptions are necessary and where applause is required. Since what constitutes meaningful ends for a people is a subject I
will discuss later, I won't dwell further on it here. Incidentally, my comments in this context are as much a criticism of our present cultural
values as of the reports, for the reports are reflections of what the planners interpret as mainstream American values, values they probably hold
themselves.

Other people and organizations have also produced ideas for economic development in Iowa. Most of these initiatives, however, can be
seen as subsets of the large frameworks sketched by SRI and the DED.

In general, both reports can be labeled "safe." Given the values of
America—and much of the world, for that matter—about the importance of economic growth, these documents are properly seen as falling
within the best traditions of American boosterism. In fact, there's almost
nothing in the reports that can be taken as patently offensive by anyone
who believes economic growth, and lots of it, is the path to nirvana.

As I said earlier, neither of the reports, or the two of them taken
together, delineates in any detail an overall vision for Iowa. Still, there is
an implied vision that can be inferred from the high-level objectives
outlined in both studies. And that vision is best characterized as more of
what we have now while viewing the natural environment as a constraint. That is, the studies carry the clear implication that material well-
being is paramount and the problem is how to get more of it while not
destroying our natural systems.

The image, then, is of a society working and playing and dying in pretty much the same manner as it does at the present time, except for the small towns, which might be in serious trouble. Aside from laboring in the service of economic development, we are seen as going to university football games on autumn Saturdays and basketball games in the winter. We'll play softball in the summer, shop at the malls for all the holidays when we are told to shop, continue to adore heroes of marginal importance and talent in popular music, and generally concentrate on doing business in new and dynamic ways, particularly in telecommunications and related fields of wonder involving emerging technologies. All of this will be done within the framework of what we like to call "progress."

In spite of the nod given toward threats from environmental degradation, the assumption is clearly implied, by the buoyant language of both reports, that we will find a way to deal with nature and consume our way toward happiness. Nothing is said about what constitutes happiness, and I would not expect the reports to examine such matters, *if* they were not so intent on either claiming to represent a vision for Iowa or implying that they do.

We are at a pivotal place in history. I suppose all people living in a given time think that. Still, there are signs of immense change around us. A deteriorating natural environment is, of course, one early warning of such change, particularly the problems of soil, air, and water, along with the decline in biodiversity. The surprising strength and durability of the New Age and animal rights movements, renewed concern for nature, the decline of traditional religions, the explosion of information technology, the aging population of Iowa and the nation, the persistent problem of drugs and crime, political and economic developments in Eastern Europe and the European Economic Community, the rise of the global corporation with its awesome potential for good or bad, and the apparent willingness of Americans to sacrifice freedom in exchange for law and order—all of these portend something other than business as usual.

Some believe the change we are going through, or are about to go through, rivals the Agricultural Revolution of the Neolithic period (ten thousand years ago, when people began sedentary agriculture, managing ecosystems to increase the output of food on a given piece of land) and the Industrial Revolution, particularly when the problems we confront with the natural environment are brought into view.

Something other than a pure extrapolation of what is currently deemed valuable is in order. In the following chapters, along with a survey of future constraints and contingencies, I'll provide a minority report on what development *should* mean. Some of my notions will mesh with those found in the SRI and DED studies; many will not.

FOR FURTHER READING

Iowa Department of Economic Development. *Directions for Iowa's Economic Future*. Des Moines: Iowa Department of Economic Development, Bureau of Planning and Research, 1989. (This is the 1989 update of an ongoing series of five-year plans. An executive summary of this plan is also available.)

_____. *Directions for Iowa's Economic Future: Action Plan, 1989 Edition*. Des Moines: Iowa Department of Economic Development, Bureau of Planning and Research, 1989. (This document contains specific guides for implementation of the strategies and initiatives covered in the five-year plan.)

SRI International. *Iowa's Future: A Quality Economy for Tomorrow* (or alternative title on title page, *Commitment to Quality: A Six-Point Action Program for Iowa's Economy*). Menlo Park, Calif.: SRI International, Center for Economic Competitiveness, 1989.

Waller, Robert James. "Going Soft Upon the Land and Down Along the Rivers." In *Just Beyond the Firelight,* by Robert James Waller. Ames: Iowa State University Press, 1988.

_____. "Lasers, Dreams, and Real Money." In *Just Beyond the Firelight,* by Robert James Waller. Ames: Iowa State University Press, 1988.

Threats and Contingencies

All discussions of the future are contaminated with value judgments and assumptions. The SRI and DED documents reviewed in Chapter Seven are not exceptions. For example, a preference for economic growth ultimately is a value judgment. And this value takes on the role of a decision criterion in the following way: That which promotes growth is good, that which detracts from growth is bad or at least suspect.

An important assumption, or rather a set of assumptions, in both documents centers on the natural environment. SRI clearly assumes, by omitting virtually any discussion of them, a relatively benign set of environmental circumstances supporting its recommendations for economic development in Iowa. To its credit, the DED does identify possible environmental problems, but still the assumption is present that we will somehow find our way to more economic growth in spite of these problems.

In this chapter a series of sketches delineate some potential constraints on Iowa development and contingencies that may affect the direction of our development. The focus here is on problems of the natural environment, though two others — changing diets and demographics — are mentioned briefly. (These latter two topics are taken up again in later chapters.) Before I begin, a warning is in order. Each of the topics discussed here has a huge literature associated with it. The reader is warned that what follows in this chapter are, at best, sketches of enormously complex issues.

ENERGY

Human life in the developed countries turns on a supply of cheap, easily available energy. The long gas lines, shortages of heating oil, and moratoriums on natural gas hookups in the 1970s are mostly forgotten, and we have come to take energy for granted once again.*

Unfortunately, things are about to change. The directions of this change lie swathed in uncertainty and complexity, subject to the behavior of a staggering array of elements, such as energy supplies, level of energy consumption, rates of economic growth throughout the world, population, the adoption rate of conservation practices, world political conditions, and the quality and timing of technological advances in energy use.

Iowans are particularly vulnerable to fluctuations in energy supplies and prices, since currently 97 percent of the energy we use—over $6 billion worth—is imported into the state. In addition, the agricultural sector is heavily dependent on oil and natural gas, not just to power tractors, but also as components in pesticides, herbicides, and fertilizers.

Oil and natural gas prices have also induced us to structure our lives and settlement patterns in ways not sustainable without inexpensive, portable energy supplies. We drive long distances for vacations or athletic events. The regional shopping centers are dependent on flexible, cheap, private transportation. We hold conferences (sometimes to discuss energy or other environmental problems), driving to them in our automobiles or flying in jet airplanes. Factories and offices are constructed with the presumption that people are able to commute sizable distances. Even school consolidation is based on the assumption of our ability to pay for the travel of yellow buses from one location to another.

Energy forecasts, typical of large threatening problems, lie along a continuum ranging from absolute doomsday to modestly reassuring. Few are overly optimistic; many analysts are quite pessimistic. Even basic data differ considerably from report to report.

The Input-Output Squeeze

We're entering what might be called the input-output squeeze in energy. Past concerns about energy have centered on supplies—on inputs

---

*This section on energy was written three months before Iraq invaded Kuwait. I see little reason for changing what I originally wrote. Here and there, however, are insertions that update the original material.

in other words. The major question before us was whether the energy inputs to power our economy would be available in the right amounts to support the desired level of economic activity.

Now we confront severe pollution problems, which constrain us on the output side of our production and consumption activities. For example, the atmosphere's ability to assimilate fossil-fuel wastes and river pollution stemming from heavy applications of nitrogen fertilizers are limiting how we use the energy available to us.

On the input side, my best guess is that insufficient oil supplies will start to cause serious problems in the next ten to twenty years, even without political instability in certain parts of the world. Natural gas resources, worldwide, will be all right for a little longer, but domestic supplies may disappear around 2020. These predictions are based purely on estimated consumption versus known reserves and assume no devastating political upheavals in regions where fossil fuels are produced.

In general, we have been seduced by market failure into a hybrid trap of the kind illustrated in Chapter Six, as, for example, when artificially low oil prices have encouraged us to overconsume gasoline, resulting in the depletion of resources, pollution, and a way of life that makes it difficult to remove ourselves from the trap. (Though, as I have pointed out, markets do not fail, cultures do, since markets are a set of circumstances devised by societies to promote the exchange of goods and services.) Prices act as signals, and the artificially low prices of oil and natural gas have resulted in consumption of these resources at a rate exceeding what would have occurred if prices had reflected the true costs of the resources. We are caught in a time-delay trap, potentially a serious one.

Suppose gasoline prices at the pump had been three dollars a gallon over the last thirty years. We would have, I'm sure, structured our lives and our settlement patterns quite differently, if that had been the case. But it's been politically expedient to keep gasoline prices low and avoid paying the *true costs* of its use.

For example, some analysts estimate we spend up to a third of our defense budget just to assure continuing supplies of foreign energy and minerals. At least $15 billion of that is spent defending our interests in the Middle East. (This amount was prior to Operation Desert Shield and Operation Desert Storm in the Persian Gulf.) That's a cost assignable to energy. In fact, Earl Revenal of Georgetown University has estimated that the annual military costs of protecting our energy interests in the Persian Gulf in recent years have annually been in excess of $450 per barrel of oil, which was eighteen times the amount we actually paid for the oil. That's a cost assignable to energy. With the Persian Gulf war running somewhere between $0.5 and $1 billion dollars per day, it's anybody's guess what the true cost of energy from this source might be. Whatever the estimate, the cost is huge.

A large chunk of America's trade imbalance is caused by energy imports. That has a cost attached to it. Then there's the environmental damage, ranging from smog to the greenhouse effect; that damage has not been included as a cost of our energy use. Finally, there are the subsidies attached to automobile travel that are not charged against the travel, such as the full costs of road building and maintenance, services by fire and police departments, and tax losses from land paved over for highway construction.

All of these are illustrations of social costs. Estimates showing that if all costs were taken into account, the price of gasoline at the pump might be as high as $4.50 per gallon are not difficult to find. That price would be in the range of what other developed countries, such as Sweden ($4.85 per gallon) already pay.

Limited supplies of oil and natural gas constitute a problem. What's being done about it? Almost nothing. I have mentioned the lack of a coherent energy policy in the United States and the potential this has for chaos in the future. In the early 1970s, when energy prices were increasing dramatically, we launched one of those crisis-driven programs that seem characteristic of humans and their governments. Crash programs in energy research and development were established to discover ways of conserving energy and alternative energy sources.

When petroleum prices eventually fell, and the ratio of real income to gas prices increased, the incentive for conservation and alternative-fuels programs evaporated. In 1990, seventeen years after the 1973 panic, little has changed in U.S. preparedness for future energy shocks. Again, the power of incentives in the form of prices is obvious. With the market no longer relaying signals via higher prices, the motivation for energy research and development declined. (Naturally, responding to crisis as we always do, recent events in the Persian Gulf have renewed cries for a forward-looking, comprehensive energy policy.)

In earlier chapters, I mentioned scheduling problems. Another one exists in the energy realm. R. Stephen Berry points out that twenty years, probably much more, are required from the time serious research and development efforts begin on an alternative energy source until that source can begin to make a noticeable contribution (say, 3 to 5 percent) to total consumption. Not only must the time horizon needed to conduct R&D match the time left before the problem arrives, but also long-range

R&D requires consistency and stability of effort. Otherwise enormous costs are incurred in new research start-ups and lost scientific momentum.

Michael Crow, former director of the Institute for Physical Research and Technology at Iowa State University, supports Berry's contentions about the inadequacy of U.S. energy policy, estimating we are fifteen to twenty years away from a synthetic fuel technology that could supply only 25 percent of our needs, even if an emergency arose today. With the distinct possibility of fuel crises over the next two decades, we already are behind.

It's hard not to be cautious about our energy future, particularly in Iowa, for these reasons. Partly because of politics, partly because of signals from the price system that do not reflect long-term concerns, U.S. energy programs come and go. What are the potential outcomes? Berry sees three possibilities:

1. U.S. firms and consumers will simply pay higher prices for maintaining a technological society when real fuel scarcity arrives. In other words, our cost of living will increase and discretionary income will have to be diverted from the purchase of nonenergy goods and services if energy consumption is to be maintained.
2. A more severe case is that the United States will become less and less competitive internationally. American consumers will find themselves relying on foreign nations to supply alternative fuels.
3. The most pessimistic scenario is that the United States will not be able to obtain enough energy to maintain its current industrial and living standards.

MIT researcher Michael Lynch is a little more sanguine. He argues that the world's proven oil reserves are thirty times current annual consumption and finds solace in that. Looked at another way, however, those reserves provide us with only thirty years of supply assuming no increases in consumption. But, for example, gasoline consumption by passenger cars has risen from about fifty billion gallons in 1950 to roughly two hundred billion gallons presently, and the use of such vehicles keeps growing (motor vehicle production increased by 30 percent in the 1980s).

Approximately 500 million autos are registered on this planet with an average fuel consumption of two gallons per day. At the current rate of increase, there will be two billion autos by 2025. Those figures alone are enough to keep you awake at night, without considering the enormous unmet demand for personal autos in countries such as the Soviet Union.

Lynch, though, is confident that oil exploration will uncover new reserves. Yet at 1980 consumption rates and with no improvement in efficiency, proven world oil reserves would have to increase by 20 percent by 2020, which is possible, but unlikely. Also, 40 percent of U.S. reserves lie in environmentally sensitive areas.

In any case, the supply is limited, and another oil crisis is as much a function of international politics as it is of supplies. That means a crisis can erupt at any time, if politics are the underlying cause (this was written in April of 1990, four months before Iraq's invasion of Kuwait). Given the projections that America will be importing 55 to 67 percent — depending on which projection you like — by the year 2000, the situation is precarious. Remember, we have not produced enough oil in the United States to cover even our transportation needs since 1976.

In the spring of 1988, the U.S. Geological Survey reduced its estimate of undiscovered oil and natural gas in the United States by 40 percent. More recently, the Department of Interior's Mineral Management Service estimated the amount of oil yet to be discovered in the United States is only 35 billion barrels, considerably lower than the Geological Survey's 1981 estimate of eighty-one billion barrels. Overall, known reserves combined with the new estimates will last until about 2005, at current rates of consumption.

A set of interviews conducted by Joseph Coates and Jennifer Jarratt with seventeen leading futurists disclosed that all of them agreed on the importance of solving the problems inherent in the transition to new energy sources. All of them see the reliance on oil as the dominant energy source ending in the next few decades, though they disagree on timing. Most of the futurists agree that disruption and turbulence, and perhaps a slowing of economic growth, will accompany the transition and that we likely will not generate a sense of urgency about solving this problem until we first exhaust the configuration of resources on which we currently depend.

It's worth recalling that Iowans are not stingy when it comes to spending energy. We use more energy per capita in our homes than forty other states. And our industries are more energy-intensive and energy-wasting than those in thirty-one other states. If that's not enough, we rank forty-sixth in terms of vehicle fuel efficiency. There's a lot to be done.

Energy Alternatives

We have been spoiled by the quality, convenience, and low price of oil and natural gas. Changing over to alternative fuels, even if intensive research were being done, which it's not, would be difficult. In terms of the future, there are two broad sets of alternatives, labeled the "hard path" and the "soft path." The hard path includes solid coal, synthetic liquid and gaseous fuels, and nuclear power. The soft path involves solar-based fuels, wind-generated power, and conservation.

THE HARD PATH

The hard path takes us along a route that has many of the same problems we presently face. Coal is not only difficult to burn cleanly, it also scars the environment in its extraction. Eventually, we may find a way to produce liquid or gaseous fuels from coal and repair the damage caused by extraction. At the moment, we're a long way from either.

Nuclear energy, based on fission, was once the great dream. "Too cheap to read the meter" and other such phrases heralded the atom as a source of power. In anything resembling the near term, the dream fades. Aside from the disposal of long-lived radioactive wastes and questions about the safety of operating the plants themselves, there are worries about dispersal of nuclear capability that can be turned into weapons and the vulnerability of nuclear plants to terrorist sabotage.

By the time the energy costs of decommissioning existing nuclear plants and permanent waste disposal are accounted for, we'll be fortunate if nuclear energy has produced more energy than it consumed. Someday, perhaps, fusion technology will fulfill the dream. For now, don't count on nuclear power.

Some Iowans, particularly in the farm community, have been excited about the prospect of ethanol as a partial substitute for gasoline. Since ethanol can be produced from corn, corn residues, or sugar cane, farmers have seen the potential for a vast grain market in the fuel sector. As a fuel, ethanol has some real advantages. It burns much cleaner and has a higher octane than conventional gasoline, produces less carbon dioxide per mile than does gasoline, and is based on a renewable resource.

Unfortunately, if used as a straight motor fuel, not as an additive, it is expensive. Moreover, growing corn for ethanol production competes with food supply. If, for instance, 40 percent of the entire United States grain harvest were used to produce ethanol, it would supply only 10 percent of the fuel consumed in the United States annually. Furthermore, a study by the Center for Agriculture and Rural Development at Iowa State University indicates that soil erosion could increase by ninefold if all crop residues were removed for the production of alcohol-based fuel.

Finally, the energy profit ratio, which is computed by dividing units of fuel extracted by units of fuel burned in the extraction process, is very low for ethanol (slightly over 1.0 and some studies indicate it's less than 1.0). This result flows from the high level of fuel usage, in tractors for example, that is used to grow the crops from which ethanol is made. And if intensive farming practices are used such that the agricultural sector can produce both food and fuel, then soil erosion and the consequent need to overcome loss of soil productivity further increases the energy requirements needed for farming.

Methanol (an alcohol fuel made from coal, wood, natural gas, or garbage) often is considered the chief candidate for replacing gasoline. It's a much cleaner fuel than gasoline and suits high-performance engines well. But a gallon of methanol will take an auto only one-half as far as a gallon of gas and does not operate well below 50 degrees Fahrenheit. Perhaps even more serious, methanol is highly toxic and dangerous to handle. Currently, the Bush administration and the U.S. Environmental Protection Agency favor methanol as the alternative automobile fuel, even though numerous studies show that, like ethanol, the energy profit ratio is close to or less than 1.0.

Brazil is often held up as an example of a country running on alcohol-based fuel. But Brazil has a large production capacity for sugar cane, a good source of alcohol. Besides, the Brazilian government has pumped $8 billion of subsidies into its ethanol program. The open market has not yet demonstrated ethanol's feasibility.

As an automotive fuel, hydrogen has potential, either in liquid or compressed gaseous form. Cost is still a major impediment and no hydrogen-powered vehicles have developed beyond the prototype stage. Canada, Japan, and West Germany have research and development programs for hydrogen fuel, but the United States lags in this area.

Coal is a mixed blessing. There's a lot of it around, particularly in the United States, China, and the Soviet Union — about 275 years' worth at current consumption rates. But half of it is extremely dirty in burning, and all coal causes environmental problems both in its extraction (for example, strip mining) and its use. Even with contemporary technology for cleaning coal-smoke emissions, carbon dioxide is still present in large amounts and is the major contributor to the greenhouse effect and acid rain. Possibilities exist for extracting gas from coal, but at present these technologies cannot compete economically with natural gas and oil, and research funding for them has been drastically reduced.

In addition, the energy profit ratio for coal has been declining, that is, increasing amounts of energy are required to get energy from coal. One major reason is that strip mining is very energy-intensive. A second is that the average heat content per pound of coal discovered is falling due to the decline in the quality of this coal.

The majority of our electric power is generated by oil, natural gas, and coal, with nuclear energy and hydroelectric installations providing smaller amounts. Eventually, electric-powered autos will become available for short trips such as urban commuting. Still, there is the output-side constraint. If the electricity is generated by processes that pollute the atmosphere, a serious problem remains.

Some believe that markets will make all the necessary adjustments for us. As oil and gas prices increase, they say, these prices will make it economical to develop other energy sources that currently cannot compete with oil and gas in terms of price. While some wisdom is contained in this point of view, there are also two problems with it.

First, as I emphasized in earlier chapters, markets do not handle the future very well. Increases in fossil-fuel prices may well signal a turn to other sources, but if it takes twenty years even to do the research on these alternatives and another ten years to develop efficient production and transportation technologies, the makings for chaos are in place. The scheduling problem again.

In addition, it's critical to understand that more than prices are involved. There are physical constraints. If a fuel has an energy ratio of less than 1.0, it doesn't matter how high fossil-fuel prices rise; that fuel is not going to be a viable option.

THE SOFT PATH

The soft path to energy development — including hydropower, wind, biomass, solar, and conservation — holds promise. Hydropower, while being one of the first places people look for cheap renewable energy, has dilemmas associated with it. First, most of the good sites already are in use. Second, the building of dams is environmentally disruptive in many different ways. Developing countries may find small installations useful.

Biomass (wood and organic waste) generates energy for much of the developing world. It's clumsy to use, compared with oil and gas, and has not only caused the deforestation of many developing countries (encouraging soil erosion, among other things), but also carries with it pollution problems on the output side.*

Biomass materials are the source for methanol and other alcohol-based fuel production. In principle, some of the polluting effects can be offset by replacing trees or plants, which will then act as carbon sinks for the pollution caused by burning the original trees or plants. On the other hand, methane gas is released in the process of using biomass-based fuels, making its own contribution to the degradation of the atmosphere.

Solar energy is, of course, renewable as long as the sun shines. Reasonably good solar technology exists for home heating requirements, though with our present low prices of oil and natural gas, it has trouble competing in the market. In the 1970s, with oil prices soaring and moratoriums on natural gas hookups in some areas, interest in solar energy escalated. The federal government established tax credits in 1978 for solar energy installations, providing homeowners with a credit of 40 percent of the cost, up to $4,000.

Also in 1978, the Iowa Solar Energy Association was formed, and Governor Robert D. Ray proclaimed May 3, 1978, as Sun Day in Iowa, praising solar energy as "the most abundant and least polluting energy source immediately adaptable to meet Iowa's energy needs." He was right about abundance and lack of pollution, but a little too optimistic about the state of solar technology.

Largely, the early solar technology was rudimentary, ill-conceived in its application, oversold by enthusiastic entrepreneurs and some outright charlatans, and not particularly successful. Most of the early interest involved active solar technology, relying on moving parts such as pumps, valves, and fans attached as a package to buildings and designed to heat air, or water, or both. The active systems were unreliable, poorly maintained, and too poorly designed to handle the dramatic temperature fluctuations Iowa experiences, along with the problem of cloudy days.

With these failures, Iowans began to examine passive solar systems based on large window areas to gather heat during the day and masses of concrete that could store the heat and release it at night. This required rather exotic looking structures that did not suit the taste of all Iowans, though some of the homes built with passive installations still are in operation. Results have been mixed.

---

*Air pollution caused by the outputs of fireplaces and wood stoves is a common problem in many areas of the United States, particularly the Rocky Mountain West. The same is true of dung pits used for heating and cooking in the Third World.

Eventually, the prices for conventional fuels dropped. As this occurred, the incentives for solar installations also disappeared, including the federal tax credit, which was scrapped as part of the Tax Reform Act of 1986. A society intent on avoiding an eventual trap would have maintained by tax credits and other incentives experiments with an alternative energy source such as solar, but that's not the way things work — when the immediate problem lessens, forget about the future.

Nonetheless, work on solar energy has continued, though at a reduced pace. The most promising development is in the area of photovoltaics (solar cells) that generate electricity directly from sunlight and already are used in watches, calculators, flashing highway signs, and satellites. The energy profit ratio for this technology has been rising dramatically, and further increases are expected. Photovoltaic costs have dropped to thirty cents per kilowatt-hour. Still, this use of solar power is more expensive than current sources of electricity (about three cents per kilowatt-hour). The hope is that developments in microelectronics and semiconductors will lower costs by increasing efficiency even further.

The soft energy path has a nice sense to it. Decentralized and independent, safe and renewable and (relatively) nonpolluting — that's the way it feels. But understand, it represents an entire restructuring of our industrial, household, transportation, and utilities infrastructure. The cost will be enormous. Moreover, solar and wind sources of power are weather-dependent. If the sun doesn't shine or the wind doesn't blow, you don't get energy.

On the other hand, the hard path commits us to more of what we already have experienced in the way of risk and pollution. In addition, as Carrying Capacity, Inc., has speculated, the hard path will require large, complex installations for nuclear energy and synfuel production, similar to what we now have with oil and natural gas, only more so. This creates a certain uneasiness. Frankly, I do not trust the executives of remote, megacorporations to care very much about me or my concerns. I'd rather have a nice solar unit on my roof that I can climb up and inspect now and then.

I am just as uneasy thinking about the possibility of some off-balance cycloid tossing a bomb into a plutonium plant. Finally, committing ourselves to the hard energy path means that, at some point, humans still must confront the transition to renewable sources as oil, gas, coal, and uranium begin to run out.

The best current strategy, which is the other half of the soft energy path, is conservation. The possibilities for greater energy efficiency in Iowa, in the United States as a whole, and the world are truly staggering.

Amory Lovins, who founded the Rocky Mountain Institute (RMI is a nonprofit research and educational foundation devoted to studying energy and related problems) and coined the "soft" and "hard" designations for energy sources, believes the good life, or something approximating it, is sustainable almost entirely on the back of energy efficiency. For example, his numbers show that the U.S. economy can lower its energy consumption by perhaps 70 percent. One interesting computation by Lovins shows that "if we spent as much to make buildings heat-tight as we now spend in one year on the military forces meant to protect the Middle Eastern oil fields, we could eliminate the need to import any oil from the Middle East (his calculations predated the 1990 Persian Gulf hostilities).

The result would be massive reductions in smog, global warming, and acid rain, along with an elimination of oil imports and monetary savings of some $300 billion annually, enough to pay off the federal deficit by the year 2000. Lovins contends that 92 percent of all electricity used for lighting can be saved, and a recent study by his institute indicates that improving electrical efficiency is nearly seven times more cost-effective than nuclear power for reducing carbon dioxide emissions.

Lovins, whom *Newsweek* has called "one of the Western world's most influential energy thinkers," is relentless about efficiency. RMI has claimed that instituting water efficiency measures in Denver could save as much water as the controversial Two Forks Dam was projected to supply. Following RMI's report, plans for the dam were dropped. Denver has instituted an aggressive water conservation program similar to that proposed by RMI.

President Ronald Reagan was skeptical about energy conservation, describing it as "being hot in the summer and cold in the winter." He also claimed, "No nation ever conserved itself to greatness." In spite of that, a number of influential figures in the energy community agree with Lovins, at least partially, that conservation is the key to solving our energy dilemma.

In a report prepared for *Scientific American,* John Gibbons et al. point out: "The industrialized world's energy intensity—the amount of energy used to produce a unit of gross national product—fell by one fifth between 1973 and 1985. In the U.S. the gross national product grew 40 percent while energy consumption remained constant."*

---

*While encouraging, numbers such as these should be viewed cautiously, since it's difficult to determine what has been accounted for and what has not. Earlier I mentioned those costs not included in GNP. Thus, if future cleanup costs requiring energy were being generated by the production of GNP, energy consumption would be understated.

The authors conclude: "Technological ingenuity can dramatically reduce the amount of energy required to provide a given level of goods and services, simultaneously cutting down on energy-driven problems. Investments in energy efficiency can help us reduce fossil-fuel demand without sacrificing economic growth." Indeed, we Americans use roughly 38 percent less oil and gas to produce a dollar of GNP than we did in 1973. And as Lovins points out, we didn't accomplish this with whiz-bang technologies, but with caulking guns, duct tape, and slight improvements in automobile fuel efficiency.

Energy can be conserved in two ways. One is by achieving the same output with less input — by becoming more efficient. The second is through curtailment of consumption. For example, savings can be accomplished by purchasing a smaller automobile that gets better gas mileage, or simply by driving less, or by some combination of the two. In terms of standards of living, efficiency means retaining current standards. Curtailment, to many people, means a reduced standard of living, though that's not always the case. Turning off the lights in an unused room does not lower one's living standards, but it curtails energy use.

The World Commission on Environment and Development cites two studies that illustrate what is possible with and without intensive energy conservation. If all future development of all kinds used the most energy-efficient technologies available in transportation, housing, industry, and other economic sectors, a 50 percent drop in energy consumption by the industrial world and a tolerable 30 percent increase in developing countries would be possible. On the other hand, if no gains in energy efficiency are assumed, the projection is for a tripling of 1980 global energy consumption by 2020. Neither of these is a likely scenario, but they are instructive as extreme cases.

Prognosis and Strategies

We will encounter serious energy problems in the next ten to fifteen years. Oil and natural gas prices will escalate at that time, perhaps dramatically.

A scramble to find alternative energy sources will follow. States and the federal government will throw money at the problem, and many of these funds will be wasted as we operate in the emotional arena of crisis. The citizenry will be angry with higher prices, inconveniences, and the lack of planning that caused the mess, blaming everyone but themselves.

As energy prices increase, consumers will have to devote a higher proportion of their budgets to energy procurement and less to other

goods and services. International tensions within the bloc of industrialized nations and between these countries and the developing countries
likely will escalate as major industrial powers try to protect their foreign
energy supplies.

When this occurs, my greatest fear is that people in the industrialized West, particularly Americans, will succumb to the blandishments of
the moment and lessen their aversion to environmentally harmful energy
sources, such as nuclear power and raw coal. Even more frightening is
the prospect of demagogues who tell Americans that their wasteful trips
to shopping malls and university athletic events, not to mention auto
racing and car rallies, are fundamental rights that should be protected
and enhanced at all costs. Humanity has a history of Faustian compacts;
running into an energy wall might goad us into cutting any deal that
promises to preserve our profligate way of life.

Avoiding calamity, or at least severe disruption, requires a two-
pronged approach, starting now (preferably twenty years ago). Research
along both the hard and soft energy paths should receive large federal
and state subsidies. The hard-path research should concentrate on synthetic fuels, primarily those derived from coal, working within stringent
environmental pollution constraints.

Advocates of nuclear power should not be trusted until the scientific
community and others outside of the scientific community are satisfied
that safety in both operation of nuclear power plants and disposal of
radioactive wastes is, indeed, technologically possible, including correc-
tions for human error. Some risk will be present, unavoidably, but executives in nuclear power companies should not be the ones assessing the
magnitude of that risk, and any forecast that has the least hint of excess
optimism flavoring it should be discarded.

Still on the input side, we should begin considering a world where a
mix of energy sources, instead of an excessive reliance on oil and natural
gas, will be the norm. Solar energy (both passive and photovoltaic), fuel
additives, biomass generators, and perhaps wind power will all be used
within the activities of a single household or business firm.

On the output side, conservation measures should be brought to
bear immediately. A major instrument here is the price system, and
energy prices, particularly fuel, should be raised to reflect the true costs
of production and consumption, with appropriate attention given to the
equity problems involving hardships for lower-income people. I say
"should," though I'm not confident that we can overcome the political
problems of getting the necessary legislation passed to raise fuel taxes.
Would you vote for a congressman who promised to raise gasoline prices

by a dollar and to send part of this back to people with lower incomes as a means of offsetting the higher prices for these people? Maybe. Another good approach is to levy high taxes on the purchase price of new fuel-inefficient autos and trucks, and this may be more palatable, politically. (I said *maybe*.)

Incentives can play critical roles in all areas of energy. Firms and individuals developing or using promising technologies that currently cannot compete with cheap oil and natural gas should receive government incentives in the form of tax credits and low-interest loans. Another alternative is to guarantee the price of fuels produced by new fuel systems until they become economically viable on their own.

At the household level, incentives are also important. As mentioned before, we've been creating a trap for ourselves by high levels of present consumption versus conserving for the future. Sometimes the road signs posted by the price system lead us awry; energy usage certainly is an illustration of this. Where markets fail, society needs to make adjustments to counter this failure. To repeat, *we need to bring the future back to the present.*

One approach is to allow tax credits for building energy-efficient homes and for retrofitting existing buildings. Such credits plus low-interest loans will encourage the purchase of energy-efficient appliances, including heating and cooling equipment. In conjunction with higher prices, these incentives will shorten the payback period for investments in energy efficiency by homeowners. Part of the problem, of course, is that poorer people simply do not have the funds to overcome the price difference between, for example, refrigerators that are low in energy use and those that are not. The low-cost loan can be a way of reducing the gap between two models for such people.

In discussing various kinds of traps, I pointed out that ignorance — that is, lack of good information — can generate its own kind of trap. It's important that consumers be provided with accurate and timely information about the availability of energy-efficient options, including payback periods based on usage. At the moment, they are not. One survey showed that 70 percent of appliance salespeople do not even discuss energy efficiency with customers. Utilities have done some of this via free energy audits, though experiences with the results of these audits have been mixed.

Communities can enforce rigorous building codes that require architects, contractors, and developers to incorporate the latest energy technology in design and construction. Even though the initial cost of the house may be a little higher, the incentives discussed above can provide for a quick payback period. Moreover, money spent on insulation, appliances, and heating and cooling equipment goes to local merchants, whereas distant suppliers of oil and gas benefit from consumers paying higher fuel prices.

It's pretty clear that the party is about over. Neither the hard-path nor the soft-path strategies will permit the kind of a world we have come to know and trust. None of the alternative energy sources, except for coal, approach the high energy profit ratios of oil and natural gas. If we are to sustain our economy at its present level, we're going to have to use a combination of new energy sources and conservation to provide the level of net energy that we now enjoy.

Implications for Agriculture

Modern agriculture is heavily dependent on oil and natural gas, directly and indirectly, for tractor fuel, grain drying, fertilizers, pesticides, and herbicides.* If energy prices increase, as I expect them to, then farmers will find themselves in even more of a cost-price pinch than they do presently. On the output side, individual Iowa farmers have no pricing power in the markets for their products, that is, they must take the price as set by market forces. On the input side, they purchase from large firms with considerable pricing power. Thus, as fuel supplies decline, we can expect to see cost increases, perhaps dramatic ones, that will be passed along directly to farmers in the form of higher input prices. The late 1970s gave us a taste of just that.

Net revenue is the result of subtracting costs from gross revenues. If operating costs increase, and these costs cannot be passed along to the product markets (which farmers do not have the power to do), then the only ways to maintain net revenue are to increase the amount of product produced or to reduce costs.

Raising production requires driving the land even harder to increase yields or bringing more land into production. In either case, the environmental repercussions could be disastrous, unless some technological breakthrough allows much higher yields with the same inputs. The battle against degradation of the Iowa countryside, in terms of soil erosion, deforestation, and loss of wetlands, is difficult enough under current conditions. Rising fuel prices promise to exacerbate these problems.

Agriculture represents another example of the input-output energy

---

*Much of this section relies heavily on *Beyond Oil,* by John Gever, et al.

squeeze. Constraints already exist on the output side in the form of soil erosion and water pollution. A decline in fuel supplies provides pressure on the input side. One hope here is the number of emerging studies showing that farmers have been using far too much in the way of nitrogen fertilizers; a decrease in their use would result in some reduction in the use of fossil fuels. Increments in knowledge about the time and placement of field chemicals could have the same effect. And, though the farm community has been slow to accept them, an increasing number of organic farming techniques suggest possible substantial reductions in other such inputs through regenerative farming and integrated pest management.

It's also possible that allowing food prices to rise can reduce cost-price pressures on the output side. It's only a possibility, however, since the cause-and-effect linkages in agriculture are complex. Some of this ties into the large and inefficient water subsidies given to farmers in the western United States, who continue to grow surplus crops on intensively irrigated land, thereby increasing supplies and holding market prices down.

Consumer food preferences also could have a profound effect on the throughput efficiencies of agriculture. Beef, for example, is a notoriously inefficient way of feeding people, due to the high caloric inputs of grain needed to produce a relatively few calories of beef. In certain parts of India and other developing countries, partly because of religion and partly because of economics, entirely adequate human diets consist mostly of vegetables and rice, plus some fish and fowl.

The fact is that it takes a lot more energy to produce meat than to use fields for food grains, though Iowa beef and hog producers approach conditions of apoplexy whenever a reduction in meat intake is even mentioned. John Robbins cites a study done by the Department of the Interior claiming that the raw materials used in the production of food from livestock exceeds the value of all oil, gas, and coal consumed in the United States. (I'll return to this issue of diet and nutrition later.)

Strategies for Iowa

Iowa should immediately examine all opportunities for energy conservation. In fact, efforts are already progressing in this area. The electrical utility in Osage has received national and international attention for its conservation efforts, particularly in the area of peak-load management. The Department of Economic Development recommends emphasis on conservation, and the Department of Natural Resource's Energy Bureau is also working toward these ends. The emphasis should be on incentives of the kind mentioned earlier in this chapter.

Settlement patterns are hard to change in the short run. One of the dilemmas Iowa faces is that we are quite spread out, geographically, with long distances between towns. Thus, fuel consumption for shopping trips, medical care, social visits, entertainment, recreation, and student transportation to educational sites is high in Iowa. Settlement patterns are a study in themselves, but it's clear that attention should be given to these patterns in light of approaching fuel problems.

One major consideration will be how to accommodate increasing preferences for living close to work, if automobile fuel prices increase two to three dollars per gallon, which is where they ought to be right now if all costs of producing fuel were taken into account. Likely, there will be swift and large changes in the demand for public transportation, as well.

While we are in a period of relative calm (this was written in April of 1990), economically and also in terms of energy, Iowa should examine the potential for a much greater diversity of transport options, including buses, rail systems, bicycles, and walking. The problem confronting mass transportation is flexibility and, consequently, convenience. That can partially be overcome by enhancing schedules and routes. The construction of grid systems could allow bike paths, to intersect with bus routes, and adopting facilities like those on bus and rail systems in Denmark, Japan, the Netherlands, and West Germany would allow bicycles to be carried on mass transit vehicles.

The blithe ignorance we exhibit in the face of serious problems is pretty amazing. Newspapers and magazines are fond of articles about the spaciousness of new homes built in the United States. Many of these houses have four thousand square feet or more, many built with little thought given to energy conservation. A recent article in the *Des Moines Register* extolled the virtues of a new home in the Des Moines area containing six thousand square feet and five fireplaces. The same day the article appeared, the United States and its allies flew two thousand or more missions in the Persian Gulf area as we worried about a continuing supply of cheap fuel. It's enough to make a temperate man into a flaming revolutionary.

In any case, there's a reasonable probability that such buildings will become the white elephants of the future, laughable in view of what it will take to heat and cool them and socially unacceptable when equity differences between rich and poor are taken into account and matched against fuel prices.

Just how much conservation is possible remains unanswered. Amory and Hunter Lovins believe it is our salvation and appear to have the data to show just that. Others are more skeptical.

There is a best-case scenario that might come to pass. It works like this: The federal government levies high taxes on fuels (reducing current demand), intensive conservation efforts are undertaken nationwide, U.S. population declines, and an all-out program to develop alternative fuels is funded. Prosperity, if not paradise as most Americans think of it, would be the result. In addition, economic problems confronted by developing countries may well have reduced their effective demand for oil and natural gas, leaving more for the industrialized countries. (Omitted from this are some profound moral issues, and the best case for Americans may, of course, not be the same for those less fortunate.)

None of the assumptions underlying the best-case scenario is currently visible. A more cautious prognosis is therefore the best one. That's why Iowa should concentrate on energy conservation and use. A study done for Carrying Capacity, Inc. (see Gever et al.), provides an example of the most pessimistic view, stating, "There are only ten or twenty years of per capita economic growth remaining before declining oil and gas production begins to drag the economy down [written in the mid-1980s]." Even if truth lies somewhere between the optimistic and pessimistic extremes, clearly this is the moment to get under way before panic closes in and chaos follows.

FOOD

As in the energy situation, the literature dealing with food supply contains arguments supporting just about any position one cares to take. Still, in spite of the surpluses familiar to Iowans, world food production seems to be entering an input-output squeeze similar to that of energy.

The adequacy of food supply can be judged only in relation to (1) the number of people who need to be fed, (2) what they eat, and (3) how much they eat. Consider the following estimates and projections of world population:

Year	World Population
1900	1 billion
1950	2.5 billion
1987	5 billion
2000	6 billion
2025	8 billion
2090	10 billion

Ninety percent of the population growth between now and 2025 will occur in less developed countries.

Next, look at the following information:

Worldwide, forty thousand children die each day, most of them from starvation, along with dehydration and its associated complications. Fifteen million people die each year from these causes. Write that on a three-by-five card and post it on your refrigerator door.

Worldwide, some 700,000,000 people do not receive enough calories to prevent stunted growth and serious health risks.

Worldwide, 1,500,000,000 people receive insufficient calories to provide energy for an active working life. According to agricultural economist John Helmuth, of Iowa State University, 50 percent of these are in developing countries, 40 percent in low-income countries, and 10 percent in middle-income countries.

Nineteen million Americans receive food stamps, which allow only the most minimal of food purchases per meal.

While many people in the United States battle obesity — and Iowa certainly is no exception — Helmuth says: "One-third of the world does not receive enough food to maintain an active working life, the economic loss is staggering, and the amount of human pain and suffering is incalculable. With all the relief efforts, government assistance, and private volunteer organizations combined, we are still in the dark ages in the battle against hunger." Juxtaposed against the ubiquitous advertisements for weight-reduction plans in the U.S., there is something incredibly perverse about all of this.

What's going on? Why the hunger? The list of reasons is a long one and, depending on the author, sometimes is a function of individual political philosophies. Here's one, drawn from several sources, including Helmuth's article:

Population growth swamping any advances in Third World food production

Economic and political policies discouraging agricultural production

The demand by industrialized countries for fuel and natural gas robbing poorer countries of needed supplies that could be used in food production

Poverty, leading to ineffective demand for food (ineffective demand means one does not have the financial capacity to purchase a good or service). A corollary of this is unequal distribution of financial resources in poor countries and rich countries alike

The wealthy of the world diverting resources from the production of basic foods by demanding luxury items, such as grapes to make wine

Greed, pride, and stupidity in developing countries leading to the construction of palaces and the like rather than using resources to feed the hungry. The same can be said of industrialized countries.

Greed and cruelty by business people who have a stake in keeping people hungry, since hungry people work for lower wages. Central and South America are usually cited here. Also U.S. and European companies with subsidiaries in poor countries are more profitable if they pay low wages to workers harvesting sugar, coffee, cotton, coconuts, pineapples, and bananas.

U.S. manufacturers who shut down U.S. plants and transfer operations to poor countries where hungry people will work for low wages

America's use of food as a weapon to get acquiescence to its policies

Vulnerability of agricultural systems in developing countries to pestation, drought, and other natural disasters

Poor food distribution systems in developing countries.

Adverse exchange rates and Third World debt reduce purchasing power of poor countries

Trade barriers and protectionist policies in general

Exploitation of less-developed countries by industrialized countries leading to land degradation, mineral and fossil-fuel depletion, and pollution

Subsidies to farmers in developed countries creating food surpluses, which are then dumped in poor countries, with the result that prices paid to local farmers are depressed, removing incentives for these indigenous farmers

The problem is nearly unsolvable, or so it seems. Solutions proposed range from rapid economic growth (the most popular) as a way of alleviating poverty and creating effective demand for food all the way to quasi-socialist collectives of poor countries organized to do battle with their industrialized masters and to look after their own interests.

All right, there's currently a wrenching inequity in world food availability. What about the future? There will be more people, a lot more. If the politics and greed and economics of food distribution are ignored, can we physically produce enough food to feed a population three to five billion larger than at the present time?

Maybe. Maybe not. Pierre Crosson and Norman Rosenberg, of Resources for the Future, believe physical food production can be raised high enough to support a growing population. That's what they call the "short answer." The long answer is that problems in the physical infrastructure of food production must be solved and care must be taken to minimize environmental damage from food production. Three subproblems are critical: soil degradation, water availability, and a general decline in genetic diversity.*

Crosson and Rosenberg represent a side of the food-supply debate that can be characterized as follows: Things will probably work out all

---

*Genetic diversity has to do with the range of plant and animal stocks in the world. The less diversity, the more danger there is of a disease attacking an important crop or type of livestock with no substitutes readily available. In colloquial terms, it means not putting all your eggs in one basket, diversifying your portfolio, and not planting your entire forest in elm trees. None of the major food crops are native to the United States, so we are dependent on other countries for a supply of genetic diversity. Monocropping, along with destruction of gene stocks in rain forests and other environments, causes concern about genetic diversity.

right, but we need to have some technological breakthroughs and rapid modification of social institutions to make them work out.

Lester Brown, head of the Worldwatch Institute, is on the other side. Brown sees destruction of the resources for producing food occurring all over the world. To support his case, Brown marshals a large amount of evidence pointing to soil erosion, salinization of irrigated land,* depletion of water stocks in aquifers, possible climate shifts, and other factors. He states, "The future of agriculture is being shaped increasingly by environmental trends and resource constraints."

Brown's conclusion is that world food production is falling, and will continue to fall, if environmental problems are ignored. Moreover, he does not believe biotechnology can make up the difference. Matched against the population statistics presented above, Brown's outlook can be considered grim. Basically, he is saying that current levels of food production are unsustainable, given the way we go about the business of agriculture.

As with energy, then, we confront uncertainty, vast uncertainty, in the future supply of food. Most (I said *most*) Americans tend to think of a variety of food, and plenty of it, as one of their inalienable rights. Yet after the two drought years of 1987 and 1988, world grain stocks had dropped to about 50 days' worth. There's not much comfort in that margin.

The two points of view just considered are typical of many other analyses. There is tempered optimism; there is unbridled pessimism. Iowa, as a world-class food producer, swirls in the whirlpool of food policy, in all of its political, physical, and economic dimensions.

WATER

Water is a gypsy resource, evaporating and falling as rain, moving down rivers and underneath the ground, lapping on beaches. The decline of freshwater quality in Iowa has received considerable attention over the last several years. Because it affects them at the level of the kitchen faucet, people become concerned about water quality once its endangerment is brought to their attention.

---

*Salinization may occur when river water or groundwater is diverted for irrigation purposes. If the excess water is not drained away, the water table rises and evaporation through the remaining inches of soil occurs, leaving salt on the surface.

Water is in the same category as energy, food, and climate (discussed below) — it's a current world problem that continues to worsen for all of the reasons discussed earlier. Difficulties in assigning property rights to transient resources such as water and air thwart the establishment of markets where the resource can be given a value.* Thus, overexploitation and, ultimately, degradation occur.

Not only are energy, food, climate, and water world-class problems by themselves, they also are interrelated with one another. *Problematique* is a French word that describes situations where serious problems are bound together in a mosaic, forming a superproblem, with each of the individual problems forming a subcomponent. It's a system of problems.

For instance, energy, in the form of fertilizers, can be used (up to a point) to compensate for the loss of topsoil. The poorer the soil, the more fertilizers derived from fossil fuels are needed. But fertilizers find their way into the water supply and pollute it. Likewise, carbon dioxide and other by-products of burning fossil fuels cause pollution of the atmosphere, resulting in acid rain and possible shifts in rainfall patterns due to climatic changes. Unsophisticated irrigation practices used in growing food result in waterlogging and salinization of the soil, which puts more agricultural pressure on other farming areas. And so on. In ecological systems, things cannot be easily separated — that's why they are called systems.

If all of the fresh water in the world's lakes, creeks, streams, and rivers is summed, the result is less than .01 percent of the total amount of water on earth. Still, that's a lot of water, and it's replenished by the evaporation-rainfall cycle. Most of the rainfall is lost as flood runoff to the seas or because it falls in uninhabited areas. Plants also use some of the rainfall. Even so, that leaves enough water from the cycle to support some twenty billion people.

There are, however, four pieces of bad news that temper this rosy outlook. First, human activity produces gases and particulate matter that contaminate much of the rainfall. Second, some of the rainfall, maybe one-eighth, falls on uninhabited areas where it cannot be used. Third, humans are polluting lakes, creeks, streams, and rivers. And, fourth, fresh water is not distributed evenly around the planet.

---

*In the American West, attempts at establishing a market in water through the sale of water rights have shown considerable promise. As cities, farmers, and other users bid against one another, something approximating a market gets established and the resource assumes greater value than previously.

That's *surface* water. Groundwater is another matter. No one is sure how much groundwater exists. Huge amounts, probably. Once again, however, human production and consumption activities are in the process of polluting these supplies or using them carelessly and needlessly. In Iowa, five sources of pollution occur at the top of the soil, according to the *Groundwater Protection News:*

1. Agricultural use of nitrogen
2. Agricultural use of pesticides
3. Land application of solid and liquid wastes
4. Storage, handling, and transportation of hazardous chemicals
5. Urban residential use of pesticides and fertilizers

In addition, there are five sources of groundwater contamination that occur within the soil by contaminants placed below ground level:

1. Abandoned dumps and unpermitted land disposal sites
2. Landfills
3. Wastewater treatment lagoons
4. Septic tank systems
5. Underground storage tanks and pipelines

How serious is the pollution? The data are sketchy. It's well established that coliform bacteria from human and animal wastes cause infections of the gastric system, dysentery, hepatitis, typhoid fever, and cholera. More subtle are the effects of chemicals. As an illustration, no one is certain what long-term exposure to even small amounts of pesticides means for humans, and two-thirds of Iowa's public drinking water supplies contain pesticides, not to mention other contaminants. Groundwater, hidden from us, is difficult to study, in terms of its movements and the source of its contaminants. And pollution of groundwater supplies is largely irreversible, for biological reasons.

Aside from pollution on the output side of our activities, some sources of water are depletable, just as are soil and petroleum and minerals. That is, we "mine" water contained in those aquifers that do not recharge at a pace equaling their depletion. The Ogallala aquifer and its depletion were mentioned earlier in the book. Estimates are that the Ogallala has about one generation's supply left, given its current mining to produce surplus crops. The same problem is occurring in the Phoenix-Scottsdale area of Arizona.

On a global basis, 73 percent of the water taken from the earth goes for agricultural purposes. World irrigation acreage currently approximates the land mass of India. A battle in California rages between farmers and urban dwellers over water. Expect these conflagrations to increase in number and escalate in intensity, worldwide.

Quality water is becoming increasingly scarce, globally, due to expansions of population, industrialization, and agriculture. That which is not mined is being polluted. Can it be cleaned up? Yes, some surface water can be reclaimed if pollution is stopped, but the cost is extremely high and the time required is long. (By the way, Americans are the most profligate users of water. A U.S. citizen uses, annually, seventy times as much water as a resident of Ghana and over four times as much as a resident of Switzerland.)

Then we have the oceans. Same story there. We dump our sewage and garbage into them, spill oil on their surfaces and shores, overexploit fishing grounds, and cram their mouths with silt (some thirteen billion tons of silt per year, worldwide). PCBs (polychlorinated biphenyls), DDT, heavy-metal compounds, and other long-lived compounds are out there percolating through the world's marine ecosystems, working their way through the food chains, even though a ban on PCBs and DDT by industrialized countries has been in effect for a dozen years. Worse, developing countries still use PCBs and DDT.

Cleaning the oceans, if not impossible, is much more difficult than restoring rivers, lakes, and inland seas, and those latter efforts are difficult, indeed. And as mineral resources on land are depleted, surely we'll turn to deep-sea mining, which will only compound already nasty problems. (If you're entertaining the thought that oceans have little to do with Iowa, read again the section on Gaia in Chapter Two.)

The general prognosis? J. W. Maurits la Riviere, one of the world's experts on water, says this: "All signals point to further deterioration in the quality of fresh and marine waters unless aggressive management programs are instituted."

For Iowa? I'm hopeful, reasonably optimistic, because of the groundwater legislation passed by the 1987 General Assembly and because of the attention that water quality receives in Iowa. The possible long-term contamination of our aquifers and the irreversibility of groundwater contamination are worrisome, though. It may be that the greatest threat to Iowa's water is on the supply side, based on forecasted changes in the world's climate.

THE ATMOSPHERE

The so-called greenhouse effect has become news. Though it may not be any more damaging to the human prospect than a dying off of zooplankton in the ocean or the decline in genetic diversity, which is to say it could be very damaging, it has a certain cachet to it. It's big, it's out there, we'll be able to feel it, and so forth. Because of the climate's daily impact on them, people pay attention when someone starts talking about climate change. Zooplankton seem further removed.

In Chapter Two, I mentioned that worries about the effects of human activity on the climate go back a century or more. But two events have recently raised the profile of this possibility. First, three years in the 1980s were the warmest years on record (1988, 1987, and 1981, in that order). These high temperatures, coupled with severe drought conditions in the American Midwest, propelled an interest in possible climate change. The second development is the availability of large-scale computers capable of handling the huge number of variables, parameters, and computations needed to model atmospheric conditions.*

These models consistently forecast a warming of the earth due to an increase in carbon dioxide and trace gases (such as chlorofluorocarbons, nitrous oxides, methane, and low-level ozone), which act very much like the glass in a greenhouse—that is, heat from the sun is allowed through, but the glass prevents some of the heat from reflecting back into space. We've always had the greenhouse effect; it's one of the conditions that makes life on earth possible. The worry is that human production and consumption activities are increasing the heat-retaining properties of the atmosphere with the consequence that the temperature of the earth will rise.

The range of human activities producing a possible increase in earth's warming is large, *profoundly* large. Fifty percent comes from carbon dioxide emissions, which in turn come from the burning of fossil

---

*"Parameter" is a term that generally refers to a *fixed* value in model building, a limit or boundary condition taken as given by the model builder, rather than something allowed to vary. In atmospheric modeling, it means, in the simplest terms, a mathematical coefficient that does not change as the model is manipulated, but influences the outcome of the model, such as $5X$, where 5 is the coefficient. As X changes in value due to cause-and-effect relationships within the model, it gets multiplied by 5, where 5 is a parameter. Thus, X might represent air temperature. If an increase in air temperature is believed to increase the amount of water vapor in the air, and water vapor in turn increases air temperature, 5 is the parameter that shows that if X increases, it will increase even more due to the feedback effect of water vapor. (The figures here are hypothetical, not actual.)

fuels within which the carbon is stored. Driving a car, using a wood stove or fireplace, burning yard leaves, operating factories and utilities with fossil fuels — all of these, and dozens of other everyday human undertakings release stored carbon in the form of carbon dioxide.

The other fifty percent of the problem comes from the trace gases noted above. Rice paddies are huge methane generators, with the plants acting as conduits for methane contained in mud (swamp gas). Apparently so are the stomachs of grass-eating animals (estimates are that our cows, sheep, goats, pigs, horses, camels, bullocks, and so forth belch seventy-three million metric tons of methane each year, a 435 percent increase since the turn of the century).

Then, as if we already don't have enough to worry about, we have termites. The methane excretion from a single termite mound may be in the range of five liters a minute, and there is roughly a half-ton of termites for every person on the planet. (I've provided several easily accessible references for further reading, so I'll not belabor the causes of the greenhouse effect here.)

How much do we really know about the warming of the earth? As I said before, atmospheric scientists tend to agree on this much:

1. There will be some warming.
2. The exact amount is not known.
3. The timing is not known.

A model constructed by Stephen Schneider, of the National Center for Atmospheric Research, indicates a doubling of carbon dioxide in the atmosphere sometime in the next century. The projected effect is a warming of the earth's average surface temperature by between 3.0 and 5.5 degrees Celsius in a period of from ten to one hundred years. Other large-scale computer models approximate Schneider's findings.

Some disagree violently with the forecasts based on Schneider's model and those similar to it. The disagreements, however, are mostly about magnitude and timing, not whether there will be a change.

Of course, modeling a system of the size and complexity of earth's atmosphere is fraught with problems. By necessity, the models are coarse, in the sense that every detail cannot be taken into account. Fundamentally, these models are based on points within a three-dimensional grid, where the points are several hundred kilometers apart horizontally and several meters apart vertically. The points represent climate, and the values of these points are the result of the model's computations.

The number of variables and their ranges is huge, the number of elements held constant is myriad, and the fastest computers available take many hours to run one version of the model, even as the computations flash along in nanoseconds. Then there are the possible feedback effects, which add even more complications. An example I've mentioned before is the possibility that an increase in global temperature will cause increases in oceanic evaporation, putting more water vapor into the air and increasing further the warming effect. Or the result could be just the opposite: more evaporation from the ocean will cause more clouds, causing a cooling effect.

Irving Mintzberg, of the World Resources Institute, has generated three scenarios he believes describe the possibilities inherent in the greenhouse effect (cited by Bill McKibben in *The End of Nature*). First is the business-as-usual case, where the conventional wisdom dominates. This is Mintzberg's base-case scenario, with a continued emphasis on economic growth, a search for technological fixes of the blind-faith type, and a general muddling around with the global energy system. As part of this, he assumes nations lag in their encouragement of energy conservation and development of renewable alternative fuels. Result: Average global warming of up to 4.7 degrees Fahrenheit by the year 2000 and up to 8.5 degrees Fahrenheit by 2030.

His next scenario assumes all of the attitudes and actions in the base case but also includes encouragement of the use of coal and synthetic fuels with polluting properties, plus continued tropical deforestation. Here Mintzberg forecasts average global temperature increases of up to 12.6 degrees Fahrenheit by 2030 and a nearly 30-degree climb by 2075. The results of this are unimaginable; the end of just about everything is a reasonable guess.

Even with Mintzberg's slow-buildup scenario, the outlook is not bright. This third set of assumptions involves strong international efforts to reduce emissions and stabilize the atmosphere, dramatic increases in the prices of fossil fuels, government emphasis on solar energy, and massive reforestation efforts. Result: If all of these efforts had begun by 1980, which they did not, a warming of between 2.5 degrees and 7.6 degrees Fahrenheit by 2075, which still would be greater than anything recorded in human history.

What about Iowa? Remember, the big computer models are coarse, not surgical enough to make accurate predictions about comparatively local conditions. Still, some projections have been made by tinkering with the models in such a way that agricultural and local climatic data are inserted into them. One, reported in *Nature,* the prestigious British scientific journal, foresees possible benefits for midwestern farmers, including crop-yield increases due to carbon dioxide escalation that more than offset declines due to higher temperatures.

Under this scenario, disaster befalls farmers in the southern United States, and more irrigation will be needed overall. In addition, it's expected that grain farming will move steadily north into regions such as Minnesota and Michigan. In general, American agriculture comes out looking pretty good in this forecast.

But the uncertainties still are massive. Under the assumption that atmospheric carbon dioxide doubles by 2035, the study projects an average annual temperature increase of eight to nine degrees Fahrenheit by that year. Do we have enough water for a large-scale increase in irrigation? What about the thin, glacial soils of Minnesota and Michigan, particularly the need to use large amounts of fertilizers to sustain increased farming, if the climate moves north?

Given the potential catastrophic effects of such a large rise in temperature, what about the rest of the United States? A redistribution of climate is a redistribution of resources and, hence, involves ethical dimensions. Can Iowa prosper in the midst of the chaos that such a large escalation in temperature surely will bring? What about heat waves during the critical pollinating time for corn?

The study just cited deals with carbon dioxide, but what about the influence of trace gases, which cause the other 50 percent of the warming trend? What about increases in air conditioning and the demand for electricity? Will the higher temperatures result in severe droughts? Will violent storms, including hail, offset the increased yields that are projected? Will far-reaching and severe measures by the federal government to combat the warming effect result in fuel rationing or limitations on driving or extremely high fuel prices? All of these will impact on Iowa in profound ways.

Other studies have indicated negative effects on the Midwest from global warming, such as increased probability of extreme, short-term heat waves, which may come at critical times in the crop cycle. Des Moines was one of eighteen sites in ten states studied by researchers at Michigan State University. With an assumed doubling of carbon dioxide, increases in average temperatures during the growing season are projected to be between 6.3 degrees and 14.4 degrees Fahrenheit at Des Moines over the next few decades, but precipitation changes are projected as minimal. Lower yields in both corn and soybeans are expected. The increased carbon dioxide, in this model, did not compensate for the decreased crop life cycles caused by the higher temperatures.

The Michigan scientists also believe the Corn Belt will shift north, with the implication that Iowa may need to consider new crops or at least new hybrids of existing crops. Other possibilities involve impacts on physical, chemical, and biological processes in the soil due to shorter freezing periods in winter and hotter soil temperatures in other seasons. The list goes on.

Humans, in general, dislike uncertainty or ambiguity. That's why we use contracts for just about all of our financial matters. If we're troubled by a rather free-floating future, global warming and its possibilities will not please us. When atmospheric shifts are combined with potential water shortages, erosion and other insults to the soil, a growing world population, and the rest of our dilemmas, the level of uncertainty rockets to unprecedented levels. Then there's the problem of biodiversity.

BIODIVERSITY

Biologist Thomas Foose calls them "riders of the last ark." The riders in that haunting phrase are those animals and plants that probably are not going to make it through what is now being called the largest mass extinction ever, without help from devices such as zoos. Humans are altering the natural environment to an extent that biological diversity is plummeting to its lowest level since the end of the Mesozoic era, sixty-five million years ago. As we blithely go about our daily business, we are destroying the biota (the earth's flora and fauna, collectively) at an unbelievable rate.

From his studies of tropical areas, Edward Wilson estimates that four thousand to six thousand species per year are being lost due to deforestation alone. He considers this calculation "very conservative." Norman Meyers, an environmental consultant, projects that by the end of this century, the rate will be one hundred species *per day* worldwide. The rate in 1974 was a laggardly one hundred per year (estimated), though even that figure is of blurring speed compared with natural rates of extinction.

By any reckoning, these figures represent virtually an instantaneous mass extinction, measured in geological time, and is far worse than the mass extinction that removed perhaps 75 percent of the earth's species, including the dinosaurs, 65 million years ago. As biologist Les Kaufman says: "Our species, then, is on the brink of causing, single-handedly, the worst mass extinction in 65 million years. The very species that provide, or might provide, a rich harvest of medicines, foods, fuels, raw materials, and even climate regulation are being driven into extinction, forever beyond our reach."

So what? Humans are doing all right, aren't they? Suppose you take that anthropocentric view. If you care only about survival of the human species, then worrying about biodiversity is the place to start, in spite of all that's been said so far about other environmental problems. The fact is this: We do not know how many species exist; therefore, we do not know what they are and what their roles might be in the great interlocked systems of ecology (this is true even for those we have identified); thus, we do not know to what extent other species provide crucial support for human existence. Remember the marine bacteria that provide an important function in balancing Earth's oxygen supply?

The problem of species extinction can be viewed from four different perspectives. First, there is the moral issue: What right do we humans have to cause another species to cease existence? The aesthetic dimension is a second concern: Most of us enjoy the rich variety of biota that nature offers us.

Third is the matter of economics: The fact is that we depend on biological diversity for all manner of necessities, not the least of which is a backup system for crop failures. In 1970, a fungus well-suited to a particular genetic trait of most of the hybrid seed corn planted in the Corn Belt reduced yields by 15 percent. A substitute seed was found, and the problem was solved.

Historically, humans have made use of some seven thousand species of plants for food. Today, we rely on fewer than twenty for most of our needs. It's estimated, however, that seventy-five thousand known plants are fully or partially edible. And some of them are remarkable.

For example, Wilson calls the winged bean, which is found in New Guinea, "a one-species supermarket." He says this about it: "The entire plant—roots, seeds, leaves, stems and flowers—is edible, and a coffelike beverage can be made from its juice. It grows rapidly, reaching a height of 15 feet in a few weeks, and has a nutritional value equal to that of soybeans." When I watch bulldozers plowing through forests on the evening news, I sometimes think of that plant and wonder how many others like it are being lost forever under the steel blade and grinding treads.

Wild plants and animals also provide or are potential providers of useful products, such as oils and fibers. One-fourth of the medicines we use come from tropical plants. Some 1,400 such species have been identified as containing substances active against cancer. The rosy periwinkle of Madagascar yields alkaloids effective in the treatment of Hodgkin's disease and acute lymphocytic leukemia, generating revenues of $100 million a year. There are many other such examples. And the metal treads keep on churning.

The fourth perspective from which biodiversity can be viewed is that of ecology: We just don't know very much about nature's complexity and where the critical linkages are in the vast ecological webs that surround us. One metaphor in the literature is that of a brick wall. We remove a brick here, another there, but the wall continues to stand. At some point, however, we may remove a brick in the lower part of the wall that's absolutely crucial for the maintenance of so-called higher life forms, including humans.

As paleontologic evidence clearly shows, those species high up in the scientific hierarchy of life forms are just as vulnerable to extinction as those further down. It's likely that the disappearance of the dinosaurs and other large reptiles made it possible for humans to be here at all, by providing an opportunity for mammals to flourish in an environment that formerly had been dominated by the big folks.

The loss of biodiversity is the ultimate irreversibility (a subject I addressed earlier in the book). In spite of claims made by some biotechnologists, it's unlikely we can retrieve lost life forms through laboratory means. Gone is gone. "Extinct" has the ring of forever. Dozens of plants and creatures are lost every day, and the richness of life on our planet slides toward impoverishment, while we worry about what Cher is wearing to the Academy Awards ceremonies.

Zoologists fret about creatures such as the snail darter or the blue spotted salamander or the starfish, while allegedly practical people, such as developers, laugh at such patent foolishness in light of "human progress." The laughter will start to fade soon. Maybe it will cease altogether. The twin prongs of climate change and habitat destruction are pinching out the life surrounding us. Just who's in charge of funeral services is not clear.

Where does Iowa fit in the biodiversity scheme? Remember that Crosson and Rosenberg listed the decline of such diversity as one of three major problems that must be overcome if world food production is to be maintained at adequate levels. Furthermore, Iowans are subject to the same potential catastrophes as other humans, and no one knows where the critical bricks are in the vast ecological structures within which we exist.

In fact, it's complexity that is our most fearsome opponent, if we consider "complexity" to mean situations with large numbers of elements subtly and intricately related to one another. Any one of the problems discussed in this chapter is staggeringly complex within itself. But obviously, these problems are merely subsets of a very large problem—the natural environment—and we talk about them as individual problems simply for convenience.

As the number of elements in a situation increases, so does the number of possible relationships among them that must be identified and studied if the system is to be completely understood. As an illustration, a system with only two elements has basically two possible cause-and-effect linkages. If A is one element and B is the second, A can impact on B, or B can impact on A, or both impacts can occur. In a system of three elements, the number of possible impacts rises to six. With four elements, the number increases to twelve, and five elements form a system with twenty possibilities. The numbers not only increase, but increase geometrically.

In attempting to understand big systems (or even relatively small ones, for that matter), researchers deal with very large numbers of elements and, hence, an incredibly high degree of complexity. The level of complexity rockets upward as subproblems—energy, food, water, the atmosphere, biodiversity—are brought together into ever more inclusive models. But identifying connections among elements is only one part of the effort. When a connection has been established, the next task is to determine at least an approximate value for how much A affects B. Finally, there's the problem of dynamics, of time. If A affects B by such and such an amount, over what time period does this occur, and what is the overall result of the weights and times in systems comprising thousands of elements?

The lack of scientific knowledge in each of the areas discussed thus far is frightening, because we are trying to drive a vehicle called Earth at high speed through a heavy rainstorm without windshield wipers. Scientists are not stupid; rather they are overwhelmed by complexity and a lack of time and funding to assault complexity. We have been more concerned over the years with producing improved toilet-bowl cleansers than with funding scientific inquiry into the operations of our planetary systems.

Iowa will be affected by each of the problems discussed here. Perhaps we will be affected profoundly by one of them or all of them acting together. (Later on, I'll talk about how Iowans can become part of the solution to the global problematique and develop ourselves at the same time. For now, the prudent person should feel, as I do, humbled by the enormity of the problems we confront and the comparative lack of knowledge we have about these problems.)

Chief Seattle, of the Duwamish and Allied Tribes of Puget Sound, said this in 1855: "Whatever happens to the beasts soon happens to man. All things are connected." Post that on your refrigerator door just below the note that says, "40,000 children die every day."

EVOLVING DIETARY HABITS

Meat production is a major industry in Iowa, and the slightest mention of lowering meat consumption in our diets drives cattle and hog producers into a frenzy. There are issues of livelihood and life-style at stake (a bad pun, and unintentional), and meat producers react angrily. That's understandable, even though the pro-meat rhetoric gets somewhat emotionally charged and overblown at times, as do the anti-meat arguments.

Nonetheless, some forces at work out there are proving to be inimical to the meat-production industry. As much as it may anger Iowa meat producers, they should pay careful attention to the changing dietary patterns of America and, eventually, the world. It's clear to me that people are beginning to substitute nonanimal for animal-based products in their diet. I expect this trend to continue and accelerate.

The medical arguments and environmental constraints (the water consumption and the clearing of rain forests needed to produce beef, along with the energy problems mentioned earlier) leading people in this direction are formidable, perhaps inexorable. Just as convincing are the data showing the inefficiencies, in terms of resource consumption, of a meat-based diet. For example, it takes approximately five pounds of grain to produce a pound of beef, along with 375 gallons of fresh water. Anyone truly concerned about a hungry world in the future will probably look elsewhere than to meat production for sustainable food supplies. This is a real threat to Iowa, a major contingency for the state's economy. (I discuss this again in Chapter 10 in terms of opportunities for Iowa.)

DEMOGRAPHICS

A 1988 report by the U.S. Census Bureau projected a decrease of 300,000 people in Iowa by the year 2000. This forecast, in a state with less than 3 million people, caused shrieks of panic from the state's industrial captains and government officials. The 1990 census results indicate Iowa's population declined by roughly 126,000 in the 1980s. Preliminary estimates from the 1990 census place Iowa in thirtieth place among the states (thirty-first if Puerto Rico is counted). Forty years ago we were twenty-second; since 1980, we have dropped three steps in the rankings.

Absolute numbers are one thing; patterns within those numbers are something quite different and are even more frightening, to anyone worried about population loss and the permanence of Iowa as it now exists. First, most of the loss has occurred in people of childbearing age and in children, who eventually will grow up to be parents. Second, rural areas have suffered a disproportionate amount of the loss.

Iowa State University sociologist Willis Goudy writes about Iowa demographics, "Growth and decline are regional; there is nothing random about the pattern of population change across the map of Iowa." One piece of data that is especially indicative is this: In 1980, only two Iowa counties had more deaths than births; in 1988, there were thirty-seven such counties.

Further concern is generated by the relatively large number of well-educated people who leave Iowa, a phenomenon popularly known as the "brain drain."

People tend to wrongly equate an increasing population with progress. But a stable or slightly declining population has its advantages — space, less competition for resources such as water, less need for social services, and so forth. Unfortunately, the pattern of Iowa's population loss also holds the prospect of unpleasant consequences, for example, fewer working young people to support the needs of the elderly, labor shortages in key industries, and voting patterns that may work against the needs of younger people. (I'll return to this problem of demographics later on with some suggestions.)

FOR FURTHER READING

Energy

Berry, R. Stephen. "Our Energy Future: Time Horizons and Instability." *Environment,* July/August 1989, pp. 5, 43–44.

Coates, Joseph F., and Jennifer Jarratt. *What Futurists Believe.* Bethesda, Md.: The World Future Society, 1989.

Council for Agricultural Science and Technology. *Energy Use and Production in Agriculture.* Report 99. Ames, Ia.: Center for Agricultural Science and

Technology, February 1984, pp. 50–51. (Cited in Gever, 1986) *Beyond Oil,* Cambridge, Mass.: Ballinger, 1986.

Crow, Michael M. "American Fuel Policy Is Running On Empty." *Des Moines Register,* August 20, 1989, p. 3C.

Gever, John, et al. *Beyond Oil.* Cambridge, Mass.: Ballinger, 1986.

Gibbons, John H., Peter D. Blair, and Holly L. Gwin. "Strategies for Energy Use." *Scientific American,* September 1989, pp. 136–43.

Kerr, Richard A. "Oil and Gas Estimates Plummet." *Science,* September 22, 1989, pp. 1330–31.

Lovins, Amory B., and L. Hunter Lovins. "The Avoidable Oil Crisis." *Atlantic,* December 1987, pp. 22–30.

Lynch, Michael. "The Next Oil Crisis." *Technology Review,* November/December 1987, pp. 38, 40–45, 66.

Martin, Randy. "Solar Energy." *Iowa Conservationist,* June 1988, pp. 18–21.

Renner, Michael. "Rethinking Transportation." *State of the World.* Worldwatch Institute, 1989.

Robbins, John. *A Diet for a New America.* Walpole, N.H.: Stillpoint, 1987.

Schoonmaker, David. "Thoughts on the Next Oil Crisis." *Mother Earth News,* November/December 1988, p. 10.

Udall, James R. "Amory Lovins: Walking the Soft Path." *Sierra,* January/February 1990, pp. 128–33.

———. "Turning Down the Heat." *Sierra,* July/August 1989, pp. 26–33.

World Commission on Economic Development. *Energy 2000.* London: Zed Books, 1987.

Food

Batie, Sandra S., and Robert G. Healy. "The Future of American Agriculture." *Scientific American,* February 1983, pp. 45–53.

Berry, Wendell. *The Unsettling of America.* San Francisco: Sierra Club, 1986.

Brown, Lester R. "Reexamining the World Food Prospect." *State of the World 1989.* New York: W. W. Norton, 1989.

Crosson, Pierre R., and Norman J. Rosenberg. "Strategies for Agriculture." *Scientific American,* September 1989, pp. 128–35.

Delp, Charles J. "Hunger—When There Is so Much Food." *Bioscience,* April 1986, p. 233.

Helmuth, John W. "World Hunger Amidst Plenty." *USA Today,* March 1989, pp. 48–50.

Hendry, Peter. "The New Causes of World Hunger." *The Futurist,* September/October 1988, p. 49.

Water

Fawcett, Richard S. "Pesticides in Groundwater—Solving the Right Problem." *Iowa Groundwater Association Newsletter,* December 1988, pp. 1, 3–4.

Groundwater Protection News, March 1988. Published as a cooperative effort by the Iowa Department of Natural Resources, Iowa Department of Agriculture and Land Stewardship, Iowa Department of Public Health, and the Iowa Board of Regents and associated institutions.

Hubert, Cynthia, and Veronica Fowler. "Concerned Iowans Taking Steps to Combat Tainted Water Supplies." *Des Moines Register,* June 3, 1990, pp. 1A, 6A.

Maurits la Riviere, J. W. "Threats to the World's Water." *Scientific American,* September 1989, pp. 80–94.

"Oceans and Coasts." *World Resources 1987.* New York: Basic Books, 1987, pp. 125–42.

The Atmosphere

Bean, Larry L., and Patricia S. Cale. *Global Climate Change—Implications for Energy Policy in Iowa.* Des Moines: Iowa Department of Natural Resources, 1989.

Detjen, Jim. "The Greenhouse Effect May Be Good for Farms." *Des Moines Register,* May 17, 1990, pp. 1A, 7A.

McKibben, Bill. *The End of Nature.* New York: Random House, 1989.

Santiago, Frank. "Greenhouse Effect Might Sizzle Iowa." *Des Moines Register,* November 8, 1987, pp. 1A, 11A.

Schneider, Stephen H. "The Changing Climate." *Scientific American,* September 1989, pp. 70–79.

Biodiversity

Kaufman, Les, and Kenneth Mallory. *The Last Extinction.* Cambridge, Mass.: MIT Press, 1986.

Waller, Robert James. "My Name Is Orange Band." In *One Good Road Is Enough,* by Robert James Waller. Ames: Iowa State University Press, 1990.

Wilson, Edward O. "Threats to Biodiversity." *Scientific American,* September 1989, pp. 108–16.

CHAPTER NINE

Development

Both the SRI and DED development plans (summarized and critiqued in Chapter Seven) contain a number of useful economic development ideas. Some of these will surface again in Chapter Ten where emerging opportunities for Iowa are surveyed. But some issues were omitted in the SRI and DED documents and other criticisms require elaboration.

THE FOLK WISDOM OF ECONOMIC DEVELOPMENT

Conventional Quantitative Measures of Economic Well-Being

The conventional lore of economic development contains a fair amount of what might be called folk wisdom. In many cases, interestingly enough, these beliefs are merely assumptions, many of which run counter to the logic and data of economics. Nonetheless, the folk wisdom persists and influences economic development efforts.

Even when these efforts appear to be succeeding, the quantitative data used to justify the efforts, generated by the efforts themselves, can lead us into traps. The folk wisdom of economic development may not only mislead, but also have unintended, negative consequences.

An increase in Iowans' per capita income is a central objective stated in the DED reports. That sounds good; everybody likes higher incomes.

Moreover, much of the current discussion surrounding economic development in Iowa emphasizes the importance of attracting high-wage jobs to the state. So the DED is in the mainstream of economic development thinking on this issue.

But wages or salaries do not exist separately from other elements. Business firms are not beneficent enterprises that gaze at deserving workers and calculate some "just wage" based on that. Business profit is computed by subtracting costs from revenues. Labor is a cost. Therefore, it's in the interest of managers to hold down labor costs. One has only to look at the movement of plants to states and countries where labor costs are low to understand this.

Why, then, would a firm pay higher wages and salaries? One reason is the cost of living. In other words, if people are considering an alternative area in which to live and work, one criterion for their choice is the comparison of earnings to the cost of living. If firms are to attract the type and quantity of labor required, wages and salaries must be competitive. And so high wages and salaries may be nothing more than a signal that the cost of living is high in a particular area, while lower wages and salaries may indicate the reverse. In short, high per capita income by itself is not a good indicator of economic well-being.

Furthermore, people move to areas for reasons other than pure monetary income. Climate and scenic beauty are examples. A state or area may attract people willing to work for less money because of locally available nonmonetary factors, yet judgments based solely on wage and salary levels will indicate the area is economically inferior.

Another example where quantitative data can lead us awry is the amount of gross business activity—a local or state GNP, so to speak. Flaws in our computations of such figures (see Chapter Four) can badly overstate how well or poorly an area is doing. Degradation of the natural environment, for example, is not shown as a cost deducted from measures of gross business activity. Therefore the general quality of life can be falling dramatically even while retail sales figures are rising.

In addition, if the sales are being made by chains with corporate headquarters located outside of Iowa, a substantial portion of the revenue generated is flowing elsewhere. And this firm likely has a large amount of its goods manufactured elsewhere in the United States or abroad, which does not benefit local residents. About the only advantage accruing to locals from such firms is the low-wage employment of clerks and the salaries paid to resident managers. Wal-Mart, Target, Kmart, and the like are capable of generating huge amounts of revenues while returning only a small portion to the communities in which they are located.

Measures of well-being based on gross income have similar problems. If business firms expand and more workers are required, it's probable that some, perhaps a majority, of these workers will come from outside the area. Thus gross income can be rising without any benefit to the original residents of the area.

In 1984, Flat Rock, Michigan, under pressure from the state of Michigan, was obliged to offer the Mazda Motor Corporation a fifteen-year, $40 million property tax break as part of an incentive package designed to attract the Japanese automaker to the area. Mazda chose Flat Rock and then imported most of its workers from elsewhere. The result? Wildly escalating tax bills and little employment for the original citizens of Flat Rock.

All right, how about per capita income? That's a popular index for indicating economic opulence. The DED claims, "The best single measure of our standard of living is Iowa's performance in terms of real per capita income—the amount of income per person, after controlling for the effects of inflation." Even this measure contains potential flaws similar to the other indicators just discussed.

The extreme case would be the per capita income of skilled construction workers building a pipeline in arctic wastelands. The per capita income would be high, but only because high wages must be paid to attract workers. Thus a high per capita income in an area can indicate there is something wrong with that area, something that requires firms to pay high wages to lure workers.

Therefore, economic development measures based on sheer quantitative data can be misleading—in fact, downright wrong—as indicators of how well an area is doing. Cheers from governors, mayors, and Chamber of Commerce officials following increases in quantitative figures such as wage rates, gross output, gross income, per capita income, and real per capita income ought to be met with considerable skepticism.

Economic development is supposedly designed to improve the well-being of those already living in an area. The pertinent question to ask when examining conventional quantitative measures of economic success is this: Are the original residents better off than they were before? If not, then why economic development?

Business Recruitment and Retention

Cities and states long have engaged in battles to lure large industrial firms. Over a hundred years ago, various local subsidies were offered to railroads in an attempt to get rail service. Hundreds of cities eventually defaulted on the financial instruments they used to generate these subsidies. In the 1980s, it all began again in earnest.

Free land, building sewers and roads for a plant, tax abatements, tax-increment financing, and other inducements have been offered in an orgy of industrial recruitment.* Basically, the incentives fall into one of three categories: (1) customized job training, (2) direct financial assistance (such as reduced utility charges or providing infrastructure needed by a firm), and (3) tax incentives.

All of these have the same objective, which is to reduce the cost of doing business in the state. Frequently, only the most rudimentary estimates of costs versus benefits and cash flows from projects have been made, and a fair amount of these estimates have been dead wrong, ludicrously so.

It can get pretty weird. For instance Toledo, Ohio, basically paid $125,000 per job in incentives to attract a commuter airline. The staggering Prairie Meadows racetrack near Des Moines is another example. The track was financed using $42 million in industrial-development bonds, and its well-publicized difficulties have become a burden on Polk County. Plenty of other similar examples exist. Nationally, state and local incentives to business now exceed $30 billion a year.

What's odd about all this is that communities make investments to lure firms that business managers would never make. Little analysis has been done, in many cases, of the magnitude, timing, and risk attached to cash flows from tax revenues intended for debt service. Moreover, until recently firms and developers being offered inducements have not been asked for any quid pro quos from their end. For example, it's reasonable to demand that any financial incentives offered be repaid to a city if the firm decides to leave town before bonds used to create the incentives have been retired. Even then, the deal may at best be a breakeven proposition for the city.

Before Iowa communities or the state government put up front-end money, the three cash-flow factors mentioned earlier (timing, magnitude, and risk) ought to be carefully analyzed. It's exactly what banks do when considering a loan application, but in their eagerness to attract

---

*Tax-increment financing arrangements (TIFs) involve the use of bonds issued to finance a redevelopment district in a city. The city estimates the tax revenues it expects the district to generate over, say, a twenty-five year period, then borrows against the projections. Taxes generated by the project are used to pay off the bonds, with nothing going to the city treasury until the bonds are retired. Technically, federal regulations restrict the use of TIFs to blighted urban areas; however, cities have circumvented this requirement by various means.

jobs, any jobs, governments and communities have been imprudent analysts of such matters.

At least four more questions should also be asked. *Who* will benefit from the inducements? *Who* will pay for them? *When* will the costs of the inducements be incurred? *When* will the benefits start to flow?

The proponents of high-risk development projects tend to be those who will benefit from them—developers and merchants. These potential beneficiaries obviously are in favor of, for example, requests that citizens pony up money in the form of property taxes to support a project. On the other hand, citizens have a right (and responsibility) to examine how they may benefit or suffer from the arrangement.

Vague expressions of, "Everybody will benefit from this" are not enough. If the advantages flow to the merchant class, workers hired from outside the community, and distant corporations, there is no reason for other local people to subsidize business recruitment. Furthermore, if the proposition is such that no tax revenues will flow into the community until bonds are retired in twenty-five years, the question of who benefits gets even murkier.

It's not that localities and states should never engage in incentives to business. Such projects, however, should be approached with the same careful scrutiny that sophisticated business analysts use in their investment calculations. If such care is exercised in these kinds of decisions, the initial enthusiasm for recruiting a business firm likely will dim in many cases as hard-headed analysis is carried out.

A fair amount of smoke-and-mirrors rhetoric often accompanies government incentive programs. Estimates tend to be overly optimistic and politically motivated, if not downright misleading. For example, the new laser research center at the University of Iowa, which may or may not be a good investment for the state, was sold on the basis that it would cost $25 million to construct and that it would provide 10,000 to 12,000 jobs for Iowans.

But the $25 million is just the face amount of the bonds issued for the project. When interest on the bonds is included, the final cost will probably be somewhere in the range of $50 to $60 million. Yet all articles, speeches, and hoopla about the center use the $25 million figure.

After financing for the laser project had been approved, questions about the source of the estimate for the number of jobs were raised. It turns out that the figure was generated by using a forecast from a *Newsweek* article some years earlier that contained some loose-jointed forecasts of high-technology jobs in the United States. This rather shaky number was then multiplied by Iowa's percentage of the U.S. population. The kindest description I can think of for this kind of salesmanship, which was carried out by university scientists, is disingenuous.

Understand, I hope the laser facility is a howling success. What I don't like, and never have liked, are the crafty methods used by university officials to sell the concept.* In all such cases where public funds are being used to finance projects, optimistic estimates provided by developers and the direct beneficiaries of the projects should be carefully scrutinized, if not heavily discounted as a matter of course.

In our past efforts to recruit new businesses, the cheapest and most certain approach to job generation has been overlooked. That is encouragement of businesses already established in Iowa. If we're going to ask potential businesses, "What can we do for you?" we ought to at least be asking the same of firms that long have been job generators in Iowa. These latter businesses have had to stand by and watch lucrative incentives being provided to new firms, some of which will be in direct competition to existing firms. It's not fair, it's short-sighted, and most of all, it's a dumb way to generate jobs.

As a former university dean, I used to talk a lot about what I called "internal recruitment," which simply meant paying at least as much attention to the good people already in place as was being lavished on faculty being recruited. Jim Flansburg, columnist for the *Register,* calls these kinds of activities "preventive maintenance." In other words, "remember to dance with who brung ya."

In fairness to Iowa, however, it should be noted that we have devoted resources to industrial retention. The form in which budgets are prepared and the number of economic development programs under way make it difficult to determine just what proportion has gone to retention versus recruitment. As one example, though, out of 267 grants made under the Community Economic Betterment Awards program from May 1986 to December 1990, 174 are listed as "expansion," 49 as "start-up," and 44 as "recruitment," leaving zero for retention. If "expansion" is considered "retention," the figures look much better.

Finally, it should be noted that the various incentive programs designed to attract and retain business tend to have certain biases built into them. In particular, there seems to be a bias against small, rural communities.

---

*See my article, "Lasers, Dreams, and Real Money," for a critical analysis of the process by which the laser center was sold. The article was originally published in the *Des Moines Register* at the time the Center was being pushed through the Iowa Legislature.

Demographics Revisited

The folk wisdom surrounding quantitative measures of economic well-being also operates in Iowa's thinking about demographic shifts. It's difficult, in fact, to separate the two topics. The presumption is that economic development providing more and better job opportunities will accomplish at least two demographic objectives: (1) people will choose to stay in Iowa or to move here; (2) we can keep the kids at home, which includes cessation of the so-called "brain drain" of relatively well-educated young people who leave the state after receiving their educations. A fair amount of empirical evidence exists showing that neither of these objectives can be accomplished by focusing only on job opportunities and neglecting other factors.

Decisions to move to or from a locality are just that—decisions. More, they are multiple-criteria decisions; people make location decisions based on a number of measures, only two of which are job opportunities and wage rates. Thomas Power has provided a simple framework for thinking about such choices that fits nicely with the multiple-criteria framework presented in Chapter Three.

$$\text{Total real income to individual} = \frac{\text{Locally available wage levels}}{\text{Local cost of goods and services}} + \text{Value of nonmarketed locally available qualities of the living environment}$$

Think back for a moment to how alternatives can be scored in terms of criteria. Here, the alternatives are various locations in which one might choose to live. The criteria are those terms on the right-hand side of the equation. (The left-hand side merely represents a summation of the scoring of an alternative relative to the criteria.)

Thus an individual considers a specific alternative (for example, to stay in Cedar Falls, Iowa) and compares it to other alternatives (such as, move to Denver) on the basis of how well it fares on the criteria relative to other alternatives.

One criterion is "Locally available wage levels" discounted or incremented based on the cost of living in the area. The term "Value of nonmarketed locally available qualities of living environment," includes such things as quality of the natural environment, recreational opportunities (some closely related to the natural environment), locally available educational opportunities, arts and cultural opportunities, condition of housing stock, crime levels, and so forth. All of these latter elements are criteria.

Again, think back to the multiple-criteria model. Alternatives are scored against criteria. For example, "Availability of scenic beauty" might be a criterion, as well as the incremented or discounted wage rate. Each alternative is scored on each criterion. The summation of scores for a given alternative is what Power calls, "Total real income to individual."

There is, perhaps, one element missing in Power's model. That is the availability of job opportunities. Possibly this is an absolute, in the language of Chapter Three. That is, before an alternative even makes it into the set of location choices for evaluation, there must be job opportunities available in the area.

Power's equation cast in the form of a multiple-criteria decision model provides a useful way of reflecting on location choices ultimately influencing demographics. Officials concerned with out-migration from Iowa have, in the past, assumed people's location decisions are made on the basis of a single criterion — jobs.

That's oversimplifying things a bit, and those who are concerned about population loss are starting to understand the existence of multiple criteria in people's location decisions. Recent reports have begun stressing quality of life, defined broadly, along with economic factors, when analyzing demographic changes. I believe this is the correct approach.

The existence of job opportunities *is* an important criterion; I'm not denying that. Power cites evidence that "Job opportunities are the one 'narrow' economic variable that analysts have had some success in using to explain population movements into particular areas." But other criteria also play critical roles.

Furthermore, Power believes that creating jobs will not keep the kids at home. This has been and continues to be a major theme of local economic development efforts in Iowa. The folk wisdom holds that if jobs are plentiful, young people will not be forced to look elsewhere for work. At first, that logic seems impeccable. Unfortunately, the data available do not support it.

What data we do have shows this, quoting Power: "Young people, in general, do not leave their hometowns because of lack of jobs or low wages. They leave because they are young, well-educated, curious, and adventuresome." This, of course, runs counter to the folk wisdom, the common belief that jobs will keep the kids around for Sunday dinner at the parental home.

Power again: "Young people who have just finished school are the people with the highest propensity to migrate. They are precisely the people who pay least attention to the availability of jobs and level of wages locally." Incidentally, some studies show that industrialization of a rural area actually increases the rate of out-migration by young people. Why? Industrialization brings about an evolution in cultural attitudes and worldliness of the young, which provides them with the curiosity and courage to see what else is out there.

In summary, Power says this:

> As noble as the impulse is to try to provide job opportunities near home for our young people, the evidence is that it will not have much impact on their tendency to explore the possibilities out there in the rest of the world. What those efforts, if successful, will do is create job opportunities for the children of other distant communities who, in their own trips of exploration happen to migrate through our communities. Job creation to assist our young will not create jobs for our own kids. It will create jobs for someone else's kids. Although that might be nice, it would not appear to have a high priority in any particular community.

Apparently, the best solution to keeping the kids at home is to raise children who are dumb, poorly educated, lack curiosity, and have no sense of adventure.

Not everybody in Iowa is worried about population loss. Some applaud it. And there's a certain rationality to that position. Increasing numbers of people bring with them a set of problems, including overcrowding, crime, and escalating demands for social services. People who prefer low population are not being antiprogress—they just recognize there is no relationship, or perhaps an inverse one, between population and what community leaders like to think of as progress.

Still, even if you're not worried about absolute numbers of people, Iowa's demographic situation is cause for apprehension because of the patterns within it (see Chapter Eight). Iowa is now the second "oldest" state in the nation, behind Florida. The United States as a whole is aging, but Iowa appears to be about fifteen years ahead of the rest of the country. Obviously, a strata of young working people is necessary for the economic vibrancy of a state.

So what's to be done about it? My argument is no different than it was in 1986 when I wrote "Going Soft Upon the Land and Down Along the Rivers," a series of eight essays that first appeared in the *Des Moines Register* the following year. I can summarize that argument in one sentence: Create a place so good that, in making their decisions about location, people will choose to stay or move here.

What this involves, of course, is treating location decisions in a multiple-criteria framework. It involves an understanding that while quantitative economic factors, such as job availability, are important, they are not the only determinant of location decisions. Moreover, as emphasized earlier, the very measures we use in judging economic growth can simultaneously be hiding a deterioration in other critical elements serving as important criteria in location decisions, such as quality of the natural environment.

Here's a strategy. A general tendency is to conduct studies of all kinds without a framework in mind that guides data collection. Then, when the data are collected, what exists are data, nothing more. Iowa might consider the following approach:

1. Think of individual location decisions in a multi-criteria framework.
2. Conduct surveys to discover exactly what criteria people use in determining whether or not to stay in Iowa, or to move here, for that matter. Also, find out how these criteria tend to be ranked and weighted and whether any of them tend to be absolutes.

   (New data collection schemes may not be necessary, since a number of studies along these lines already have been collected. Often, in problem solving, the tendency is to begin with data collection, when data already are available. Gathering data is always a good excuse for putting off hard analysis and policy decisions.)
3. In the same surveys, attempt to discover what alternatives people consider in these decisions and what kind of information they use in generating their alternatives.
4. Then, formulate a marketing strategy for convincing people that Iowa is a good place to live, based on the findings from these surveys. Focus especially on the content of the criteria set, the rankings of the criteria, and the weights assigned to the criteria.

In other words, since location decisions are just that—decisions— organize the effort in a framework based on decision making. People calculate trade-offs, implicitly or explicitly. Often they do this rather poorly. Therefore, if we believe Iowa has some real advantages as a place to live, and it does, we can formulate our strategy in terms of these trade-offs.

A place where people err in computing trade-offs is an excessive focusing on wage and salary levels without fully comprehending the effect of local prices and their impact on spendable income. Standard cost-of-living indices can be used, of course, and should be. But there are more subtle costs attached to living in certain areas. These costs are not usually considered very thoroughly, if at all. I know from experience that university seniors in a large college of business ignore both cost of living and more subtle costs in selecting a job.

One such cost is commuting. A second is the level of crime and violence. Protecting oneself from unpleasantries has its costs, both psychological and financial. A third is the cost of traveling home to visit friends and family. Such costs easily can absorb a salary differential appearing quite sizable when all costs are not taken into account and can have dramatic effects on outcome estimation when alternatives are matched against criteria, that is, how alternatives are scored against criteria.

When viewed separately, the elements of this modest proposal are not news to anyone involved in marketing Iowa as a good place to live. In dealing with citizen retention and recruitment, we already think in these terms, in a vague sort of way. What we ordinarily don't do is to capture the entire strategy in a decision-making framework. Iowa has enough to offer, in spite of its legendary winters, to hold its own in any such analysis. More than that, if the salary-wage differential between Iowa and other locations can be lessened through careful analysis of *all* costs, Iowa looks very good on a number of softer criteria.

One area in which we do not glisten is support for the arts. A second is groundwater purity, though recent legislative measures to protect groundwater should improve conditions eventually. A marketing strategy for the state based on a formal decision model has the advantage of discovering weaknesses, confronting these weaknesses, and devising strategies for overcoming them.

Clearly, people must be aware of alternatives for intelligent decision making. Governor Terry Branstad has proposed the creation of a "job bank" that will provide information on job alternatives in Iowa. This strikes me as a very good idea, one that fits nicely with the decision-making approach sketched in this section.

In addition, Iowans would do well to look at our neighboring states of Minnesota, Wisconsin, and Missouri, along with Kansas. Each of these states has gained population since 1950. Hence, the old arguments about economic difficulties in the Midwest driving people out are open to some challenge, given the experience of these neighboring states with economies similar to Iowa's.

I cannot close this section without mentioning two characteristics damaging Iowa's efforts to attract and retain people. These are a product of my own observations, my own opinion, nothing more.

First, we have a self-imposed sense, an unwarranted one, of inferiority. Where it comes from I'm not sure. But I have heard, over and over again in various forms, Iowans saying to newcomers or prospective immigrants, "Why would you want to come *here?*"

It's a little dance I have come to call the "Iowa Backstep," a shuffling of feet while intoning the lyrics, "Aw, there's not much here and we're not very good" or "I'm just from Iowa." My only conclusion is that Iowans believe what others of superficial sophistication say about us and that we have not traveled enough to understand how many virtues this place of ours possesses.

Second, there is a tendency, and I'm not the only one who has made this observation, to "eat our babies." That is, we seem to view highly successful Iowans with a mixture of envy and something almost akin to hostility. As soon as a person—or a city or a region—begins to exhibit success, we start subtle campaigns to discredit them, to pull them down to a lower level, to applaud, in a way, any warts or weaknesses they may exhibit. I don't know where this attitude comes from, and I don't know what to do about it. But it's there, and it hurts us as a people.

Tastes evolve, life-style preferences change. The coasts are sinking under the success of their own development, because they did not pay attention to quality-of-life considerations. It's possible that Iowa will start to look very good to people fed up with long commutes, crowds, violence, and smog.

One student of such matters, Jack Lessinger, believes there are subtle, long-run demographic tendencies indicating such a migration already is under way. Peter Drucker, the old warhorse of management and futurist thinking, tends to agree. If Lessinger and Drucker are correct, Iowa's problem eventually will be one of handling population growth, not worrying about its decline.

Perhaps, as part of our population recruitment efforts, we should refocus our marketing thrust. If we are bent on providing first-class educations for our young people, and if well-educated young people have a propensity to emigrate from Iowa, then maybe we're targeting the wrong demographic strata in our efforts to encourage people to move here.

It would be worthwhile to construct a profile of those people most likely to want the kind of life-style Iowa offers and direct our attention at them. I suggest this is likely to be a youngish family with children, concerned about a stable social environment and a good educational system.

In our early recruitment efforts at the University of Northern Iowa

College of Business, we found targeting our recruiting efforts at professors fitting this profile a productive way of recruiting. These were people who already had taken one academic job and were dissatisfied, often for social and educational reasons, with their location.

Maybe Iowa should think about a similar profile. We tend to offer a quiet life, whereas young people just graduating from high school or college apparently desire city lights or the equivalent. We might just be trying to attract the wrong people to live in Iowa, and our marketing efforts will be wasted, if this is the case.

Finally, it's important to remember that systems have a way of achieving equilibriums, or at least moving toward them. If people are mobile, which characterizes most of the U.S. population, there will be a tendency for demographics to even out, over time. As population streams into an area, wages and quality-of-life factors tend to decline. Eventually, other places will start looking better and better to those disenchanted with these declines. I think that's what Lessinger and Drucker are saying.

While we're worrying about population loss, Iowans will do well to make sure we are maintaining and improving those elements comprising what Power calls "non-marketed locally available qualities of [the] living environment." In the end, these will make the difference.

(For more detail on the issues of economic development discussed here, as well as other useful material, I highly recommend Thomas Power's book. Power lives in Montana, a state that has experienced many of the same problems Iowa has confronted over the last decade. Overall, it's the best reference I've come across on the general subject of economic development and the fallacies surrounding it in conventional thinking.)

ANOTHER KIND OF DEVELOPMENT

Growing Our Own

Iowa reacted to the economic crisis of the 1980s in the same way as many other states, by launching an embarrassing program of smoke-stack chasing. The idea was — and still is, to some extent — to court large industrial firms by obsequious marketing efforts and a focus on improving local "business climate." The emphasis, always, was on *jobs*. Any jobs.

The real source of new jobs in the United States, however, is not large firms, but rather small businesses, many employing twenty people or less. The consensus seems to be that in the decade of the 1990s, half of all new jobs will be generated by businesses employing less than one hundred people; some put the figure higher than that. From 1980 to 1989, Fortune 500 companies cut 3.5 million jobs. In that same period, small businesses created 20 million new jobs. It's also important to note that female entrepreneurs launch more than half of the new small businesses.

As the state courted outside industry, the owners of locally owned businesses felt neglected, left out of the state's economic development push. They had every right to feel this way, watching grants, low-interest loans, and offers of free or cheap land flowing to outside firms.

There are several things wrong with this type of strategy. First, relatively few large firms are seeking to build new plants at any given time. Hence, with thousands of economic development groups courting them, the probability of landing a new plant is very low. Second, some of these large firms are industrial gypsies who could care less about Iowa or the community in which they are located. Plant managers come and go, profits are transported out of the state to a home office that might be located in Zurich, inputs are purchased from underdeveloped countries, and locals are given the task of final assembly at low wage rates.

Third, and this is something not often recognized by local economic development groups, hooking into large firms, many of them with an international scope, increases a community's vulnerability to national and international economic fluctuations. Fourth (this is closely related to the previous point), one never likes a community's economic structure to be highly dependent on one or two large firms. If conditions dictate that Chrysler close a plant employing 6,500 workers, as it did in Kenosha, Wisconsin, in 1988, the results are devastating. The John Deere staff reductions in Waterloo, Iowa, during the 1980s had a similar effect.

Fifth, large plants are generally seen as providing thousands of assembly-line jobs. But the robots are coming. In 1989, about 30,000 robots were working in U.S. assembly plants. That doesn't seem like a particularly large number, but automation eliminated two-thirds of all assembly-line jobs from 1980 to 1989, according to Marvin Cetron and Owen Davies. They further predict that by the year 2000, 250,000 more robots will replace another 4 million workers.

Sixth, improving the business climate — as it has been defined in the past — usually means giving business what it wants. Providing incentives, in other words. As is obvious, I'm all for an incentive-based approach to things. What I am not in favor of are decreases in local quality of life disguised as incentives.

Economic development officials like to caution locals that being competitive means holding down taxes on business while providing the same or increased levels of services, accepting low wages, enduring environmental degradation, and generally standing around with their hats in their hands hoping that Big Firm will choose them. Once Big Firm has arrived, local residents are continually reminded that the cushy circumstances must be continued, lest the Zurich or Tokyo decision makers decide to close things down. Thus, in the face of overwhelming evidence about the harmful effects of chlorofluorocarbons on the ozone layer, statewide efforts to ban styrofoam containers are trashed by the loss of *jobs* promised by Big Firm manufacturing the containers.

Business people dislike confronting monopoly power on the input side. If you have only one supplier of a key input, you are at the mercy of that supplier. A community depending on one or two large firms for its employment opportunities is in the same situation. The community supplies labor; the large firms supply jobs and wield considerable power by threatening to move or cut back on employment.

Ideally, then, a community's economic development efforts should be focused on the creation of many smaller enterprises, particularly those that can make use of locally produced resources. Looked at another way, the community should move toward becoming more self-contained. Though participating in the global economy—a favorite admonition of economic development cheerleaders—has a certain element of being modern and contemporary attached to it, the more a community is tied in with the global economy, the more it will suffer from economic fluctuations and decisions occurring in distant places.

Moreover, the problem of energy will have profound consequences for Iowa communities. Long commutes, Sunday shopping in the regional malls, and school consolidations involving unceasing travel by yellow school buses all are going to become less attractive as gasoline prices reach and exceed $3 per gallon. Much of our societal decision making is predicated on continuing access to cheap, portable fuels for our vehicles. When such fuels cease to be available, and that is going to occur, we will confront an entire restructuring of the way we carry out our daily affairs. One aspect of this restructuring will be the need for living on a more local basis.

Who, then, will provide the jobs and stores close to home? Partly those small businesses that have managed to survive in spite of the emphasis placed on attracting large firms and the marching orders favoring membership in the global economy. Partly small-business franchises, such as Hardee's and McDonald's and Casey's General Store, that depend on local traffic for their business. Who else? Entrepreneurs.

Several years ago I published an essay in which I predicted that entrepreneurship would be the next great trend in Iowa economic development thinking. I strongly believed I was correct then; I believe it even more strongly now. (The original essay appears as an appendix to this chapter.)

The major points to keep in mind about entrepreneurs are these: (1) they have an idea for a product or service, (2) they generally need capital, and (3) they generally lack good business management skills. Entrepreneurship is a complex mixture of personal vision and personal energy, often combined with technical skills of some kind. Just where and how the entrepreneurial drive arises is not clear. Much of it seems to be a product of personal gifts or environmental nurturing or a combination of the two. Entrepreneurship is difficult to teach. What can be taught, however, are basic management skills necessary for survival of the entrepreneurial enterprise.

One update to the essay is required. A great deal more attention is now being paid to capital generation for entrepreneurial businesses. Such venture capital is still hard to acquire, however, and the DED report discusses this problem in some detail (see Chapter Seven).

In addition, first-class consulting services are an absolute for the beginning entrepreneur, particularly in the areas of sorting through which enterprises have the earmarks of future success and the basic skills necessary for preparing business plans as a prerequisite for attaining capital from banks or venture capitalists. The best of the Small Business Development Centers, which provide free advice to small-business people, are valuable in these tasks of evaluation and skill development.

In sum, while "participate-in-the-global-economy-or-perish" is the currently fashionable dictum, I tend to be less enamored of this approach to economic survival. Obviously certain events in the world economy will influence Iowa's economic health. But to the extent that we encourage self-sufficiency in our communities, and as a state, we can cushion ourselves against the arbitrariness of world economic forces that care nothing for the happiness and economic well-being of Iowans. Each time we plug into the national or global economy, we subject ourselves to fluctuations; the dog surely wags the tail in such cases.

The Content of Economic Growth and Criteria for Development

In the SRI and DED plans, the content of production is not an issue. In fact, virtually all discussions of economic development/growth are couched in terms of magnitude—*more*. But the output of an economy can be judged in light of its content, as well as its magnitude.

For example, we can decide to produce pet rocks or we can choose to produce better hospital care. Economists don't like to talk about such matters. They prefer to take individual tastes as given and to focus on how the price system allocates goods and services based on these tastes. To discuss tastes is to discuss values, and economists long have seen values as lying outside the realm of economic science.

Thus, discussions of economic development appear largely amoral.* *More* is the issue in such plans, not *more of what?* In other words, if it sells and provides employment, it must be good, and the market itself should be the judge. But markets are not capable of moral judgments.

When thinking about the future of Iowa, we should carefully consider the content of our economic output; we should pay attention to the *mix* of goods and services, both private and public, that we strive to produce. In general, we should seek to produce goods and services that lie at the core of human existence, not at the fringes. More than that, we should also examine *how* the goods and services are produced. Put bluntly, we should make moral judgments about what we produce and how we produce it.

As a start, I offer the following criteria. Any firm seeking our applause and perhaps our financial support should meet these criteria. Those that do not should be ignored, if not discouraged, from doing business in Iowa.

1. We should strive to produce goods and services that lie at the core of human existence. We should concentrate on basic human needs and shy away from the trivial and transitory.
2. We should encourage firms whose management is concerned with a sustainable natural environment. As a subcomponent of this criterion, no endangered species and no irreplaceable natural areas should be threatened as a part of Iowa's economic activities. We, as

---

*Notice I said "appear." It's a little more subtle than mere amorality. All discussions of social and economic policy contain values, as I have pointed out previously. The apparent lack of moral judgment about the content of production in economic development plans is, in fact, a moral judgment via abstention. To refrain from making such judgments only implies tacit approval of what is being produced.

citizens, should be prepared to go into the streets, if necessary, to ensure this criterion is met.

3. We should encourage firms whose management treats employees in an enlightened fashion. This includes such matters as employee participation in company decisions, bargaining in good faith with employees, provisions for continued employee training and development, handicapped accessibility, equal employment opportunities, worker safety, and, overall, treating employees as adults.

4. We should encourage firms whose management demonstrates sensitivity to the communities in which they are located. Civic involvement and charitable contributions to community betterment are sub-criteria here.

5. Any firm doing business in Iowa should be expected to pay the full costs of its operation, including all social and environmental costs incurred. Those firms not meeting this criterion should be openly discouraged from operating in the state.

   Most of these costs are obvious, but some are less so. An example of one cost currently ignored is the social cost externalized by telemarketing firms. When my phone rings in the evening, after I have spent a long day working, I am not interested in hearing a pitch for house siding or family portraits or whatever. This constitutes, clearly, an invasion of my privacy, which is a social cost. If such firms are to operate in Iowa, they should agree to solicit only from those people who are willing to be solicited. This restriction eventually will be applied nationwide, in any case, and Iowa should be a leader in all such matters.

6. Product safety should be of utmost concern to firms producing goods or services in Iowa.

7. Other things being approximately equal, we should support and encourage businesses that decrease our vulnerability to external social, political, and economic fluctuations.

8. We should not engage in weapons manufacture. We already have some such firms, successful ones, but we should not encourage additional ones.

9. We should not encourage firms who do business with oppressive regimes.

10. We should encourage those enterprises dedicated specifically to improving the condition of the natural environment.

In case you find this list excessively restrictive, similar criteria are employed by both the Calvert Social Investment Fund and the Parnassus

Fund, two of the leading social investment funds. Both of these funds are predicated on the belief that long-run economic success flows from enlightened management.

Whether these criteria are appropriate for Iowa is open to public debate; I do not speak for all Iowans. What I'm saying is that we should not be morally flat when thinking about economic development in Iowa. A published list of such criteria would capture the attention of the kind of firms we wish to attract and encourage.

In addition, such criteria are very much qualitative. Judgment will be required in generating and applying them. And that's called enlightenment, recognizing that everything in the realm of economic development cannot be subjected to rigorous, quantitative measurement.

A Zen Approach to Development

The thinking on Iowa economic development by various agencies and commissions, thus far, has been excessively self-focused. That's understandable. With the foundations shaking underfoot, as they did in the 1980s and promise to continue doing that in the 1990s, it's natural for a people to concern themselves with their own survival. At some point, however, such attention to personal desires becomes unseemly, and selfishness generates its own kind of myopia.

Therefore, it is worthwhile to consider an old Zen expression: To obtain a thing, you must first stop wanting it. The way of Zen is indirect, an unusual kind of thought for Western minds committed to linear, rational thinking. I came across this idea years ago, puzzled over it, and finally began to give it my own interpretations. For Iowa, it might be seen in the following way: By helping others, by concentrating on their problems, we will help ourselves, even though personal gain is not the motivation for our behavior.

Here's an example. Dominica (pronounced Dom-a-NEE-ka) is a mountainous Caribbean island, about 250 miles southeast of Puerto Rico. Eighty-three thousand people live there on 290 square miles. Its economy, based on bananas, coconuts, and citrus, is in bad shape, with export markets disappearing, and its waters overfished. The language spoken is primarily English mixed with a little local dialect. Britain granted Dominica its independence in 1978.

Dominica exhibits some similarities to Iowa, or at least where Iowa was at one time. Basically, it's a monocrop economy, with bananas as its primary output. The government has urged and attempted to support economic diversification. One such effort involved the production of mangos, but markets have been difficult to establish, and the fruit often rots on the ground. Another crop, aloe, has shown some promise. Agricultural production costs also are a serious problem. Oddly enough, in the dry Caribbean, Dominica's 365 rivers (at least the islanders claim that many rivers) allow it to export water to its neighbors.

Lennox Honychurch, a former member of the Dominican parliament, says this: "Dominica is a rural farming community. People cannot expect it to provide them with the U.S. life-style they see on TV. When Dominicans talk about their standard of living, they don't tend to take into account natural things, like being able to dive into a river and drink the water they're swimming in. What we have to do is narrow the gap between expectations and reality, through tourism but more through agro-processing—getting away from our monocrop and making products from our raw materials. Keep the money here and provide employment." That last sentence could have been taken from any number of economic development proposals in Iowa.

Suppose, through arrangements with the island's government, Iowa forms a partnership with Dominica. Suppose, furthermore, we study its culture, vacation there, and send our agriculture and natural resource experts to provide assistance. And suppose that we bring to bear on the problems of Dominica all that we have learned and are learning about economic development in Iowa, including our successes and our failures.

It's possible that some kind of barter arrangement can be struck with Dominica for its agricultural and fish products in return for our grains and manufactured products. Our high school and college students could spend summers or semesters there, both teaching and learning. Our medical expertise, particularly that of the new tropical medicine department at the University of Iowa, could be applied. And our engineering departments could help with road building and bridge construction. Our efforts should be noncolonialist in texture and designed to help Dominica become sustainable in the way that it chooses to become.

How might Iowa profit from such an arrangement? First of all, the image of the state would rocket upward. We would be seen as a place of enlightenment, as cosmopolitan, as a people willing to share its expertise and learn about another culture at the same time. We would come not as typical arrogant Americans, but as students of a world different from our own.

Iowans would begin to watch the weather in the Caribbean, and the price of bananas on the world market. Iowa school children would generate pen-pal relationships with their counterparts in Dominica. We might even develop a taste for mangos. We would, in short, be thinking about something beyond ourselves. And, I suspect, *Time* would do a laudatory article about our efforts.

Because of the commonality of language, start-up time on all projects with Dominica would be lessened. Probably there are grant institutions that would help us defray whatever minimal costs we might incur in such an enterprise. Even if there are not such funds available, my guess is that we would experience financial and spiritual revenues far beyond whatever resources we might put into such an endeavor. We also would surely learn something of value to us in our own rural development efforts.

I used Dominica merely as an example here, though I think it's a good one. Perhaps there are other, better candidates for such an arrangement, such as a state in Mexico. That's not the issue. The point is this: Instead of worrying so much about helping Des Moines commuters get into the city from its western suburbs, it might be worthwhile to expend a little effort in helping other people increase their range of options. In the process, we'll expand our own range of options and ourselves as well.

An Economy Based on Caring

A sustainable society must, along with treating the natural environment kindly, be a caring society. An area of particular concern to Iowans is care of the elderly. Economically, it's tough. Psychologically, it's distressing to think about, especially in a society counseling and promoting youthful beauty and fun as a way of life.

Iowa should address both the economic and psychological aspects of health care for the elderly. With our aging population, we will be forced to do it, whether we want to or not. And while we're doing it, we should become nationally known as sensitive care givers. There is a huge industry that can be built around the idea of being a place that knows how to care for the elderly. At the moment, given the limits of Medicare funding, the problem appears virtually intractable, particularly for those people without private resources, because care costs exceed Medicare payments.

Still, we should study the situation, carefully. If we can find a way to operate quality nursing homes in a caring fashion that is also economically viable, we can transform what seems like a burden into an economic virtue for the state. In a nation that is growing older, with people concerned about care for themselves eventually and for their aging relatives presently, care of the elderly can be looked upon as an industry. Perhaps we can become a place that cares, truly cares, and in the process provide new jobs ranging from orderlies to nurses to physicians and mental-health experts. (I will discuss this possibility further in Chapter Ten.)

By the way, our efforts here should not be limited to the elderly. The same comments apply to the homeless, the mentally ill, the indigent, and others.

An Economy Based on Craftsmanship

The SRI report suggests that Iowa develop a "quality economy." After mentioning the importance of quality, however, the language of the report drifts into conventional ideas of economic stability, a balance between rural and urban growth, and a higher standard of living, without clearly linking these objectives to the notion of quality. Nonetheless, quality is an important notion, and the general admonition by SRI that Iowa emphasize quality fits well with the ideas in this section.

When business people (and writers of economic development reports) talk about quality, the focus is on the level of excellence exhibited by a product or service. Quality, in other words, is a continuum, and a product or service is judged by where it resides on the continuum, from the low end to the high end.

The essence of quality lies in a word that is used infrequently these day, *craftsmanship.* * The word implies proficiency, expertness. Quality, therefore, flows from craftsmanship.

Craftsmanship is a product of knowledge, skill, *and* attitude. When the business community or governments talk about improving education so that America might better compete in the world economy, it's the knowledge and skill dimensions of craftsmanship upon which attention is focused. Business wants knowledge and skills. So do governments and parents who provide schooling for their children.

Yet knowledge and skills alone are not enough to produce craftsmanlike work. One must also possess a mental attitude that values perfection, that pushes one toward producing the best possible work. In my senior-level course, I emphasize the development of a craftsmanlike attitude. A very high percentage of my students — perhaps 80 percent — have no idea of what craftsmanship really means. The papers they are asked to write come to me full of typos, poorly organized thoughts, and sloppy

---

*I apologize for the gender bias in this word. Women are not excluded from what I'm talking about. Quite the contrary. And though I happen to live with a very good craftsperson, I find "craftspersonship" just too bulky for my taste.

writing in general. Some of this is a lack of skill; mostly, though, the students simply do not understand what it means to do craftsmanlike work.

So I demand they redo the work. And redo it again. And again, if need be. Still, the attitude persists: Make it just good enough to get by. These are people who have spent seventeen or eighteen years in our educational system. And they still do not possess a craftsmanlike attitude.

The same is true, I might add, of many of their instructors in both teaching and research endeavors. Recently, three professors who had coauthored a research paper asked me to review it prior to its submission to a professional journal. It was, well, junk, a perfect example of doing just enough to get by, of not driving toward a product exhibiting the quality of being completely finished. The knowledge was there, the skill was there, the attitude was not.

Why is this so? Because as a society we do not generally honor the notion of craftsmanship. We honor *output*. But craftsmanship involves a love of process as much as the finished product. The Japanese understand this, I think, and that is a major source of their quality we strive so hard to imitate.

How does one develop a craftsmanlike attitude? Some people seem to acquire it almost naturally, regardless of what they pursue. Most do not. For those in the latter category, the way to develop craftsmanship is to study the arts and crafts.

And I don't mean learning to make corn-husk dolls. I mean studying one or more of the arts or crafts in a serious way as an integral part of education.* Incidentally, I include writing—poetry, essays, fiction, for example—as part of this.

Personally, I don't believe any student should be granted a diploma from an Iowa high school or college without being able to demonstrate a reasonable level of competence in both a manual skill (for example, welding) and a skill in music or writing or drawing or photography or watercolor painting or sculpture or weaving or ceramics or any of several

---

*A long-running debate exists in aesthetic fields over the supposed difference between art and crafts. For example, oil painting is considered to be an art, while woodworking is a craft. Hence, oil painting is to be held in higher esteem than woodworking. This is an example of what pseudointellectuals talk about while drinking brandy on Friday afternoons. It's nonsense and is not worth serious consideration here. One can easily find artistic woodworking and uncraftsmanlike oil painting. When I use the term "arts and crafts," I am only following convention, but no pejorative connotation is attached to the work of those in fields outside of what are deemed to be the "fine arts."

other fields. I don't care whether the student eventually plans to become a lawyer or a plumber or an accountant or a farmer. The need for a craftsmanlike attitude cuts across all fields.

In addition to learning the elements of craftsmanship, other benefits accrue from this kind of study, each of them contributing directly to Iowa's ability to compete in the world economy. Some of these benefits are design skills, composition skills, facility in making qualitative judgments and decisions, writing skills, and a sense of competence demonstrable in a medium other than standardized tests.

Moreover, craftsmanship is related intimately to what is being produced. Over twenty years ago I wrote an article titled "Job Satisfaction and the Throwaway Society," in which I argued that if one is asked to produce junk, one will work with an attitude commensurate with that output. I still believe that to be true. You are what you make, and making useless things well is a contradiction in terms. Only robots can do that over the long haul.

This returns us to the economic mix, the content of our output. Business people talk about quality without considering what is being produced. In my estimation, a quality economy is based on a culture that thinks carefully about not only how it produces something, but also about what it wants to produce. As I said before, Iowa should concentrate on producing products and services not on the fringes but rather at the core of people's lives. If we have a sense that what we are producing is truly important, it will be much easier to achieve quality in that production.

Tied in with all of this is the question of producing art/crafts as products in and of themselves. Iowa has not been kind to the arts, ranking somewhere around dead last among the states in per capita support. I would like to believe that Iowa could sustain itself by producing nothing but ceramics, wood carvings, paintings, and so forth. I doubt that is possible.

What *is* possible, however, is the encouragement of our arts/crafts such that they play a more important role in our economic structure than they do currently. There are several advantages to this. First, young people will implicitly understand that craftsmanship is valued. Second, the fume of good craftsmanship will float through all of what Iowa does. Third, in a state worried about its image, a healthy arts/crafts sector of the economy will lend a certain gloss to our image.

And, fourth, in a society wedded to huge markets supplied via mass production, there still are plenty of customers for the products of people skilled in the crafts. For example, Tom McNeil of Preston, Iowa, is a former hog farmer who now specializes in creating wood products, primarily rolltop desks. He advertises in *The New Yorker*, and his work sells in a price range of $2,500 to $12,000. Good potters are regularly able to sell clay work for $100 to $300 or more, sometimes higher.

Appalachicola, Florida, is basing a substantial portion of its economic development effort on the arts. That community is even offering incentives and relocation assistance to arts and crafts people. And author Edward Lucie-Smith points out: "[The] craftsman is valued by contemporary Japanese as the symbol of the best their society can produce, to the point where certain individuals are officially designated as Living Cultural Treasures. The term may seem to us quaint, but the attitude of mind which it embodies is surely something we ought to find admirable."

Ireland exempts artists from paying taxes and feels the financial benefits far outweigh the costs of doing so. Perhaps Iowa might consider a system similar to Ireland's on a state level. The articles extolling our level of artistic commitment that subsequently would appear in national magazines would send waves of approval our way. Our image as a place devoted to creativity and craftsmanship would soar, far offsetting any losses in tax revenues.

North Dakota's Small Business Development Centers have established a home-based business development program providing technical assistance and marketing services to people who start businesses in their homes. At a certain stage, a business may be designated as "market ready." When that occurs, the state will help market the products. In addition, craftsmen with similar skills are grouped into "pods" and given the opportunity to fill orders, on a national scale, which have been obtained by the SBDCs. Iowa's home-based business program is in its beginning stages and should be encouraged.

Iowa ought to be looked upon as a place where quality is pervasive — in its products, in its care of the elderly and others, in its treatment of nature, in all things. And craftsmanship is the key to quality. In short, we should develop a culture based on the idea of craftsmanship.

OTHER ISSUES AND SUGGESTIONS

Taxes

Many of the problems we confront lie outside the normal activities of the market system. Examples are national defense, aid to the indigent, and correcting environmental degradation. We fund such activities through the tax system. Yet, the very word "taxes" is enough to rile the populace and swing presidential elections.

The reason is not hard to understand on an emotional level: taxes decrease our discretionary income and, therefore, run counter to the ethic of high consumption. If we are conditioned to the pursuit of more private consumption, then whatever detracts from that pursuit is to be condemned. From this viewpoint, taxes are bad and one should do whatever is necessary to avoid paying them.

Of course, taxes are neither good nor bad. It's all a matter of how we wish to spend our money; it's a matter of what mix of products and services—the *content* of our economic output, social versus private—we choose. Incidentally, I would not presume to argue against privatization. I think it's a good idea in many cases. Given what I said in earlier chapters about incentives, I would have difficulty feeling otherwise. Those of us who recall the weeks required to receive a battered package through the U.S. Postal Service are amazed, continually, at the efficiency and effectiveness of United Parcel Service. And there is nothing to prevent the use of private firms in the production of social goods and services.

But to rail against taxes as simply being bad, in and of themselves, is to misunderstand the limits of the market system. The fact is that we have things that need to be done that will not be done by private interests; for example, public education, care of the homeless, or maintenance of our physical infrastructure. If there was a buck to be made in these areas, someone would be doing it.

My wise colleague, John Warfield, has suggested that we should stop talking about taxes and use the term "public investment" instead. There is merit to that suggestion, for it focuses attention on the fact that we are spending money in areas neglected by private markets instead of simply removing discretionary income from people's hands, which is always what the word "taxes" connotes, as we have been conditioned to interpret it.

We tend to be concerned not just with how much taxes we pay, but also how these monies are spent. Voting for politicians is an extremely indirect and unreliable way of expressing preferences for the expenditures of public revenues. Perhaps there will come a time when each of us, within limits, can designate on our tax returns how we prefer to have a portion of our taxes spent. That, I think, might revive some interest in the practice of democratic government.

Taxes, however, have another important role to play, one that is denigrated by many politicians who don't think very deeply about human behavior. As noted in Chapter Six, a popular phrase in considering revisions in the tax code is, "Taxes should not be used as an instrument of social policy."

That's a ludicrous argument. First of all, every tax is, in one way or another, a judgment about social policy. Some people benefit, others lose. In addition, taxes or the lack of them can act as powerful incentives while still allowing people to make their own decisions. A three-dollar-a-gallon tax on gasoline or on a carton of cigarettes or a tax credit for installing energy-saving devices in the home are all surgical instruments for influencing behavior while still permitting freedom of choice. There was a fair amount of discussion of this earlier in the book, so I'll not belabor it anymore here, except to say that the incentive component of taxes should always be a consideration in deciding upon the quantity and type of taxes levied.

Education

Since I am filing a minority report on economic development, let me state my somewhat radical views rather succinctly: I do not believe education should be put at the service of economic development. *Period!*

Recently, the business community has advanced some bold proposals for getting itself involved in education, mostly under the rubric of the Iowa Future Project. These proposals tend to sound good and emphasize an output-oriented approach to education. That is, educators can approach education in whatever form they wish, as long as certain outputs are produced. Furthermore, educators are encouraged to see students as products and business as the customers for these products.

I am empathetic with the frustrations of the business community about the quality of education. Business people see themselves competing in a global economy with countries such as Japan and view, rightly or wrongly, our work force as inferior to those countries with whom they must compete. Naturally then, since humans are a key input in the production of goods and services, business wants better quality in these inputs. In the jargon used by both the SRI and DED reports, business wants better human capital.

Here are a few observations, mostly about the relationship of education to economic development. A rehashing of the debate surrounding educational improvement is a swamp I prefer to avoid.

Given a student who falls within the wide range of what might be termed a "normal learner," education is not all that difficult. It requires, at minimum, the following:

1. Students who are ready to learn.
2. Teachers who are academically prepared, who possess some reasonable skills in presentation, and who are patient and equitable in their classroom practices.
3. A recognition that students learn in different ways and at different rates. Some people acquire information best through reading, some through verbal explanation, some through visual means, and so forth.
4. An understanding that the training of a mind is a combination of teacher explanation and private study and being around those who value the intellect — in both its logical and artistic dimensions.
5. Rigorous standards.

Those who counsel an emphasis on the three R's, hackneyed though that sounds, are not necessarily wrong; they are just being incomplete. If you can read, can communicate with others, and have a basic grounding in mathematics, you can participate at some useful level in the market economy, or at least be trained to do it relatively easily.

What's wrong then? Why the commotion about our educational system? The answers are not hard to find.

First, we ask our schools to do more than educate students. We want them to provide babysitting while parents are at work, nutritious food, social and academic counseling, entertainment for the public at large, and a range of other services. Because we so object to taxes, we tend to underfund the schools in terms of the ancillary services we ask from them.

Second, people respond to incentives. Teachers are no different. We don't complain about business people earning $100,000 per year, even if this income is derived from the production of trinkets. The market has blessed this income.

But we would complain bitterly if property taxes were raised enough to pay teachers salaries competitive with those earned in business. Somehow, teachers are supposed to substitute missionary zeal for money. And many of them do. But let's not create a mystery where there is none: If you want the best and brightest people to be in education, make sure their salaries and perquisites are commensurate with their opportunities elsewhere. This, of course, requires a willingness to substitute public investment for private consumption.

Third, elementary and secondary school teachers are asked to be all things to all people. If you want them to teach, let them teach. Taking tickets at football games, bus duty, janitorial duties, keeping track of lunch tickets and performing lunchroom duties, passing out promotional materials from local service organizations, recess duty, as well as making do without clerical help, all hinder the educational process and should not be part of it. In addition, many of these teachers carry instructional loads that are far too heavy to allow for adequate preparation, additional study in their fields, and thoughtful grading of homework and examinations.

Fourth, get rid of the self-serving bureaucracy that controls American education. The state departments of public instruction, or whatever they may be called, have been tightly interlocked with the university departments producing teachers. This results in an incestuous relationship that has made teacher-education programs jokes at most institutions of higher learning. If people have the subject-matter knowledge and skills to teach, they should be allowed to teach without all the current nonsense attached to teacher certification. A written and oral test of basic competence should be enough.

Fifth, most of the complaint about education centers on some combination of students, teachers, and curricula. Little is said about the quality of academic management. Though I think some improvement is noticeable, the management of our educational institutions in the past has been characterized by a range of sins. Incompetence is one of them. The cozy relationships within the educational bureaucracy mentioned above are nowhere more evident than in the superintendent–school board–teacher college–state department of education coalition. The good ol' boys, on the whole, have been bad managers.

Sixth, the arts and music are undervalued in education, are seen as impractical and dilettantish. That's balderdash. Concentrated study in artistic fields is the best way of developing creativity, design skills, the ability to synthesize, and many other desirable attributes. These areas of study should be given time and funding equal to the traditional academic subjects. (See my essays on frontiers, in *One Good Road Is Enough,* for elaboration on this point.)

Ultimately, our schools are what we want them to be and reflect society's commitment, or lack of it, to education. Insufficient funding, minimal parental involvement, and a society that devalues intellectual and artistic accomplishment will lead to bad schools. It's not much more complicated than that.

Into this arena comes now the business community with its own ideas for education. American business people, driven by what they see as market pressures, have engaged in an orgy of short-run thinking over the decades. Suddenly they want to be involved in the educational process, an enterprise that is distinctly long-run and whose production process is far more subtle than most industrial processes.

The current problems with our educational system have been developing over a long time. Studies, reports, articles, and speeches warned of this. Where was the business community while the problems were being discussed? By and large, not paying attention, because they had not yet felt the impact of the problems. By and large, looking to locate in states with the lowest taxes. By and large, luring students to minimum-wage jobs that detract from study time.

By and large, advocating a high-consumption society that distrusts and scorns the contemplative kind of existence needed for fine education. By and large, transferring families at the discretion of corporate whim, ignoring the impacts on the family structure and its stability and the relation of that to education. By and large, demanding that parents work long hours, which detracts from exactly the kind of parental involvement that contributes to education.

While I am empathetic toward the needs of business, I am not sympathetic. American business, aside from periodic cries of alarm about student writing skills or the lack of young people entering certain technical fields, has contributed little to the solution of our educational dilemmas. Now, experiencing the results of problems in our schools, they want to contribute.

That's commendable. The business community should be welcomed as a participant in improving our nation's education. But it should not be trusted to provide the kind of vision it will take to produce a first-class educational system. Why? The short run, always the short run. The same thing I have discussed over and over again in this book.

If you put business people in charge of defining the outputs for education, you'll get outputs defined in terms of what business thinks it needs at any particular time. The arts, for example, have always suffered because employers are much more interested in how many accounting or mathematics courses students have completed than in whether the student is a decent watercolorist or has developed some skills in poetry.

High-level corporate executives are fond of citing the virtues of a broad-based, liberal arts education. When they send out their recruiters to universities, however, they belie this viewpoint by specifically citing their needs in finance or operations management or accounting. Students get the message; so do teachers. Cut back on poetry, load up on accounting.

Remember the input-transformation-output model in Chapter One? If we allow business to define the desirable outputs of education, implicitly we will allow the market to determine educational transformation processes and what inputs to the processes are valued. And what the market thinks it needs at any given time bears no particular relationship to those human qualities required for a sustainable culture.

The bare fact is this: A first-class education is really what the business community wants in our students. It wants people who can read, write, compute (defined broadly), think, and create. If that's what business people are talking about when they strive to define outputs, I'm on their side. But market pressures determine business preferences, and markets are amoral, attaching no value to human dignity and personal happiness.

If we are to attain the goal of an enlightened civilization, we must look to broader guidance than the market. I grieve over the potential outcomes if we do not. Education should not be the servant of economic growth. It should provide people with the wherewithal for leading happy and productive lives. If it does that, education automatically will contribute to economic development without becoming its vassal.

Information and Brokerage

The DED report emphasizes the importance of information networks. I wish to second that idea here. In a rural state, such as Iowa, such networks are critical to providing information to those removed from the information resources available to urban dwellers.

Electronic devices — computers and telecommunications and the like — usually receive the primary attention in any discussion of information networks. I grant that such modern wonders are, indeed, critical. Most small towns, as well as large ones, already contain the makings of an information center. It's called the library. And I contend that libraries are going to be key institutions in creating a sustainable Iowa. Educational institutions, outside of the research enterprises in our universities where new knowledge is generated, are information brokers. So are libraries.

The idea of brokerage, as a general concept, is worth focusing on. Herbert Simon, Nobel laureate, once described human problem solving as a three-stage process: intelligence, design, and choice. Before you can choose, you must design alternatives and criteria. Intelligence, in the sense of information gathering, provides the grist for this design as well as data for estimating the outcomes of alternatives. Assisting people in the stages of intelligence, design, and choice is a task of libraries.

With the aid of telecommunications, interlibrary loan services, and computer-assisted information search capabilities, one can live anywhere and acquire in rapid fashion the information necessary for intelligent decision making. Libraries have a key role in brokering this kind of activity.

The High-Consumption Society

The SRI and DED plans are predicated on several assumptions, axioms really. The dominant assumption underlying both plans is that economic growth (or economic development, whichever you prefer) is good. On the surface of it, as mentioned before, that assumption seems unchallengeable. As evidence of the benefits of economic growth, proponents customarily cite such things as improved medical care, access to education, and a considerable array of goods and services available to consumers.

Yet, economic growth has its costs, both present and future. Degradation of the natural environment is one such cost, a huge one. Moreover, the argument that growth is a way of handling poverty—the rising-tide-lifts-all-boats argument—is not holding up to careful scrutiny. The data clearly show a concentration of benefits from recent growth at the upper income levels, both in the United States and when the wealthier nations are compared with the poorer ones. In other words, the "trickle-down" theory is not working. Many boats are not rising, while some are bobbing up quite rapidly.

Those of us some distance above the poverty line, and that includes a large number of Iowans, must begin to struggle with a profound question, a question that strikes at the very heart of our human existence: "What is the purpose of economic growth?" In the past, the answer was obvious: To lift ourselves out of the stark and brutish conditions imposed upon us by a natural world that gave no quarter.

The cold of winter was unforgiving out here on the prairies. Our clothing was rough, our food supplies uncertain. Women and babies died at childbirth. People became bent and worn from their labors at a fairly early age. My maternal grandfather dug field-tile ditches for a living, by hand, with a tiling spade, sleeping in a pup tent at night. I often think of him standing at the beginning of an endless stretch of cropland, in the summer heat of Iowa, looking at the task before him and at the spade in his hands. That image gives me no cause to yearn for the good old days.

So, early on, the reasons for growth were clear. But those reasons have become increasingly muddled as our standard of living has increased. Yet, the DED baldly states that improving the standard of living is the goal of economic development. That objective is no different from the objective of other states and the United States as a whole. To what end, though?

That's not clear, at least for those of us who have surmounted the hurdle of poverty and the hammering effects of coarse, repetitive labor at low wages. The only answer seems to be "More." More what? Well, larger houses, real big ones, for starters. And saunas and hot tubs and autos with expensive stereos. More comfort and more stuff. How much more? Where is the end? What's the point of it all?

Those are uncomfortable questions. What's even more uncomfortable is that the entire American economy (and the economies of other industrialized nations) is built on the premise of high-intensity purchasing by something called "consumers." In Chapter Two I quoted William Leiss's argument that the legitimacy of modern societies now rests upon the expectation of permanently rising levels of consumption, that individual well-being has become synonymous with increases in per capita GNP.

It's starting to get a little frightening. You can find people out there earning $100,000 a year with nothing in the bank, a suffocating mortgage, and $20,000 in short-term debt on top of it, a legacy of pulling out the plastic too many times.

Still the pressures mount for ever more consumption. Economists, business people, and government officials worry constantly about current and projected levels of consumer buying, with heavy emphasis on the Christmas holidays. Textbooks on consumer behavior point out that consumers "must be constantly stimulated," lest we purchase less than is necessary to keep the economy running at high levels so we can purchase even more. To keep us from faltering in our appointed tasks, we are bombarded relentlessly by advertising, peer-group pressures, and the general celebration of high-intensity consumption in all of its forms.

We no longer are viewed as citizens, but as the foundation of an industrial machine that has no purpose except to reproduce itself in ever-larger versions. We are, in the language of contemporary hucksterism, targets for units.

Something is wrong, dead wrong. This is not how it was supposed to turn out. Thirty years ago sociologists fretted over the question of how people would spend the projected large amounts of leisure time that would eventually stretch before us as we steadily solved the problem of subsistence. Now we fight for leisure hours; leisure has become a scarce commodity in its own right for many people.

All of this might be tolerable, though perhaps not laudatory, if it were not for the problems confronting us.

In the United States, a woman is raped every six minutes, according to the Senate Judiciary Committee.

Violence is becoming more pervasive and more deadly, reaching into pockets of rural quietude. The number one cause of injury to women in our advanced industrialized society is domestic violence. Thirty-five percent of all female homicide victims older than fifteen years of age are killed by their husbands or intimate partners.

Over two million of us are hooked on cocaine, though some experts view that as a conservative estimate. Iowa is believed to have about eight thousand such addicts. Gangs equipped with automatic weapons terrorize neighborhoods. Seventy to eighty thousand people in Los Angeles County alone belong to gangs.

Children are killing other children to obtain their designer jackets and expensive tennis shoes.

Teen-age suicides, though not as rampant as some would have us believe, are prevalent, often occurring for no apparent reason.

Executives are looting savings and loan institutions.

Neglect and abuse of the mentally ill and the elderly are widespread. A recent report by the National Alliance for the Mentally Ill and Public Citizen ranked Iowa thirty-eighth in quality of services for the mentally ill.

A majority of Americans, according to a recent study, are sleeping sixty to ninety minutes less per night than they should to maintain full cognitive alertness.

Another survey shows that 79 percent of American parents feel guilty about not spending more time with their children.

A fifth or more of the U.S. population is functionally illiterate. And the standards for measuring such illiteracy are not particularly rigorous. In terms of the ability to read anything approaching serious writing, the figure certainly is higher.

And there is no question that our natural support systems are in serious trouble.

The above list is a short one. Still it leads us back to the essential question surrounding economic growth based on high-intensity consumption: What is the point of it all? If you back off a few steps and look at what's going on, it all appears pretty mindless. That's the temperate judgment.

The harsher position is that we are destroying ourselves and our planet for nothing more than the acquisition of trinkets. We grow fat, physically and mentally, and stupefied in pursuit of the trivial and transitory while our human and natural support systems crumble. And some call it progress; others call it economic development.

Clearly, in my estimation, we are going to change, and change dramatically, in the way we live and the things we value. This will occur for one, or both, of two reasons.

First, and perhaps this will seem a.little judgmental, we are a floundering culture. Even if it's not stated that boldly, I think many people sense we have lost our way in a melange of selfishness and infantile demands for fleeting, shallow pleasures. I suggest that slowly, ever so slowly, we are turning, or will begin to turn, toward more emphasis on personal and family growth and less emphasis on high-intensity consumption.

"Born to Shop," the bumper sticker, is the most tragic statement of our human condition I can possibly imagine. Though marketers undoubtedly applaud that ghastly self-incrimination, that implicit admission of having given oneself over to cheap and transitory and ultimately meaningless pastimes, I take it as a signal of an empty life and, more generally, of a society about to capsize.

Such a proclamation is clear surrender to the forces of environmental destruction and liquidation of the human spirit. Born, yes, but not to shop. Born to create and explore and think and leave something more

behind than auctioneers holding up tattered doodads for a snickering
crowd as the bidding tops off at a quarter. Gradually, I believe we are
coming to recognize that a life based on material consumption is, clearly,
a wasted life. At least I want to believe we are drawing closer to that
realization.

Second, even if I am wrong about what I just said, the natural
environment is not going to support our high-consumption life-style into
perpetuity, in spite of promised technological fixes and doing away with
plastic garbage bags. If you mix population growth with demands for
industrialized life-styles with the complex of problems discussed in
Chapter Eight, it's difficult to see how we can continue to exist at our
current rapacious levels. We are not living in a sustainable fashion, either
in human or environmental terms, and no amount of civic or statewide
boosterism can change that.

I have talked about the decline of options before. For instance,
species extinction, a massive problem, decreases our options, economically and aesthetically. Perhaps in terms of our own survival as well.
Rampant development, the unfettered kind we have witnessed in the
United States, narrows our range of options, particularly those connected with the natural environment.

But other critical options are also decreasing. For example, the
freedom to move about unchecked by fear of violence, or the option to
secure potable water at a reasonable price. The mentally ill and destitute
elderly confront a distressingly narrow range of options. The same can
be said of disadvantaged young people.

With the coming decline of cheap and portable energy in the form of
fossil fuels, our options to travel will disappear. In the winter of 1991 we
spent roughly $1 billion a day in the Persian Gulf area, attempting to
maintain these options. And rising prices for fossil fuels along with the
climatic effects of the greenhouse effect may well reduce our agricultural
options in Iowa.

If liberty is to have any meaning, choices must be present, not just
politically, but in all areas of our lives. We have been trading increased
choice in the consumption arena for decreased options elsewhere. Doors
of questionable value open while other doors of inestimable value click
shut behind us.

At any given time, we confront a range of choices, a set of options.
For example, what car to purchase, what apartment to rent or home to
buy, whether to drop out of high school or attend college, whether to
join a country club or a street gang.

We would, of course, like to have everything. But we cannot, and the reason is a combination of scarcity and constraints on our set of choices. Thus the limits of our own lives, the fact that we can't be in two places at once, financial constraints, physical constraints, legal restrictions, and social conventions prevent us from having it all, even though purveyors of something called "the good life" might like us to believe otherwise. "You can have it all!" the advertisements shriek.

Scarcity and constraints place restrictions on us, dividing our set of choices into roughly two categories at a specific moment: the attainable and the unattainable. Where the attainable set meets the unattainable, we confront borders. Just this side of the borders, we live within settled regions — it's where we are at a particular time with our thoughts and our skills and our ability to acquire things.

As I said before, the dominant frontier of American life is economic consumption. We are urged by our peers, by the media, by the constant bombardment of advertising, and even by our federal and state governments to push ever further into the realm of material acquisition. This activity is defined as progress, as economic development.

LP records were apparently not good enough. Thus audiocassettes came along. Still not good enough. So compact discs were introduced. Remember, consumers must be constantly stimulated. And all of this for a population that can't discern the difference between a major third and a minor fifth in music. All of this for Madonna. All of this not just in the interest of better audio quality, but to stimulate consumers to buy.

Manufacturers believe our television screens are not adequate. So high-definition sets are on the way, which will enable us to better view sporting events and evangelistic advertisements for improved car wax. The old AM/FM radio in our autos is giving way to costly, sophisticated stereo systems capable of pounding out music at high decibel levels. This is called increased choice.

In other words, we are urged to launch tireless assaults on the border between what material goods we have now and those that might be possible for us to obtain in the future. We are goaded, pushed, to reach ever-outward into the frontiers of materialism, in the name of economic development.

Eventually, almost everything is judged in terms of what it will or won't do for economic development. Nature loses any intrinsic value and, instead, is viewed as a set of constraints that must be overcome, or at least held in abeyance so they don't interfere with more economic development. Highways, athletic events, the operation of local schools, and education itself — all are viewed in terms of their contribution to economic development, which is based, ultimately, on higher and higher levels of consumption. (If you don't believe that last statement about the proper role of education, read the SRI and DED reports.)

Instead of a means to higher ends, economic development has become the end. For reasons that nobody seems to question, more is better and less — or the status quo — is worse. If it sells, it's good. If it doesn't, try something else.

But there are other frontiers. And it is toward these alternative frontiers we must begin to move. Plato called them the "fair and immortal children of the mind." They possess a number of important characteristics and are accessible to almost everyone.

1. They have a lower impact on the natural environment than high-intensity material consumption.
2. They encourage personal growth, a plumbing of the richness that can be found in the reservoirs of the human mind and body and spirit.
3. Most require relatively little in the way of financial resources. Some are within the economic capabilities of everyone.
4. They promote a craftsmanlike work ethic.
5. They develop a "designing culture" in which all of us become sensitive to and responsible for how our products appear and function.
6. They result in a more discriminating culture, a society of intelligent buyers, who disdain shoddy products and glitter.
7. They foster a "learning culture," where the acquisition of knowledge and skills becomes a natural part of the daily cycle of life.
8. Most of all, they result in personal and cultural growth.

Here's a partial list of such frontiers: intellectual pursuits, the visual arts, music, writing, theater, dance. You will no doubt have others in mind.

We must stop talking about economic development as the sole end of society and begin looking at development in a broader context. *We must discard the adjective "economic" and start thinking about development as a multidimensional concept.*

As part of this, we must redefine abundance. Recent evidence indicates that many early peoples, those described as "primitive" in the textbooks we all were privileged to read, in fact had large amounts of leisure time and were able to provide for their basic needs by working comparatively few hours per week. As we redefine abundance and development, we will also be redefining what it means to be successful, what it means to lead a life that is rich and full.

As with just about everything else, it's a multiple-criteria problem of the kind mentioned throughout this book. That is, at the borders of our attainable and unattainable sets, we have choices about the frontiers we choose to pursue. Those who favor high-intensity consumption insist that we focus on the single criterion of increasing our stock of purchased goods and services. This, in turn, results in the selection of alternatives designed to do just that.

Suppose, however, we approach our personal and political decision making with a more balanced set of criteria that includes concern for the natural environment, kindness to animals, time for personal development in an artistic field, time to spend with our children, and concern for the elderly, the poor, and the mentally ill. That's only a sample list.

If criteria such as these are given heavy weight in our decision making, then other alternatives aside from "work more hours to get more money" (or however it's stated) will increasingly be favored. The purveyors of the high-consumption ethic find this kind of thinking distressing, if not downright subversive. It means that people might just select a more balanced life, that we might decide to stay home and play with the kids or do an oil painting on a Sunday afternoon instead of aimlessly wandering the shopping malls in search of fribbles that eventually will find their way into the neighborhood garage sale.

In a world of people running hard, trying to balance work and children and care of aging parents, all of this probably seems more than a trifle naive. Remember, though, I am not writing about today or even next week, but rather about the kind of society I believe we will have to create in the next few decades.

In addition, anxiety about caring for ourselves in our later years plays a critical role in life-style choices, including the choice of more and more work in exchange for the other things I have mentioned. Thus, the creation of a comprehensive system of medical, hospital, and retirement benefits for the elderly must be designed and implemented, probably at the national level.

In spite of the cynicism engendered by the well-publicized problems with our current Social Security arrangements, such a system is feasible and is needed. The highly successful Teachers Insurance and Annuity Association/College Retirement Equities Fund, developed for university professors, might serve as a useful model.

SUMMARY

Some argue that we, humankind in general, are about to enter a period of the most profound changes in the history of human life on earth. The rhetoric holds that the era we are moving into will be more dramatic than the changes wrought by the Agricultural Revolution and the Industrial Revolution. This is pretty strong stuff, but it's starting to take on the appearance of being right on target.

For decades we have tried to deny the basic tenet of economics: scarcity. Through economic growth fueled by huge government deficits and high levels of consumer spending and inattention to our natural support systems, it has seemed that we could outrun scarcity, that we could provide everything for everyone. Clearly, we cannot, though it's difficult to find politicians who will stand and say, "The choices are difficult, but they are inescapable, and we must make them."

What are the choices? Much of it boils down to one issue: We will not be able to sustain high levels of economic consumption of what fundamentally amounts to trinkets and still take care of the other problems confronting us. There simply are not enough resources available to purchase $150 sneakers for whining young people and still provide adequate care for the elderly. There are not enough resources to lumber around in motor homes and high-performance autos and still provide clean air and fuel to heat our dwellings.

I wish it were not so. I like my life pretty well, and I'm not excited about the prospect of giving up discretionary income to solve the pressing social and environmental problems we confront. But I see no other alternative.

If we are going to take care of the environment, we must begin to pay the true costs of our products and services. If we are going to care for the elderly and others who need help, we're going to have to pay for it by decreasing our consumption of other goods and services. If we are going to rebuild and maintain our physical infrastructure, we're going to have to make the necessary social investments. The list goes on.

It's a mess. We have caused the mess, however, and getting out of it is going to be grinding, at least until we discover that most of the real pleasures in life lie in our minds and not in our bank accounts.

Iowa should, in my opinion, concentrate on things fundamental to human existence. We should focus on producing goods and services at the core of existence and not at the trivial fringes.

Food and fiber are fundamental, and we are admirably equipped to produce them, providing we get our water quality and soil erosion problems under control. A decade ago some of us were arguing for more value-added processing of agricultural products in Iowa, rather than sending our raw materials somewhere else for processing. That viewpoint seems to have caught on in the last few years.

Craftsmanship, as a general concept, also is fundamental. A people working with intelligence and a craft ethic will dominate in the world economy.

Iowa should look carefully at which industries it wishes to encourage via its state programs. Those who meet the criteria of environmental concern, fair treatment of employees, and who produce products at the core of human existence should be encouraged. Quality care for the elderly of all income levels potentially is one such industry. Those who insist on producing products or services of little worth should be ignored, if not discouraged. We could do worse than follow the criteria employed by the more progressive social investment funds, such as the Calvert Social Investment Fund.

I have cited evolving dietary habits as a possible contingency for Iowa. In spite of the pressures that will be exerted by meat producers, we should attempt to take a clear view of what is coming toward us. After all, we have rich soil and other resources for producing food and fiber that do not involve the consumption of animal flesh. As with any industry whose products become obsolete over time, it's possible, perhaps likely, we will have to shift our mix of agricultural outputs. Denial and politics will not change this, only blind us once again to critical shifts in our economic environment.

We are caught in a way of thinking where development is interpreted to mean economic development and where economic development is synonymous with progress. Development, however, is a broad term, and we should use it without the adjective "economic" attached to it. Forests fall to the saw, highways and shopping centers cover productive farmland, and the disadvantaged among us are sacrificed to the dubious pleasures of improved toilet-bowl cleansers and designer clothing.

This returns us to the vision issue. It's important for us—Iowans and everyone else—to define in reasonably crisp terms what we mean by development. We still have not done that, in spite of numerous documents containing the word "vision" on their mastheads. For example, what is it we mean by the word "economic" when we talk about economic development? Thomas Power suggests the following:

   a. The availability of useful and satisfying work for members of the community

b. Security for members of the community in access to biological and
   social necessities
c. Stability in the community
d. Access to the qualities that make life varied, stimulating, and satisfying
e. A thriving, vital community

Power emphasizes this is not just another version of "jobs and income" cast in a different form. The discussion of these matters in his
book is worth reading. Basically, Power and I believe the same thing:
Jobs and income are one thing, improvements in the quality of life for
local residents who are supposed to benefit from economic development
is quite another. The state can claim success in attracting industry by
celebrating the opening of a chicken-processing operation paying the
minimum wage or close to it, where people exist in a daily blood bath.
But whether a community is better off, overall, for attracting that plant
is questionable. And therein lies the issue of quality, not just quantity.

It's time to shift our view of what constitutes the good life. More
than that, I don't think we have any choice; we have closed down many
of our options already by the search for happiness through consumption. It's time now to open up other options for ourselves, options that
involve developing the mind and the spirit—to begin another kind of
progress, the kind we started out to create before we lost our way. In the
end, love, respect, and home-grown tomatoes are all that really matter,
and it's possible that heaven and hell are what we leave behind, not what
we enter at the closing of our lives. Economic development officials
would do well to think about that.

APPENDIX

Entrepreneurship and the Value of the Small Increment

Entrepreneur. The very word, coming from the Old French, and
meaning "to undertake," has a ring of romance and daring about it. In
the minds of most people it fairly thunders of risk and creation and the
molding of enterprise, of change and innovation and jobs where there

---

This essay was originally published in the *Des Moines Register,* April 19, 1987, pp.
1C, 3C. Reprinted by permission of the Iowa State University Press from my book, *Just
Beyond the Firelight.*

were none before. It will, I predict, be the next word of the hour in Iowa.

It's about time. So, let's talk about entrepreneurship — what it is, who does it, where it comes from, and how we might go about encouraging it at both the state and local levels.

We have been a while getting to this point, and it's worth looking at our recent history in the area of economic development, for it is a history of youth and the failures of youth, some of which we may live with for a long time.

In the process of personal development, you first try for maturity. Then you hope for wisdom. And slowly, slowly then, you begin to understand the quick kill you longed for when you were young comes only now and then, as a matter of luck, and cannot be counted on. The way up, it seems, is more like building a fine piece of cabinetry than plopping it all down on red and watching the big wheel turn.

So, call it wisdom, or call it simply understanding the value of the small increment — pursuing quality each day, learning from this pursuit, and trusting that the small gains will somehow amount to something. And they do. Eventually, it becomes clear that a different and more subtle algebra is at work, where things added together equal something greater than their arithmetic sum. So it is, slowly, and almost with reluctance it seems, that Iowa approaches wisdom.

We started off, like the young and the gambler, looking for the quick kill, trying to lure big firms with big employment. "Chasing smokestacks" it was called, and it was pathetic. We were unprepared and amateurish. We bowed and scraped and cut taxes and offered gifts of money. Most of the time we looked like rubes in $10 suits peddling costume jewelry to rich folks. And the big firms smiled down at the supplicants and said, "We'll see, we'll see."

Then came high tech. Nobody seemed to know exactly what it was, but it looked dazzling and seductive and, well, current. Besides, it offered politicians the chance for bold strokes, and risk comes easily with other people's money. Never mind that high tech is expected to create only about one-sixth of the new jobs in the United States during the 1990s. Never mind that the gestation period from high-tech invention to employment is long and tenuous. And ignore the fact that high-tech jobs, aside from those in management and the laboratory, are often minimum-wage jobs involving routine assembly operations.

So the universities lined up at the trough with high-tech proposals, did some bad arithmetic on even worse data, made promises they should not have made, and generally behaved in a fashion unbefitting the supposed intellectual leaders of the state. The legislature made no serious attempts at checking the proposals against either fact or logic, and a $130 million bonding bill, with a mortgage for twenty-five years attached, flew through both houses like a fat duck. High tech sometimes resembles high cheek, it seems.

That done, we turned to gambling. Flashy, very flashy. Surprised? No reason to be. It's a natural lurch for those bereft of money or bankrupt of ideas or both. What does the list look like? Lotteries, dog racing, horse racing, table games. How about slot machines in the grocery stores and airports? Even the Mesquakies have a "tribal bingo committee."

Unless the gambling attracts a large number of non-Iowans, we'll just be churning each other's money through casino drop boxes. The result will be a new and reasonably subtle mode of state and local tribute with a little more entertainment value attached than the usual forms of taxation. (By the way, you should know that, as a serious blackjack player, a moralist I am not.) Moreover, we are going to restrict casino gambling to the rivers and lakes. Apparently, water serves in certain instances as a prophylactic for protecting innocence and virtue.

Yet, here and there, the maturity and wisdom one expects from Iowans begins to surface. People are starting to ask, "What about small business?" "What about entrepreneurs?" "Maybe we ought to be a little more patient and rebuild this place a piece at a time."

My colleagues at the University of Northern Iowa, Neil Wilson and Al Pelham and Paul Winter and Earl Brooks and David Wheelock, all of them former business executives with a mountain of experience, have been arguing in favor of this approach for years. And while, with great success, they quietly have been training and counseling hundreds of small-business people and entrepreneurs, their ideas have not been heard in the larger forum of policymaking; their voices have been submerged in high-tech, big-kill bombast and a faint roar from the crap tables.

Now comes entrepreneurship. What does an entrepreneur look like? Trying to get a handle on the salient personality characteristics of entrepreneurs is like trying to identify the attributes of great leaders or great teachers. It's like grabbing smoke. As soon as you construct what you think is a good list of such characteristics you find a hundred people who are successful in these areas and don't fit the list very well.

But let's try. John Burch, a fellow who has done a fair amount of writing on the subject, lists the following characteristics of entrepreneurs: a desire to achieve; capacity for hard work; a tendency to nurture quality in all things; the acceptance of responsibility; a desire to be rewarded handsomely for their work, not just in monetary terms, but also in recognition and respect; an optimistic bent (any time is the best of times and anything is possible); an orientation toward excellence; good at organizing with a take-charge attitude; a strong desire for profit as a way of metering achievement and performance.

Checking yourself out to see how you fit the list? People of any competence at all will have several or most of these characteristics. My own observation is that taking responsibility (I mean *really* taking it), the attitude that anything is possible, an ability at organizing complex systems, the drive for excellence (getting it done right, once and for all), and the nurturing of quality are the behaviors in shortest supply out there.

Now, if Burch is even approximately correct, and his list is as plausible as the next, here's something to notice: All of the characteristics save one are what might be called "genetic/environmental." They are personal aspects of behavior that are acquired by poorly understood processes in places other than our formal educational systems or even in organizations in general.

The one characteristic that seems to be teachable, in the usual sense, and it is a critical one, is "good at organizing," though the "take-charge attitude" portion of this is up for grabs. (I'll come back to this matter of organizing later on.)

Notice that the idea of risk has been absent from everything I have said, even though there is a tendency to equate risk-taking with entrepreneurship, and the early writers on the subject did just that. Yet some empirical studies show no difference between ordinary managers and those people we would classify as entrepreneurs.

Other writers downplay the importance of risk in entrepreneurial ventures, arguing that most of these enterprises start very small and are bootstrapped upward a little at a time, with minimal risk being present at any particular stage. The evidence is not conclusive on the matter of risk-taking and entrepreneurship.

Where are entrepreneurs found? Where opportunities exist for innovation, that's where. Entrepreneurship is not limited to business. There are entrepreneurs in all walks of life, in education, government, and health care delivery, as well as business, though the dynamism of entrepreneurial people often is throttled in large organizations grown conservative by age and attainment.

Peter Drucker, the respected old warhorse of management philosophy and practice, has been studying entrepreneurs for thirty years and, in his book, *Innovation and Entrepreneurship,* has boiled this work down into seven sources of entrepreneurial opportunity. Some of his categories are a little hazy, and some overlap, but they are still worth looking at. I present them along with some examples of my own that relate to Iowa.

The Unexpected. Drucker considers this the richest source of entrepreneurial opportunity. In its own way, the unexpected agricultural crisis coupled with the change in Americans' eating habits away from red meat has provided an opportunity for a return to the broiler-hen business. Farm families desire to supplement their farm incomes, there are empty facilities on the farms, and Americans are demonstrating a preference for poultry versus pork or beef. One north Iowa community is investigating the feasibility of a major investment in a poultry-processing plant because of these unexpected developments.

Incongruities. Goat ranches, lettuce fields, catfish farms, and the like usually are not considered as having much to do with tourism. Yet *Country* magazine finds its tours to these places, normally thought of as rather dull vacation stops, booked solid. There is apparently a strong desire by people to see the more-or-less ordinary transactions of life in rural areas. In short, the magazine discovered a discrepancy between what really exists and what everybody assumes to be true. Anyone in Iowa contacted *Country?*

Here's another example. In a world seemingly devoted to concrete, circuit boards, and the roar of jet airplanes, Maurice and Herbert Frink of Waterloo saw the need for, of all things, flowers. Now, their Flowerama of America, Inc., has one hundred franchises in twenty-four states. Flowers. Just flowers. And a lot of money and a lot of jobs.

Need for a change in process. Robotics, quality circles, and the use of lasers for cataract surgery are examples here. One of the nastiest problems in Iowa is how to keep rural communities vital by maintaining their schools while affording young people the opportunities for a rich and diversified educational experience. There is a glitch in the educational process, in other words, that is having broad and severe social ramifications. Somebody's going to clean up by figuring out how to use the power of modern electronics and telecommunications to remove this discrepancy.

Changes in industry and market structures plus demographic shifts plus changes in perception. I lump these three together because they so directly relate to the phenomenon of an aging Iowa. Obviously, this trend has to be moderated if the state is going to be viable in the long run. On the other hand, there are opportunities galore in the current direction. Older people have more disposable income, have different tastes, and require different services than younger folks.

People of age travel, often to exotic destinations. And when they aren't traveling, it seems they are moving somewhere else to retire. Retirement is an industry in and of itself. Ask Arkansas. Moreover, it tends to be a stable, quiet, nonpolluting, and low-crime industry. Iowa is not even listed in books on desirable places to retire, even though Illinois and Wisconsin are, and that's pitiful.

It is howling testimony to the uncreative way in which the state has perceived and pursued economic development, lamenting the "brain drain" from Iowa while ignoring the economic impact of the older segments of our population. One exception here: Some private firms have recognized this opportunity, such as Charles Colby's The Lodge of Ashworth, a retirement community in Des Moines, and innovators in home health care delivery.

Thus right before us we have changes in market structure and demographic shifts. Now, all we need is a change in perception from the bottle being half empty to it being half-full.

Knowledge-based innovation. This category is a little hard to deal with, since all innovations flow, in one way or the other, from knowledge. Basically, Drucker is talking about that elusive thing called "high tech" and other innovations in such fields as health care and financial services. Iowa is attempting to enter the areas of laser technology and molecular biology via the pathways mentioned earlier in connection with university efforts.

Drucker has rather harsh words to say about the high-tech field as a source of entrepreneurial opportunity. While acknowledging that high tech reigns as a "superstar" in the eyes of the public because of the publicity it gets and the venture capital it attracts, he points out, "More people have probably become rich building such prosaic businesses as shoe-polish or a watchmaking company than have become rich through high-tech business."

Furthermore, he warns of the substantial casualty rate in high-tech ventures, the long time span between the emergence of new knowledge and its applicability to technology, the extreme turbulence and consequent shakeouts in high-tech industries, and the constant need to plow more and more money back into research, technical development, and technical services to stay in the race. There is more, and our public officials in Iowa are well advised to at least read Drucker's arguments.

It's also interesting to look at the *INC.* magazine list of the one hundred fastest growing companies in America, a list that is updated and published each year. In 1986, only about thirty of the companies listed are directly in the high-tech field.

And, since *INC.*'s list is limited to publicly owned companies, there is, as Drucker points out, a natural bias toward high tech, which because it is fashionable, "has easy access to underwriters, to stock market money, and to being traded on one of the stock exchanges or over the counter." Even with these advantages in making the list, the high-tech firms accounted for only about 30 percent of *INC.*'s tabulation.

Let's put all of this together. In the 1978–1986 period, Iowa ranked forty-ninth among the fifty states in job growth, according to a study by the Federal Reserve Bank of Chicago. Among the causes listed for this miserable performance was the lack of small-business growth. And entrepreneurship is certainly an important part of small-business growth. (Not all small businesses are entrepreneurial. The key differentiating factor is innovation.)

Presumably, then, Iowa wants to encourage entrepreneurship. If we do, there are four elements to the problem. First, people with entrepreneurial capabilities must be recognized and assisted. One way or the other, these people tend to identify themselves.

If the list of entrepreneurial characteristics presented earlier is at all accurate, and it seems to echo the content of most such lists, then the major area where help can be given is in the organizational sphere, since the other characteristics apparently are either inherited or the product of one's general environment. Therefore, a second aspect of the problem is helping entrepreneurs acquire organizational skills, including how to search for and acquire capital.

This skill is as important as any of the other abilities listed. In fact, it is often the Achilles' heel of entrepreneurs. I personally have been acquainted with two small Iowa firms, both of which had considerable promise and employed a total of approximately one hundred people, that have fallen on hard times. In each case, the businesses were so successful that, paradoxically, they grew beyond the organizational skills of the original entrepreneurs and suffered greatly for it.

Entrepreneurs tend to be production-oriented. That is, they are good at the core technology, and maybe the marketing, aspects of the business. Many of them, however, lack the necessary management skills to handle the business once it has grown past the point where the entrepreneur can supervise everything that's going on. And to be quite blunt about it, a fair number of entrepreneurs find the tasks of purely managing an operation to be tedious. They grew up in the shop, so to speak.

A third element in encouraging entrepreneurship is the provision of venture capital, and sources for this capital must be established in both the private and public sectors. Some of this has already been accomplished, with the creation of the Iowa Fund, The Iowa Business Development Corporation, and the Invest America Venture Group, Inc., in Cedar Rapids, though I have no idea of the activity level of these funds in supporting Iowa entrepreneurship.

Finally, there are the sources for entrepreneurial innovation I talked about earlier. Many of these opportunities are in relatively mundane places we surely will neglect if overcommitment is made to alluring, let's-bet-it-all areas, such as high tech.

Entrepreneurs have a way of finding opportunities themselves. Yet, there are an abundance of opportunities out there at any time that will go unnoticed if left to the forces of chance discovery.

Several years ago, I proposed the establishment of a think tank for Iowa — a small, politically independent, state-funded research unit staffed with hard-headed people possessing practical and theoretical knowledge, whose task would be to exercise what one of my old professors used to call "opportunistic surveillance." The job of this group would be to constantly scan the world for opportunities of potential interest to Iowa, evaluate these opportunities, and forward its findings to the public at large, including state officials. I still think this idea-generator might be a good idea.

The entrepreneurial opportunities available to Iowa are staggering in number. Most of them require no heavy expenditures at the outset and will become self-sustaining as they grow. As we mature, as we acquire wisdom, we will begin to understand the value of the small increment and the power of innovation. We will come to appreciate that things of worth are built day by day and do not require the largess of panicked state officials, whose current munificence will become the future burden of ourselves and our children.

FOR FURTHER READING

"Best Jobs for the Future." *U.S. News & World Report,* September 25, 1989, pp. 60–71.

Booth, Robert. "Dominica." *National Geographic,* June 1990, pp. 101–20.

Center for Rural Affairs. *Half a Glass of Water—State Economic Development Policies and the Small Agricultural Communities of the Middle Border.* Walthill, Nebr.: Center for Rural Affairs, 1990.

Cetron, Marvin, and Owen Davies. *American Renaissance.* New York: St. Martin's, 1989.

Diamonstein, Barbaralee. *Handmade in America.* New York: Harry N. Abrams, 1983.

Drucker, Peter. "Facing the 'Totally New and Dynamic.' " *Time,* January 22, 1990, pp. 6–7.

Guskind, Robert. "Where Have All the Good Jobs Gone?" *Des Moines Register,* June 10, 1990, pp. 1C, 3C.

Leiss, William. *The Limits to Satisfaction: An Essay on the Problem of Needs and Commodities.* Toronto: University of Toronto Press, 1976.

Lessinger, Jack. "Emerging Region of Opportunity." *American Demographics,* June 1987, pp. 33 ff.

National Geographic Society. *The Craftsman in America.* Washington, D.C.: National Geographic Society, 1975.

Pins, Kenneth. "Census Drops Iowa to No. 30 in U.S. Rankings." *Des Moines Register,* September 3, 1990, p. 1A.

Power, Thomas Michael. *The Pursuit of Economic Quality.* Armonk, N.Y.: M.E. Sharpe, 1988.

Waller, Robert James. "Frontiers, Part I" and "Frontiers, Part II." In *One Good Road Is Enough,* by Robert James Waller. Ames: Iowa State University Press, 1990.

_____. "Going Soft Upon the Land and Down Along the Rivers." In *Just Beyond the Firelight,* by Robert James Waller. Ames: Iowa State University Press, 1988.

_____. "Lasers, Dreams, and Real Money." In *Just Beyond the Firelight,* by Robert James Waller. Ames: Iowa State University Press, 1988.

Westphal, David. "Census Projection Is Wrong, Experts Say." *Des Moines Register,* April 10, 1988, pp. 1A, 8A.

Woolson, Eric. "Iowa Mental Health Care Comes under Heavy Fire." *Waterloo Courier,* September 12, 1990, p. A5.

Yepsen, David. "Branstad: Job Bank Needed to Bring Iowa Alumni Back to State." *Des Moines Register,* September 28, 1990, p. 2A.

CHAPTER TEN

Opportunities

The tendency in discussing business opportunities is to focus exclusively on new domains of commercial activity. To do so would be a serious error. For example, while lasers may be an important new technology that Iowa should examine for opportunities, that does not mean we should ignore insurance or agriculture, two industries that have been at the core of Iowa's economic well-being for decades.

Excitement about the new and emerging should not be cause for neglecting HON Industries' furniture and Amana Refrigeration's appliances (twenty-nine hundred employees and sales of $400 million a year) and Maytag's laundry equipment and Meredith's publications and Bandag's tire retreading and Viking Pump's pumps and H & H's custom machine tools and Waterloo Industries' toolboxes and John Deere's agricultural implements. In other words, it's entirely possible that much of our future lies in simply doing better what we already do, rather than seeking always to embrace the newfangled.

Moreover, the thinking of Iowans tilts toward goods rather than services. We have, I think, had a production mentality, rather than a service orientation. Yet the service sector has been and will continue to be a rapidly growing segment of the American economy. The Iowa Department of Employment Services forecasts that service occupations will increase by 22.6 percent by the year 2000, while semiskilled production occupations will increase only 1.3 percent and farm careers along with related occupations will drop 4.8 percent.

One service sector offering many opportunities for Iowa is consulting of all types. Sophisticated consulting firms can range from one-person operations to organizations employing hundreds of highly paid specialists. For example, Stanley Consultants Group in Muscatine employs four hundred people. One can sell knowledge as well as products. Keep that in mind when I mention consulting opportunities in the discussions below.

I have tried not to duplicate too closely the popular recommendations for Iowa's economic development that continue to appear in various reports and newspaper articles. One of the most talked about areas, high technology — an umbrella term covering microelectronics, biotechnology, robotics, and telecommunications — has been a favorite of Governors Robert Ray and Terry Branstad. Ray talked about the promise of high technology in 1982, and Branstad has made it a key economic development target over the last eight years.

For all of the noise, however, Iowa has yet to benefit much in job creation from high technology; we rank thirty-first in scientists and engineers per one thousand workers. Still, proponents of this thrust argue that we have only laid the foundation, with the benefits yet to come. I remain a healthy skeptic about the employment benefits of high technology in Iowa — not negative, but skeptical . . . and hopeful.

A subject seldom discussed by those for whom high technology is nearly a religion is the cost per job created. If high technology contributes to our gloss of being advanced and contemporary, that's one thing. But the investments in this field are usually justified in terms of jobs. At the moment, the cost-benefit equation is nowhere in balance, particularly when the opportunity cost of monetary interest on state investments in high technology is taken into account, which it never is.

In this chapter, my intent is to present some possibilities that deserve consideration and further exploration. Basically, I have employed four criteria in devising my list. First, the products and services ought to be at the core of people's lives, rather than at the fringes. Second, I underscore certain opportunities where aid can be given to our suffering natural environment.

Third, many of my suggestions, while comparatively mundane, involve areas where a lot of money can be made with only small investments and minimal risk, lending themselves to entrepreneurial bootstrapping. And, fourth, I emphasize trends that seem inexorable, that are not going to disappear with the next smashing technological breakthrough.

One area I do not talk about, intentionally, is weapons manufacture.

Iowa has some good corporate citizens in this field already, such as Chamberlain Manufacturing in Waterloo, but I do not believe we should become any more involved in the production of killing machines than we already are. Others may do it and make a fortune. Let them. My vision for Iowa emphasizes sustainability and caring, not destruction, regardless of the boyish enthusiasm one can find for the potential of new "smart" weapons. In addition to the morality question, weapons manufacturing is an economically volatile area, and from a strict value-added perspective in terms of an economy's stock of productive wealth, it adds nothing and contributes to inflationary pressures.

Relying on current trends as a means of looking at the future has its liabilities. Trends have a way of disappearing after a while as societal shifts in values or technology, or both, alter them. Others go unnoticed or are ignored until they reach a critical state. The degradation of the natural environment is a good example of this latter trend. Still, several trends seem sure to influence our future as a state. And though some of them appear to involve rather nasty problems, these problems also offer opportunities.

I call these "TAO opportunities" (with apologies to those of Taoist philosophical leanings). TAO is my acronym for "two things at once." I have stolen the idea from the old French epigram "Never do just one thing," which has some benefits not only for getting along in life, but also in economic development. The idea is this: In dealing with the problems we will confront, we should figure out how to profit from our work on these problems, since we have to deal with them anyway. Thus, the TAO approach to economic development—solve a problem and make money doing it.

Conceptually, this is quite different from the ordinary strategy, if it can be called a strategy, of looking to find new businesses that can generate tax revenues to solve various problems. That's treating problems and opportunities as being in separate boxes, which is not a very efficient way to do things. The TAO strategy puts them into the same box and stirs them together—two things at once.

PROBLEMS WITH THE NATURAL ENVIRONMENT

One trend clearly is the degradation of the natural environment and the search for solutions to environmental problems. Already, Iowa is recognized as a leader in groundwater legislation and research. We should try to package our expertise in this area and sell it to other areas of the nation and world having similar problems. Our opportunities here range from the sale of consulting services to better water filters to well-drilling equipment to nitrate removal systems.

A second natural environment problem is air pollution. The federal Clean Air Act of 1990 contains several goals for the year 2000: Cut acid rain pollutants by half, reduce dramatically urban smog, and eliminate most of the toxic emissions from industrial plants. As noted previously, the estimated cost of meeting these goals is $25 billion per year.

These costs will present problems for Iowa and its industries. But the requirements of the act also offer opportunities. While we're working on helping everyone from power plants to dry cleaners to meet the new standards, we should be looking at possible products and services connected with cleaning up the air that we can market. Scrubbers are one example. Disposal units for those firms using volatile chemicals are another. A third is environmentally acceptable incineration units for hospitals. A fourth example is alternative fuels for automobiles.

Sustainable agriculture is another field ripe for solving our own problems and exporting our technical knowledge to other areas at the same time. As we devise new methods of planting, cultivating, and harvesting, including biotechnology, we should simultaneously be thinking about how our innovations can be turned into exports. My guess is that John Deere already is doing this; if they're not, they should be. Every idea, every innovation, no matter how small it may seem initially, is a possible product or service.

Moreover, Iowa ranks first among the states in the amount of pesticides used per person — 26.2 pounds. We're also first in the percentage of pesticide contamination of our groundwater, at 75 percent. Since we have the toughest problems in these areas, we should become the best at low-input agriculture and then sell our expertise to others.

Then there's the energy problem. The opportunities here are numerous. And, again, these opportunities are a perfect example of the TAO approach to development. Because of our relatively harsh climate and the importation of 97 percent of our energy supplies, Iowa should be at the forefront in research and development of energy conservation and alternative energy.

We are not, in spite of some trial programs in selected cities and the widely applauded work of Wes Birdsall at the Osage Municipal Utilities. The Iowa Department of Natural Resources reports that Iowans use more energy per person than forty other states, and we rank forty-sixth in the gas mileage of the cars we choose to drive.

We have bet $50–$60 million (a cost of $25 million plus the cost of amortizing the bonds) on the laser research center at the University of Iowa. Lasers certainly appear to be a promising high-tech industry, but it's a gamble nonetheless. I would have preferred that $50 million be given to the university for research on energy alternatives for Iowa and how these alternatives could be commercialized for export while solving Iowa's energy problems.

Some forecasts indicate that, in the next ten to twenty years, photovoltaics (solar-generated electricity) will become competitive with electrical power currently generated by conventional energy sources. As that occurs, the worldwide markets for solar generators and all the components used in their construction will escalate.

Even if it turns out that solar energy is a relatively small part of Iowa's energy future, funds spent on research and development in the solar field could have large payoffs. The earth must support roughly eight billion people by 2030, most of them in underdeveloped countries, and these people are going to need simple alternatives to fossil fuels for heating and cooking. Is there a market here for Iowa quality and ingenuity? Of course.

What are the possibilities? Innovations in caulking and weatherstripping and insulation, high-efficiency lighting, and just about anything else you can conjure up. Iowans spend too much time traveling to "safe" destinations, such as Europe and Hawaii. We send trade missions to obvious places such as Japan and China. What we don't seem to do is visit underdeveloped countries, get to know average citizens there, and get outside the westernized hotels to see how people really live. If we did, we would have been manufacturing inexpensive solar generators or other devices in the alternative energy arena, the best ones in the world, long ago. On your fifth straight night in south India without a hot shower, you start thinking about solar water heaters and the huge potential market for them.

We should form a public-private organization called the Iowa Energy Corporation whose job it is to prepare Iowa for the new age of energy that's coming and, simultaneously, to develop export markets for the technologies we develop or adapt for ourselves. This corporation would have three functions:

1. Develop a long-range plan for Iowa's energy needs
2. Based on the plan, allocate research contracts to universities and

firms for studying various alternative energy sources and technologies
3. Provide start-up funds to Iowa firms showing promise in the energy
field

The payoff from this corporation would be relatively fast. First, we'd be saving on energy consumption in Iowa, which is the same as cutting back on imports to the state that send money outward across our borders. Second, we'd discover what technologies are most promising for export to other areas of the nation and world. We're already behind in this area, but we can catch up and forge ahead, if we have the will. We're going to have to change our ways in the energy domain, so we might as well commercialize our efforts while we're doing it. Otherwise, we'll still be importing our energy, either in raw materials or in assembled energy-generating units from elsewhere.

The rich field of environmental consulting also should not be overlooked. This activity meshes perfectly with the high-paying, white-collar jobs Iowa has been trying to attract. For example, Malcolm Pirnie, Inc., an environmental consulting firm based in White Plains, New York, employs some seven hundred engineers. I'm pretty sure Iowa would love to have such a firm, and there's nothing stopping us from doing it. The Stanley Consultants Group, mentioned earlier, includes environmental problems as one of its four operational areas.

How can it be done? It's not all that difficult, with some front-end leadership from the state. We should define what types of environmental consulting appear to be required over the next few decades. Then we should design an organization that can handle the work. The design should be matched against expertise already existing in the state, with gaps closed through recruiting. The state should provide start-up funds via a public corporation strategy and subsidies. Eventually, as sufficient revenues are generated, the firm's linkages with state government could be severed.

In addition, the state should form an environmental products and services clearinghouse. Ideas from Iowans and others can then be examined for commercialization possibilities. This easily could be a function of the Wallace Technology Transfer Foundation discussed later in this chapter.

The coming shortages of fossil fuels and other environmental constraints are going to require massive changes in the way the world functions on a daily basis. The TAO opportunities in dealing with these problems are enough to propel a set of Iowa industries for decades.

RECYCLING AND RELATED STRATEGIES

The ideas in this section properly belong under the natural environment heading. So much attention, however, is being lavished on recycling that it deserves a section all its own. (Figure 2.1 in Chapter Two will be helpful in conceptualizing much of what I say here.)

Recycling, in the broadest sense, is a strategy for dealing with what I have called the "input-output squeeze" in earlier chapters. This squeeze is really just another way of talking about scarcity. That is, we confront pressures on two sides in our production and consumption processes.

First, there is the limited quantity of resources available to the peoples of the world. As eight billion of us, the round-figure forecast for world population by 2030 or a little later, try to live at the level of comfort sought by Americans, the drawdown of critical resources such as copper, cobalt, molybdenum, nickel, and petroleum will be severe. The simple fact of scarcity in certain resource stocks already is evident and promises to worsen, given existing technologies. That's the input side of the squeeze. It's the problem we've worried about for decades.

Only recently have most people begun to recognize the output side of the squeeze, which involves having places to put the offal from our production and consumption processes. Americans produce approximately 160 million tons of trash each year, over thirteen hundred pounds from every American, enough to fill a line of ten-ton garbage trucks stretching halfway to the moon. Landfills fill and limited space for new ones results in cities shipping wastes hundreds of miles to remote sites, nuclear wastes sitting in rusting barrels while we fret over proper disposal, rivers becoming polluted, acid rain falling, and carbon dioxide pumping into the heavens. These are only a few examples of the output side of the problem.

Since matter can neither be created nor destroyed, an ideal economic system would function much like a natural ecosystem, where the outputs of one process become the inputs for another. Thus the system would be closed, with little or no loss of anything outside of the system. In nature, plants synthesize nutrients. In turn, herbivores feed on the plants, carnivores eat the herbivores, and the wastes and decaying bodies of carnivores eventually return nutrients to the soil for plant use. This is nature's approach to recycling.

In human economic systems, we now are seeking to emulate such cyclical processes, calling the approach "industrial ecology." All such efforts involve technological innovation in its purest form. Because of the diverse production and consumption processes existing in industrialized economies, the opportunities for innovation are myriad. And, understand, these are business opportunities—the new idea for reusing waste, the new valve that aids this reuse, better initial product design that facilitates recycling, collection units for consumer recyclables—all of these offer Iowans emerging opportunities for profitable businesses.

One intriguing idea is that of "engineered scrap." Here, products and their production are designed in such a way that waste from manufacturing can be fed directly back into the process just completed or to another process that uses the waste from the first process as an input. This already is occurring in certain areas of metal and plastics manufacturing and long has been a practice in iron production (GM's four foundries operate entirely on scrap steel from other GM processes and scrap iron from the casting process itself). Another example, though still controversial to many environmentalists, is using wastes as inputs for steam or electricity generation via high-efficiency incinerators. Nature can engineer scrap, in a matter of speaking; we can do the same.

Problems Inhibiting Recycling

Recycling seems like a good idea. More than that, the input-output squeeze demands that it be done. Why, then, has the United States, in particular, been slow to adopt recycling strategies? There are several reasons, all of them interrelated.

One reason is a combination of sheer economics and technological innovation. For example, the concept of engineered scrap is a matter of both product design and alterations in production processes. As I have emphasized over and over, incentives drive decision making. As long as resources were relatively plentiful, as long as we felt unhindered in pumping our wastes into a natural environment with no cost for such behavior, the incentives for recycling have not been present. Hence, the pressures for technical changes in product design and manufacture have also been absent.

Given two alternatives, recycle or don't recycle, business chooses the alternative that reduces costs and maximizes profits. If resources are plentiful and relatively cheap, and if there is no charge for dumping wastes into nature, the nonrecycling alternative is favored. When, however, resource costs rise and charges or restrictions, or both, are applied to waste disposal, the recycling alternative begins to compete with the nonrecycling alternative.

A woman who is a recent convert to environmentalism called me recently. She was excited about the possibilities of recycling and was frustrated at the lack of such activity in the city where I live. "Why don't we collect plastic milk bottles and rubber tires and newspapers?" she asked. "Let's get something going!" Of course I applaud both recycling and her enthusiasm for it, but I tried, unsuccessfully I think, to explain the problem of markets to her.

In a capitalistic system, it takes both buyers and sellers to establish a market. Thus if plastic milk bottles are to be converted into park benches, someone must be willing to undertake the conversion process. If the bottles can be collected and processed at a cost less than the price for which the park benches can be produced and sold, then the possibility for a market exists. If not, recycling languishes, unless government subsidies are forthcoming to support the effort, or unless cities, as an act of conscience, are willing to pay more for plastic park benches than metal ones. (However, if a technological innovation emerges allowing cheaper conversion of plastic bottles into other products, such as park benches, the process may become economically feasible.)

Then there's the problem of governments and how they influence decision making via incentives. For instance, if stringent regulations about the handling of hazardous wastes in recycling are instituted, it may be cheaper for business firms not to engage in recycling and simply pay whatever costs are necessary to dispose of the wastes. In designing regulations, as pointed out before, it's critical that the explicit or implicit incentives present in the regulations be carefully studied prior to implementation.

At the consumer level, many obstacles exist that thwart recycling. If recycling is to work, sorting of trash is necessary prior to collection. That takes time and effort. Some will do this because they believe it is a good thing to do. For others, it's a matter of incentives. Charges for trash removal and disposal, while appealing to the logic of pay-as-you-go, can act as a disincentive. The result is rubber tires and old refrigerators along the roadsides. Iowa's deposit system on bottles and cans has worked well as a litter-control measure because consumers have a monetary incentive to return the containers.

Still other disincentives, perverse ones, operate to prevent recycling. Firms that produce virgin products are not anxious to see their markets decline because of recycling. The same thing is true of those who haul trash as a business. Then there's the problem of scale. A city may not produce enough trash to make the construction of an incinerator or recycling plant feasible. Is the solution, then, to produce more trash?

As a society, America appears slothful in its consumption and recycling efforts compared with other countries. For example, a resident of New York City generates twice as much waste every day as does a resident of Hamburg, Germany. Perhaps consciousness-raising will accomplish recycling. I hope so; but I prefer to rely on incentives while we're getting our consciousnesses raised.

Intuitively, recycling sounds like a workable answer to some of our resource and disposal problems. Eventually, it will become a way of life for both consumers and manufacturers. Still, the realities of markets must be recognized. As Jeff Buer, of Container Recovery, Inc. (a Des Moines firm), says: "The idea of recycling is fine and dandy, but what do you do with the stuff once it gets segregated. The trend to recycle products is happening so fast, the industry can't keep up with it."

Opportunities in Recycling

In complex systems, second-order effects exist. That is, one pushes a policy button to deal with a problem and unintended effects occur beyond what was envisioned by the original policymakers. Iowa's bottle-deposit law, passed by the Iowa Legislature in 1979, was intended as a litter-control measure; recycling was not an issue.

Suddenly, beverage distributors were forced to collect the containers and found themselves with huge amounts of returned cans and bottles. Initially, they simply crushed the containers and hauled them to landfills, because no market existed to absorb the empties. At least two businesses have now been established in Iowa that handle collection and resale of the containers to aluminum and glass manufacturers who recycle the material into new cans and bottles.

One of these firms, employing ninety people, also has designed and patented equipment for crushing cans and bottles, for baling aluminum, and for cleaning glass. The sale of this equipment provides those distributors who wish to collect and resell their own cans and bottles a feasible way of handling these tasks. One result is that 85 percent of the aluminum cans sold in Iowa are now recycled, compared with an average of 55 percent nationally.

The entire issue of recycling involves fascinating problems that strike at the heart of market system economics. I expect the business opportunities in this arena to escalate dramatically as the input-output squeeze tightens. Because of the difficulties involved in the start-up phase, which is where we are currently, it's an area that is a prime candidate for state subsidies.

Such funds can jumpstart recycling efforts where they might

otherwise languish. Those who solve the basic problems and obtain patents on their ideas, particularly in the area of equipment and process, will confront the pleasant prospect of worldwide markets for their products.

Recycling obviously is one answer to our waste dilemma and fits well with the TAO approach to economic development. Iowans, like everyone else, confront waste disposal problems. While we're solving these problems, we should think about how our solutions can be converted into products and services.

There are business opportunities in recycling now; more will come later. Still, we should recognize that recycling, viewed in another way, is just one more attempt to enable the continuation of a high-consumption society, a technological fix that suits the status quo. A society that uses less would have less need for recycling. Ultimately, that will be the solution to our waste problem, and I think we'll be happier for it.

One final note. California and a few other areas of the United States have waste information exchanges whereby those who produce waste can locate those who can make use of it, and vice versa. Such a network has been started in ten southeast Iowa counties. It's a concept whose usage will undoubtedly spread and should be encouraged.

DIET AND NUTRITION

Here's another example of economic development in the TAO mode, one that I've alluded to before. Clearly, fat derived from ordinary foods plays a major role in both cancer and heart disease. That much we know. And, slowly, the American diet is changing toward foods lower in fat. In addition, the animal rights and vegetarian movements, though still small, are beginning to generate momentum. Dr. Walter Willett, professor of epidemiology and nutrition at the Harvard School of Public Health, who directed a large, recent study implicating red meat consumption in the development of colon cancer, has this to say about eating red meat: "At most, it should be eaten only occasionally. And it may be maximally effective not to eat red meat at all." Such trends and comments are potentially dismal for a state whose agricultural industry, one way or another, is primarily involved in producing animal flesh for human consumption.

We can choose to fight a rearguard action and denounce those who choose nutritional styles that do not fit our way of doing things, or we can become world leaders in the field of nutrition and food production designed to satisfy the demand for low-fat diets. Iowa agriculture (to generalize a bit) is notoriously conservative toward change. The attitude long has been one of, "Here's what *we want* to produce; now let's find a way to sell it."

A better approach is to examine what people may demand in the way of food and then attempt to produce those foods. That's called the marketing concept. It gets you out on the frontiers, rather than grumbling around in the dust while markets disappear.

The decision by Nichi Co., Ltd., to build a soybean-processing plant in Jefferson, Iowa, is a good example. The plant will produce soybean flakes, which function as a building block in the manufacture of tofu, the high-protein soybean curd. Tofu long has been a staple in oriental and domestic vegetarian diets and shows signs of attaining global popularity.

The plant will accomplish three things for Iowa. First, the raw material will be processed here. That's called "value-added" because it adds additional stages of income to the Iowa economy that would be lost if the beans were shipped elsewhere for processing. It's exactly what many of us have been arguing for since the 1970s—raise crops *and* process them here.

Second, it increases the demand for soybeans. Third, it gives us a foothold in markets catering to evolving dietary preferences, rather than simply running more advertisements cajoling people toward increased meat consumption. One supposes that folks in Jefferson and on surrounding grain farms might now applaud vegetarians, rather than scoffing at them. It's amazing how easily opinions can shift given the right monetary incentives.

In any case, the Nichi plant is a move in the right direction for Iowa. We should take more such steps. We should start looking clearly at what's occurring out there, in terms of consumer demand, rather than whining at the local cafe about vegetarians and their impact on the meat industry.

If we're going to think clearly about the future, we need to be able to think the unthinkable as part of our planning. It's what I like to call the high probability of the improbable. Thus the Iowa agricultural industry should ask, "What would happen if 50 percent of Americans no longer eat meat by the year 2010?"

The answers will be illuminating, even if the proportion is not that high. First of all, it starts people thinking about alternatives to a flesh-based agricultural industry. And in those alternatives will be strategies for exporting to the billions of people already alive who do not eat meat, either by preference or because of its cost. India, for instance, will soon become the most populous country on earth, and large portions of its population are vegetarians. At the moment, India is self-sustaining in food production, but that may change given its population explosion mixed with the environmental decline evident there. Markets exist or are emerging that we will miss by clinging only to the old ways of doing things.

The issue of meatless or cheeseless or milkless diets, or even cutting back on the consumption of these products, is generally an explosive one in Iowa. Our view of the future should not be clouded by fear of controversy. Only those with minds unprepared for the future avoid searching for the truth or, worse yet, try to suppress it. They are not part of Iowa's enhanced future and should be ignored.

OUR AGING POPULATION

We fret about the increasing proportion of Iowans who can be classified as elderly. Second only to Florida in this category, as mentioned earlier, we are approximately fifteen years ahead of other states. Strictly from the viewpoint of economics, our struggles to manage a population with a high proportion of elderly offer many opportunities for financial gain. In a way that seems slightly crass at first glance, but is not, we might think of caring for the elderly as an industry itself. This also falls under the heading of a TAO opportunity. It's a problem we're going to have to deal with; we may as well market our solutions to others.

Opportunities here include the following:

1. Innovative programs in insurance and social services
2. The development of care systems for use in Iowa that can be exported. Computer software for record-keeping, nursing home management strategies, and nursing home construction are examples. Nursing homes now outnumber hospitals in the United States by two to one and will be hiring increasing numbers of both health-care professionals and unskilled labor. Due to low birth rates during the Great Depression of the 1930s, a temporary slowing of the over-sixty-five population will occur in the 1990s. But, by 2010, as *U.S. News &*

World Report predicts, "a deluge of new retirees from the baby-boom generation will cause elder care to surpass child care as a national priority and career market."

3. Hardware, such as special beds, prosthetics, railings for wheelchair ramps, and physical therapy equipment; medical supply in general.*
4. Foods designed especially for elderly people. This meshes nicely with the diet and nutrition opportunities mentioned in the previous section.
5. Consulting services in a wide range of fields. Examples are physical therapy, hospital management, recordkeeping, and medical-supply systems.
6. Catering to the needs of elderly adults who either cannot or do not wish to continue doing certain basic tasks. Balancing checkbooks, handling investments, and dealing with the complexities of medical insurance are illustrations. Firms are cropping up in this field in other parts of the country, and at least one Iowa attorney is already providing such services. Fees range from fifty to one hundred dollars per hour for such work. There's a critical service component included here, for it allows many elderly to maintain their independence for additional years.

Here's another possibility, worth mentioning again. Can Iowa become a haven for the elderly? Retirement is an industry all by itself. Ask Arkansas and Texas and Florida. Moreover, it tends to be a quiet, stable, nonpolluting, low-crime industry, with substantial amounts of disposable income (though, admittedly, a large proportion of our elderly are not in good shape, financially). Why isn't Iowa listed in books on desirable places to retire, along with Illinois and Wisconsin?

Winter weather can be countered by self-contained retirement complexes under a single roof or connected by enclosed walkways. Atrium areas help. Larger areas, including swimming pools and gardens, are possible with domed construction and miniature but complete ecosystems that are self-sustaining.

We have lamented the "brain drain" and exodus of young people from the state while ignoring the economic impact of the older segments of our population. I'm generalizing a bit here, but it's mostly true. What

---

*A good example of physical therapy equipment is a small hassocklike product over which people recline while doing certain exercises for neck rehabilitation. My local hospital uses a Swedish-made device for this and has trouble getting them. The device, with a simple design and construction, sells for several hundred dollars.

we need is a change in perception from the bottle being half empty to it being half full. In 1990, more than 50 million Americans were over fifty-five. Expenditures by this group accounted for $800 billion in consumption expenditures annually, which was 42 percent of all consumer demand.

Suppose we welcome the elderly from everywhere. Suppose we become known as a place hospitable to the elderly, where retirement communities and nursing homes are designed and managed better than anywhere else in the world. Suppose we are smart enough to figure out the difficult economics of caring for healthy elderly, as well as the infirm and helpless. What might happen? Carried out correctly, this would provide jobs for a range of people, including doctors, nurses, orderlies, recreational specialists, and physical therapists. We would become famous as a place of caring and, in the process, provide a lot of jobs for Iowans.

SMALL THINGS FOR LARGE MARKETS

As I mentioned earlier, lasers, biotechnology, robotics, and microelectronics are popular (and obvious) buzzwords for Iowa economic development. Getting involved in high-technology fields such as these gives the impression of being contemporary, of being industrially sophisticated and out at the frontiers of big-time commerce. Yet enormous opportunities exist in making simple, basic products for which there is a large demand.

The underdeveloped countries account for much of the world's population; this proportion will increase as population rises over the next few decades. What do these people need on a daily, or at least frequent, basis that Iowans can supply? Footwear, water filters, high-efficiency wood stoves, and bicycles are just a few of the thousands of examples worth exploring.

In the manufacture of footwear and similar items, we cannot compete in terms of labor costs with these countries; I have watched Indian women sew leather uppers for famous American shoe brands at a wage rate of sixty cents per day. But what we might be able to do is supply components, for example, sandal buckles. We worry about designing lasers. Can we not also design a better buckle for sandals and produce these buckles or the machines for making them?

Suppose five billion people, by the year 2010, wear sandals. Suppose, furthermore, that each person purchases one sandal buckle per year, either as a replacement or as part of a new pair of sandals. If the buckle costs five cents, that's $250 million per year. If Iowa has only 10 percent of that market, it still amounts to $25 million per year, which is a decent-sized business.

Don't like the idea of sandal buckles? Then how about glue for holding pieces of the shoe together. It might surprise some Iowans to know that high-quality glues are not found worldwide. If we supply glue for holding parts of the shoe together at a nickel per pair of shoes, we have another $250 million industry.

With no other alternatives before them, more than half of the world's people use wood, charcoal, animal wastes, and crop residues as cooking fuel. This practice is environmentally devastating. Hence, a number of new designs for high-efficiency cooking stoves that burn organic products have emerged in the last decade. Half of the world's current population is 2.5 billion. Can Iowa make better stoves than anyone else, or even just make the equipment for metal stamping components for the stoves?

As the earth's water supply continues to degrade, underdeveloped countries with limited funds face serious problems in supplying clean drinking water. It's hard to overestimate how serious this problem is becoming. Again, there's the possibility for developing the world's best water filter or a simple, inexpensive pump and marketing either the product itself or the equipment to produce it.

With the energy problem bearing down upon us, bicycles will continue to increase in use. Iowa already has something of a reputation in the world and national bicycling community via the *Register*'s Annual Great Bike Ride Across Iowa (RAGBRAI), our network of bike trails, and some custom frame fabricators. Perhaps we can design and manufacture the world's best low-tech bicycle for a world that will demand more and more of these vehicles. It should be simple, durable, easily repairable, amenable to being hung off of buses and trains, and generally suitable for daily commuting. The market for bicycles, or just the critical components, is going to be huge—it's huge already. Perhaps we can manufacture only the gears or the seats or some other subcomponent for major manufacturers already established.

Maybe sandal buckles and footwear glue, or stoves and water filters and bicycles, are not good examples. That's not really the point. What I'm driving at is that we have a tendency to focus on sexy technology and ignore the market potential of small, simple things.

Vern Schield, Waverly (Iowa) industrialist and inventor, is a good resource for thinking of this kind. The founder of Self Help, an organization dedicated to the design and use of appropriate technology in developing countries, Schield probably has enough good ideas on small things for large markets to keep Iowans busy for a long time.

A perfect example of this was invented by a plumber who also happened to be a volunteer fireman. He recognized correctly that most fire-related deaths are caused by smoke inhalation, not flames. As a plumber, he knew that an unlimited supply of breathable air is always available from sink drainpipes. Therefore, connecting a hose from the drainpipe to masks that people can wear would prevent smoke inhalation. Nice, simple. Every major hotel in the world will eventually have these.

I mentioned India before. It's a country in which I have spent considerable time. Currently the United States is pushing India to become more flexible in its restraints on international trade. That will happen eventually, and India, with a population approaching one billion, offers a vast market for low-cost, high-quality products.

Produce a basic item needed by people in India or other developing countries and you have the potential of an industry that can support twenty or more small Iowa communities. An efficient wind generator for electricity or just a small part in such a generator will create large revenue flows to Iowa.

Start-up capital for all of the products I've mentioned is minimal, except perhaps for large-scale bicycle manufacturing. With the increasing world population, the potential markets for small items are huge. And while we are helping ourselves, we can also be helping others, another example of what I call a zen approach to development (see Chapter Nine).

COMPONENTS

In casting around for business opportunities, there is a rather natural tendency to look at finished products. Sometimes, however, as touched on in the previous section, component manufacturing can provide substantial opportunities for economic development. For a state such as Iowa, with many small towns looking for ways to survive economically, the production of finished products may be asking too much, whereas the manufacture of small parts for larger products *is* feasible.

One strategy, then, is to examine basic and enduring products already being produced, as well as potential new products having promise, for critical parts well suited to small fabrication operations. In a complex economy, particularly a worldwide economy, the possibilities are large in number. For example, Edge Technologies, Inc., of Ames has begun manufacturing powerful magnets for use in cars, loudspeakers, power tools, and other assorted applications.

This fits well with the TAO approach and also my suggestions about developing small products for large markets. For example, we might concentrate only on frames for solar collectors. At an even smaller level, we could focus on devices for fastening the collectors to the frames or critical components of the device(s) used to store the collected heat.

A good way to begin the search for opportunities in component manufacturing is to take virtually any product whose market is already established or has strong promise of developing and ask the final assembler what components are the most difficult to obtain at a reasonable price or quality. The Iowa DED easily could do this and put the results in a newsletter, call it "Opportunities in Component Manufacturing," which could be distributed throughout the state.

The opportunities, small and large, are in the hundreds of thousands here. In the millions, more accurately. And it's an area that lends itself well to entrepreneurs in smaller communities. I suggest an emphasis on high-end products, in terms of quality and price, where Iowa's intelligent work force can be used to advantage.

Products break down into hierarchical structures, much like organization charts. As an illustration, a camera body can be broken down into shutter, film transport, and light meter. The meter can be further subdivided into the various mechanisms for metering light or the type of meter, center-weighted or spot or matrix. Visual drawings of complex products can show both components and connections among components. Business opportunities can be found merely by looking at the parts and the connections among them.

Sophisticated Japanese firms have a history of purchasing components from smaller vendors. For example, Komatsu, Ltd., a world leader in construction equipment and machinery, still makes use of smaller vendors from the small community where it began. Japanese firms are known to be demanding when it comes to quality, and smaller vendors work closely with the final assembler to ensure that their outputs meet unforgiving specifications.

Vendor selection by the firm assembling components is a multiple-criteria decision. Typical criteria are price, vendor quality, and vendor history of delivering on time. A small firm wishing to supply components can ask the larger firm's management what criteria are used in vendor selection, along with how they are ranked in importance, and then analyze these criteria carefully to formulate a marketing strategy. Do it better, do it cheaper, and in most cases the contract is forthcoming.

MINIATURIZATION

Out of the processes used to produce microchips for computers and other electronic gear, a new set of tools is emerging. These are tiny moving parts, micromachines the size of sand grains, made up of lilliputian valves, gears, springs, levers, lenses, and ball bearings. For example, at the University of California in Berkeley, a research team has constructed a silicon motor slightly wider than an eyelash with the capability of rotating five hundred times a minute.

To examine an exciting area of robotics, this is the place to look. Imagine a robot the size of a gnat that can perform surgery inside the human body or operate minuscule space capsules. A 1988 report prepared for the National Science Foundation cited a number of uses for micromachines. Some of these are: micro-optical systems precisely focusing lasers in fiber-optic communication systems; miniature parts for tape recorders, camcorders, and computers; and pills that combine medication, a silicon thermometer, and the electronics necessary to send moment-by-moment temperature readings to an external recording device. One of the main areas of application, in terms of present thinking, seems to be in sensing devices of all types for implantation in structures as diverse as the human body and automobile engines.

A little further out, timewise, is something called nanotechnology, which involves items measured in billionths of a meter (nanometers). In the visions of nanotechnologists, buildings and cheeseburgers and airplanes are built atom by atom.

The economics get a little strange in the field of miniaturization. The front-end development costs are huge, but because copies of a workable prototype can be easily made, economies of scale are quickly reached. Miniaturization looks like one of the next quantum leaps in the high-technology sector.

VALUE-ADDED OPPORTUNITIES IN AGRICULTURE

This is an old topic in Iowa economic development. Well, ten or fifteen years old, anyway. Some of us were passionately arguing for an emphasis on value-added production derived from agricultural products a decade ago. Progress has been made, but not nearly as much as is possible.

As in other areas, we operate in a more or less random search mode, like an amoeba squishing around on a glass laboratory slide looking for food. One hopes for dazzling bursts of creativity, but it's not necessary to depend entirely on the old "Eureka!" effect. Diligent, structured search is a way of making creative possibilities surface.

A simple approach to developing ideas is called forced juxtaposition. It's a technique used by designers in many fields. For example, Iowa produces corn. Juxtapose corn against a long list of ideas; most of them will be nonsensical and discarded, but like panning for gold, a few useful nuggets will often be left at the end of the process.

Thus we might have a partial list that looks like this: corn cars, corn paper, corn computers, corn shoes, corn dolls, corn fuel, corn glue, corn foods. Fuel and food already are produced from corn. So focus on the subcategory of food, for example, and continue the process: corn drink, corn steak, corn sweetener, corn pepper, corn jelly, corn salad, corn tomatoes, corn yogurt, corn cheese. Then look at some of the interesting possibilities. Corn salad, for instance.

What does this mean? I don't know. But it might be worth exploring. We already have corn relish. Can we do something else with corn that turns it into a staple offering in homes and restaurants, one that could substitute part of the time for the familiar lettuce salad? Maybe. All creative people understand one simple fact: Failure is part of the process of creating something new — you throw away a lot more ideas than you keep. But those ideas retained may offer potential.

The largest producer of chickens in the United States is Tyson Foods, located in Springdale, Arkansas. While everybody else was shipping fresh broilers to market, Don Tyson was looking for ways to add value to his chickens, partly to avoid commodity market fluctuations. So he developed and marketed chicken nuggets, patties, and other processed chicken products to food service and fast food companies.

The result? Tyson Foods alone generates $2 billion each year in the $16 billion industry, and profits climbed 800 percent between 1978 and 1988 to $81 million. Nothing very fancy here; nothing very high tech. Why didn't we do this in Iowa?

Of course, fuels or fuel additives made from grain, such as ethanol, offer potential, depending on several variables. One is the price of oil. A second is the efficiency with which these fuels can be produced. A third is the environmental impact on the land from intensive cultivation and the inputs used in grain production. One study predicts that $360 million of investment in Iowa ethanol production facilities would occur if this product was used extensively to reduce auto emissions.

I don't believe we have yet explored the opportunities in value-added manufacturing using Iowa's farm products in a truly systematic, exhaustive fashion. Frankly, young schoolchildren might be a good source of such ideas, since their view of the world is still relatively untainted, in terms of what is and is not possible. Somewhere out there in the schools of Iowa is a kid who once thought about "chicken popcorn." If we had captured that idea and elaborated on it a little, chicken nuggets would have been ours.

AGRICULTURE – OLD PRODUCTS, NEW MARKETS

As I'm writing this, world grain supplies are at their lowest level in the last fourteen years. This, together with the opening of new European markets in the next decade, offers possibilities for Iowa's traditional grain products. Craig Carver, food industry analyst for Dain Bosworth, Inc., of Minneapolis believes no industry will have more opportunities than agriculture.

But forecasting anything in agriculture, affected as it is by politics and national security concerns and climate, is a dicey proposition. Changes in subsidy structures within and among countries, evolving food preferences, food health-and-safety issues, breakthroughs in biotechnology, and world-class environmental problems make this just about the murkiest area of all, one that lies far outside of my range of expertise. For that matter, probably outside the range of just about everyone's forecasting abilities.

Optimists see a world of open markets with expanded trade and riches for all. The darker side is a global pattern of trading blocs, economic protectionism, and economic failure. The global rules for agricultural trade, as U.S. Trade Representative Carla Hills observes, are "loose or nonexistent."

MARKETS AND THE LAND

It's hard to think in new ways; it's even harder to strike out in new directions, given the uncertainty of markets and the certainty of interest payments on borrowed capital. Yet, we must stop thinking solely of Iowa agriculture as corn, soybeans, hogs, and cattle. Those may be our basics now, and possibly they will remain our basics.

But, in light of shifting consumer tastes and potential climatic changes, a different perspective is in order. We should respond to markets rather than producing those products with which we're comfortable and attempting always to shape markets to our production preferences. That's the output side.

The land that is ours, land that is rich and expansive, is a multiproduct resource, even though it's not usually thought of that way. Just as a computer can perform various tasks, so the land is capable of multiple uses in the production of goods and services.

Since 1984 the U.S. Department of Agriculture, on a limited basis, has begun to talk about the feasibility and profitability of alternative crops. Particular attention is being paid to crops that have industrial markets, instead of being consumed as food. Examples are meadowfoam, jojoba, lesquerella, kenaf, rapeseed, and guayule. Current estimates are that new crops and their use in products could add as much as $15 to $20 billion per year to farmers' income in the United States.

On this land of ours we can provide recreation and gentle leisure activities. We can also raise amaranth and angora goats and llamas and ostriches and sheep and fallow deer, open bed-and-breakfast operations, and produce canola and Christmas trees and fish and firewood and grapes and herbs and honey and navy beans and sweetcorn and buckwheat and berries. At one time, Iowa was considered to have the highest-quality apple industry in America. In spite of lip service given to alternative crops, my sense is that a great deal more attention has been given to attracting smokestacks than to exploring, intensively and thoroughly, the possibilities offered by the land, particularly those that are environmentally sensitive.

INFRASTRUCTURE REPAIR AND CONSTRUCTION

We forget about what's underground. Our water and sewer systems for example. In our tendency to favor the short run over the long run, the United States has badly neglected the maintenance of its basic infrastructure. It's another one of those deficits we have created for ourselves while spending our money on consumer goods for which there is a questionable need. And good opportunities for the TAO approach to economic development exist here.

The bill is coming due. Massive, and I mean truly massive, repair and reconstruction of our basic infrastructure must occur. Already, streets are collapsing in some cities, bridges are being abandoned or their stress loads reduced, and steam pipes in New York are blowing up. Contemporary definitions of infrastructure now include airports, fiber optic networks, and telecommunication facilities.

The business opportunities in the entire infrastructure area appear to be many. And as is the case with just about everything else, there are possibilities for component manufacturing and consulting. The Vermeer Company in Pella is an example of an Iowa firm positioned well to supply equipment for infrastructure work, particularly in highway construction.

Adequate housing for a state or nation's population is also a kind of infrastructure. The housing stock in Iowa is, according to all reports, not in very good shape, especially in smaller communities. Can Iowa become a leader in the construction of quality, low-cost housing construction? We need to solve this problem within the state. Can our expertise or our materials, or both, be made into exportable products? The TAO outlook has many applications here, particularly in the area of small-scale energy production (for example, home solar and wind units) and conservation.

Moreover, there's not much of a gamble in tooling up for this kind of work, since it has to be done; there's no alternative. Good, attractive, energy-efficient housing is needed. Somebody's going to do it. Iowans might just as well be the ones.

Also, and this relates directly to the issue of an aging population, it's possible that radically different home designs will be needed. This is true both for new homes and remodeling of existing homes to house trigenerational families with mom, dad, children, and grandparents in one dwelling.

Furthermore, U.S. population trends indicate fewer new households will be formed. Exactly what this means in terms of home construction and remodeling is anybody's guess.

LANDSCAPING

I feel quite certain about the opportunities discussed thus far in the chapter, since they are based on trends unlikely to change quickly, such as the aging population. I am less certain about what to say in this section, but I think it's worth mentioning.

My guess is that an aging population and younger people scrambling to find more leisure time in their busy schedules will disdain traditional lawn care of the mowing/raking variety. Moreover, I expect concerns for the environment will propel opposition to lawn fertilizers and create an interest in providing micro habitats for wildlife; that's already occurring to some extent. Then there already are new laws prohibiting yard waste from being hauled to landfills. Given Iowa's expertise in growing things, all kinds of things, and the presence in the state of several large nurseries, we might consider developing a high level of production and marketing capability in the area of business and residential landscaping.

This is a case where we have to help people see the alternatives. The idea is to show how distinctive, attractive, low-care natural environments can be created within the confines of business or residential property. Furthermore, business firms are becoming increasingly conscious of their image vis-a-vis the natural environment. Sensitive landscaping is one way of fostering this image. It's possible that owners of adjacent properties might wish to cooperate, creating the opportunity for even larger, multiproperty landscaping designs. A pheasant outside the windows of the marketing department, deer in the woods outside the employee lunchroom. Those look like desirable possibilities.

As I said, the probabilities of demand here are a bit shaky. If, however, Iowa is truly "A Place to Grow," we might choose to demonstrate it by marketing alternatives to the acres of empty grass and concrete covering the residential yards and business properties of America.

INFORMATION

Another TAO opportunity exists here. Clearly, if our communities and farms are going to survive, let alone prosper, it's necessary they be linked to larger worlds in terms of information exchange and coupled into the economic mainstream. This is particularly true of rural schools and rural industry. Citibank's decision to relocate its credit card operation from Manhattan to South Dakota is an example of the powerful economic changes that the information revolution promises to bring.

Such information linkages require expertise in hardware, software, and systems design. Quite simply, Iowa should become a leader in this area, the core of which seems to be fiber optics. As with earlier TAO possibilities, we're going to do it anyway; therefore we might as well become experts and earn a profit while we're doing it.

Fiber optics, I must admit, is beginning to take on the appearance of being the latest economic development craze, supplanting the old smokestack chasing of the 1980s as the darling of state officials. And there are downside risks. For instance, a state might invest considerable monies in sophisticated devices, such as satellite uplinks, only to discover that its industries now can shift data-processing jobs to less-developed countries with lower wages. A systems of incentives might help prevent this shift.

In a related field, the emphasis on upgrading skills through employee training should create a boom in the markets for films, audiotapes, and professional trainers. In 1988, corporate America spent $30 billion on formal training for employees, including instructor pay, materials, and equipment ranging from the low-tech filmstrip to interactive computer systems and satellites. Another $180 billion was spent on informal training, such as on-the-job training conducted by supervisors. Over the years, I've been involved in training corporate executives in other states, and I've brought a fair amount of money back to Iowa with me. That's called exporting.

TOURISM

First off, let's understand that tourism is the third largest industry in Iowa. It accounted for over fifty thousand Iowa jobs paying a total of roughly $450 million in 1988. For every $41,000 spent by travelers, a job is generated for an Iowan. The three-day Sturgis Falls Festival in Cedar Falls brings in $2 million or more to that community. All such numbers related to tourism have been growing over the last decade.

As an industry, tourism is a rather neat kind of export when dollars are spent by out-of-state people in Iowa. To the extent that Iowans choose to travel locally, it's also a way of keeping Iowa dollars from being spent on the products and services of other states.

Tourism is also an area where Iowans tend to demonstrate an almost unbelievable level of ignorance and lack of knowledge about their own state. A common reaction is, "Why would anyone want to come here?" Or, "Iowa cannot develop a tourist industry, so our economic development dollars should be spent on other things." That's unadulterated nonsense.

Like most other choices, the decision to visit a place and tour there is a multiple-criteria decision. Unfortunately, many Iowans seem to believe that the presence of mountains or a seacoast is the key ingredient for attracting tourists. Maybe that's because Iowans go to those places.

But people travel for many reasons, to satisfy many criteria. Not the least of such reasons is peace and quiet, a diversion from the roar of city life and city hassle. As mentioned earlier, *Country* and *Country Woman* magazines have a travel division marketing tours to what most Iowans view as rather common destinations, such as goat farms and draft-horse breeding operations. They're booked up solid.

Among other things, Iowa offers quiet. But we also offer a great deal more, most of which is underappreciated by Iowans themselves.

Recently, Iowa was mentioned in an issue of *Outside* magazine, a national publication targeted toward upscale travelers, as having one of the thirty best campsites in America (the Upper Iowa River area). The same publication, two months earlier, cited the Wabash Trace trail in southwest Iowa as one of the best mountain bike trails in the United States—yes, *mountain biking!* (I should note that the praise was a little premature, since the trail was not yet complete when the article was published.) In the same month, a photograph of RAGBRAI appeared in *National Geographic.*

People from other states marvel at our bike and hiking trails, which we have managed to construct in spite of rural fears about the trails being frequented by hippies, thugs, and vermin in general. We are unsophisticated at times, incredibly so. In fact, Iowa bids fair to become the bike-and-nature-trail capital of the United States. From a straight economic point of view, bicyclers and hikers are about the best kind of tourists you can hope to attract, in terms of dollars spent and courteous deportment.

Several years ago, I proposed that Iowa become known as a place of parks and ponds and prairies. First-class tourism on a smaller scale, in other words. I further suggested we put that on our license plates as a motto—Parks and Ponds and Prairies. The point is, you don't have to have mountains and oceans. What you do have to provide is service, trails, interesting places to stay, good food, and the other things that sensitive travelers request. Iowans are naturally hospitable; we just need to focus this attitude on providing service to visitors.

An example is Pheasants Galore, a bed-and-breakfast network operating in southwest Iowa. The idea has attracted hunters and fisherfolk who stay with farm families. I am opposed, personally, to sport hunting, so I present the idea here merely as an illustration of what can be done in the area of small-scale tourism.

With the overcrowding of our national parks, helicopters buzzing the Grand Canyon, and increasing gasoline prices, Iowa's small-scale tourism will become even more popular. You can drive into lovely Iowa parks on almost any summer weekday and virtually have the place to yourself. People from other places are discovering our peace and quiet, and I expect this trend to continue. Economic development in Jackson County has featured tourism as an important component. Mike Jones, formerly the county's economic development official, and his associates have demonstrated what can be done by focusing on Iowa's natural gifts and service to travelers. Theirs is a model worth emulating.

My only plea is for better food, particularly in rural areas. I am aware that most of the clientele for these establishments prefer high-fat diets. But one menu option, just one, could at least be prepared and frozen for those of us who choose to eat differently. If nothing else, offer to prepare a nice salad with an oil-based dressing (and without the cheese on top, please!). It's a wilderness out there when it comes to eating decently on the road in Iowa. We'll learn that eventually; it's part of providing service in a service-based economy. It's part of attracting tourists, a fair proportion of whom do not share the eating habits of rural Iowans.

THE QUALITY ECONOMY

Being out on the frontiers of anything has a certain romance connected with it, but it's also risky. A less expensive, less risky approach is simply to observe what appears to be a large and ongoing market, then produce that product or service *better* than anyone else. The University of Northern Iowa program in accounting is similar in structure to many other programs that prepare certified public accountants. Yet UNI's program has attained national prominence by simply doing a better job than most other schools with similar curriculums.

Thus, we might examine what is being produced in the energy domain, whether it's a high-efficiency shower nozzle or just a part for the nozzle, and then become the high-quality, low-cost producer. Doing business well is not all that complicated.

I've used the example of solar hot water heaters before. A high-quality, simple (little maintenance required), inexpensive heater could practically carry a portion of the Iowa economy on its back, even though such heaters already are in production throughout the world. Our task, then, is to make a better one or a similar one at a lower cost. The same is true of high-efficiency wood stoves for cooking and of small tractors that run on locally produced biomass or solar-generated electricity.

From general reading, one gets a pretty strong sense that Americans are turning more and more toward quality as opposed to glitz. If we Iowans are as smart and productive as we like to claim we are, then we should find almost limitless opportunities in simply making common products better.

That's not strong enough. We won't just make products better or services better, we'll make them *perfect, zero defects.* The Japanese understand this, and it's part of the reason for their rocketing economic success. I like the following illustration.

Siecor International, a North Carolina telecommunications firm, sold 15,600 miles of fiber-optics cable to Japanese customers in 1988. Before that could happen, Siecor had to learn something about Japanese standards. One of them was this: No scratches on the cable, none, even though it's going in the ground where nobody will ever see it. That's demanding quality.

The giant forest-products conglomerate, Weyerhaeuser, finally entered into a joint venture with a Japanese papermaker after five years of negotiations. That's a long time. But then it took *another five years* for the joint venture to simply meet the quality criteria of Japanese publishers. And, as a Weyerhaeuser executive remarked in trying to put the quality requirements into perspective, "This isn't a Space Age product, but it shows the enormous commitment you need to compete in this market."

Here's a third example. Karen Bonomolo operates the Klaytonian Bed & Breakfast in Clayton, Iowa. During my first stay at the inn, she asked what time I wanted breakfast. I told her not to bother, since I would be leaving about six A.M. to do some photography. At a quarter to six the next morning, with the temperature well below freezing, she rapped on my outside door with a tray containing orange juice, coffee, and a bran muffin. I since have spent many nights at her inn while photographing northeast Iowa. You see, Karen Bonomolo understands quality.

Iowa likes to talk about the quality of its people and its outputs. In the markets to come, and in many that are already here, perfection will be demanded. Nothing less. This relates to the attitude of craftsmanship I mentioned earlier, for craftsmanship is just another way of talking about a compulsion for making things perfect. To the extent we become perfectionists in our products and services, we will prosper. Quality offers more opportunities, in its own way, than everything else combined.

TECHNOLOGY TRANSFER AND OPPORTUNISTIC SURVEILLANCE

Some years ago, I proposed the establishment of a small, politically independent, state-funded research unit staffed with hard-headed people possessing practical and theoretical knowledge. A think tank, in other words. The sole task of the organization would be to conduct what one of my old professors used to call "opportunistic surveillance." The job of this group would be to constantly scan the world for commercial opportunities of potential interest to Iowa, evaluate these opportunities, and then forward its findings to the public at large, including state officials.

I still think it's a good idea. Basic research is expensive, the results uncertain. It's much cheaper to let other people spend money on such research and then make use of their findings through innovation and application of the research to specific markets. That would be one function of the proposed think tank, along with evaluating more basic research ideas.

Economic development officials, and the public in general, have been quite naive in the past about the capabilities of state universities to supply useful products through basic research. I sense this naivete is declining, a little. University researchers are driven by priorities, such as tenure and accolades for scholarship, that don't necessarily coincide with economic development. Moreover, there is no guarantee that the output of academic labs will translate into marketable products or that Iowa will be the beneficiary if this translation does occur.

That doesn't mean university-based research should be summarily halted. The long-range perspective provided by academia is necessary for discoveries of the most fundamental kind. That kind of effort, however, does not automatically lead to economic benefits for Iowa in anything resembling the near term, if at all.

The newly created Henry Wallace Technology Transfer Foundation appears to be Iowa's attempt at forming the kind of opportunistic-surveillance organization mentioned above. I know for sure, absolutely, ideas and products already exist that could carry Iowa in style and comfort for the next thirty years. The problem is one of identifying markets and matching these markets with existing or emerging products and services. If the Wallace Foundation does only that, it will be a howling success.

Similarly, Edge Technologies, Inc., of Ames, mentioned earlier, was founded in 1987 with the explicit intent of commercializing inventions at Iowa State University. Though it remains small in terms of employment, it's an example of one type of structure that can be used to bridge the chasm between invention and commercialization.

The Leopold Center for Sustainable Agriculture at Iowa State University holds great promise for enhancing Iowa's leadership role in world agriculture. With the incentives being provided by ISU to researchers in sustainable agriculture, along with the center's own activities, I expect the Leopold Center to achieve world-class status, not only as an environmentally beneficial institution, but also as a source of TAO opportunities for Iowa.

A key ingredient for the success of such an organization is political independence. In the absence of such independence, a technology transfer center gradually becomes a tool for those in positions of power, usually funding power, and loses its ability to make critical judgments in the process.

LOOKING FOR THE INTERSECTIONS

When thinking about trends, there is a tendency to see events as parallel to one another. That is, people are getting older and computers are getting ever more smaller and sophisticated — two unrelated parallel trends. Interesting things begin to happen, however, when trends are considered as perpendicular to one another and allowed to intersect. That's where many opportunities for innovation and commercialization of products lie.

Thus suppose we visualize the *intersection* of an aging population and microcomputers. What kinds of opportunities can be found at this intersection? We might think of computerized methods for monitoring the condition of the infirm elderly, or computer software for nursing home care and record keeping, or electronic networks that enable those confined to their homes to stay in touch with the world, or computer-aided design of prosthetic devices or miniature computers for monitoring a fluttering heart.

A completely different view is also possible. As the traditional labor force shrinks, perhaps elderly people will be employed as computer operators or word-processing workers.

The intersection of more than two trends enriches the possibilities. Evolving preferences in diet/nutrition can be juxtaposed with an aging population and the search for agricultural markets as government subsidies to farmers shrink. Can Iowa farmers produce specialized crops that serve as basic inputs for the manufacture of high-nutrition foods designed especially for the dietary needs of older people?

Such an approach is just another version of the forced juxtaposition technique discussed earlier, under the heading of value-added opportunities in agriculture. Simple computer programs can be designed, in about an hour or two, that will print every possible combination in however many dimensions are being explored.

As an illustration, we might list agricultural products followed by the nutritional needs of the elderly (or the young or the middle-aged, for that matter). The computer will produce a long list, in two dimensions, of possibilities, for example, oats/need for fiber in the diet. When these two-dimensional possibilities have been examined, a third dimension can be added, such as computers. Hence, one category out of dozens or hundreds or thousands that might emerge is computers/oats/need for fiber in diet. In this case, we could explore the use of computer models of human nutritional requirements for ways of integrating oats into diets for the elderly.

What I'm saying, and said earlier, is that one does not always have to sit around and wait for grand explosions of creativity. There are methods for generating ideas that can be analyzed for potential products and services. Along with forced juxtaposition, "morphological boxes" and "synectics" are other approaches to such idea generation. (Any general book on creativity will provide information on such techniques, and most of them focus on intersections. Some of the best opportunities lie in those places where trends crosshatch with one another.)

CLASSIFYING OPPORTUNITIES

A useful organizing framework for business opportunities can be generated from the input-transformation-output scheme used earlier in this book. This requires thinking in four dimensions (see Figure 10.1). The dimensions are as follows:

Whether the product/service already exists or is new

Whether the market for the product/service already exists or is new

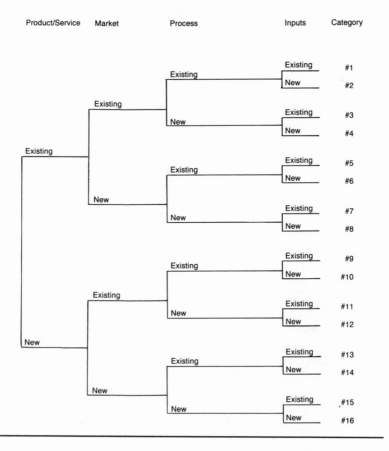

10.1. Categories of business opportunities.

Whether the transformation process used to produce the product/service already exists or is new

Whether the inputs used in the transformation process already exist or are new

The value of this classification is that it provides a systematic way to search for opportunities over these four dimensions, which combine to form sixteen opportunity categories. For an even more surgical approach, goods and services can be separated, providing thirty-two categories, and then markets can be divided into domestic and foreign, which provides a total of sixty-four categories. Further subdivisions can be created within each dimension, if even more detail is desired. Or a given product or service or basic consumer need can be chosen for analysis and opportunities explored in the market, transformation process, and input categories.

Following are examples of each of the sixteen categories listed, though it should be noted that changes in inputs are sometimes difficult to separate from changes in transformation processes. Also, some categories are much richer in opportunities than others. Refer to Figure 10.1 as you read the list.

1. The production of finely crafted rolltop desks
2. Biotechnology applications creating new seed stocks; use of recycled materials in homes and businesses
3. Innovations in nursing home operations or component manufacturing or industrial ecology
4. Innovations in nursing home record keeping using newly developed software
5. A shift in production mix from high-fat to low-fat foods
6. Penetration of foreign markets with gasoline-alcohol mixes
7. Penetration of Third World markets with new and superior solar hot water heaters using conventional manufacturing techniques
8. Penetration of Third World markets with new and superior solar hot water heaters manufactured with robots
9. Design of a "Parks and Ponds and Prairies" route for tourism in Iowa
10. Redesigning lawn care to create low-maintenance, wildlife-friendly habitats in place of conventional lawns
11. More efficient manufacturing techniques for wood-fired food stoves
12. Communication networks tying rural schools and communities into

larger information bases. Miniaturization is also a good example here, as is freeze-drying flowers.

13. Marketing Iowa as a mecca for retirement
14. Using new varieties of soybeans to produce tofu and other meat substitutes for untapped domestic and foreign markets
15. High-efficiency manufacture of small agricultural implements for developing countries
16. Same as number 14, but using new processes to improve the taste or texture of the product

And, of course, categories can be combined. For example, canola oil is an existing product that can be produced in existing ways, using existing inputs, for *both* existing and new markets.

SUMMARY

I have discussed the following business opportunities in this chapter: those connected with the natural environment and its problems (including recycling), those associated with our aging population, opportunities in diet and nutrition, small things for large markets, component manufacturing, value added in manufacturing, infrastructure repair and construction, landscaping, consulting of all types, tourism, and the general strategies of opportunistic surveillance and looking for commercial possibilities at the places where various trends intersect.

Your favorite emerging opportunity probably has been omitted. For example, I have not discussed biotechnology (only briefly mentioned), robotics (except for applications in miniaturization), and other glamour fields. That doesn't mean I believe these fields hold no opportunities. Quite the opposite, in fact.

What I have tried to accomplish is to focus mostly on very basic areas that seem to have little risk attached to them, in the sense that they are part of inexorable trends (the brief mention of landscaping is an exception). The "hot" fields listed in the previous paragraph are already common knowledge and appear in just about every economic development report prepared for all fifty states plus all countries of the world.

The key idea in this chapter, which also is applicable to commercial opportunities not discussed, is the TAO approach to economic development. I like efficiency. And one way to be efficient is to carry out two or more things simultaneously. That's the notion underlying the TAO attitude. There are things that must be done, such as care of the elderly, and we should be creative enough to apply our knowledge gained from problems that must be solved in such a way that we generate commercial opportunities for the state. In common parlance, it's called getting the biggest bang for the buck.

My choices also are biased by the criteria I listed at the beginning of this chapter. And, quite frankly, I have a bias toward what I call the "value of the small increment." Most of what I have found to be workable and lasting is the product of doing small things well, building on the successes flowing from this quality-based approach, and doing more of it. I'm aware of the big kills possible in high-technology fields. I'm also aware of the big kills possible in Las Vegas.

But as management guru Peter Drucker once pointed out, more people have become rich manufacturing everyday items we never stop to consider than have gained their wealth through dazzling technological breakthroughs. We hear much about the latter, however, and that tends to unduly influence our decisions in economic development.

There is, it seems, no shortage of opportunities for Iowa. What always is in short supply, however, are the skills, open-mindedness, and vision to take advantage of the opportunities that array themselves before us.

FOR FURTHER READING

Amoco Chemical Company. "Recycling." Chicago: Amoco Chemical Company, 1989. (Public relations brochure)

Bartimo, Jim. "On a Clear Day You Can Guess Forever." *Business Week,* January 22, 1990, p. 14.

"Best Jobs for the Future." *U.S. News & World Report,* September 25, 1989, pp. 60–71.

Bolten, Kathy A. "Can-Recovery Firm Spawned by Deposit Law." *Des Moines Register,* August 7, 1989, p. 8S.

_____. "Flower-Preserving Blooms into High-Tech Business." *Des Moines Register,* December 25, 1989, p. 6S.

Cetron, Marvin, and Owen Davies. "Future Trends." *Omni,* October 1989, pp. 114–18.

Coates, Joseph F., and Jennifer Jarratt. *What Futurists Believe.* Bethesda, Md.: The World Future Society, 1989.

Elmer-DeWitt, Philip. "The Incredible Shrinking Machine." *Time,* November 20, 1989, pp. 108, 110, 112.

Fowler, Veronica. "Sustainable Ag No Longer a Novelty." *Des Moines Register,* January 20, 1991, pp. 1J, 2J.

Henderson, Carrol. "Landscaping for Wildlife." Available from the Minnesota Documents Division, 117 University Ave., St. Paul, MN 55155.

Hills, Carla A. "How to Plan Global Trade for a New Century." *Des Moines Register,* February 11, 1990, p. 3C.

Kanfer, Stefan. "Millennial Megababble." *Time,* January 8, 1990. (Review of John Naisbitt and Patricia Aburdene, *Megatrends 2000,* 1990, Morrow)

Kiplinger, Austin H., and Knight Kiplinger. "America's Bright Global Future." *Changing Times,* October 1989, pp. 111–12, 114.

Roos, Jonathan. "Middle Class Torn by Shift in Job Trends." *Des Moines Register,* April 12, 1987, pp. 1B, 5B.

"Zen and the Art of Being a Stickler for Perfection." *U.S. News & World Report,* November 27, 1989, pp. 58–59.

CHAPTER ELEVEN

Town and Country

I grew up in Rockford, Iowa, a town of just under a thousand people. My father operated a produce business, purchasing chickens and eggs from farmers for resale, and for a number of years raised large flocks of turkeys. So our family not only had daily contact with the farm community, but also lived with the vagaries of markets and shifts in consumer preferences.

For me, growing up in a rural environment had a number of advantages, and elsewhere I have written fondly of my boyhood days there. There were also disadvantages, some of which I was aware of as a young man and others that only became apparent to me after I left Rockford and entered a larger world. In other words, I claim some reasonably accurate sense of what transpires in rural communities, since all such communities have similarities to one another. On the other hand, I do not consider myself an expert, or anything close to it, in contemporary rural development strategies.*

---

*My original intent was to research and write a rather thorough survey of economic development and its relationship to rural communities. But, in the course of my research, I discovered a 1990 report prepared by the Center for Rural Affairs in Walthill, Nebraska (zip code 68067), titled *Half a Glass of Water — State Economic Development Policies and the Small Agricultural Communities of the Middle Border.* The report, 129 pages in length, contains a useful discussion of exactly what the title promises and comes very close to what I would have said here. I see no reason to rewrite what has already been done. The report costs only $8, and it should be required reading for anyone trying to handle the nasty dilemmas faced by small, rural communities.

287

Following only a brief sketch of the problems confronted by small rural communities, I aim to do three things in this chapter. First, I'll offer some observations, which will not be met with uniform applause, about the cultural barriers inhibiting the sustainability of rural communities. Second, I'll repeat the basic recommendations in the 1990 Center for Rural Affairs (CRA) report, with minimal discussion. Third, I'll present a workable vision for a group of rural communities operating in a cooperative fashion with one another.

A one-chapter analysis of rural problems should be viewed as, at best, a bare minimum. At worst, I risk oversimplification. Nonetheless, a book dealing with the future of Iowa somehow doesn't seem complete without at least a mention, no matter how superficial, of the dilemmas confronting our smaller communities.

THE SET OF PROBLEMS

Rural communities across the United States all face a problematique — a set of interlocked problems — whose appearance varies only slightly from one community to the next. The small town in Maine or Kansas or New Mexico is troubled by the same configuration of problems as that confronted by Iowa communities.

First, there's population. Our overall perception is that rural population is declining. The Census Bureau, under its definition of "rural," however, estimates that rural population in 1989 was stable or up slightly compared with 1988. This is part of a long-term trend, according to the Bureau, with rural population increasing by 12 million people since 1950.

This conflicts with our casual observations about the demographics of Iowa's rural communities. It's a matter of definition. The Census Bureau's figures include those people living in the outlying areas of urban communities, though not in what are ordinarily defined as suburbs. Thus a number of small towns within commuting distance of Des Moines are, in fact, showing population increases or at least population stability. Urban sprawl and the willingness of people to commute greater distances to work in cities have propped up the Bureau's numbers.

The CRA report concentrates on what it calls "farm-based communities." Here, raw demographic data support the casual observations about decline. John Keller, professor of regional and community planning at Kansas State University, has stated: "Many of these communities peaked in 1890. This has been the longest deathbed scene in history."

In 1986 and 1987, alone, one million people left these farm-based rural areas for urban ones (note this is similar to what is occurring in underdeveloped countries). Between 1982 and 1986, more than half of the nonmetropolitan counties in the United States lost population. The proportion of population living in what the CRA study labels farm-based counties is only 15 percent in Iowa.

Of course, the decline in farm population itself has been a major contributor to the exodus of people from truly rural areas. The 1900 census showed 29.9 million people living on farms, which was 39.3 percent of the U.S. population of 76 million. In 1980, 6.1 million were living on farms, or 2.7 percent of the nation's 221.7 million people. By 1989, farm population had dropped to 4.8 million, which makes up 1.9 percent of the U.S. population of 248.2 million.

Also, farm people tend to be older than the general nonfarm population. The median age is 38 years compared to 32.5 years for nonfarm residents. Through all of this, it's crucial to remember that farm-based communities have been declining in population for the last one hundred years, though the economic difficulties of the late 1970s and early 1980s accelerated the decline.

Obviously, those most willing and able to leave a rural community tend to be younger people. And with them go the children who attend school. Over the period 1969–1986, school enrollment in Iowa's metropolitan counties dropped 33 percent, while the loss in rural counties was 49 percent.

As the Iowa Rural Development Task Force's 1987 report to the governor notes,

During the years of 1979 to 1986, rural areas in Iowa lost:

35 percent of their gas stations
20 percent of their grocery stores
29 percent of their variety stores
35 percent of their men's and boys' apparel stores
22 percent of their movie theaters

Most of these losses occurred in towns below 5,000 population.

In rural areas, unemployment rates run as much as 30 percent higher than those found in urban areas (this difference has been declining recently), and rural per capita income averages 25 percent lower. One study even indicated that rural schools have higher dropout rates than their urban and suburban counterparts, though this seems a little hard to believe on the face of it.

Rural communities tend to have a disproportionate number of older residents, which requires greater expenditures per capita on health care. In case you doubt the demographic mix just mentioned, ask a small-town banker about what percentage of the bank's deposits are social security checks and other forms of transfer payments to the elderly. Moreover, a high proportion of incomes, about 40 percent in the farm-based counties in the CRA study, is from what is technically labeled "unearned income."

Unearned income flows mostly from passive investments (rent, dividends, and interest) and government transfers in the form of farm program payments, social security, and welfare. In farm-based counties, surprisingly enough, passive investments account for a higher portion of income than government transfer payments, which indicates that some people in farm-based counties have large amounts of capital invested. A fair chunk of this capital undoubtedly is in the form of land.

Moreover, according to the CRA, poverty rates are higher in farm-based counties than in all other kinds of counties in the United States and, in fact, are twice those of metropolitan areas. One-third of the households, on average, have incomes under $15,000.

In general, then, rural areas, particularly those that are primarily agriculturally based, are in serious trouble. That will not surprise anyone who travels Iowa and sees the tattered main streets of many small towns. Yet these communities, measured strictly in terms of number of towns, not population, account for a large percentage of America's communities. Half of the thirty-nine thousand towns in the United States have a population of under one thousand, and 86 percent are under ten thousand. So, culturally at least, the small community is an important part of American life.

THE SOURCES OF DECLINE

There is no one problem here, but rather a set of them. The passion for deregulation under Presidents Carter and Reagan, in spite of their rhetorical admiration for small-town life, hammered the small towns in terms of rail, truck, bus, and airline service. The dissolution of the Bell telephone system added to the problems.

For various reasons, a lack of jobs being one of them, small communities have suffered an exodus of people, as noted earlier. The rise of regional shopping malls and large discount stores (Wal-Mart is usually cited as the chief culprit) has drained consumer expenditures from rural areas, and with this decline has come a loss of jobs formerly provided by small-town merchants.

One large store, such as a Wal-Mart, is enough to damage the economies of a dozen or more communities. In addition, the economic factors of medical care, including Medicare and Medicaid reimbursements tilted in favor of city doctors, have resulted in difficulties for small towns in obtaining doctors, not to mention the closing of smaller hospitals, which have also been sources of jobs for rural residents.

Then, of course, there has been the trend toward larger and larger farms. Fewer farmers mean fewer customers for local merchants and hence fewer merchants and hence less local employment and hence a population loss and hence fewer customers for the remaining stores. The cycle goes on . . . and on . . . and on. With the current downward direction of farm subsidies, the situation promises to worsen, at least in the short run.

Overall, American farm policy has been no friend to small communities. Quite the opposite. As the CRA study points out, "National agricultural policy has generally worked against these communities by encouraging crop specialization and farm consolidation, narrowing their economic base and depleting their population base."

That's true of the last twenty or thirty years. Fifty years ago, when most rural residents were farmers, farm programs and rural development were basically the same thing. As Richard Doak points out, "That's no longer true, but policies have never changed with the times."

State-level policies have also contributed greatly to the decline of small Iowa towns. Economic development has been focused on creating jobs in urban areas, which only hastens the exodus of people from rural areas as, out of necessity, they follow the movement of jobs. In addition, changes in educational policy and law are stripping smaller communities of their schools. And the local school has long served as a cultural rallying point for small towns.

Tied in with all of this is a leadership vacuum in many rural communities. The old guard that helped take the towns through the middle decades of this century have died or retired, and the exodus of younger people has left a dearth of replacements.

As population has declined, so has political clout. This has not been all that obvious up to this point, since farm lobbies in particular have been able to amplify their political influence out of proportion to their numbers by good organizing skills. Those times are over, and recent cuts in farm subsidies are examples of a decline in political influence.

The U.S. Department of Agriculture estimates that only 46 of the 435 congressional districts are farm-oriented. In Iowa, based on the USDA's definition of a farming-dependent county (at least 20 percent of the labor and proprietor income is contributed by agriculture), farming-dependent counties have declined from ninety-one in 1950 to thirty-seven in 1986. Nationally, only one in six counties is agriculturally dependent. In 1950, this figure was two of every three.

And understand this: Decision making is at the heart of the entire rural problematique. When it was decided to deregulate transportation and communication industries, small towns suffered. When decisions were made to focus economic development efforts on large industries in larger communities, which results in a magnet for people seeking work, small towns suffered. Some of the decisions that have battered and are battering small towns are market decisions; others are political.

If profit is not to be found, the market sends resources elsewhere, unless regulatory barriers proclaim otherwise. Hence, Greyhound removes bus services critical to small-town life and business. The decision to deregulate transportation was a political one; subsequent decisions to remove bus service were market-driven.

As a people, we can decide to interfere with markets or leave them unfettered. Those are political decisions. When rural America had more political clout, political decisions were made that promoted its interests, mostly through market interference in the form of subsidies designed to support its transportation, communication, and agricultural infrastructure. As that influence declined, so did the policies that favored rural interests. Intervention in market processes declined, and rural America began its downhill slide.

What's important here is to recognize that, as a state or a nation, we *can decide* to have a set of policies that enhances rural life or we can choose not to. Early on, we made the former type of decisions. More recently, we have made the latter.

Presently the U.S. Postal Service is considering the abandonment of overnight mail delivery within Iowa. That's both a political and business decision. The Postal Service is a public entity that attempts, in some ways, to operate in a businesslike fashion. Cost pressures, apparently, are driving the proposal to drop overnight mail within the state. Overnight delivery could be retained if we as a people *decided* it was important enough to pay for in the form of increased taxes. The same is true of the level of medical care we decide to offer through the Medicare system.

But we don't like taxes. So we decide that overnight mail delivery is less important than paying more taxes to retain it. My guess is that many small-town residents are among the strongest opponents of additional taxes. The problem is scarcity, and there is no free lunch.

Magic and uncontrollable forces are not at work here.* Again, it's a matter of decision making, in both the political and business spheres. In fact, there's a vague similarity between degradation of the natural environment and the decline in rural America's fortunes. Left to the dictates of the market, both suffer. As a people, we can *decide* to regulate, provide appropriate incentives, and offer subsidies that enhance the natural environment. That is, we can choose to pay the cost of a clean environment.

We can make the same choices about the survival of our small towns in rural areas. At the moment, we have decided, sometimes unintentionally, not to insure the viability of rural communities through market intervention.

The plight of farm-based communities is a good example of something I've mentioned before — a lack of vision. We, nationally and at the state level, do not have a coherent image of what kind of America or Iowa we desire for the future. So we tout the virtues of small-town life and bemoan the migration of people to urban areas while, at the same time, making a series of seemingly unrelated decisions that exacerbate the very things we are worrying about.

In the words of a French poet, "We touch a flower and disturb a star." That comes, at least partly, from a lack of vision.

CULTURAL BARRIERS TO ECONOMIC DEVELOPMENT IN RURAL COMMUNITIES

I debated whether to include this section, not because some of the observations I present will be unpopular, but rather because it borders on half-baked sociology. Still, in talking extensively with people over the last several years, I'm convinced there are real and serious cultural barriers to small-town development that are integral to the existing cultures

---

*I need to qualify this statement. Some uncontrollable forces do operate with regard to specific communities. Some lack certain historical or locational advantages, such as a college in the town, being near a large city, having an interstate highway close by, or being located in a particularly scenic area.

of these places. I should also point out that most studies of rural problems focus strictly on economic matters and ignore the role of culture as it relates to economics.

My view is something other than the bucolic, lemonade-on-the-front-porch-swing image held by urban dwellers and fostered by Norman Rockwell and others who have seen small-town life through a soft-focus lens. There are good things and things not so good in all kinds of life-styles and environments. I'm talking about negative things here, things that I believe have hampered and are hampering the sustainability of these communities. Incidentally, some of these cultural barriers are also present in urban life.

Cultures have their own beliefs, their own values, and attempt to transmit these from one generation to the next. These beliefs, these values, some of which are mythical in character, have the effect of defining acceptable behavior and binding a group of people into a unified, functioning whole. There's nothing wrong with that, in general, and it's one of the ways groups weather times of great change.

To the extent that a group is an isolated tribe and the natural environment on which they depend is stable, the attributes of culture perform their tasks of cohesion and sustainability. When new elements are injected into the system, however, beliefs can become outmoded and useful myths evolve into damaging lies.

One reaction to such events is denial. "There's nothing wrong with us; it's the outside world that's causing our problems." That may or may not be the case. Usually it's a combination of the two. To refuse acceptance of any responsibility for a troublesome situation or an unwillingness to examine the situation objectively is to exercise denial.

So, in response to population declines, small-town people have shouted, "But this is a great place to live." Maybe, maybe not. And, "It's a great place to raise kids." To the latter, I always respond, "But is it a good place to raise and sustain adults?"

Like everything else, the choice of a place to live and work is a multiple-criteria problem. If small towns were so wonderful, they would be overwhelmed by population pressures. Bright, clever people of all stripes would find a way to earn a living in these places. The fact that they currently do not flood to small towns indicates there is something amiss besides the lack of jobs.

Here's a list of their cultural barriers I believe small towns must face with brutal honesty if they are to survive.

1. The lack of interest in the arts and intellectual accomplishment.

Denigration or distrust might be better, though harsher, words than the phrase "lack of interest." The won-lost record of athletic teams has little to do with a town's attractiveness, and the sign at the entrance to a town proclaiming, "State Boys 2A Track Champions, 1982," is an embarrassment.

Worse, it tells people the town has damn little to offer if that's the main accomplishment in the last decade or so. In a choice between hiring a teacher with first-rate academic credentials and one less qualified but who also can coach an athletic team, the decision often is made in favor of athletics. The kind of dynamic people that small towns need to attract will not be impressed by high school athletics; they more likely will be impressed by a town that takes pride in its artistic and intellectual accomplishments.

2. An almost complete lack of consideration given to environmental matters. Notice I said "almost." Urban areas are just as guilty, but I'm not talking about urban areas here.

3. A lack of concern, in Iowa particularly, for the matters of tradition that surround us. There are those, of course, who work mightily to establish museums and refurbish old railroad depots. As they are well aware, however, they do so in the face of apathy or subtle sabotage in the form of derision. Twice, in recent months, while photographing old rural schoolhouses, I have had locals stop and ask in the exact same words, "Why in the world would you want to take a picture of that old thing?"

4. Development without a change in culture. Even the Saudi Arabians, with considerable financial resources but a dictatorial political system, are finding this impossible. If development is desired, be prepared to change. Cultural change fosters development, and development will bring more cultural change.

5. A tendency to smooth over conflict, to avoid direct discussion of pressing issues in an effort to keep from "blowing the town wide open," until it boils over into anger and divisive adversarial relationships. Conflict resolution at the outset is the answer. The problems we confront are tough. Change and divided opinion about change are part of solving these problems. Anger and hate have no place in problem solving.

6. The use of economic boycotts as a means of expressing disagreement. Overall, I'm in favor of boycotts when dealing with large organizations unresponsive to public opinion. In small towns, it doesn't work, and it stifles open debate on critical issues. The woman who runs the gas station may not share your opinion on

sewer repair, but that's not a sufficient reason to buy your gas somewhere else.

Related to this is the problem of getting people to run for office and serve the community at low pay rates. It's not so much money that's a problem. Rather, it's the grief suffered by city council members and the mayor, all of whom are probably serving out of a sense of community spirit. Public officials must deal with the toughest kind of trade-offs in decision making, and those who disagree with their decisions should at least try to be empathetic about the difficulty of making such decisions in the face of multiple constituencies.

7. Pressures for conformity in a world where people increasingly are trying to express their individuality. The most interesting and dynamic people, those who can make a community thrive, probably won't look and act the way old conventions dictate. Not everyone wants to belong to a church or attend the high school football games.

8. The lack of anonymity, the prevalance of gossip. It's not critical to know what everyone is doing all of the time.

9. Distrust of the new, the innovative, including soil conservation methods and alternative agriculture. I'm talking about distrust that exceeds healthy skepticism.

10. Lack of appreciation for the reality of mental problems. Farmers and local merchants should not be ashamed to seek help for such problems.

11. Sexism of the worst kind. Women are here to stay. What's more, they're just as good as men at the tasks that need to be accomplished for development, maybe better, and it's time to accept that.

12. The pressures that prevent local newspapers from playing a central role in town development. This is linked with items 5 and 6 above. A newspaper can be a vital force in getting issues aired, opinions expressed, and generally serving as a forum and propellant for the things that need to be accomplished, instead of just being a record of deaths, births, marriages, and the like. Refusing to advertise in a local newspaper or dropping a subscription because of disagreement with the editor's position on a local issue hurts not only the paper but the town as well.

13. Lack of support for law enforcement. One of the first things small-town kids learn when they move to the cities is that the local police show up with helmets and shotguns, and they don't care who your parents are. Drunken driving is drunken driving, but the locals seem to think they're immune from such matters and small-town officers

suffer criticism and even harassment for their law enforcement efforts. In some cases, enforcement of the law seems to be cause for dismissal.

14. Finally, there appears to be a general negativity, sometimes in the form of outright scoffing, toward those with innovative development ideas. It's almost as if certain communities have a death wish. Over and over again I have seen situations where a few people are trying to push a town forward, but are hampered by the attitudes of "Nothing can be done" and "Who do they think they are, anyway?"

Urban life is not necessarily superior to rural life. Cities have their own serious problems. But some of us who live in urban areas get a little tired of the smugness we find in smaller communities. The point is that small towns need to examine themselves carefully and to honestly face up to those cultural elements that cause these places difficulty in development efforts. The 1950s are not going to return.

Furthermore, smaller communities fall into the same trap that urban areas and, in fact, organizations in general tend to encounter. Ordinarily, by the time a community decides to get organized and develop itself, things have already declined precipitously. At this point, there is a natural bias toward action and away from reflection.

Yet pure action, lacking the guidance that reflection provides, usually leads to chaos and failure. Time spent in thinking about a vision for the community provides a large payoff eventually. A community that identifies "a clean, safe environment" as one of its key objectives will be less likely to accept the first medical-waste-disposal plant that appears on the horizon offering a few jobs.

A good example of this kind of thinking is evident in Craig Mitchell's study of 101 smaller Iowa communities. As part of a thorough survey, Mitchell asked communities to list the goals they were pursuing in their economic development activities. General quality-of-life considerations, such as "beautification" (only six communities listed this as a goal) and "improve housing" (twelve listed this one) were ranked low, while goals such as "recruit new industry" were ranked high.

Apparently, based on Mitchell's data, smaller communities do not see the relationships among various elements that must all be combined for successful development. For example, it's unlikely that new industry can be recruited if there is insufficient housing in which workers can live. One interesting finding is that eleven communities professing to be interested in development did not list any development goals. There's something quite strange and contradictory about that.

In thirty-seven of the communities surveyed, the following was cited as a major obstacle to successful development: apathy or lack of support from the community's citizenry, local government, and local businesses. This is consistent with item 14 in the list of cultural barriers.

THE CRA RECOMMENDATIONS

As background for the recommendations presented below, it's important to understand that state and federal development efforts have not, *for the most part,* been directed toward small communities. It's partly a case of the rich-get-richer syndrome. That is, given limited state development funds, the tendency has been to put the money into those communities that show the greatest promise for development. Some programs exist that are focused on rural areas, and a few more are coming along, but these communities largely have been ignored in the great economic development flurry of the 1980s.

The CRA recommends the following. (The CRA made a number of recommendations regarding economic development in general. Included here are only those most pertinent to the salvaging of smaller communities. My clarifications or elaborations are in brackets.)

1. The states should collaborate to establish a common development policy for small communities. [The idea here is to act regionally in order to take advantage of large, global markets.]
2. The objective of development policy toward small agricultural communities should be to sustain them. [The CRA believes it is unrealistic to expect these communities to grow and development policies based on that objective are likely to fail, which only furthers the decline already in progress.]
3. The states, through their respective universities, should establish a cooperative institutional research capacity to address the needs of small communities. [The CRA is talking here about grouping people in universities who have an interest in rural development, rather than hindering their work by keeping them apart in various academic departments.]
4. On-going planning assistance should be available to small communities.
5. Small communities would be better served by reorienting the state development model from competitiveness to cooperation.
6. The states should strengthen programs aimed at improving the development capacity of small communities through inter-local

cooperation. [This is basicallly what has come to be known as "clustering," where several smaller communities work in cooperation with one another.]

7. The states could sponsor interchanges of ideas about small community development strategies, including a regional fair of development ideas aimed specifically at small communities.

8. State technical assistance to communities should be focused at the community level, not the program level. [In other words, the needs of a community should be the focus, not fitting community needs into an existing program.]

9. States should consolidate application processes and forms so that all assistance can be requested with a single set of documents. [Minnesota has a model approach in this regard.]

10. The states should collaborate to provide small communities with technical assistance in specialized program areas such as water and wastewater treatment services, solid waste disposal, and housing assistance. [This is the infrastructure problem mentioned several times in this book.]

11. States should expand efforts to reduce purchased inputs and conserve resources in agriculture. [This is the sustainable agricultural model.]

12. States should support efforts to develop nonfarm businesses and secondary farm enterprises that spring from import substitution strategies being employed by farmers. [Iowa already has given significant attention to new agricultural product developments. The CRA's point here is that a TAO strategy should be followed. As farmers learn to reduce inputs and hence rely less on imported chemicals and the like, the strategies they are using should be packaged for export either as services or as products. An example would be the use of solar collectors for drying grain.]

13. States should establish or strengthen programs to aid beginning farmers, focusing on opportunities available in the disposal of land from federal agencies and capitalizing on the shift to sustainable agriculture. [The view here is that a farm is a business, and a new farm is a new business for the community.]

14. States should develop programs that build on the self-employment sector, both farm and non-farm. [Iowa is getting under way in this area, with the encouragement of home-based businesses. The idea is to foster a number of small victories for communities, even though state officials may not be able to participate in ribbon-cutting ceremonies of the kind reserved for new industrial plants and highways.]

15. States should expand their small business development centers for the specific purpose of encouraging new business formation in small rural communities.

16. Self-employment and small business strategies should be designed to tap the potential role of local banks and locally owned capital in financing the self-development of people.
17. States should develop the capacity to provide small communities with technical assistance to determine the viablility of cooperative or employee ownership strategies for business retention and start-up.
18. The federal government should increase rural development assistance to states that use such assistance in collaboration with other states to address the special needs of small communities affected by long term structural changes in agriculture.
19. The federal government should establish a regionally based national rural development policy.

A VISION FOR RURAL AMERICA

Smaller communities basically have followed or are following some mix of four development strategies. The first is to attract a reasonably large manufacturing plant of some kind that will provide jobs. Eventually, recognition emerges that a town of, say, a thousand people does not have the resources to make this happen by itself.

Thus a second approach is the clustering concept, whereby several smaller communities band together to share resources and ideas. One of the earlier attempts in Iowa is the Area Community Commonwealth, involving Chapin, Dougherty, Meservey, Rockwell, Sheffield, Swaledale, and Thornton, located in the north-central part of the state. Clustering also meshes with research findings that indicate a critical mass of about twenty-five hundred people is necessary for survival. And in his survey of 101 smaller Iowa communities, Craig Mitchell notes, "Smaller communities seemed to have a more difficult time of instituting an effective economic development plan."

A third strategy is to take advantage of a community's location near a major employment center and simply declare the town will become a suburb, maybe a distant one, for those working in the metropolitan area but who prefer a small town for living. Vinton, Iowa, has adopted this approach.

Implicit in this strategy is the assumption that the town will provide a certain set of goods and services, along with housing. In general, this seems to be a viable strategy, except for one hitch: Serious problems may develop in the supply and price of portable fuels for commuting. If this happens, as I expect it will, then alternatives to conventional automobile travel will become necessary.

The fourth strategy, if it can be called that, is to engage in hand-wringing and hope the state provides help, any kind of help. The state has not and is not going to do this without some effort by the community on its own behalf. On the contrary, certain state-level initiatives such as school consolidation have worked against the survival of smaller communities.

At first glance, things look a little gloomy out there. I used to think the situation was hopeless for most small communities, but I'm not so sure now. It's just possible that in their own way, through their trials and their reflection on what needs to be done to overcome the problems before them, a number of small towns may emerge as vital forces in the future of Iowa.

As the coasts and other urban areas become less and less livable, as people begin to search for places that offer a sense of community and a quieter life-style, those clusters that have learned to cooperate with one another or those communities that find a particular niche, such as declaring themselves a suburb, may be on the leading edge of social and economic trends in this country.

One hypothetical portrait of success might be as follows (I'll use the term "Commonwealth" for a hypothetical cluster, but most of this also could apply to a single community acting by itself):

The communities in the Commonwealth have learned to fully cooperate with one another, sharing schools, recreational facilities, volume purchasing power, and ideas. Sophistication has been gained in dealing with state bureaucracies for development money and ways to use this money.

Support is given to local entrepreneurs whose work promises to offer results. Some of these people are successful and open small plants that employ five to twenty people. At the same time, considerable emphasis is placed on home-grown, home-based enterprises. Every person who employs himself or herself has created a job. The Commonwealth has established relationships with a first-class small-business development center that can help entrepreneurs in management problems and in preparing business plans.

The Commonwealth resists the temptation to focus only on recruitment of new business. Existing businesses, their survival and expansion, are given equal if not greater attention. Home-based enterprises are encouraged.

Larger industrial areas within reasonable distance are scanned for opportunities where residents of the Commonwealth can operate cottage industries, working at home to produce all or part of certain products needed by the industries identified. Transportation of raw materials and finished goods is handled by a Commonwealth transportation system.

Similarly, opportunities for component manufacturing (of the kind discussed in Chapter Ten) are surveyed, with the intent of opening small plants that supply larger manufactuers with high-quality, high-value-added components.

Local bankers operate individually and together as sources of funds for the Commonwealth. Those people who currently have funds passively invested are encouraged to supply at least small amounts of venture capital for Commonwealth enterprises. It doesn't take much for many small businesses to get under way.

The TAO approach to development is emphasized. Every problem the Commonwealth faces is faced by other small communities around the nation and, for that matter, the world. In solving its own problems, the Commonwealth continually asks how its experience can be commercialized into goods or services needed by others.

Opportunities for cooperatives are examined. Perhaps a grocery store or two serving the Commonwealth can be operated on a cooperative basis. Whenever possible, local residents shop at Commonwealth stores, recognizing that paying slightly higher prices at small, community-based stores is merely a form of investment in the community.

Information is a key. Local libraries act in coordination with other libraries in the Commonwealth and as part of a state library system. The library becomes a focal point of the community, serving as a center for information relevant to an assortment of problems and interests: better farming techniques, home-based business opportunities, guidance through the maze of state programs for social assistance, and of course, artistic and intellectual development.

Though local newspapers still exist for recording the comings and goings of the towns, a Commonwealth-level paper is established and supported. The paper is viewed as a forum for debate and opportunities. First Amendment rights are not threatened by economic boycotts stemming from unpopular positions.

Farmers are encouraged to share any innovations they make, no matter how small, with the Commonwealth's "Opportunity Committee," which, in conjunction with local libraries, acts as a clearinghouse for possible new products and services.

Carpooling and bus service is provided for those residents of the Commonwealth working in nearby metropolitan areas. A portion of the transportation expenses (such as, bus fares) are forgiven if people shop at Commonwealth stores.

The Commonwealth forms a political action committee that monitors how local politicians are treating the member communities and seeks to further the well-being of the Commonwealth through political channels.

The Commonwealth agrees on a standard set of zoning restrictions for the towns constituting it. Intense efforts are made in environmental protection and resource conservation. Rivers, prairies, and streams are viewed as local treasures and are treated as such. Opportunities for outdoor recreation are emphasized, and tourists are encouraged to visit the "Villages of the Commonwealth." Waste disposal and recycling are dealt with in a cooperative fashion.

Artists and serious craftspeople are encouraged to relocate to the Commonwealth. Incentives can be in the form of low-rent or free housing and studio space. In exchange, the artists and craftspeople conduct classes in the arts and crafts for members of the Commonwealth. An annual or semiannual art fair is held where members of the Commonwealth can display their work.

A concert series is established for the Commonwealth. Universities and colleges, or local people, are contacted about providing concerts. Residents of the Commonwealth hold receptions for the visiting musicians.

Emphasis is placed on forming a collective community memory. The individual communities treasure their own heritage even while they are changing to something new, and the Commonwealth supports and encourages a respect for the saga, for the history, of its constituent communities.

Attention is given to upgrading rural health care. The Commonwealth emphasizes emergency medical services, outpatient care, and medical transportation and communication. The Commonwealth joins with other such clusters in lobbying the Iowa Legislature to provide incentives encouraging medical school graduates to establish practices that increase the quality of rural health care. Support systems are established that allow elderly residents to remain in their own homes.

Like many urban people, rural families have come to rely on multiple incomes, with both parents working. Therefore, provisions for child care are instituted by the Commonwealth.

The Commonwealth emphasizes self-sustaining activities. Where possible, decoupling from a volatile external environment that cares nothing for the life or death of the communities is undertaken. In other words, imports are cut.

If the Commonwealth can afford it, a professional manager is appointed. The manager's job is to coordinate the diverse activities of the Commonwealth and to operate as project manager for new initiatives by the Commonwealth. Without ongoing coordination, by relying strictly on volunteer leadership, the strong possibility exists that promising projects would not receive the constant and consistent attention needed.

One of the best managerial ideas of this century is that of a project management organizational structure overlaid on the more traditional hierarchical form. (Discussions of this organizational form—called "matrix organization" at one time—can be found in standard management texts. I have used it over and over again in my own consulting and managerial activities. It works.) The use of a project management structure is adaptable to those communities and commonwealths that cannot afford a professional, full-time manager of development activities.

In addition, much of the volunteer help from smaller communities is from people accustomed to operating their own businesses, including farms. Development, however, requires organizational and managerial skills of a particular kind not ordinarily learned in traditional small-business management. The design and management of large-scale projects involving multiple and diverse constituencies is an example. If a professional manager cannot be hired, help is sought from agencies such as the University of Northern Iowa's Institute for Decision Making that specialize in such matters.

The Commonwealth forms a local development corporation, compiles labor statistics, prepares a community profile and fact book, completes a five-year economic development plan and a five-year capital improvement plan, along with a one-year work plan that builds toward the objectives of the five-year plans, and creates a business retention strategy. The Commonwealth even considers producing a video presentation for prospective businesses and conducting mock presentations as preparation for dealing with those seeking industrial sites. (What I've just listed are the requirements for participation in Minnesota's Star Cities program.)

Flowcharts of all activities required for the start-up of new businesses and the expansion of existing ones are created. The Commonwealth examines the flowcharts and identifies those resources already existing within the Commonwealth and those that must be obtained from outside. For example, some local financing might be available within the Commonwealth, but sophisticated photographic services for advertising might not be available.

Intense and continuing efforts are made to involve all members of communities within the Commonwealth in development planning and activities.

The overall vision is one of cooperation and of doing many small things well. While the rest of the world suffers overcrowding, pollution, and a general decline in amenities, the Commonwealth not only survives, but flourishes. In short, the Commonwealth becomes a model of life as it ought to be lived.

The success of the Commonwealth depends on face-to-face contact by people in that dreaded institution called the "meeting." (Use the meeting format in the Appendix of this book, and most of the frustration experienced in the traditional meeting format will disappear.)

Oh, yes, three more minor suggestions. All signs touting distant successes of athletic teams are burned at a picnic celebrating the entrance into a new world of enlightenment and development. Also, each cafe in the Commonwealth agrees to offer one nonmeat, low-fat menu item. Finally, all street signs on country roads in Iowa that say "270th St. South" or some such nonsense are removed as a testament to the decline of delusions of grandeur.

Can it be done? Certainly. It requires changes in attitudes, competent management, cooperation, tolerance, and possibly reorganization of county governments. Obviously, certain cultural barriers also must be dismantled as part of the process. But it's possible.

And it's not all that difficult. I estimate the development time from ground zero to what I've just sketched at five to ten years, depending on the energy and creativity of the residents. For those rare places composed entirely of dunderheads, the time span is infinity.

In spite of the rhetoric about the values of small-town life and advertisements that push "good, old-fashioned country cooking" in the form of TV dinners, relatively few people outside of rural communities really care whether these communities survive. Those small communities that do survive will do so because the people in them want them to survive. Nobody else cares much one way or the other. Small-town residents will have to do it themselves.

The CRA report emphasizes the self-help approach also. But notice in the recommendations I listed from the report, virtually every one is couched in terms of public assistance, i.e., that the state should do this, the state should do that. Clearly, in spite of the do-it-yourself rhetoric, the CRA believes action at the state or multistate level is necessary for small-town viability.

Earlier I said there's no magic involved in all of this. That's true. It's a matter of political and market-driven decision making. For example, the costs of operating a first-class school in a community are paid through taxes. If a community wants first-class schools, it can lobby the state and itself to provide them.

If the state refuses to provide sufficient resources and demands that certain costly educational standards be met, then the community must decide whether to supply those resources through additional public investment in the form of local taxes. Again, you get what you pay for.

But if local resources are simply not available, then the kind of community, or commonwealth, I have sketched in this section must be developed so that the resources are present. Additionally, residents must *decide* to devote the resources to education through taxes, if they want first-class schools. To the extent that older populations do not support higher taxes for education, either because of self-interest or the inability to pay, they will vote against such public investment. The cycles roll on and on. Through our private and public decision making, we decide whether the spirals will be up or down. It's not magic; it's decision making.

In a world of scarcity, it's possible that a triage system will be forthcoming in deciding which communities to support and which ones to ignore. Such an outlook is already present, though it's mostly implicit. Thus some communities will be selected for much state assistance, some will receive a little, and some will be left to die. Even though the smart money flows toward investments with the highest probability of success, communities themselves have a fair amount of control over the category in which they will be placed. Imagination, planning, and cooperation are the key elements.

The triage perspective is a harsh one, reeking as it does of social Darwinism, with only the fittest surviving. Whether small towns, which in many ways have defined the culture of Iowa, should be saved is a matter of politics, not just markets. But little has been forthcoming at the state level in terms of how rural Iowa fits into some grand future vision. That's partly because there is no such vision. No clear portrait of a desirable Iowa future, in all of its social and economic dimensions, has emerged.

SMALL BUSINESSES IN SMALL COMMUNITIES

Data clearly show that small business is the source of most new jobs in the United States. In spite of this, states have focused on attracting and supporting large enterprises. Much of this attention is a combination of naivete and politics, mostly the latter. If a local merchant hires one additional person, it's hardly worth the governor's time to come by with a ribbon-cutting ceremony and a speech. But a new chicken-plucking plant employing a hundred people offers the possibility for politicians of all stripes to gather for an afternoon of coffee and mutual self-congratulation.*

*It's the same reason why new highway construction can receive funding, but repair of existing highways goes wanting. New roads provide the opportunity for a political splash. Highway repair, or the repair of any existing infrastructure for that matter, is a much less glamorous event.

Aside from politics, small businesses suffer from other biases. If rural communities are to survive, maybe even prosper, these biases must be addressed. (An entire book could be written on cultural shifts and policies favoring large businesses at the expense of small ones; I'll mention only a few here.)

Originally, fair trade laws were designed to prevent large discounters from undercutting smaller firms. I don't like fair trade laws. Not many people who truly believe in the efficiency benefits of competition are in favor of them. One has only to look at the rigid pricing practices of state-owned Soviet firms to understand the damages wrought by not allowing the price system to execute its signals. So we remove fair trade laws, but we have still allowed the existence of practices that favor large firms over and above those of normal competitive pricing.

For example, beverage distributors are allowed to exercise differential pricing based on the class system. Thus a restaurant in St. Ansgar pays 33 percent more for pop than does a large grocery store in Mason City, because a resturant is in one class and the grocery store is in another. If the restaurant and grocery store are in competition for bulk sales of pop, people naturally gravitate toward the lower price.

Likewise, a grocery chain, such as Hy-Vee, can sell a product at one price in a market where it has little competition and use its overall profits to subsidize less-than-cost sales in another market. The small, independent merchant does not have this option.

My father, after thirty years in the produce business, finally was driven out of it because the Greater Atlantic and Pacific Tea Company (A & P) moved in with its economic power and paid a slightly higher rate to farmers for their eggs. That's called competition, of course, and all good free-marketers applaud it. I'll wager that most small-town people vote for presidents who wave the free-market flag. Still, my father closed his doors, and another small-town business employing several people was gone. When he and others like him were driven out of business, the chains no longer had competition and were free to pay any price they wished.

Similar problems exist within our liability laws. Litigation and damages awarded have gotten out of hand. Ask just about any small-business person, including a rural physician, about this abomination of the market system. Liability is a cost of doing business and is no different from paying wages or buying inputs for the firm.

Even moderate-sized firms suffer from the costs of liability, but in some cases they are able to at least self-insure their operations or pay the premiums and pass on the increased costs through market power they possess. The effects of liability costs are insidious, and much of their impact goes unnoticed, in spite of the ballyhoo. What's hard to measure is the number of small businesses that never get started because of the daunting costs of liability insurance.

Not all the problems of small-town businesses, however, are a result of laws and regulations. Even in the absence of such market interferences, larger firms have an advantage. One of them is volume purchasing at discount prices. That's why I recommended that the Commonwealth look for such opportunities in cooperative buying.

Even the marginally lower prices of metropolitan firms should not be enough to lure consumers from small-town main streets to city malls *if* people compute their travel costs and sacrifices in personal time expended in driving. It's a curious phenomenon. Apparently many people do not make such computations. If they did, much of the perceived price differentials would disappear.

Gasoline prices in the range of $4 to $5 per gallon, which is about where such prices ought to be right now if all private and social costs incurred in obtaining and converting crude oil to fuel were taken into account, would change some shopping habits. In other words, the artificially low price of automobile fuels in this country works against merchants in small communities.

Then there's the tough problem of store hours. Small businesses in small communities have operated in a way more suited to the traditional farm-based community than to a world where both husbands and wives work at off-farm jobs or where local residents commute to cities. The fact is that these people cannot shop during the standard eight-to-five business hours established decades ago. If the local grocery store closes at five, people will shop in the city on their way home.

Let's be frank: Large, metropolitan stores have their advantages. Price is only one of them, and that advantage eventually will lessen as fuel costs increase. Another advantage that's more difficult for small merchants to counter is selection—the variety of goods. Wal-Mart offers a cornucopia of goods beyond what any small-town merchant can hope to duplicate.

Thus the smaller communities must base their retail sector on the provision of good service and filling niches that larger stores do not offer. I like doing business at places where I know the owner. Others feel the same. It's incumbent on small towns to look for unique opportunities where they have an advantage. Personal service is one of them.

Residents of small towns have not thought very clearly about just what it is they want. Having spent their Sunday shopping at a regional mall, over Monday coffee at the struggling local cafe they bemoan the decline of their business district—a rather curious lack of connection between their shopping habits and the welfare of the town they profess to love.

Like many things, it's a multiple-criteria decision problem. When evaluating two alternatives, shopping at a regional mall or shopping locally, price and selection are two criteria. But a third criterion might well be "survival of the small town in which I live." All right, suppose both the mall and the local merchant have an item in stock, but the mall sells it for considerably less.

If price is the dominant criterion, the purchase will be made at the mall. If, however, survival of the town is heavily weighted in the decision process, then the purchase might be made at the local store. You see, it's a matter of decision making, once again.

Paying a higher price at the local store is a form of subsidy, or a tax, depending on how you wish to view it. In that sense, it's no different from agreeing to higher property taxes to support first-class schools.

Small-town residents can choose to support their local merchants and help ensure the town's survival or they can choose to shop at the regional mall. It's not much more complicated than that. Anyone who insists on making the decision in favor of the mall has thin grounds for complaining about his or her town's dissolution.

FOR FURTHER READING

Center for Rural Affairs. *Half a Glass of Water—State Development Policies and the Small Agricultural Communities of the Middle Border.* Walthill, Nebr.: Center for Rural Affairs, 1990.

Doak, Richard. "How to Develop Rural America," *Des Moines Register,* March 25, 1989, p. 4A.

Iowa Rural Development Task Force. *Report to the Governor.* September 1987.

Mitchell, Craig K. "A Study of Economic Development in Iowa's Smaller Cities." Research Paper, University of Northern Iowa College of Business, 1989.

Petroski, William. "Greyhound Drops 18 Cities." *Des Moines Register,* May 8, 1990, pp. 1A, 3A.

Santiago, Frank. "Postal Service Looks at Axing Overnight Delivery." *Des Moines Register,* May 8, 1990, pp. 1A, 3A.

Schwab, Jim. "Small Towns, Big Dreams." *Planning,* November 1986.

CHAPTER TWELVE

An Emerging Vision

By profession, I am not a futurist. I said that a long way back in the Preface. But I'm pretty certain that things are going to get rough before they get better. Too many problems are beginning to hit us at once—"us" being Iowans and the world in general.

If I had to choose one word to describe what we now are confronting, it would be *scarcity*. We are running into shortages of conventional energy supplies. Fresh, potable water will become scarce in many areas before long; it's already a problem in some parts of the world. Our soil washes into rivers or blows away in the wind.

Those examples are on the input side of what I've called the "input-output squeeze" in this book. On the output side of our production and consumption processes, we are running out of places to put the waste from these processes—the heavens are beginning to choke, as are the seas and the rivers.

Yet the natural environment is not the only place where scarcity exists. We also, I think, face shortages of compassion and caring. And we steadily find that time itself is a scarce commodity. Perhaps the greatest scarcity of all is that of imagination, of being able to see different ways of living, ways that are more abundant while less damaging to our environment and social structure.

Huge social problems are matched against our unwillingness to devote monetary resources to their solutions. In my judgment, incidentally, the degradation of our natural systems is a social problem, not a

technical/scientific one. We try to approach it as the latter, with technological fixes of various kinds, but fundamentally it's a social problem.

We wring our hands over the sick and old and homeless, over the
decay of our infrastructures, over illiteracy, over violence in our streets.
All the while, we refuse to recognize the scarcity that confronts us.
Everything cannot be done; hard choices must be made.

The tallyman is coming. The bill is due.

We have sought escapes from ourselves in the form of high consumption and low reflection on what it means to be human, in all of its
dimensions. A large portion of modern industrial output is designed to
keep us from confronting ourselves, from standing in the darkness just
before sunrise, staring up at the heavens, and asking, "Who are we and
what is the point of our being here?"

But Iowa has a chance to show the world something about how life
ought to be lived. We, in this place between the rivers, have our own
failings, own serious problems — mostly because we have created them
for ourselves. Still, through some combination of skill, intelligence, and
just plain good luck, we yet have the personal and natural resources to
create our own Eden.

Suppose we made a decision, or rather a set of decisions, about the
future. Suppose we Iowans decide to create a world of enlightenment for
ourselves. By, say, 2020 the following is a sketch of what I think we
ought to look like. Everything is not mentioned here, since this whole
book lays out a vision for the future. This should be viewed as a best-
case portrait of how we might appear. Even so, it is attainable.

Sustainability is the overriding criterion for everything we do. If an
activity, any activity, degrades future prospects, we don't do it, even
though it may require economic and personal sacrifice.

In fostering sustainability, attention is constantly focused on the use
of incentives in combination with education and lawmaking. Always, we
ask, "How can we solve this problem by expanding people's choices,
rather than diminishing them?" Liberty and concern for democratic values dominate.

We have, by this future time, finally come to realize that the role of
education is to help people live happy and productive lives, not just the
latter in its narrow sense of contributing to economic development. Thus
the arts are treated with the same importance in our schools and lives as
mathematics and science.

In 2020, we understand that our agricultural land really belongs to
everyone, though farm owners may temporarily hold title. Our agricultural activities are designed to restore and maintain the productivity

of our soil. If an agricultural practice results in a net decline in productivity because of resource degradation, the practice is stopped, either through the proper use of incentives or law or negotiation. The same is true of our water and air; we see them as community property in the long term, and we manage them in that fashion.

Some of the small Iowa towns are gone; perhaps a third of them. With this decline, and with the rise of strong rural commonwealths cutting across old county lines, our former system of county government has changed and shrunk. The commonwealths exhibit all the characteristics sketched in Chapter Eleven and manage themselves for the most part.

Moreover, communities with a mutual interest, such as a river flowing through them, have interlocking governing boards so that resource considerations are handled on a coordinated basis. In other words, a microregionalism is present.

Iowa has focused its efforts on the creation of many small firms rather than huge industrial complexes. The go-go rhetoric of the 1980s has been shown to be hollow and debilitating to both humans and nature. Our firms produce products, or components of products, and services that contribute to the solution of problems and foster sustainability. Furthermore, our attention is devoted to products and services at the core of human existence, rather than at the fringes. We monitor our internal and external environments for opportunities, and through well-designed research and innovation programs, we continually are at the front of developments instead of lagging behind them.

Our business firms and public organizations are managed in a way that combines toughness of intellect with genuine concerns for humans and nature. We have come to see that no contradiction exists between being profitable and being kind. Quite the opposite. Women managers have played an important role in this transition. Furthermore, we operate by a business code based on criteria such as those listed in Chapter Nine. In particular, Iowa businesses pay the full costs — operational and social — of their production activities.

Connected with this is an output orientation to management. We have come to understand that work is something we accomplish, not just a place we go to. People are judged by their output, not the number of hours they spend in an office tower. In 2020, many people work at home part of the time, which has reduced environmental pollution due to commuting, not to mention the need for more intracity highways and the loss of productive time spent in commuting.

Iowans have parlayed the tradition of a strong belief in education into a genuine comparative advantage. In the 1990s, Iowa began to emphasize craftsmanship in all of its thinking and commercial activities. By 2020, we have developed a reputation worldwide as a place of quality in everything we do. Appreciation for the arts and the manual skills has created a work force that understands what it means to work in a craftsmanlike way.

The term "economic development" has been replaced by "development." Development from an economic perspective is based on precepts such as those of Thomas Power, which were presented in Chapter Nine.

Though state government activities are still organized along traditional hierarchical forms (departments), we recognize that our activities do not define themselves so neatly. We finally have grasped the systemic nature of our world and see education, culture, the arts, economics, and nature as intertwined and inseparable in policymaking.

Hence, a formal overlay of managerial relationships and citizen groups provides linkages between the various departments so that a systems point of view is dominant. For example, we recognize that environmental concerns cannot be separated from transportation and economic initiatives. Even though routine activities may be managed hierarchically on a day-to-day basis, larger issues are dealt with in a way that encompasses their true scope.

Iowa has become known, in the year 2020, for its low-impact (on the natural and social environments) recreational opportunities. We have become a state of parks and ponds and prairies and wild spaces. Strong emphasis on the preservation of our historic structures and natural places, coupled with the best hiking and bicycling infrastructure in the nation, has made us a favored tourist destination. We have taken small things and made them significant. As part of this, major portions of Iowa have been reforested and wetlands have been restored through a combination of incentives and law.

We also have come to treasure what Plato called "the fair and immortal children of the mind." Along with our opportunities for healthy recreation, we understand that craftsmanship is just as important in recreation as it is in commercial activities. Our large athletic stadiums sit empty now, as people pursue leisure time activities that contribute to self-development and community richness. Competitive athletics has been put in perspective and college sports are played at a club level. Monday night football is no longer carried by Iowa television stations because nobody is watching. Nobody is watching much television, period, since people have been taught personal skills and philosophies that have enabled them to substitute the fair and immortal children of the mind for spectator activities. The *Des Moines Register* sports section has become a single page.

Sport hunting is no longer practiced. Slowly, over several decades, we began to understand that recreational killing is not recreation in any fundamental sense of the word. In an enlightened society, the stopping of another beating heart for personal pleasure is seen, correctly, as a contradiction in terms. Overpopulation of game animals is now handled by other means.

Small towns, as well as large ones, have learned to treasure both their professional and amateur art and crafts. High standards are brought to bear on such accomplishments. Amateurs in these fields seek to work at a professional level, even though they earn their livings elsewhere. Concerts, art shows, demonstrations of craftsmanship, and the like are daily activities in all neighborhoods and communities. Our small-town restaurants and taverns have taken on some of the characteristics of English pubs and have become gathering places for community affairs and thoughtful discussion.

By the way, drunken driving has all but disappeared. Neighborhood pubs, public scorn, and heavy penalties for drunken driving have taken care of that. Public transportation and a return to walking as exercise have also helped bring about this change.

Energy use by Iowans has been cut by 75 percent through efficiency measures. Most of the energy used is produced within Iowa by a combination of wind, solar, biomass, and alcohol generated from agricultural crops. Experiments with synthetic fuels are well under way, as well. The "life-style" pages of our newspapers feature well-designed, modest-sized homes that are functional and energy-efficient. Social disapproval, coupled with high energy costs, has relegated conspicuous consumption via large, ostentatious houses to the category of relics.

The fields of Iowa farmers are no longer neat and tidy, but they are productive. Iowa has become the world leader in sustainable and low-input agriculture. Our ditches are managed as wild prairies, providing both beauty and cover for wildlife. Substantial reforesting has taken place, and certain crops are raised within the forests instead of replacing them. Warming of the climate has caused some problems, and Iowa has become known for its research and expertise in alternative crops and water conservation as ways of dealing with the change.

Through a combination of enlightenment and wise use of incentives, the Iowans of 2020 pay considerable attention not just to their natural environment, but also to their social environment. Elderly Iowans are treated humanely and with respect. "Zero Poverty" and "Zero Hunger" are two of our state goals. The less fortunate among us are appropriately provided for, and those who are able are assisted into self-sufficiency. Some of this has been made possible by a gradual evolution in the willingness to trade trivial consumption for social well-being. In addition, Iowa has become famous as a place where the elderly are treated well, and this has become a major industry for Iowans. In all care of the elderly, the emphasis is on independent living for as long as possible.

In 2020, Iowa communities operate as much as is feasible in a self-sustaining fashion. While always looking at global markets as possibilities, a central question continually asked in decision making is this: To what extent does this activity expose us to the instabilities of global politics and economics?

Population overall and specific demographic strata are no longer a concern in 2020. First, Iowa understands that numbers are not a reflection of life quality. Second, the state has become known as a desirable place to live and work, and consequently in-migration has even begun to pose a problem.

Iowans of 2020, finally, have come to realize that scarcity is a relative matter. If the trinkets of contemporary civilization are no longer desired, they are no longer scarce. In other words, less has become more, as less time is devoted to high consumption and the means to attain the trivial and transitory and more time is available for seeking the abundant pleasures of the mind and spirit.

In 2020, enlightenment is dawning, and things are beginning to fall into place. We have come to understand that, though our personal time here is short, the future is long. We no longer are butterflies who flutter for a single day and think it is forever. We have learned to love that day without neglecting forever in the process.

Nominal Group Technique

For managing effective and efficient meetings of small groups, use the following steps. It is essential that you not deviate from them. If you do deviate, *disaster follows.*

Make sure everyone has coffee or whatever and is seated at the table; nobody should be up and walking around as the procedure begins.

A "trigger question" has been prepared by the meeting facilitator. Typically, the question is of the general form, "In your opinion, what . . ." Here are four examples. "In your opinion, what should our community look like, in all of its dimensions, in the year 2020?" "In your opinion, what are the major opportunities for small-scale manufacturing available in our community?" "In your opinion, what are the most critical infrastructure problems our community faces in its attempt to attract new businesses or expand existing businesses?" "In your opinion, what should be done to improve the overall beauty of our community?"

1. Everyone answers the question provided, writing answers on a separate sheet of paper (any number of answers are acceptable). They do this in silence. Individuals who have finished sit quietly until everyone at the table has finished.
2. Collect the ideas as follows:
   a. Go around the table taking one idea from one person at a time. Do not let any person read off more than one of his or her ideas per turn.

    b. Write the ideas on a flip chart and number them.

    c. When a sheet on the chart gets full, hang it on the wall with masking tape.

    d. Individuals who run out of ideas on their sheets just say "pass" when their turn comes round. If, however, they come up with other ideas in the course of listening to group members, they can jump in when their turns come again.

    e. Withhold criticism of the ideas at this stage.

    f. Make sure the ideas get written on the flip chart just the way they are presented.

    g. Don't worry about overlaps at this stage. We'll take care of them later.

    h. Work as rapidly as possible. Print in a reasonably neat way. (If you don't print well, appoint someone in your group to do it for you.)

3. Now is the time for clarification and analysis. Go through each item and make sure everyone has a clear idea of what it means. At the same time, feel free to criticize the idea or support it. Now is a good time to remove overlaps. Ask two questions about each item.

    a. Clarification. Does everyone understand what this item means? Let's make sure. Write down a definition if necessary. (In situations where there's a lot riding on the meeting, I use a secretary with a word processor to provide a record of meanings/definitions.)

    b. Analysis. Is this a good idea or a bad idea? Why? Does it overlap with any other ideas? If so should we combine them or keep them separate? Is the idea a subset of another larger idea? If so, should we subsume it under the larger idea? The subsuming of one idea under another larger idea often is critical. Watch for these opportunities; this procedure will help eliminate confusion. Here's an example. You have two elements: "inventory cost" and "cost." If you try to determine which of these is more important than the other, confusion results, since inventory cost is really a subset of the larger idea of cost.

4. Ranking. Instruct each person to do this individually.

    a. Take seven 3 × 5 cards.

    b. Choose what you think are the seven most important issues/ideas from the flip chart sheets before you. Write ONE on each card.

    c. Array the cards before you and rank the issues/ideas from most important to least important by lining up the cards. Ties are allowed. To make sure there is no confusion, write the ranking of the issue/idea in the upper-left-hand corner of the card.

5. Fill out the rating form provided, as follows (do not put your name on it):

   a. Write the number of the issue/idea in the "flip chart #" blank space. Start with your top-ranked idea. Then score it on a 0–10 scale, with 10 the most importance you can give to an item and 1 the least importance. You must give the top-ranked item a score of 10.

   b. Consider your second-ranked issue/idea. Ask: "Is this 90 percent as important as the top-ranked item, or 50 percent as important, or what?" Suppose you decide it is 70 percent as important. Score the item with a 7.

   c. Continue the process of scoring the ideas/issues relative to the top-ranked item until you have scored all seven.

6. Collect the scoring sheets. Appoint a member of the group to help you total as follows:

   a. Put a mark on the first sheet to avoid counting sheets twice.

   b. Have your assistant read off the item numbers and their scores.

   c. Write down the item numbers and their scores on a clean flip chart sheet.

   d. Continue until you have all times on all sheets.

   e. Sum the scores for each item.

   f. On another clean sheet of flip chart paper, write down the number of the top-ranked item, then the name of the issue/idea item, then its score.

   g. Continue until the scores start to "dribble off" noticeably. If you're unsure about this, write down all items and their scores.

7. Stop and take a break.

Now, here's a warning, a critical one. The voting procedure used in NGT is something of a sledgehammer approach. Each person is ranking and rating based on his or her own personal preferences, with the scores summed to reach a group total. Yet, one of the values of group deliberation is the opportunity to learn from other members of the group, which produces a higher, more accurate level of consensus. NGT does provide for such learning, but only at the clarification and analysis stage, not at the voting stage.

There are more surgical approaches than the one used in NGT for obtaining the final rankings of the items. I often use the first three steps of NGT as listed, then switch to one of these other methods for obtaining the final rankings. These alternative approaches, however, are a bit too complicated to explain here. Therefore, when using NGT as outlined above, the rankings obtained by the group members voting independently should not be viewed as having pinpoint accuracy. On the contrary. Treat the results as a rough-hewn, first approximation of the group's rankings.

For example, suppose eight items receive comparatively high scores in the NGT voting. The differences in scores received by these items should not be viewed as highly accurate when comparing one score with another. What has been produced is a set of high-ranking items that is a good, but somewhat imprecise, indication of those items the group feels are important. If one item receives, for instance, a 70, a second receives 56, and a third receives a 50, treat all three items as approximately equal and worthy of further examination, nothing more.

Does this warning mean you should not have confidence in using the NGT? No. The power of the technique is that it enables the group to move through complicated issues, generate ideas, learn from one another during the clarification and analysis phase, and arrive at a first approximation of a consensus. Further discussion of the top-ranked items will yield a more precise representation of the group's overall feeling about the relative importance of the items.

For a general reference with more detail on the Nominal Group Technique, see Andre L. Delbecq et al., *Group Techniques for Program Planning,* from Greenbriar Press, 1986.

RELATIVE IMPORTANCE

FLIP CHART #	DESCRIPTION	NOT IMPORTANT							IMPORTANT		
_____	_____	1	2	3	4	5	6	7	8	9	10
_____	_____	1	2	3	4	5	6	7	8	9	10
_____	_____	1	2	3	4	5	6	7	8	9	10
_____	_____	1	2	3	4	5	6	7	8	9	10
_____	_____	1	2	3	4	5	6	7	8	9	10
_____	_____	1	2	3	4	5	6	7	8	9	10
_____	_____	1	2	3	4	5	6	7	8	9	10
_____	_____	1	2	3	4	5	6	7	8	9	10
_____	_____	1	2	3	4	5	6	7	8	9	10
_____	_____	1	2	3	4	5	6	7	8	9	10

Scoring sheet for Nominal Group Technique

About the Author

ROBERT JAMES WALLER grew up in Rockford, Iowa, and was educated at the University of Northern Iowa and Indiana University. He has
taught management at the University of Northern Iowa since 1968, and
from 1979 to 1986 he served as dean of UNI's College of Business. He
has lectured and published widely in the fields of problem solving and
decision making and has worked as a consultant to business corporations and governmental institutions throughout the United States and
around the world. His essay collections, *Just Beyond the Firelight* (1988)
and *One Good Road Is Enough* (1990), were both published by the Iowa
State University Press. His first novel will be published by Warner Books
in 1992. Waller also has performed extensively as a singer and guitarist,
starred in basketball at the high school and college levels, and is a serious
photographer who travels Iowa and the world for his photographic im-
ages.